HISTORIC LONDON

STEPHEN INWOOD was born in London in 1947, the son of a taxi driver. After studying at Balliol and St Antony's College, Oxford, he was for many years a university history lecturer before becoming a professional writer after publication of his highly acclaimed *A History of London* in 1999. He lives in Richmond, West London, with his wife and sons.

STEPHEN INWOOD

HISTORIC LONDON

An Explorer's Guide

MACMILLAN

First published 2008 by Macmillan
an imprint of Pan Macmillan Ltd
Pan Macmillan, 20 New Wharf Road, London N1 9RR
Basingstoke and Oxford
Associated companies throughout the world
www.panmacmillan.com

ISBN 978-0-230-70598-2

Typeset by SetSystems Ltd, Saffron Walden, Essex
Printed and bound in Great Britain by
Mackays of Chatham plc, Chatham, Kent

Visit www.panmacmillan.com to read more about all our books
and to buy them. You will also find features, author interviews and
news of any author events, and you can sign up for e-newsletters
so that you're always first to hear about our new releases.

Contents

Acknowledgements vii

Introduction xi

ONE: ROMAN AND MEDIEVAL LONDON *1*

TWO: PLEASURE GARDENS AND COFFEE HOUSES *39*

Walking Quiz: From Pillar to Post 57

THREE: LONDON HOUSES *63*

FOUR: PLANNED LONDON *121*

Walking Quiz: Lawyers, Printers and Monks 167

FIVE: MUSICAL LONDON *173*

SIX: LONDON PUBS *207*

SEVEN: SHOPS AND MARKETS *235*

EIGHT: CRIMINAL LONDON *275*

Walking Quiz: Underneath the Arches 325

NINE: DICKENS'S LONDON *331*

TEN: LONDON SCIENCE *345*

ELEVEN: LONDON'S WATERWAYS *373*

Answers to the Walking Quizzes 397

Bibliography 402

Index 405

Acknowledgements

I have been exploring London and studying its history for a long time, and many people have encouraged and helped me over the years. My students have joined me on walks around the town, and my family and friends have cheerfully taken part in my quizzes and mystery tours. My son Joe helped me to investigate London pubs and tested their beer for me, without complaint. The churches I had to do alone. My wife Anne-Marie joined me in walking some of London's rivers and canals, and did her best to stop me turning into a London bore. I leave you to judge whether she succeeded. I am grateful to my agent, David Godwin, for his friendly and effective support and to my editor at Macmillan, George Morley, for her patience and encouragement.

Two universities have sustained me intellectually and financially during the years in which I have tried to earn a living through writing. New York University in London, directed by Professor David-Hillel Ruben, has given me every assistance, a pleasant working environment in central London, and the opportunity to teach its excellent students. Kingston University has supported me for several years as a research fellow. I am especially grateful to Dr Chris French, Director of the Centre for Local History Studies and MA in Local History, and to Professor Peter Beck.

Readers may notice the extent of my debt to the late Nikolaus Pevsner and the publishers and architectural scholars who have brought his *Buildings of England* series up to date in the last few years. The six volumes on London have been my constant companion while I was preparing this book, helping me to identify and describe many buildings I would not otherwise have noticed. No city and no country are as well served as London and the United Kingdom are by such wonderful books.

Picture sources for the plate sections

1: anonymous photograph, 2006
2, 12: *The Queen's London* (1897)
3: *London Past and Present*, ed. C. Holme (1916)
4, 12, 18, 19, 27, 31: photographs by Stephen Inwood, 2007
6, 9, 14, 17, 22, 24, 28, 29: *Round London* (1896)
7: *London, a Souvenir*, W.H. Watts (1911)
8, 23: anonymous contemporary engravings
10, 11, 26: *The History of London*, ed. W.G. Fearnside, engravings by
    John Woods (1838)
13: *Londoners Then and Now*, M.C. Salaman (1920)
15, 20: *The Second Country Life Picture Book of London*, G.F. Allen (1953)
16, 25: *Dickens Landmarks in London*, Arthur Moreland (1931)
30: photograph by G. Lynch, 2006
32: *Select Illustrated Topography of Thirty Miles Around London*, W.E.
    Trotter (1840)

Cockney feet
Mark the beat of history.
Every street
Pins a memory down.

Noël Coward, 'London Pride'

Introduction

I could start this book by saying, as people often do, that I have lived in London all my life, as if that were some sort of guarantee that I know the place well. But as we all know it is perfectly possible to live in a city, and especially one of London's enormous size and complexity, without ever learning much about its history. There are visitors who live here for a few months – and I include my own students in this – who see as much of historic London during their stay as many residents see in a lifetime. My aim in writing this book is to awaken Londoners, both temporary and permanent, to London's rich but often forgotten past, and to encourage them to study it not just on paper, as they could by reading my *History of London* or one of its competitors, but on foot, by looking again at familiar streets and suburbs, and visiting unfamiliar ones, in a spirit of historical discovery.

I have been teaching the history of London for the past thirty years, and writing books on it since about 1990, and I have never grown tired of it. There are several reasons for this, but the most important is that my subject is here, beneath my feet, outside my door. When I am tired of reading, writing or lecturing about it I can step outside, with my students or by myself, and walk its confusing and historic streets. I teach in aristocratic Bedford Square, which still looks almost as it did when it was built in the 1780s. A five-minute walk to the south brings me to St Giles, the most famous and frightful of London slums or rookeries, whose horrors inspired Hogarth and Dickens, and ten minutes brings me to Covent Garden or Soho, each of them with a history so rich it defies brief summary. Five minutes to the west, and I am crossing the old furniture district of Tottenham Court Road and entering the lower reaches of Fitzrovia, famous as a haunt of artists and intellectuals in the 1930s, 1940s and 1950s. To the east the squares of Bloomsbury coexist with the colleges of London University, including Senate House, London's only pre-war skyscraper. Next door to Senate House, the British Museum has wonderful collections illustrating the Roman and Saxon history of London, as well as artefacts left in the area by the pre-Roman inhabitants. The British Museum's Reading Room, the centre of London's intellectual life for 150 years, is now open to all. Many other starting points could illustrate the wealth of London's history just as well as this.

What we see as we walk around may not be beautiful or old or well kept, but it is undeniably interesting, alive and changing. London is a place where history has been made for thousands of years, and where it is still being made today. This is not a city frozen in time, preserved in its ancient or medieval pomp through later centuries of stagnation and insignificance, but a place that has been at or near the centre of national life for a thousand years, and at the forefront of international political, economic and cultural history for each of the past five centuries. While Granada, Venice and Bruges offer us historical snapshots, London gives us a moving picture (with sound) of its whole unfinished history. Sometimes it seems that the new has overwhelmed the old, and that all we can see is a modern and often ugly city, but remember that every Londoner throughout its history has lived in modern London, regretting, no doubt, that they had missed its golden days. The Tower of London was as new, unfamiliar and dominating a presence in 1100 as the giant gherkin, or Swiss Re building, is today. So enjoy the riches we still have left, without too many regrets for what has been lost.

London is a busy, prosperous, crowded and ever-changing city, and its historic past does not overwhelm you as soon as you look around, as Amsterdam's or Siena's does. But take the time to stop and look, to turn off the main shopping streets into the narrow alleys and backstreets, to lift your eyes from the shop windows to the houses above them, to go into the churches and local museums that you generally hurry past, to spend a day in suburbs that your usual journey does not take you to, and you will begin to see that though London has been burned, bombed, burned again and bulldozed, its two thousand years of history have not been wiped away, and that streets that seem humdrum or familiar can be interesting again. London's history could be told as a story of destruction, but we can see it too as a story of survival – stretches of Roman wall that survived four hundred years of quarrying; medieval churches and Tudor houses that survived the Great Fire; monastic buildings that survived the Reformation; street markets that survived the hostility of police and local residents; seventeenth- and eighteenth-century streets and squares that survived the urge to replace them with hotels and offices; and Wren churches, Victorian terraces and Inns of Court that survived the Blitz.

There can hardly be a city in the world with richer historical and cultural associations than London's. Every king and queen of England, every courtier, adviser, archbishop and minister lived in London, and very many of the decisions and events that shaped the history of the kingdom took place in London. There are buildings or streets in London built for the Emperor Hadrian, Alfred the Great, William the Conqueror and Henry III, houses where Wolsey, Henry VIII, Charles II, Marlborough, Handel, Dickens and Wellington lived, courtrooms where Sir Thomas More, Anne Boleyn, Lady Jane Grey, Guy Fawkes, Charles I and Oscar Wilde were tried and condemned. In its time London was the greatest industrial and trading city in the world, a concentration of population far beyond anything the world had ever seen, and the unrivalled international centre of political and financial power.

When Britain ruled the world's largest empire, as it did in the nineteenth and twentieth centuries, it did so from London, the supreme imperial city. At the same time it offered refuge or education to some of the most important opponents of state or imperial power, from Voltaire and Benjamin Franklin to Marx, Lenin, Gandhi, Ho Chi Minh, Kwame Nkrumah and Jomo Kenyatta. Almost every English painter, composer, architect, actor, scientist and writer spent some of his or her working life in London. Many were London-born: Chaucer, More, Spenser, Jonson, Bacon, Inigo Jones, Donne, Milton, Vanbrugh, Pepys, Purcell, Defoe, Pope, Hogarth, Blake, Keats, Byron, Faraday, Turner, Trollope, Virginia Woolf and Charlie Chaplin. Others, including Shakespeare, Marlowe, Boyle, Wren, Dryden, Newton, Handel, Fielding, Samuel Johnson, Garrick, John Wesley, Shelley, Constable, Nelson, Dickens, Darwin, Marx, George Eliot, Henry James, Wilde, Pissarro, Shaw, Wells, Vaughan Williams, T.S. Eliot and George Orwell, made it their home. Often we can enjoy London more if we identify the places where they lived or worked, the streets they wrote about, the scenes they painted or the buildings they designed. As we walk down Cheapside or Borough High Street we can remember the London of Chaucer, Shakespeare, Johnson and Dickens, as we walk along the Embankment we can share the river that was painted by Canaletto, Whistler and Monet, and all around the town we can see the work of Inigo Jones, Christopher Wren, Nicholas Hawksmoor, Robert Adam, John Nash and Norman Shaw.

*

This book is organized by themes or subjects, which have been chosen because of their importance in London's history and because they are still fairly well represented in its surviving fabric. By following the suggested walks and visits in the book you can explore and understand the history of London's houses, shops, pubs, pleasure gardens, rivers, canals, squares and medieval remains, and learn more about the history of crime, music and science in London. Where possible I have grouped my suggested visits together in convenient geographical ways, linking them in a walk or neighbourhood, but I have not excluded places of interest because they do not fit into a conventional walking tour. There are fascinating places in distant corners of London, in Waltham Abbey, Twickenham, Eltham, Cheam, Merton, Pinner, Hoxton, Bow, Harmondsworth and Enfield, for example, which should not be forgotten, and I have mentioned them in their proper place. Many other themes might have been chosen with equal validity, but walkers do not want thousand-page books, and I hope that the subjects I have selected give a fair impression of the breadth of London's history, and take my readers into some interesting and unfamiliar parts of the town.

This is not a comprehensive or conventional guidebook, and I have not concentrated my attention on London's greatest tourist attractions, though I have not deliberately avoided them. Visits to the great galleries, the British Museum, the Museum of London, Westminster Abbey, the Tower of London, the Victoria and Albert Museum, can be safely left to your own good sense. Instead, I have tried to alert you to the odd, the out of the way, and some places you might otherwise have missed. I hope that by following some of my leads you will explore new areas, and see familiar places in a different way. I have given the best information I could find on opening times and prices, but these change, and it is easy to get the latest information from websites, which I have identified. I have described particular places in enough detail to enable you to decide whether or not to go to them, but fuller descriptions will often be available on the spot.

I have suggested how you might get from central London to the more remote places, but I am aware that individual journeys do not often start at Charing Cross. So my best advice is to phone London Travel Information on 020 7222 1234, or to go to www.tfl.gov.uk and click on journey planner, taking care to temper their advice with some common sense. Remember that in central London it is often quicker, and usually more interesting, to walk than to take the bus or Tube. A map is always useful, and I recommend one of the fold-out maps published by the A to Z company. The 6 inch to a mile *Map of London*, ISBN 978-1-84348-354-0, is good for the central area, the 9 inch to a mile *Super Scale London Street Map*, ISBN 978-0-85039-928-8, is even better (though harder to fit in your pocket) and the 3 inch to a mile *Master Map of Central London*, ISBN 978-1-84348-379-3, goes out as far as Wimbledon, Greenwich, Hampstead and Crystal Palace.

*

Enjoying historic London need not be a serious business. The city is like a giant four-dimensional maze, with mysterious passages leading you from noisy streets to quiet and unsuspected courtyards, famous residents remembered on the walls of obscure buildings, seventeenth-century houses above twentieth-century shopfronts, medieval cellars beneath seventeenth-century churches, and reminders everywhere of London's eventful history. For several years now I have been devising walks for my friends which involve following clues, looking for information and solving puzzles. The verses I use have no literary merit, but simply give the puzzles an extra cryptic twist. In case you might enjoy them too, I have included three central London quiz walks in this book. These walks can be done alone or in groups, but seem to work best for a party of twenty or so divided up into groups of three or four. The competition is not about speed – though there might be a time limit of about two hours – but about the number of correct answers. The groups finish at a meeting place specified in the verse, where they get the answers and perhaps a prize from the organizer. The puzzles do not test – though they might increase – your knowledge of London, but only your perceptiveness, your eyesight and your problem-solving skills.

The walks were devised and checked in early 2007. It is surprising how quickly what appear to be permanent features of the London streetscape change – pubs close down, buildings are demolished, restaurants and theatres change their names, alleys are blocked by office buildings. Over time, some of these changes may affect the walks, making some instructions impossible to follow. I have been careful, though, to make sure that these changes do not make it difficult to complete the walks. With a map, it will always be possible to keep on track and get to the end.

Nobody can know London, a vast city of nearly eight million people, as Samuel Johnson knew it in the 1760s, when there were about 700,000 Londoners, mostly living between Westminster and Limehouse. But we can still follow the advice he gave to James Boswell: 'Sir, if you wish to have a just notion of the magnitude of this city, you must not be satisfied with seeing its great streets and squares, but must survey the innumerable little lanes and courts. It is not in the showy evolutions of buildings, but in the multiplicity of human habitations which are crowded together, that the wonderful immensity of London consists.'

Boswell had his own thoughts on the many ways in which this wonderful city could be enjoyed:

I have often amused myself with thinking how different a place London is to different people. They, whose narrow minds are contracted to the consideration of some one particular pursuit, view it only through that medium. A politician thinks of it merely as the seat of government in its different departments; a grazier, as a vast market for cattle; a mercantile man, as a place where a prodigious deal of business is done upon 'Change; a dramatick enthusiast, as the grand scene of theatrical entertainments; a man of pleasure, as an assemblage of taverns, and the great emporium for ladies of easy virtue. But the intellectual man is struck with it, as comprehending the whole of human life in all its variety, the contemplation of which is inexhaustible.

So, whether your interest is in crime, science, music, shopping, medieval remains, pleasure gardens, pubs, coffee houses, waterways, Dickens, town planning or just getting lost in fascinating places, I hope that you will find something to stimulate you in this book.

CHAPTER ONE

*

ROMAN AND MEDIEVAL LONDON

St Bartholomew the Great, 1900

LONDON IS ALMOST two thousand years old, but it does not look its age. Centuries of decay, fire, warfare, demolition and rebuilding mean that we have to look quite carefully to find visible reminders of London's ancient and medieval history. Outside of museums, all we can see of the period of Roman settlement, which lasted from about AD 43 to 410, are sections of the walls that protected Londinium from about 200, part of the fort built around 100 or 120 as barracks for Roman troops, a temple to the god Mithras, the remains of a great amphitheatre, and some scattered scraps of flooring and pavement.

The walls were probably built during or shortly after the struggle between the Emperor Septimius Severus and the overambitious governor of Britain, Clodius Albinus, who was defeated and killed in 197. They were maintained for over a thousand years, until they were abandoned and partly demolished in the middle of the eighteenth century, when the threats from Saxons, Danes, Normans and rebellious barons or peasants were long gone, and when, in any case, most Londoners lived outside the walls. What we see today is a mixture of Roman, medieval and Tudor brick and stonework. One of the best places to see Roman and medieval wall is Tower Hill. Outside the Underground station, on your left, there is an impressive section, of which the bottom three metres are the Roman wall, with its distinctive red tile courses, and the rest medieval. The statue of Trajan is a copy, as is the tombstone of Gaius Julius Classicianus, the Roman Procurator Fiscal (treasurer) of Britannia in the 60s. The restored original, which was found near here, is in the British

Museum, which has a fine collection of pre-Roman, Roman and Saxon artefacts from the London area.

Go down into the walkway leading to the Tower of London, and soon you will see a well-preserved postern gate, probably built in the late thirteenth century, when skilful masons were at work on the Tower. This was the eastern gate into the medieval city, defended by archers (the arrow loops are still there), wooden gates and a portcullis. The slot through which the portcullis was raised and lowered is easy to see, on the north-eastern corner of the tower. If you pay to go into the Tower of London, you can see a large section of the riverside wall, part of fourth-century London's defences against the Saxons, which was discovered in 1977. Instead, you could retrace your steps to Tower Hill, and walk up Cooper's Row, to the left of the station. About 50 metres along, on the right, in the courtyard of a modern hotel, there is a stretch of Roman and medieval wall about 10 metres high (almost its full medieval height) and 30 metres long, which survived as the wall of an old warehouse. The lower section of the wall, about 4.4 metres, is Roman, and above that there is the medieval wall, with the remains of the double staircase leading up to the wooden sentry walk, which was supported by posts fixed in the square holes in the present masonry. The broken sections of the wall help you to see how it was constructed, with finished stone on the outside and rough Kentish ragstone filling within. Go through the archway to see what the attacker would have seen, over 6 metres of solid stone, made even more impregnable by the ditch dug against the outer wall.

There is one more piece of the wall in this part of the City, but it is not as impressive as the two stretches we have just seen. Continue along Cooper's Row, under the lines coming from Fenchurch Street station, and turn right into Crosswall. On your right is a large office building called 1 America Square, which was built over the wall. Look into the basement offices at the far end of the building (a few steps short of America Square) and see what is left of the wall here.

To see more of the wall, follow Jewry Street north to Aldgate, the site of one of the Roman gates in the wall, and, in the nineteenth century, of the famous Aldgate Pump. Cross Aldgate and go almost straight ahead into Duke's Place, which runs to the east of the site of twelfth-century Holy Trinity Priory, the first of the London religious houses to be seized and destroyed by Henry VIII, in 1532. Duke's Place becomes Bevis Marks and then Camomile Street, Wormwood Street and London Wall, curving westward in line with the Roman wall. Our next glimpse of the wall comes near the beginning of the road called London Wall (near Old Broad Street), where the church of All Hallows on the Wall is, logically enough, actually built on the foundations of the Roman wall. The vestry is semicircular, reflecting the shape of the bastion on which it rests. This beautiful church was the first work of George Dance the Younger, John Soane's first employer and teacher. It was built in 1766, when Dance was 24. To the west of the church, another part of the medieval wall acts as the northern wall of the churchyard. Much further along London Wall, near the Museum of London, the ruined tower of St Alphage, which can be seen from the road or the highwalk, stands alongside a very good and high stretch of the wall, in quiet St Alphage Garden, the old churchyard. Only the base is Roman, and the chequered red brick battlements are prob- ably from the rebuilding of the wall in 1476.

For economy's sake this north-west corner of the City wall followed and reinforced the outer wall of the older fort, which had been built around 120, perhaps at the time of the Emperor Hadrian's visit in 122. You can see remnants of the wall and fort from the Bastion Highwalk (on the northern side of London Wall) by the huge office block at 140 London Wall, and there are impressive sections in the gardens around the church of St Giles Cripplegate, which can be reached by going down into St Alphage Garden, walking north on Wood Street towards the distinctive church tower (a cupola on top of red brick), and turning left when Fore Street goes right. The two semicircular thirteenth-century bastions are built on the outside of the Roman wall. The wall turned at a right angle here, following the square of the fort into Monkwell Square. St Giles church was built in 1394, but though it avoided the Great Fire of 1666 it suffered its own fires in 1594 and 1897, as well as very severe damage in 1940, so now it looks rather spacious and bare, without the wealth of monuments that makes some London churches so fascinating. The wall survived here because it was the southern boundary of the churchyard.

You can see more traces of the wall from inside the Museum of London, whose entrance is on London Wall. Finally, cross London Wall by the walkway and come down in Noble Street. Walking south on the right-hand (west) side of Noble Street, before reaching the church of St Anne and St Agnes (with a golden A on its weathervane) you will see the remains of the south-western corner of the fort, and the thicker City wall turning westward towards Newgate, where it turned south along the ridge before the Fleet valley, through the site of the Old Bailey, where its remains have been found, to reach the Thames just to the east of Blackfriars station. Looking down on the City wall and fort as they diverge, you can see the brick-lined Roman drainage tunnel, which prevented the wall from being undermined by water, and the remains of two square turrets. Looking north, the line of the two walls (of the City and the fort) is easy to see, with the remains of houses destroyed in the Blitz built on top of them. It was only this wartime destruction of Noble Street that made possible the discovery of the previously unknown fort after the Second World War. The fort covered twelve acres, and you can get a sense of its size by looking back to St Giles Cripplegate, where you saw its northern wall.

Nearby, you can see the remains of one of London's newest (or most recently discovered) Roman buildings, the amphitheatre. A short walk east on Gresham Street brings you to the courtyard of the medieval Guildhall, in which part of a large tiled circle marks the line of the inner perimeter of the huge arena discovered here in 1987, during the building of the Guildhall Art Gallery. Inside the gallery (free on Fridays and after 3.30) some of these remains have been preserved and displayed, giving as good an impression of life in the Roman city as you can find anywhere else in London. You can see the footings of the eastern entrance of the gladiators, and the waiting or dressing rooms under the tiers of seating, from which the performers emerged to fight in the arena. Bones of the losers, both animal and human, have been found here.

*

The Guildhall is a good place to begin an exploration of London's scattered medieval remains. The great hall lost its roof and most of its interior fittings in the Great Fire of 1666 and again in the bombing of 1940–1, the disasters which between them wiped out most of medieval London. But its mighty walls survived, and the Guildhall remains today as a reminder of the skills of the master mason John Croxton (who built the hall between 1411 and 1429) and of the great power of the City's governors, the Mayor and aldermen. Sixteenth-century pictures and maps show that after St Paul's the Guildhall was the medieval City's biggest and finest building. Only one medieval hall in London, the king's great hall in Westminster, is bigger or more impressive than this. Inside the Guildhall, the masonry as high as the tops of the windows is essentially Croxton's work, though the roof, rebuilt in the 1950s, is not as he intended it. The elaborate oriental and Gothic porch was designed by George Dance in 1788–9, with fifteenth-century masonry at its base. Underneath the hall is one of the hidden treasures of medieval London, the crypt or undercroft. If you visit the Guildhall on one of the very few days when the crypt is open, you will see two great rooms, one, the eastern crypt, built by Croxton in the 1410s, and the other, the simpler western crypt, a beautiful remnant of the earlier Guildhall, built in the decades around 1300. Scraps of an earlier plastered wall in the north wall of the western crypt are probably from the first guildhall, built in the twelfth or thirteenth century.

Of the other secular institutions of medieval London, very little remains. Although the City still has many livery company halls, most of which have late medieval origins, only one hall, that of the Merchant Taylors, managed to preserve any of its medieval buildings from the Great Fire and the Blitz. The late-fourteenth-century Hall and crypt, and the fifteenth-century Great Kitchen, still survive, but they are not easy to visit, and the entrance on Threadneedle Street gives no hint of what is inside.

Between about 1050 and 1400 over twenty religious communities, monasteries, priories, nunneries, abbeys, friaries and hospitals, were founded in and around the City of London, usually by wealthy or royal benefactors. The pre-Norman communities were Westminster Abbey, St Paul's Cathedral and St Martin-le-Grand. Westminster Abbey has mysterious and partly fictional origins in the Saxon centuries, and was refounded by Edward the Confessor as a Benedictine abbey around 1050. St Paul's Cathedral, which began as a wooden Saxon church in 604, was rebuilt after a fire in 1087, and the College of St Martin-le-Grand, now no more than a street name on the western edge of the City, was founded around 1056, and remained a place of power and influence – as well as a sanctuary for criminals – throughout the Middle Ages. In 1189 William II (Rufus) founded a Cluniac priory in Bermondsey, and in the twelfth century a growing fashion for founding communities associated with one or other of the great monastic orders led to the creation of monasteries and priories all around the City. There were three Augustinian foundations, St Mary Overie (1106, now Southwark Cathedral), Holy Trinity Priory (1108), and St Bartholomew Hospital and Priory (1123), and the crusading orders, the Hospitallers and the Templars, each established a London community in the middle of the century. Both of these knightly orders built a church with a round nave, in imitation of the Church of the Holy Sepulchre in Jerusalem. Jordan de Bricett, the wealthy landlord who paid for the Hospitallers' Hospital or Priory of St John of Jerusalem in 1145, also founded the Nunnery of St Mary Clerkenwell, just north of Clerkenwell Green, of which hardly anything now survives.

In the thirteenth century the new mendicant orders of friars settled in England, and established communities in London. The Greyfriars (Franciscans) settled at the western end of the walled City in 1225, the Whitefriars (Carmelites) and Austin Friars arrived in 1253, and the powerful Blackfriars (Dominicans), who enjoyed great royal favour, had the City walls moved west to accommodate their new friary in 1275. The Friars of the Holy Cross, or Crutched Friars, settled inside the City walls, north of the Tower, in 1296. There were no important new foundations after 1371, when the Carthusian monastery, Charterhouse, was built at the expense of the soldier and courtier Sir Walter de Manny, but monastic communities continued to be enlarged and rebuilt up to the early sixteenth century, funded by the generosity of rich benefactors and the wills of pious citizens.

By the 1530s, when Henry VIII took control of the national church and repudiated the authority of the Pope, there were 23 religious communities in London, eleven inside the walls and the rest outside, in Southwark, Clerkenwell, Holborn, Westminster, Bermondsey and Stepney, occupying land with a growing commercial value. The King's assault on the monastic system began with the seizure of one of the most venerable communities, Holy Trinity Priory, Aldgate, in 1532, progressed to the closure of the friaries in 1538, and culminated in the 1539 Act of Dissolution, which led to the abolition of all the rest. Most of the monastic estates were sold or given to wealthy Londoners or royal favourites, and in many cases the medieval buildings were demolished and used as quarries for the secular buildings that replaced them. But the destruction was not complete. Some monastic hospitals and asylums were retained, under new management, because of their value to the City, and several monastic churches were saved because they were also used for parish worship. Some new owners decided to retain the old buildings for their own use, and some monastic fragments were preserved because they were incorporated into the new buildings that replaced them. Westminster Abbey and St Paul's Cathedral were untouchable, because of their importance in national and royal life, though St Paul's lost many of its surrounding auxiliary buildings.

Fire (especially the Great Fire of 1666), road-building, commercial redevelopment and the bombing of 1940–1 have removed much of what was saved after the Dissolution, but London's monastic remnants are still impressive and numerous. To start with the grandest of all, Westminster Abbey not only survived intact, but many of the medieval buildings in its precincts are still there, some of them surviving from the original eleventh-century abbey, and others from its thirteenth-century rebuilding. The abbey is open to visitors every day but Sunday (worship only), but you must arrive before 3.45, or 1.45 on Saturdays and 6.00 on Wednesdays. See www.westminster-abbey.org for accurate information. Westminster Abbey has some of the finest medieval architecture in London and the monumental tombs of some of England's greatest monarchs, including Edward the Confessor, who built the mid-eleventh-century abbey, and Henry III, who built most of the present abbey between 1246 and 1272, along with Edward I, Edward III, Richard II, Henry V, Henry VII (who built the wonderful Lady Chapel between 1503 and 1510), Elizabeth I and Mary I, 'partners both in throne and grave'. Also, there are the tombs and memorials of some of the greatest figures in the arts, science and politics, and those of dozens of courtiers and aristocrats, who often built themselves more ostentatious monuments than their monarchs.

Some of the buildings in the abbey precinct are accessible to the public without a ticket. Beyond the west end of the abbey (the end furthest from Parliament), a little past the abbey shop, an archway on the left leads into Dean's Yard, a large grassed square surrounded by medieval and later buildings. If you go left, you pass, at the next corner, part of what was once the abbot's house, a large medieval house built between the 1360s and the early sixteenth century. The entrance to the Great Cloister on this corner is the 1360s parlour of the abbot's house, but the rest of the house is inaccessible. For the moment, go right to see the east side of Dean's Yard. The buildings you pass are the Cellarer's Building, the Guesthouse and the Treasurer and Monk Bailiff's hospice, all built about 1390. The entrance on the left is to Little Dean's Yard and Westminster School, which has been in existence since the four-teenth century, and occupies abbey buildings of that date. It is never open to the general public. So go back a few metres to the north-east corner and go through the gateway into the Parlour and the Great Cloister. Go left and all round the Great Cloister, which was rebuilt in the mid-twelfth century (and again after a fire in 1298) following the shape, and sometimes using the walls, of Edward the Confessor's cloister. This is rich in interesting memorials. In the middle of the third (eastern) side you will see the entrance to the octagonal Chapter House, one of the finest and most interesting rooms in London. In 1257, about seven years after its completion, the Chapter House was used by Henry III for meetings of his Great Council (the first 'parliament'), and the early House of Commons usually met here between about 1350 and 1395. The building is notable for its very large tiled floor of *c.* 1255, and the wall paint-ings, dating from the decades around 1400.

As you leave through the vestibule of the Chapter House, take a look at the modest door with the uneven top on your left. This has been here since about 1050, making it the oldest door in England. After this, continue round the cloister to find the Chapel of the Pyx, a royal treasury or strongroom, with two immensely strong doors that were fitted after a burglary in 1303. A pyx was a small box containing examples of gold and silver coins, for testing. The chapel and the museum next door were originally two parts of the same room, the undercroft of the Dormitory, dating from around 1066. The wall dividing them was built in the late twelfth century. The museum has interesting fragments of abbey masonry, the late-thirteenth-century Westminster Retable, the oldest altarpiece in England and the finest of its date in northern Europe. Much of the painting is damaged, but you can see scenes of Jesus' miracles, and pictures of Mary, Jesus and various disciples. The altarpiece survived the destruction of such things in the Reformation and Civil War because it was used as the roof of a display case. The most striking exhibit is the set of wooden funeral effigies of Henry VII and several medieval queens, and wax effigies of William and Mary, Nelson and the Elder Pitt. Go left out of the museum and turn left to see the Little Cloister, a pretty garden surrounded by an arcade of 1680, on the site of the monastic infirmary. On the far side there are the ruins of the twelfth-century Infirmary Chapel of St Katherine. On Tuesday, Wednesday and Thursday the Little Cloister is the way into the Abbey Garden, which was first cultivated as the Infirmary garden in the eleventh century. On your left as you enter the garden are the fourteenth-century precinct walls of the abbey, and on your right is Lord Burlington's 1720s dormitory building for Westminster School. The Great Cloister is open daily from 8.00 to 6.00, and the Chapter House, Pyx and museum are usually open from 10.30 to 4.00. The Abbey (or College) Garden is open on Tuesday, Wednesday and Thursday from 10.00 to 4.00 in winter and till 6.00 from April to September. The abbey website, www.westminster-abbey.org, has full details and an excellent guide. Westminster Hall and the Jewel Tower are described in Chapter Three.

The remnants of medieval St Paul's are much thinner; even though substantial parts survived the Great Fire of 1666, they had to be demolished afterwards. If you walk round the outside of the cathedral, you will see that the lower walls, those of the crypt, are made from stone rescued from the earlier cathedral. In a garden next to the southern side of the nave there were some visible remains of the fourteenth-century chapter house, and work in 2004–6 exposed more fully the shape of this and the old cloister. This layout will probably be marked out in new stones when the garden is reopened, leaving the medieval ones buried for preservation.

All around the north-eastern part of the City, until the Dissolution in the late 1530s and the 1540s, there were large abbeys, priories, friaries and nunneries. Some of these have disappeared altogether, remembered only in street names and sometimes in the pattern of streets once within the monastic property. There is nothing left of St Martin-le-Grand, one of the most important medieval foundations, except the name of the street on which it stood. But walk a little further north-west, along Little Britain, where the church of St Botolph, the Anglo-Saxon patron saint of travellers, reminds us that one of the City gates, Aldersgate, was here until 1761, towards West Smithfield. Now you are entering the precincts of the Priory and Hospital of St Bartholomew the Great, founded by the courtier Rahere in 1123. Bartholomew Close and the tiny side-alleys running off it follow the course of the paths within the old precinct. On the left is the hospital, which was saved from the general destruction when Henry VIII agreed to refound it in 1546. His early-eighteenth-century statue stands over the entrance of the hospital in West Smithfield, commemorating his generous endowment in more ways than one. The hospital is medieval, but the buildings are not, except for the fifteenth-century tower and vestry of its church, St Bartholomew the Less.

But St Bartholomew the Great, on your right as Little Britain reaches West Smithfield, is another matter. This was the huge monastic church founded by Rahere in 1123. In the Reformation Henry yielded to the pleas of local churchgoers, and allowed them to keep the transept, choir and Lady Chapel as their parish church. The nave, except for its doorway and an eastern fragment, was demolished to make the present churchyard. You enter the churchyard through the original thirteenth-century doorway, which has a fine half-timbered house (1595) built over it. The church, which is usually open (for a fee of £4), is the finest Norman church in London. The transepts were reconstructed, smaller than the medieval originals, in the late nineteenth century, but the mighty columns and arches of the choir are twelfth century, and so is the monks' ambulatory above them. The fourteenth-century Lady Chapel at the east end was used for houses and workshops until it was rescued and reconstructed by Aston Webb in the 1890s.

A few minutes' walk away there is a more complete, though not grander, monastic remnant. Walking towards Smithfield Market, take the first right turn into Cloth Fair, a street which reminds us of the fair and market that was held in Smithfield from the twelfth century until 1855. Number 41 is a merchant's house dating from the early seventeenth century, representing the transition from the timber-framed houses of the sixteenth century (of which the gate-house of St Bartholomew is a good example) to the fashionable brick houses that became compulsory after 1666. Turn left next to the Rising Sun pub, and cross into Charterhouse Square, the site of one of the burial pits created after the Black Death of 1348, and then of the cemetery of the Carthusian monastery founded here by Sir Walter Manny in 1371. Unlike those who bought most of the London monasteries, the successive owners of Charterhouse after the Dissolution did not destroy the medieval buildings, but retained them for domestic and institutional use. In 1611 Sir Thomas Sutton bought the house and made it into a school for poor boys and a home or hospital for 80 poor gentlemen. The school moved out to Godalming in 1872, but 40 pensioners still live here.

The Blitz destroyed many of the monastic buildings, but if you visit Charterhouse on a Wednesday during the spring and summer, you will be able (for a fee) to see the buildings that survived or were restored, including the seventeenth-century library and Great Hall, and the fourteenth-century Chapter House, now a chapel. The tour information line is 020 7251 5002. If Charterhouse is closed go a few metres past (not through) its main gate and look through the railings. You can see the fenced tomb of the founder, Walter Manny, and the wall of the chapel (the Chapter House) ahead of you, and that of the master's court, the mansion built by the new owners in the sixteenth century, to the left. The top of the chapel tower, which you can see behind the chapel, was built in 1613.

Leave Charterhouse Square by Charterhouse Street, to the west, and turn right to take St John's Street, and then a left fork into St John's Lane, going north into Clerkenwell. After about 200 metres you will come to the gatehouse (built in 1504) leading into another of London's lost religious houses, the Priory or Hospital of St John of Jerusalem. This was founded in 1144 by the wealthy Suffolk landlord Jordan de Bricett as a community for the Knights Hospitaller, a crusading order dedicated to the care of sick and injured pilgrims. The precinct covered about six acres, between St John Street and Clerkenwell Green, and Turnmill Street and Cowcross Street. Like the Knights Templar, the Hospitallers built themselves a church with a round nave, but unlike the Templars' church that of the Hospitallers no longer survives. After nearly six hundred years of misfortune, starting with its destruction in the Peasants' Revolt of 1381 and ending with further damage in the Blitz, little remains of the old church above ground, though the outline of its nave is marked in St John's Square, which is reached by crossing Clerkenwell Road. But underground two twelfth-century crypts survive, one from about 1150, when the first church was built, and another from 1185, when the choir was enlarged. The contrast between the semicircular vaults of the first choir and the rib vaulting and pointed arches of the second shows the transition from the Norman to the early Gothic style that was taking place in these years.

Inside the church there are some good sixteenth-century monuments, including an alabaster effigy of a Knight of St John, with his son or page, brought from Valladolid in 1914 and (according to Pevsner) 'of a quality unsurpassed in London or England'. The Hospitallers' crypts are entered just by the Tudor gatehouse, and the gatehouse itself, which was once a coffee house run by William Hogarth's father, has a museum of the history of the order. The priory and museum are open every day except Sundays and bank holiday weekends, and there are guided tours on Tuesdays, Fridays and Saturdays at 11.00 and 2.30. See www.sja.org.uk/museum for details.

Jordan de Bricett's other foundation in the 1140s, the nunnery of St Mary Clerkenwell, was directly north of the priory, and could be reached from St John's Square by going north through Jerusalem Passage. Hardly anything remains of the medieval buildings, except for the footings of the cloister walk in the gardens of St James' church, which was built in the 1780s on the site of the nunnery choir. But the area north of Clerkenwell Green still carries the imprint of the nunnery in the pattern of its streets. The meandering path of Clerkenwell Close follows the outlines of the nunnery buildings, and arrives eventually at Sans Walk, where Museum of London archaeologists found walls, trenches, paths and rubbish pits belonging to the medieval nunnery. As you wander these little streets and alleys, you might stop for a drink at the early-nineteenth-century Horseshoe pub in Clerkenwell Close, or look at the 1830s–40s Sekforde estate (Sekforde and Woodbridge Streets) and the 1883 Peabody blocks of Pear Tree Court, two contrasting solutions to the homelessness created by local slum clearance. The car park and little playground on Corporation Row are all that is left of Spa Fields, where radicals and rioters used to gather.

*

There are monasteries and friaries in London that seem to have been completely destroyed but of which tantalizing fragments remain which the careful urban explorer can find. Elsing Spital, a small Augustinian hospital for the blind, was the only London community dissolved under the earlier Dissolution Act of 1536. Its priory church, built against the Roman wall, was retained as a parish church, St Alphage London Wall. Most of the church was rebuilt in the 1770s and demolished in 1923, and the ruin we see today – the early-fourteenth-century tower and north transept – is all that survived the Blitz. It can be seen from the highwalk above London Wall, near Wood Street, or from the road below.

Holy Trinity Priory, Aldgate, was one of the oldest and most distinguished communities in medieval London, but it was also the first to be dissolved by Henry VIII. It was seized in 1532 and sold to his Lord Chancellor, Lord Audley, who demolished most of it for building material. In the little streets and courts to the north of Leadenhall Street we can still see the shape of the vanished priory. Bury Street and the southern part of Creechurch Lane follow the boundary between the priory and the mansion of the Abbot of Bury St Edmunds, Mitre Square (the site of one of the Jack the Ripper murders in 1888) occupies the site of the old cloisters, and Mitre Street marks the centre of the priory church. Creechurch Place is where the priory's outer court used to be, and Duke's Place, nearby, is named after Thomas Howard, Duke of Norfolk, who inherited the house built on the site of the priory by Thomas Audley in the 1530s. The destruction of Holy Trinity Priory was not quite complete. In the lobby and basement of an office building, 76 Leadenhall Street, on the corner of Mitre Street, there is a tall arch (c. 1400) from the choir of the Augustinian church, with some twelfth-century traces. Some of the foundations of the south wall and south transept of the twelfth-century church were also found, and are in a room off the foyer.

Blackfriars, one of the greatest and most important of the friaries, is almost completely gone, but you can find traces if you take Pageantmaster Court, a small turning off Ludgate Hill, on your right as you walk towards St Paul's. Go ahead into Ludgate Broadway and Blackfriars Lane to find Apothecaries' Hall. This beautiful hall was built on the site of the demolished friary after the Great Fire, and incorporates parts of the medieval guesthouse, some of them only visible from the inside. Just past the Hall, take Playhouse Yard (named from James and Richard Burbage's theatre built in the friary in 1596) to Ireland Yard, and turn right into a little courtyard, which was the site of the Principal's Hall. Return to Playhouse Yard and turn right into Church Entry, which follows the line of the passage between the choir and nave of the Dominican church. The old burial ground on your left occupies the site of the nave of the old church. There is another piece of the church (a column and part of the choir wall) in St Dominic church, Camden Town, to which it was moved in 1925.

Bermondsey Priory (which became a Benedictine abbey in the fourteenth century) fared no better. Most of it was demolished by Sir Thomas Pope in 1540 to make way for his own mansion. The buildings that he retained, including the gatehouse and cloister, mostly vanished when Pope's mansion was pulled down in the nineteenth century, and now only a part of the gatehouse, incorporated into three houses, remains at numbers 5, 6 and 7 Grange Walk (between Abbey Street and Grange Road). The grange was the abbey farm. The abbey church stood roughly where Abbey Street meets Tower Bridge Road, and the square near this junction, Bermondsey Square, occupies the site of the inner court, which lies just below the modern road surface. Recent excavations in this area have exposed some of the remaining walls of the abbey, and clarified its size and plan, but there is not much here for the public to see.

To the west of Blackfriars the Carmelites, or Whitefriars, had their community from about 1253 to 1539. Nothing remains now except for a fourteenth-century vaulted undercroft, which can be seen under the Freshfields office building in Bouverie Street, off Fleet Street. Take Magpie Alley, on the left, and follow the steps down to the cellar level, where the medieval remnant is displayed behind a glass screen. The crypt is not where it was or what it was, since it was moved westward in the 1980s and now seems to have more nineteenth-century brickwork than fourteenth-century stonework. The interior is too dark to see.

The medieval remains left by the Templars, the crusading order which occupied the next riverside site to the west from 1160 to 1312, are much more impressive. Walking west along Fleet Street, turn left through the Inner Temple gateway opposite Chancery Lane into Inner Temple Lane, under the fine Jacobean building (1610–11) which contains the beautiful chamber known as Prince

Henry's Room. Shortly, you will come to the magnificent late Norman and Gothic Temple Church of St Mary. The round part of the church is the nave, which was built around 1160, when the Norman style was just beginning to give way to the Gothic. The chancel, the rectangular area that now has seating in it, was built between 1220 and 1240, replacing an earlier chancel of which only a crypt remains. The whole building has been much restored over the centuries, especially in the nineteenth century and after severe bomb damage in 1941. Much of the internal and external stonework has been renewed, along with the windows and the round wooden roof of the nave, but this is still an impressive and beautiful building.

The large piers in the nave represent the first known use of Purbeck marble in London, and the famous thirteenth-century effigies of knights, though sadly damaged in the Blitz, are of great interest. The men they depict, leading supporters of the Templars, were some of the greatest figures in early medieval London: Geoffrey de Mandeville (died 1144), Constable of the Tower of London and betrayer of King Stephen and the Empress Matilda; William Marshal (died 1219), right-hand man of Kings Richard I and John, and regent of England in 1216; and his son William Marshal (died 1231), one of the leading baronial supporters of Henry III. The only other surviving medieval building in the Temple is the four-teenth-century buttery, a remnant of the old Inner Temple Hall, the rest of which was demolished in 1865. You will find it by taking the path from Church Court (outside the church) into Elm Court, to the south-west. This is also the way to reach the other great treasure of the Temple, the Middle Temple Hall (1562–70), a wonderful Elizabethan hall and the only remaining place in London where one of Shakespeare's plays was performed in his lifetime. Elizabeth I saw the first recorded performance of *Twelfth Night* here, perhaps with Shakespeare in the cast, in 1602.

The church of the Austin Friars, which was spared after the Dissolution for the use of Dutch Protestants in London, was destroyed by a direct hit in 1940, and has been replaced by a

modern church. Christchurch, Newgate Street, which was originally the chancel of the huge church of the Greyfriars (Franciscans),
was rebuilt after the Great Fire by Wren, and ruined in the Blitz.
The beautiful tower, built around 1700, remains, and parts of the
remaining walls incorporate some medieval stonework. This leaves
St Helen Bishopsgate as the only church within the City walls
which once belonged to a medieval religious community. Great St
Helen was the church of a Benedictine nunnery (founded just after
1200) and survived the Dissolution because it was attached to a
twelfth-century parish church. That is why the church has two
naves and an unusually wide and open interior. The church escaped
the Great Fire, because the blaze did not spread into the north-
eastern section of the City, and was damaged but not destroyed
by IRA bombs in 1992 and 1993. The outside walls of the church
bear the marks of over eight hundred years of history. There are
sections of twelfth-century stonework on the south wall of the nave
(near its corner with the one remaining transept), and the west and
north walls (and much of the east wall) are thirteenth century. The
scars and patches represent centuries of additions, demolitions and
amendments, windows added and filled in, and repairs after bomb
damage. Inside, this fascinating variety of styles and materials has
been rather obscured by the new paving, rendering and repainting
inflicted on the church after the recent bombs. The remains of a
fifteenth-century arcade mark the division between the nunnery
church, to the north, and the parish church, with a transept with a
seventeenth-century Gothic window.

There is some beautiful woodwork in the church – a pulpit and
a marvellous doorcase in the Inigo Jones style (inscribed 'the Gate of
Heaven'), both probably 1630s, against the south wall, and another
doorway, reflecting different early-seventeenth-century styles, in the
transept, and thirteen fifteenth-century choir stalls. The roof, unusually for a City church, is partly original, and the church has a fine
collection of medieval and pre-Fire monuments and fifteenth-century
brasses. Near the transept, look for the tomb chest and effigy of Sir

John Crosby (died 1475), merchant, MP and alderman, whose great mansion was located nearby until it was moved to Chelsea, where it still stands. Two important Elizabethan Londoners are buried here in impressive tombs, Sir Thomas Gresham (died 1579), the founder of Gresham College and the Royal Exchange, and Sir William Pickering (died 1575), a courtier, diplomat and lieutenant of London. The church is open every morning, from Monday to Friday.

The City of London was once staggeringly rich in churches. In 1173 William FitzStephen reckoned that there were 139 churches in the City and its immediate surroundings. The Reformation, the Great Fire (and other fires), deliberate demolition, and bombing have reduced the number (depending on definitions) to about thirty-nine. Some of the best survivors are in the eastern part of the City, part of which escaped the Great Fire. A short walk from St Helen Bishopsgate will take you to five medieval or partly medieval parish churches. First, you could go north to Bishopsgate to see the little fourteenth-century church of St Ethelburga, rebuilt now as a replica of what it was before the IRA destroyed it in 1993, a simple little late-medieval parish church. It is open between 11.00 and 3.00 every Friday. Then go back past St Helen to the junction of St Mary Axe and Leadenhall Street, to see St Andrew Undershaft, which was rebuilt in the 1520s, just before the Reformation, and still has a fifteenth-century tower. Inside, if you find the church open, there is seventeenth-century stained glass (though much was lost to IRA attacks in 1992 and 1993) and some good sixteenth- and seventeenth-century monuments. For lovers of London's history, the most important of these is the tomb of London's first great historian, John Stow (1525?–1605), which has an effigy of the scholar, sitting at his desk holding a quill pen, which is renewed by the Lord Mayor in an annual ceremony on 5 April.

Cross Leadenhall and go left (east), turn down Billiter Street and Mark Lane, go past the fifteenth-century tower of All Hallows Staining, and turn left into Hart Street to find the lovely little church of St Olave. This was the parish church of Samuel Pepys ('our own church'), who is buried there, along with his poor wife, Elizabeth, who looks down from above the altar. The tower and most of the church were rebuilt in the mid-fifteenth century, but the crypt and part of the west end date from 1270. The church is usually open on weekdays, but if it is shut the churchyard and the grim gateway on Seething Lane (a rare piece of 1650s churchwork) are still worth a look. Continue down Seething Lane and cross Byward Street (there is an underpass) to reach All Hallows Barking, so named from its association with Barking Abbey. This largely fifteenth-century church was ruined in the Blitz and rebuilt in the 1950s, but the bombing revealed London's oldest churchwork, a section of Saxon wall and arch at the west end of the church, now thought to be eleventh century. There are other medieval remnants in the church, including a tiled floor and the fourteenth-century crypt, which can be visited.

Southwark Cathedral, just across London Bridge, was until 1905 the church of St Saviour and St Mary Overie (over the water), and began life in the early twelfth century as the church of the Augustinian priory of St Mary Overie. There are remains of the Norman church in the covered passageway along the north side of the church and inside, in a doorway in the north wall of the nave and in the east chapel of the north transept. Most of the church is the result of rebuilding after a fire in 1212, except for the nave, which was demolished in 1838 and rebuilt in 1839 and again in the 1890s. Externally, the most striking feature of Southwark Cathedral is its beautiful fourteenth- and fifteenth-century tower. Inside, the most interesting parts of the cathedral are its thirteenth-century choir and retrochoir (east of the altar) with beautiful tracery, its transepts, and the crossing, with a ceiling composed of bosses from the demolished medieval nave. Of the many tombs and monuments, the best are the painted (and repainted) tomb of the writer John Gower (died 1408), a contemporary of Chaucer, in the north aisle, the allegorical Austin monument of 1633 in the north transept, the tombs of John Trehearne ('Gentleman Portar to James I') and Alderman Richard Humble (and family) in the north choir aisle, and the tomb of the saintly Bishop Lancelot Andrewes of Winchester (died 1626) in the south choir aisle. There is a plaque to the Bohemian engraver Wenceslaus Hollar (1607–77), who drew some of the finest views of London from the vantage point of this church, on a pillar in the south aisle.

In the choir of the cathedral there is a rather battered model showing the church and its surrounding buildings before the destruction of the priory. Most of the buildings shown are long gone, but if you walk west from the cathedral, passing the ancient landing place, St Mary Overy Dock, on your right, and walk a few metres along Clink Street, you will see on the left the remains of Winchester Palace, the bishop's town house. What remains are the foundations and lower walls of the great hall of the palace, together with the west wall of the hall, with its beautiful rose window. This, according to Pevsner, is unique in design, and appears to be early fourteenth century. The palace was occupied by Bishop Andrewes until 1626, but was used as a prison in the Civil War, and was in such a bad state in 1660 that the new bishop had it converted into tenements and found a new house in Chelsea. Over time the palace buildings were consumed by the cheap domestic and commercial buildings that were built in the grounds, and the wall with the rose window was only rediscovered after a fire in 1814. Until the 1970s it did duty as the east wall of a warehouse. The palace courtyard is now Winchester Square, just behind the great hall. A little further along Clink Street you will find a faded plaque explaining that this is the site of the bishop's prison, whose name, the Clink, has been used as a colloquial term for jails in general.

Winchester Palace is a remnant of one of the many mansions that important barons and churchmen owned in medieval London to keep in touch with the centre of power and patronage. Lambeth Palace, the Archbishop of Canterbury's house across the river from the royal Palace of Westminster, is the outstanding surviving example. Oliver Cromwell, Victorian restorers and Adolf Hitler have done their work on Lambeth Palace, but what is left is a large and interesting domestic building which includes structures added by some of the greatest medieval, Tudor and seventeenth-century archbishops. The red brick gatehouse was built around 1495 by Archbishop John Morton, Henry VII's Lord Chancellor and tax collector (who caught potential taxpayers in the two prongs of 'Morton's Fork'). The late-fourteenth-century church next to it, St Mary's, is now a museum of garden history, and three Tradescants, the great seventeenth-century gardeners and botanists, are buried in its churchyard. The fine red brick hall of the palace, which you can see, with its pretty golden lantern and weathervane, behind the gatehouse, was rebuilt by Archbishop Juxon in the Gothic style in the 1660s after its destruction in the 1650s, and is now the library. The early-thirteenth-century chapel, though gutted in the Blitz and restored in the 1950s, has some good medieval features and a vaulted undercroft which dates back to the 1220s, when the great scholar and statesman Stephen Langton was archbishop. The chapel connects the four-storey ragstone and red brick Water Tower or Lollards' Tower, finished by Archbishop Chichele in 1435, which is on the roadside, with the sixteenth-century brick tower, which is known as Cranmer's Tower, after the archbishop who guided the Protestant Reformation under Henry VIII and Edward VI. Until 2000 we could only see these buildings from the road outside, but now, thanks to Archbishop Carey, it is possible to get permission to see parts of the palace or to work in the library.

There is another survivor of the great medieval episcopal palaces a few metres from Holborn Circus. The Bishop of Ely had his London mansion in Ely Place, and much of it, including its great hall, cloister and gatehouse, lasted into the eighteenth century. All that is left now is the late-thirteenth-century chapel, which survived first as a Welsh chapel, and then (from 1873) as a Catholic church, St Etheldreda. The church is on two storeys, an upper chapel with five bays, well-restored tracery and windows and arches in the late-thirteenth-century Gothic style, and a simpler but equally impressive crypt, which is usually open. If all this medievalism has made you thirsty, try the Old Mitre, an eighteenth-century pub in Ely Court, a little alley a few yards from the church.

Crypts often survived when churches were destroyed by fire or bombs, and there are two that are especially worth a visit. St Mary-le-Bow, the only surviving church on Cheapside, was destroyed in 1666 and ruined by bombing in 1941, but its wonderful crypt survives. The crypt was built by William the Conqueror's Archbishop of Canterbury, Lanfranc, in the 1080s as his London headquarters, and it is still the meeting place of the ancient Court of Arches (named from the arches or bows in the crypt) and the place where newly elected diocesan bishops take their oath of allegiance before the archbishop. The crypt is London's oldest church room, rivalled in antiquity only by the Chapel of St John in the White Tower of the Tower of London, which was built around the same time. The nave and north aisle of the crypt are now used as a restaurant, but you will get a better sense of the medieval building if you enter the south aisle by going down the steps on the outer wall of the church, near the statue of John Smith.

The second important City crypt is that of St Bride's, which is near Ludgate Circus, set back from Fleet Street. Like St Mary-le-Bow, St Bride was destroyed in 1666 and ruined in the Blitz, but the second destruction made it possible for archaeologists, led by Professor William Grimes, to expose the history of the site, and the many rebuildings and enlargements of the church since the Saxons first built here, perhaps as early as the sixth century. The crypt is now a museum, and in it you can see remains of a Roman villa, Saxon, Norman and several medieval churches, as well as part of Wren's present building. There could hardly be a better practical demonstration of London's continuity and regeneration, or of its land as a palimpsest, a slate written on and wiped (almost) clean over and over again.

Above their crypts, St Bride and St Mary-le-Bow, beautiful as they look, are a little disappointing because they were gutted, like most City churches, during the Second World War. To see some

Wren churches that still look more or less as he meant them to, without Victorian redesign or excessive war damage, go to St Mary Aldermary, St James Garlickhythe, St Mary Abchurch and St Mary-at-Hill, which are all a short walk from each other. Starting at St Mary-le-Bow, walk down Bow Lane and left into Watling Street. St Mary Aldermary, with its lovely fan-vaulted ceiling, is regarded (by Pevsner) as one of the two most important late-seventeenth-century Gothic churches in England. It is open Monday, Wednesday and Thursday from 11.00 to 3.00. Go back to Bow Lane and follow it directly south to find Garlick Hill, which leads down to St James Garlickhythe. This is full of fine workmanship by Wren's craftsmen – stalls, pews, sword rests, hat stands, font, pulpit, staircase, gallery and organ case. It is open Tuesday to Thursday, 10.00 to 3.00.

Now follow Skinners Lane and College Street to Dowgate Hill, passing three fine livery company halls, the Innholders, Skinners and Dyers, on the way. Go left, then right, into Cannon Street, and left into Abchurch Lane, to find St Mary Abchurch in a quiet square that was once its churchyard. Though the church was badly damaged in the Blitz it still has its unusual painted dome and a wonderful reredos by Grinling Gibbons, reassembled like a huge jigsaw after the war. There is some very fine 1670s and 1680s woodwork, and a gilded copper pelican that was once the church's weathervane. The church is only open on Tuesdays, 11.00 to 3.00, but there are services on Wednesdays at 12.30 and Thursdays at 6.00. Phone 020 7626 0306 for details. Then return to Cannon Street, continue east into Eastcheap, and turn right into St Mary-at-Hill, to find the church of that name. This is a medieval church repaired and redesigned by Wren in the 1670s to an unusual square Byzantine plan. It had a fine collection of late-seventeenth-century woodwork until a serious fire in 1988, but much was rescued and is gradually being reinstated. The ceiling, west screen and gallery have been restored, but the box pews and reredos are still in store. It is open Monday to Friday, 11.00 to 4.00. Details of all the City churches can be found on the website of the Friends of the City Churches, www.london-city-churches.org.uk.

*

We hear a great deal about the City of London churches, but very little about London's other great collection of wonderful churches, scattered throughout its outer suburbs. As the capital expanded it absorbed many existing towns and villages which had their own churches, many of which have survived while other medieval buildings have been lost. Most of these were built in the twelfth or thirteenth century, sometimes replacing simple wooden Saxon churches, and extended by the addition of side aisles, chancels (the area reserved for the officiating clergy, at the eastern end of the church), chapels and towers later in the Middle Ages. Most of these churches were repaired and restored in the nineteenth century, sometimes undoing centuries of neglect, and often overlaying original structures with features that Victorians thought a medieval church ought to have. Nevertheless, many are still worth the trouble of a trip to a distant suburb, especially if this is combined with a visit to other interesting buildings in the neighbourhood. Nowadays, parish churches are often shut, so it is worth contacting the parish office ahead of your journey or going to a Sunday service.

Sometimes, apparently dull commercial or residential districts in outer London have an old village or an old parish church hidden and half forgotten in their centre. In east London, for instance, there are medieval churches in Barking, Stepney, East and West Ham, Walthamstow, Ilford, Dagenham, Hornchurch, Upminster and Bow. St Mary's in Little Ilford is a charming little twelfth-century church, with some good seventeenth- and eighteenth-century monuments, and St Mary's Walthamstow, a medieval church badly battered by centuries of restorers and improvers, has a fine collection of tombs and monuments, showing that it served a wealthy rural community in the sixteenth and seventeenth centuries. It is in Vinegar Alley, in the interesting old village of Walthamstow, which you reach by taking Church Hill from Hoe Street, near Walthamstow Central station. The Monoux almshouses in Vinegar Alley date back to the sixteenth century, though the apparently Elizabethan part was rebuilt in 1955 after war damage. In Church Lane, near the churchyard, the Ancient House lives up to its name. The timber-framed hall house was built in the fifteenth century, and restored in 2001–2. St Mary Magdalene in East Ham is a complete twelfth-century Norman church with a thirteenth-century tower and wall paintings damaged by whitewashing in the 1960s. The church has three Norman windows, an early-twelfth-century apse (at the eastern end of the church) with thirteenth-century wall paintings and a very rare Norman timber roof, exposed and unaltered. It is in a wild park-sized churchyard (the biggest in England) at the corner of High Street South and Newham Way, half a mile from the Beckton terminus of the Docklands Light Railway. To arrange a visit, you could call the parish office on 020 8470 0011.

Barking lost its abbey in 1541, but a few remnants survived, including the two-storied fifteenth-century East Gate or Curfew Tower, which now stands at the entrance of the parish church-yard. The present parish church, St Margaret, is a large fourteenth- and fifteenth-century building rather spoiled by eighteenth- and nineteenth-century restoration work. It has plenty of old and inter-esting monuments inside, including the 1328 tomb of the first vicar of Barking, the lovely 1625 tomb of Sir Charles Montague, a fine naval tribute to John Bennett, a sea captain who died in 1705, and the tomb of the nicely named Sir Crisp Gascoyne (1700–61), the first Lord Mayor of London to occupy the Mansion House, and Bamber's forefather. The church and the abbey remains are between Abbey Road and Broadway, a short walk from Barking station. Hornchurch's parish church, St Andrew, still has a horned bull's head (in stone and copper) on its outer east wall, continuing a tradition that seems to have begun before 1222, and which gave the village its name. The present church was rebuilt in the thirteenth century, and improved by William of Wyckham, founder of New College, Oxford, after 1400. The nave is thirteenth century, with a fine fifteenth-century roof, and the tower and spire (once a beacon for shipping) are fifteenth century. Even Dagenham has a thirteenth-century parish church, St Peter and St Paul, nestling between the vast Becontree housing estate and the Ford factory, though much of it was rebuilt when the tower collapsed in 1800. There are good monuments, including the Urswyck family's brass, in the fifteenth-century north chapel. If you have ventured so far east, you might go a little further, beyond the Metropolitan Police District, where Rainham has one of the best Norman churches in the London area. St Helen and St Giles was built by Richard de Lucy, Henry II's Justiciar and son-in-law, in 1178, and thanks to skilful restoration in 1897 it still looks like a Norman church, with some later medieval additions. There is some medieval wall painting in the nave and chancel, and a drawing of a boat done by a graffiti artist around 1500. If you visit the church on a Wednesday or Saturday afternoon, you might be able also to visit Rainham Hall, a fine house built for a merchant and shipowner in 1729.

All Saints, West Ham, which is on Church Street, off West Ham Lane, is a medieval church, was begun in the twelfth century, altered and enlarged in the later Middle Ages, and restored in the 1840s. The nave is thirteenth century, the tower is fifteenth century, and the church is full of good sixteenth- and seventeenth-century monuments. St Mary, Bow, which is in the middle of the noisy Bow Road as it approaches the Blackwall Tunnel Northern Approach and the Lea, is an altered and repaired fifteenth-century church which was saved from destruction in 1896 by the Society for the Protection of Ancient Buildings. It is the last standing reminder of the medieval riverside village of Bow. The other medieval church in Tower Hamlets, St Dunstan and All Saints in Stepney High Street, is a much more important and impressive building. Restoration has given it a Victorian appearance, but in essence it is a very large fifteenth-century Perpendicular (English Gothic) church with some thirteenth-

and fourteenth-century remnants in the chancel. Near the altar, the survival of a weather-worn carved Saxon stone panel showing the crucifixion seems to support the story that the church was built by St Dunstan, Abbot of Glastonbury and future Archbishop of Canterbury, in 952. The profusion of monuments to the prominent citizens of pre-industrial Stepney is a reminder that this was not always a working-class suburb in which wealthy Londoners would not want to be seen dead.

In north London, St Pancras has an exceptionally old church, in Pancras Road, north of the station. Early-nineteenth-century restoration in the Romanesque style makes it hard to spot the real Norman work, but its early-seventh-century altar stone shows its great antiquity, and there are visible remnants of the old church in the nave and chancel. The burial ground outside the church is worth visiting for Sir John Soane's fantastic monument to his wife Elizabeth, as well as the plain tomb of William Godwin and Mary Wollstonecraft, pioneers of the rights of men and women. Enfield, a country town on the Lea until late-Victorian London engulfed it, has the fine medieval church of St Andrew in its marketplace, dating back at least to 1200. The walls at the east end, behind the chancel, are thirteenth century, the tower and nave are fourteenth century, and the north aisle is fifteenth century. The tomb of Lady Tiptoft (died 1446) is fine, and so is that of the Lord Mayor of London, Sir Nicholas Raynton (died 1646), and his family. Raynton built Forty Hall, one of London's great Jacobean houses, which, together with the church, makes the long trip to Enfield worthwhile. It is open Wednesdays to Sundays, 11.00 to 4.00. Not far away, St Mary's in East Barnet (in Church Hill Road) is a plain and well-preserved Norman church which was built by St Albans Abbey, but the Norman features of St James, Friern Barnet's twelfth-century church (in Friern Barnet Lane), are rather lost amid the 1850 rebuilding. All Saints in Church Street, Edmonton, is a fifteenth-century church, well restored in the 1880s, with plenty of good sixteenth-, seventeenth- and eighteenth-century monuments.

Waltham Abbey, on the River Lea near the north-eastern corner of the Metropolitan Police District, is one of the best medieval sites in Greater London. The abbey was dissolved in 1540, but the nave of its huge Norman church was saved from demolition, and survived as a parish church. The church existed in 1030, and was rebuilt in the 1050s by Harold, later King of England. Most of the church, including the present nave, was rebuilt in the twelfth century by Henry II, who also founded the abbey here. What survives today is the 33-metre Norman nave, a 1345 south chapel, a tower built in the 1550s when the medieval tower collapsed, a Lady Chapel and undercroft of 1345, and a wealth of medieval and later monuments.

Outside, there are remains of the late-twelfth-century cloisters, the supposed burial place of King Harold and a late-fourteenth-century abbey gatehouse and bridge, north of the church. While you are here, you should look at the marketplace and Sun Street, both of which were originally laid out by the abbey around 1200. There are some good old pubs and some Tudor houses, including number 41, now Epping Forest Museum, open Friday to Tuesday afternoons, without charge. Finally, if you walk back to the church and past Waltham Cross station along Eleanor Cross Road, you will eventually come to the cross that gave the town its name. When Edward I carried his wife Eleanor of Castile's body from Lincoln to Westminster in December 1290 he marked her twelve stopping places with huge and elaborate crosses. Only three survive, and one of these is at Waltham. Careful restoration means that little or nothing of the thirteenth-century stone survives, but three of the original statues of the queen are in the Victoria and Albert Museum. The cross outside Charing Cross station was made in the 1860s, but Eleanor's wonderful tomb is still in Westminster Abbey. Waltham Cross station is about 30 minutes from Liverpool Street, but there is still some walking to do when you get there.

In suburban west London, where dozens of villages and country towns were absorbed into Greater London between 1880 and 1939, there are many medieval churches, some of which have not been overwhelmed by later additions. In the borough of Brent there are medieval churches in Kingsbury and Willesden. St Andrew, in Old Church Lane, Kingsbury, the oldest building in Brent, is a simple twelfth-century church, restored in the 1880s, and now no longer used for worship. It incorporates some Roman building materials, and in the churchyard there are the remains of medieval earthworks. The church of St Mary, Neasden Lane, is almost the only remnant of old Willesden. Restoration has obscured the medieval nave and chancel, but the tower dates from 1400, the south door is a little earlier, and the Norman font is a rarity. In the borough of Harrow there are medieval churches in Pinner and Harrow-on-the-Hill. St John the Baptist on Church Lane, Pinner, is a simple fourteenth-century church with a fifteenth-century tower and east window, and a Victorian roof and south aisle. A short and pleasant walk from the church, in Moss Lane, stands one of the best medieval farmhouses in Greater London, East End Farm Cottage. In the fifteenth century this was an open hall building with a central hearth, but in the next two centuries the house was modernized and divided by walls and floors to meet changing demands for privacy and domestic segregation. One of these internal walls was painted with a large hunting scene, and parts of this still exist, a unique survival in Greater London. The house is privately owned and occupied, but may be open to visitors on some occasions, including the annual Open House weekend in September. It is well described in its website, www.eastendfarmcottage.com. St Mary on Church Hill, Harrow-on-the-Hill, is an interesting and important church. It was founded and consecrated by two eleventh-century Archbishops of Canterbury, Lanfranc and St Anselm, and rebuilt in the twelfth and thirteenth centuries. The lower part of the tower dates from about 1140; the nave, like the transepts, is thirteenth century with a fifteenth-century roof, the Purbeck marble font is Norman, and there are many old brasses in the church, dating from between 1370 and 1600.

Ealing contains several old village centres, some of which still have their medieval parish churches. The church of St Mary on

Northolt Green, near Northolt station, is a simple little early-fourteenth-century building, which was given a chancel and a new roof in the early sixteenth century. The three windows at the western end of the nave have fine tracery, now rather worn, and there is a fourteenth-century font and some good sixteenth-century brasses. St Mary, Norwood, on Tentelow Lane (near the M4) is slightly older, but it has suffered more frequent and intrusive restorations. St Mary in Perivale Lane, near Perivale station and Western Avenue, is a Norman church with a thirteenth-century chancel, a nave with a fifteenth-century roof and gallery, some good sixteenth-century brasses (to the Mylett family) and a very pretty sixteenth-century weatherboarded tower. There is another weatherboarded tower on the old church of Holy Cross, Greenford, which is on Oldfield Lane South.

Hillingdon, London's westernmost borough, is rich in medieval parish churches, several of which are worth making an effort to see. St Mary, Harefield, right on London's western edge, is a charming old church, mostly fourteenth century, with an early-Tudor tower and north aisle. It is famous for the number and beauty of its fifteenth-, sixteenth- and seventeenth-century monuments, most of which were built by the Newdigate and Ashby families, the main local landowners. The four-poster tomb of the Countess of Derby, Alice Spencer (died 1637), is probably the pick of a very rich collection. St Martin in Ruislip High Street, two miles to the south-east, is a thirteenth-century church with fifteenth-century chancel and tower, a Norman font, some faded late-medieval wall paintings and a good collection of monuments. St Giles, Ickenham, on the corner of Swakeleys Road and the High Road (near West Ruislip station), is a fourteenth-century church with a Tudor north aisle and a 1640s mortuary chapel, and very fine late-medieval roofs in the nave and chancel. St John the Baptist, Hillingdon, on the Uxbridge Road, is a thirteenth- and fourteenth-century church with Victorian additions and an unusually fine thirteenth-century chancel arch decorated with an assortment of gargoyles and monsters. The church also has excellent sixteenth-century brasses and seventeenth- and eight-eenth-century monuments to rich local families. In Church Road, Cowley, St Lawrence is a small, simple and surprisingly unspoiled twelfth- and thirteenth-century church, with a medieval roof and medieval pews in the chancel. St Mary's in Church Road, Hayes, is a thirteenth-century church with a fifteenth-century tower and north aisle, and medieval roofs throughout. Its most distinctive feature is a large wall painting of St Christopher, with a boy fishing in a river full of monsters and mermaids. The artist, working around 1500, was plainly not in touch with the latest developments in Italian painting. St Dunstan, in Cranford, a lovely medieval church with a fifteenth-century tower and chancel and an early-eighteenth-century nave, once belonged to the Knights Templar. The little church is crowded with monuments, many of which have great historical and artistic interest. Harlington, Cranford's neighbour on the M4, has the church of St Peter and St Paul, which has a Norman nave and a lovely Norman doorway decorated with long-tongued cats. Inside there is a fourteenth-century chancel with its original roof, a Norman font and some good monuments. And in Harmondsworth, between the M4 and Heathrow, there is another church, St Mary, to which every century since 1100 has made its contribution. There is a Norman nave and a very fine doorway, thirteenth-century arcading, a fourteenth-century chapel, chancel and nave roof, lovely pews from about 1500, seventeenth- and eighteenth-century monuments, an eighteenth-century cupola, Victorian glass and restraint in not turning the church into a Gothic fake, and twentieth-century floor tiles. The contribution of the twenty-first century is a planned third Heathrow runway, which threatens to destroy the work of almost a thousand years.

An even better reason for going to Harmondsworth is to see Greater London's finest medieval barn, which stands near the church. Manor Farm Barn, which was built by Winchester College in 1427, is over 58 metres long, and is one of the biggest and best timber-framed barns in England. At the time of writing it is threatened by the Heathrow third runway, and may be dismantled and re-erected, divorced from its historical context. The village of Harmondsworth has many interesting sixteenth-, seventeenth- and eighteenth-century houses, and some fine medieval and Tudor walls, and along the road in Sipson, also threatened by the airport, the William IV pub occupies a quite well preserved medieval hall house.

The borough of Hounslow has not been so fortunate in retaining its medieval buildings. Medieval churches in Feltham and Hanworth were replaced in 1812, and those in Hounslow and Isleworth were burned down in 1943. The latter has been well rebuilt, using the fifteenth-century tower and early-eighteenth-century nave walls. The medieval church of St Leonard, Heston, was needlessly demolished and rebuilt in the 1860s, leaving only its tower, west doorway and monuments. The fifteenth-century church of St Lawrence, Brentford, has been left to rot, and the parish church of Chiswick, St Nicholas, by the river in Church Street, was rebuilt, apart from its fifteenth-century tower, in the 1880s. It has good seventeenth- and eighteenth-century monuments, and interesting tombs in its churchyard, including those of the painters William Hogarth and Philip de Loutherbourg (died 1812), whose mausoleum is by John Soane. Of London's suburban churches, only St Anne, Kew, which has the bodies of Gainsborough and Johann Zoffany, has a churchyard so full of artistic talent. Hounslow's best medieval church is in the far west of the borough in East Bedfont. St Mary was originally a twelfth-century church, and it still has a Norman doorway, windows and chancel arch. The chancel and the nave and chancel roofs are fifteenth century, and there are plenty of Victorian additions. The best things in the church were discovered by Victorian restorers. In recesses on the north and east walls of the nave there are exceptional mid-thirteenth-century wall paintings of the Last Judgement and the Crucifixion, bright and clear after three hundred years hidden under limewash to save them from Puritan zealots. The church is in Hatton Road, hidden from the busy Staines Road by the trees in its churchyard.

South London has a scattering of good medieval churches, including a few worth making an effort to see. Starting with those along the Thames, All Saints, Kingston (just off Clarence Street), is a big medieval church with some Norman and thirteenth-century remnants, a fourteenth-century nave and transepts and a fifteenth-century chancel. The Victorians covered the whole building in flint, but do not be put off. Outside in the churchyard are the excavated foundations of the Saxon chapel in which it is thought the tenth-century kings of Wessex, from Edward the Elder to Ethelred the Unready, were crowned. The stone which is said to have been used in these coronations is now on display next to the Guildhall, in the High Street. Moving east along the river, the lovely church of St Peter, Petersham, has a thirteenth-century chancel, but is otherwise sixteenth, seventeenth and eighteenth century, not heavily Victorianized. Richmond's St Mary Magdalene, off George Street, has a 1507 tower, but is otherwise mid-eighteenth century, with very fine monuments. St Anne, Kew (on the Green), was built in 1710, and St Mary, Barnes, is a medieval church rebuilt after a disastrous fire in 1978, but retaining some interesting medieval features including a Norman doorway and traces of wall painting on the south wall of the old nave. St Mary, Putney, also gutted by fire in the 1970s, has a fifteenth-century tower and a rare and beautiful fan-vaulted chantry chapel, built by Bishop West of Ely in the 1520s.

St Mary, Merton, in Church Lane (near Merton Park station) is a Norman church with a fine thirteenth-century chancel, a fifteenth-century porch and much Victorian remodelling. In the churchyard there is a doorway from Merton Priory, which disappeared in the Reformation. Further south, Cheam has the Lumley Chapel, in the churchyard of St Dunstan, off Malden Road, near Cheam station. This is the chancel of the old parish church, a twelfth-century structure with a fine 1592 ceiling, a very good collection of medieval brasses and some fine monuments to the members of the Lumley family who died between 1577 and 1617. All Saints in Carshalton High Street is a late-twelfth-century (Norman and

Early English) church hidden in a late-Victorian rebuilding. The medieval nave is now the south aisle, the early-thirteenth-century chancel is now the Lady Chapel, and there is Saxon work in the lower part of the tower. There are some good monuments, but what catches the eye is the decorative work of Sir Ninian Comper the 1930s: the west gallery, the organ case and the painted reredos, rood and screen. A little further east, St Mary in Church Road, Beddington, is a medieval church with a late-fourteenth-century nave, tower and chancel, and a very well-preserved early Tudor chapel off the chancel, built by the Carew family, whose house next door is now a school. The chancel has good medieval brasses, and choir stalls with misericords, perhaps from Merton Abbey. Going east again, Croydon has the Archbishop's Palace (*see* Chapter Three) but no medieval churches, so the next good medieval church is All Saints, on Church Hill, Orpington. This little building, dwarfed now by the new church to which it serves as an ante-chapel, seems to have been a Saxon church remodelled around 1200. The tower, chancel arch and west doorway are of this date. The west porch was built by the rector Nicholas (died 1370), who asked to be buried there and got his wish. The most unusual feature of the church is a very rare Saxon sundial, which was discovered in 1957 set upside down into a pillar in the old nave. The Latin letters OR ... UM suggest the word *orologium*, and part of the Anglo-Saxon runic inscription has been translated as 'for him who knows how to seek out how'.

In the outer suburbs of south-east London there are three medieval churches. St Nicholas in Church Lane, Chislehurst, is a fifteenth-century church partly rebuilt in the nineteenth century. The tower, north aisle and north chapel date from about 1460, and there is possible Saxon material in the west wall of the nave. St Mary the Virgin in Bexley High Street was built around 1200 (the date of the tower) but was heavily disguised by restoration in the 1880s. St Paulinus, Crayford, is probably the most interesting of the three. It is a Norman church, one of the few in England which have two naves served equally by one chancel. The north nave was originally an aisleless nave, built around 1100, and the south nave was added about 90 years later. The church was given its chancel soon after 1300, the tower around 1400, and its south porch and two side chapels and its reconstructed central arcade in the fifteenth century. There are many interesting monuments, including the 1650s Draper family monument in the north chapel, which unusually shows their stillborn child.

CHAPTER TWO

PLEASURE GARDENS AND
COFFEE HOUSES

Marylebone Gardens in 1755

EACH AGE DEVELOPS its characteristic leisure institutions, reflecting, among other things, the technological, social and cultural circumstances of the day. In London between the Restoration of Charles II in 1660 and the French Revolutionary Wars of the 1790s, a wide range of new commercial leisure activities developed, creating a vibrant and varied metropolitan cultural life. Some of these innovations have survived into our own time. We owe to London in this period the novel, the periodical or magazine, the musical play, the daily newspaper, the commercial concert and the public art gallery and museum. Two of London's most important recreational institutions, the coffee house and the commercial pleasure garden, faded away in the nineteenth century, leaving little trace of their existence in the London of today, but we can find some remnants of these fascinating and important places if we know where to look.

*

Pleasure gardens were privately owned parks which offered entertainment, illuminations, music, fireworks, dancing, skittles and walks, in return, usually, for a small entry fee. In some you could picnic, others sold refreshments. Some were full-sized pleasure gardens, offering all these facilities in extensive and well-managed grounds. Vauxhall, Ranelagh, Marylebone Gardens and Cuper's Gardens were the leaders, setting the standard for others to imitate. Some of the rest (there were over fifty in eighteenth-century London) were modest tea gardens, others were the garden of a public house, and others offered medicinal waters from their own springs and wells. Ticket prices determined the social level of those using the gardens, but most were cheap enough for Londoners of most classes, from the rich to shopkeepers and working men, to visit them at least occasionally.

Although the great age of pleasure gardens was the eighteenth century, most were founded in the late 1600s. Some, including the original Spring Gardens, west of Charing Cross (now remembered in a street near Admiralty Arch), and Mulberry Gardens, on the site of Buckingham Palace, came and went before 1700. Marylebone Gardens, which were just to the east of Marylebone High Street, roughly between Weymouth and Devonshire Streets, started in 1650 and lasted until 1778. The most famous and long-lasting of all the gardens, Vauxhall, opened in 1661, and was one of the last to close, 198 years later. Cuper's Gardens, now covered by the southern approach to Waterloo Bridge, opened at around the same time and closed in 1760, and Ranelagh, which displaced Vauxhall as London's most fashionable garden, opened in 1742 and lasted for sixty years. Even in the dying decades of the gardens some new ones were opened, notably Cremorne Gardens, between King's Road, Chelsea, and the river, which opened in 1843 and closed in 1877. Its site is now occupied by the World's End estate, but a scrap of land, still known as Cremorne Gardens, survives by the river, next to Lots Road and Cheyne Walk.

Many of the smaller gardens were clustered together in Clerkenwell, between Farringdon Road and St John's Street, where there were medicinal chalybeate (iron-rich) springs, mostly associated with the River Fleet. Bagnigge Wells, Islington Spa and Mulberry Garden were all close to each other, and one of the group, Sadlers Wells, remains a place of entertainment today. Bagnigge Wells was on the Fleet, on the road now known as King's Cross Road, a little south of its junction with Wharton Street. If you go down the steps from Granville Square and cross King's Cross Road, going a little to the right, you will see an old carved white stone set in the wall of number 61, reading, 'This is Bagnigge House, neare the Pinder a

Wakefeilde. 1680'. The stone was supposedly taken from the house
of Nell Gwynn, which was nearby, and seems to be on the western
edge of the gardens. The Pindar of Wakefield was a public house at
328 Gray's Inn Road, nearby, and it still exists but is now known
as the Water Rats, the headquarters of the theatrical charity the
Grand Order of Water Rats. The pub's musical back room hosted
Bob Dylan's first London performance in 1962.

There was another group of gardens in the easily accessible
countryside just north of the New Road (now Euston and Pentonville Roads), between King's Cross and Islington, and several others
scattered further north, in Islington, Hornsey and Highgate. White
Conduit House, an alehouse west of Islington High Street, had a
fenced pleasure garden in the 1750s, with a fish pond, walks,
arbours, and a field for playing cricket with bats and balls lent
by the owner of the public house, Robert Bartholomew. Since they
were a short walk from the City, the gardens were popular with
middle-class Londoners, whether they wanted to flirt, walk, play or
drink tea and eat the famous White Conduit loaves. White Conduit
Gardens were advertised as the 'New Minor Vauxhall', but the
spread of working-class housing into Pentonville in the 1820s
and 1830s undermined their fashionable appeal, and most of their
customers were artisans, clerks and apprentices, who were given
fairly coarse entertainment. The gardens were sold for development
in 1849, and rows of houses built between White Conduit Street
(the northern section of which is now Cloudesley Road) and
Barnsbury Road, a little north of Chapel Market. White Conduit
House, in Barnsbury Road, became an ordinary public house again,
and remained there, rebuilt and renamed the Penny Farthing, until
2006. In one respect the legacy of White Conduit Gardens has
been more lasting. In 1786 a young man employed as an attendant
at the gardens, Thomas Lord, an excellent underarm bowler, was
asked by some aristocratic players in the team to find them a more
private cricket ground. Using their money, Lord took a lease on
Dorset Fields on the Portman Estate in Marylebone. This site is

now Dorset Square, next to the station. This is where, in 1787–8, the White Conduit Club merged with the Marylebone Club and formalized the rules of cricket. The club moved in 1811, and again, to its present ground in St John's Wood, in 1814.

Hampstead, then and still a favourite escape from the dirt of London, had four or five gardens or spas. From about 1700 Hampstead's spring water, which emerged in Well Walk, was believed to have healing properties, and in the early eighteenth century Hampstead Wells became a fashionable health and pleasure resort, London's answer to Tunbridge. Interest in the wells had faded before 1800, when Cheltenham and Harrogate had greater fashionable appeal, but, as is often the case, pubs survived when other social institutions disappeared. The Flask Tavern in Flask Walk is a reminder of Hampstead's history as a spa: the spring water was sold at 3d a flask in the Thatched House pub, which was rebuilt as the Flask in 1874. Well Walk, which begins at the northern end of Flask Walk, was once the centre of Hampstead's fashionable social life, and still has some fine late-Georgian houses. The painter John Constable, a great lover of Hampstead, lived at number 40, and the socialist H.M. Hyndman lived over the road, in a house (number 13) which the poet John Masefield also occupied. The first Long Room, or assembly room, was converted into a chapel in the 1720s and demolished in 1882. The house known as Wellside was built on the site ten years later. There is an 1882 stone drinking fountain opposite, with an inscription commemorating the gift in 1698 of the chalybeate well and six acres of land to the poor of Hampstead. A second Long Room was built down the road next to Burgh House, on the corner of New End Square, but that is also gone.

There was a third concentration of gardens south of the Thames, north of a line drawn from Vauxhall Bridge to London Bridge. One of these, Lambeth Wells, was on the road then called Three Coney Walk, which is now Lambeth Walk. There was a fourth group in Chelsea, near Ranelagh and the canals and reservoirs of the Chelsea waterworks, which was established a little to the east of the Royal Hospital (roughly at the northern end of Chelsea Bridge) in 1723.

Nearly all these gardens were on the edge of town, and the land they occupied was bound to be sold as building plots as London grew in the eighteenth and early nineteenth centuries, just as the market gardens, pastures, tenter grounds and osier beds were. In most cases nothing now remains except perhaps a street name, a plaque or a pub, but, as it happens, the two most important gardens, Vauxhall and Ranelagh, are still open spaces today, and we can still walk where Samuel Pepys, Dr Johnson and Horace Walpole walked, though without the flirtation and fireworks. Ranelagh Gardens were closed in 1803 and the great Rotunda demolished in 1805, but the grounds were not sold for development. Instead, they eventually passed into the ownership of the Chelsea Royal Hospital. The gardens are open in daylight hours but closed on Sunday mornings and every lunchtime from 12.30 to 2.00. You can get into them from Royal Hospital Road or the Chelsea Embankment. The wooded hills and twisting paths are reminiscent of an old pleasure garden, but they cannot recreate the atmosphere of Ranelagh in its great days, when (according to Horace Walpole) everybody went there. 'The floor is all of beaten princes ... You can't set your foot without treading on a Prince or Duke of Cumberland.' The company of a few Chelsea pensioners is not quite the same thing.

After nearly two hundred years the twelve acres of Vauxhall Gardens were finally sold off for building in 1859, and soon nothing was left of them except the names given to the new streets built on the land. On a modern map the site of the gardens is marked on three sides by Goding Street, St Oswald's Place and Kennington Lane, and nearby Tyers Street and Jonathan Street commemorate the most famous owner of the gardens, Jonathan Tyers. But German bombers and Lambeth Council between them have cleared much of this land again, and in recent years Spring Gardens have been reborn, right next to Vauxhall railway station. This is a useful open space in an area crowded with flats, workshops and offices, and watched over by the huge MI5 building on the river, but without trees, music or entertainers it has nothing to remind us of the pleasures that once took place here: 'Women squeak and men drunk fall / Sweet enjoyment at Vauxhall'.

For these reminders we have to look elsewhere. As the commercial gardens faded, they were replaced by public parks which offered recreations not unlike those once found at Ranelagh and Vauxhall – brass band concerts, bowling greens, boating lakes, flower gardens and so on. Regent's Park, which was laid out in the 1820s, had a zoo from 1826 and a botanical garden (inside the Inner Circle) which held weekly musical promenades from 1839. The botanical garden moved out in 1932, and now Queen Mary's Gardens and the open-air theatre occupy its site. Queen Mary's Gardens have an enormous variety of different labelled roses, some interesting statues, a waterfall, a water garden, a sunken garden and some fine trees. You might prefer the seclusion of the gardens of St John's Lodge, which are to the north-east of Queen Mary's Gardens, tucked away down an arched alley off the Inner Circle. These pretty gardens have pools, fountains, 1930s statuary and a hidden garden surrounded by a circle of trees.

Battersea Park, which was created from riverside marshes, a fairground and market gardens in the 1850s, was designed as a replacement for the lost pleasure gardens and was often called a pleasure ground. It had an artificial lake (pumped from the Thames by a steam engine) with spectacular cascades, a wonderful four-acre subtropical garden, refreshment rooms, carriage drives, plantations, shrubberies and parade grounds. The park's designer, James Pennethorne, raised the level of the whole park, and created hills, banks and interesting contours, including the peninsula in the lake, by using a thousand cubic yards of soil taken from the excavation of the Victoria Docks at Canning Town.

Many of these original features remain, but the park bears the marks of a further 150 years of innovation in the field of public recreation. Some of the trees planted by its first curator are still there, grown now to enormous size. Look for the massive black walnut tree near the Albert Gate entrance just north of the car park, and the strawberry tree near the Pump House. The park accommodated the new sports that Londoners took up in the nineteenth century, including bowls, cricket, football, trap-ball, rounders and cycling, and it still serves the community in this way. Its gardens were redesigned according to the tastes of new generations. The subtropical garden is still there, smaller and less impressive than it once was, and the two herb gardens, looking a little unkempt, are still there, too. The walled Old English Garden, which replaced a botanic garden in 1912, is still charming and peaceful, and there is a Horticultural Therapy Garden (to encourage gardening among the disabled), the 1970s' contribution to the rich cultural mix of Battersea Park.

After the Second World War Battersea's status as a pleasure park was renewed by its selection as one of the main sites for the 1951 Festival of Britain. While the South Bank hosted the more educational exhibits, Battersea got a funfair, a Grand Vista, a crazy railway, a fantastic Guinness clock and a huge marquee ballroom. The funfair remained until the 1970s, long after the Festival of Britain was over, but only some of its foundations are left now. Between the Old English Garden and the Peace Pagoda (a gift to London from Japanese Buddhists in 1984) you will find the Grand Vista (not looking too grand now), with fountains, pools, cascades and a colonnade, which was the contribution of the artists Osbert Lancaster and John Piper to the Festival of Britain site, which stretched from here to the east end of the park. A path through the old herb garden takes you to some more survivors of 1951, an aviary and a children's zoo.

It is pleasant to walk round the lake, one of the original features of the Victorian park. Following the lake anticlockwise from the East Carriage Drive, you will come to the Victorian cascade, which is more likely to be flowing at the weekend. The Pump House, on the northern edge of the lake, was built in 1861 to house the steam engine that raised water for the cascades and the lake, and is now a gallery. Beyond this is the strawberry tree, and a three-figure sculpture by Henry Moore which has been here since 1948 when a pioneering outdoor sculpture exhibition was held in the park. On the western edge of the lake you come to the showpiece of the Victorian park, the subtropical garden, which still has some palms and other trees that have to be wrapped up in the winter. The old splendour is gone, but its protective banks, winding paths, fine trees and lawns are still there and well maintained. Finally, passing Barbara Hepworth's 1961 tribute to Dag Hammarskjöld, you come to an enclosure for deer, wallabies and peacocks which was constructed in 1888.

A more powerful competitor with the last pleasure gardens was the new park at Sydenham Heights, which was renamed after the 1851 Great Exhibition glasshouse, the Crystal Palace, when it was moved from Hyde Park and reopened there in 1854. For over eighty years the Palace was one of London's greatest attractions, drawing visitors and suburban settlers to this remote part of south London. Crystal Palace burnt down in a spectacular fire on 30 November 1936, but some scraps remain, and some of the other attractions installed here for public education and delight can still be seen. Go into the gardens at Boundaries Gate, on the roundabout between Anerley Road and Crystal Palace Parade, the terminus of several bus routes, including some from central London. To your left, towards the BBC mast, is the vast site of the Palace, which still has extensive foundations, two grand vaulted terraces, sets of great granite steps at the centre and sides, the High Level station subway which took visitors from the station to the Palace, and several statues and constructions saved from the fire. The statue of a nymph in the flower garden here is one of the many statues that once adorned the Palace grounds, and the round brick stump over to the right, near Anerley Road, is the base of one of the two huge water towers, built by Isambard Kingdom Brunel, which once supplied the hundreds of powerful fountains that cooled the terraces, pumped from an artesian well deep below the park. The six sphinxes on this terrace, in rather poor condition now, were copies of an Egyptian original in the Louvre.

When you have admired the fine views into and out of London from the Upper Terrace, go down the steps to the Lower Terrace, which was once occupied by a formal Italian garden. Down the steps from the Lower Terrace, past the large bust of Sir Joseph Paxton, the creator of the Crystal Palace, is the National Sports Centre, built in the 1960s on the site of a motor racing track which in turn took the place of a sports stadium in which FA Cup finals were played between 1895 and 1914. If you turn left along the bottom of the Lower Terrace, passing a statue of Dante, you will come to a concert bowl, a lily pond and a hornbeam maze, one of the largest in Britain. If you carry on around the outside of the sports centre, or go right instead of left, you will come to the most interesting part of the Victorian park, its south-eastern corner.

Here the founders of the park created an outdoor lesson in the history of the earth for visitors. The boating lake was once called the Tidal Lake, because it rose and fell to meet the demands of Paxton's waterworks. As you walk across the lake, via two bridges, you will see huge life-sized models of prehistoric animals, made by Benjamin Waterhouse Hawkins, director of the Crystal Palace fossil department, under the supervision of Sir Richard Owen, the creator of the Natural History Museum and a powerful opponent of Darwin's *Origin of Species*. The elks, iguanodons, pterodactyls, ichthyosaurs, dinosaurs (a word coined by Owen) and amphibians lurking in the woods around the lake were based on the fossil discoveries of the early nineteenth century, not on the ideas of Darwin, which were not made public until 1858, and some of the reconstructions were not accurate. Still, they represent the best scientific understanding of prehistoric creatures right at the end of the pre-Darwinian period, and both here and in the Natural History Museum Owen had as great an influence as Darwin on Victorian perceptions of the prehistoric world. The models, constructed in brick, iron, tile and stone, are set among replicas of geological strata, including coal seams, sandstone and chalk, to introduce day trippers to the science of geology. On your way back to the Boundaries Gate, you could visit the children's zoo, or urban farm, which has been a feature of the park since 1952.

If you have made the journey out to Crystal Palace, you could visit Sydenham Wells Park, which is less than a mile from the Sydenham exit from the grounds (near the maze). Sydenham Wells Park is a survivor from the many gardens with medicinal waters that were popular in the seventeenth and eighteenth centuries. Waters were found here around 1640, when this was part of Sydenham Common. Many wells were dug to satisfy the demands of the Londoners who visited Sydenham, who included, on one occasion, George III. The wells fell out of favour in the nineteenth century and most of the common was built over, but this beautiful park was saved. It still has its wells and springs, and now children play in its newly created water features. For adults not so keen on water, the Greyhound Inn, which is on Kirkdale, near Sydenham station, has served visitors to the wells since about 1720, and is still serving them today. The inn used to be on the edge of Sydenham Common, but now it is half a mile from Sydenham Wells, a measure of how much of the common was lost to suburban development.

*

At the height of their popularity, between the late seventeenth and early nineteenth centuries, there were hundreds of coffee houses in London. William Maitland's *History of London*, published in 1739, reckoned that there were 551. Bryant Lillywhite's exhaustive study of London coffee houses lists over 2,000 but many of these were short-lived or of uncertain authenticity. England's first coffee house opened in Oxford in 1650, and the first in London was supposedly opened by a Turkish Greek, Pasqua Rosee, in 1652, on the corner of St Michael's Alley and Castle Court, just behind St Michael's church in Cornhill. In fact the written record (in the shape of John Aubrey's *Brief Lives*) suggests that the founder and owner of Pasqua Rosee's Head was Christopher Bowman, the coachman to a Turkey merchant, Mr Hodges, who set him up in the business, presumably to increase the sales of a commodity he imported. It was destroyed in the Great Fire of 1666, and its replacement on the site was the Jamaica Coffee House, which became a favourite with London merchants involved in the West Indies trade.

It was common for coffee houses to attract specialized clienteles – merchants, brokers, marine insurers, wits, gamblers, politicians – and thus, in time, to form the basis of exclusive organizations dedicated to a specific economic or social pursuit. Lloyd's, the marine and general insurers that began in Edward Lloyd's Coffee House, is a famous example, and the Stock Exchange, which started as Jonathan's Coffee House in Change Alley (near the Jamaica Coffee House), is another. By the 1840s the Jamaica Coffee House was charging a subscription to its members, and in 1869 it changed its name to the Jamaica Wine House, which it is still called today. The present building, an odd construction in red Mansfield stone, dates from 1885, and the place still serves coffee. Whether it is like the seventeenth-century stuff, 'made the Turkish way, in little china dishes, as hot as you can suffer it, black as soot and tasting not unlike it', I leave you to discover. There are two more historic refreshment places near the Jamaica Wine House. One, Simpson's Tavern, between Cornhill and Castle Court, has been here since the fire of 1748, with an authentic-looking shopfront added in 1900. The other, the George and Vulture in Castle Court, was also rebuilt after the 1748 fire, but has seventeenth-century origins. Robert Hooke, the scientist, City Surveyor and architect, met his clients here in the 1670s, and in *Pickwick Papers* Dickens had Mr Pickwick staying here while he defended himself against Mrs Bardell's breach of promise suit. There was another George and Vulture round the corner in George Yard, but the surviving establishment, with its richly panelled walls, reeks of history.

This triangle of little alleys between Cornhill, Lombard Street and Gracechurch Street was one of the heartlands of the coffee house in its heyday, especially those that served the merchants and financiers whose business was in the Royal Exchange and the Bank of England. The Jerusalem Coffee House, which began in the early eighteenth century and became a subscription house for East Indies merchants in the 1840s, was situated in Cowper's Court (between Birchin Lane and Cornhill) until the 1890s, and one of the greatest and longest-lasting houses, Garraway's, was here, as a carved plaque high on a wall in Change Alley reminds us. Its founder, Thomas Garraway (or Garway), made his mark on English history in the early 1670s by being the first person to sell tea, in leaf or liquid form, in this country. Garraway's opened in Change Alley in or around 1670, when the alleys and the nearby Royal Exchange were rebuilt after the Great Fire. It was rebuilt after the 1748 fire, and lasted for over two hundred years as a coffee and commercial auction house. It closed for business in 1872, when it was demolished to make way for a bank. Jonathan's, which also has a plaque, in another branch of Change Alley, lasted from 1677 (the plaque date is wrong) to 1778, when it was destroyed in another fire. From the mid-nineteenth century large banking headquarters dominated these streets, turning the Cornhill alleys into white-tiled canyons. Now, oddly enough, many of these banking buildings, too large for modern needs, have been converted into bars, selling many of the same things that Garraway's and Jonathan's sold 250 years ago.

Coffee houses were still thriving in the early nineteenth century, but in the 1840s and 1850s several developments, including the growth of clubs, financial institutions, restaurants and hotels, and the introduction of the penny post, undermined them. Some coffee houses lasted until late in the century, but their great days were over when Garraway's closed in 1872. Some of the buildings survive, of course, and some are still places of refreshment. The Grecian Coffee House, one of the houses from which Joseph Addison and Richard Steele wrote their famous letters on coffee house life for the *Spectator* between 1711 and 1714, still exists, but as a pub not a coffee house. It is in Devereux Court, a lane at the western end of the south side of Fleet Street, leading into Essex Court and Fountain Court, in Middle Temple. The Devereux public house is named after Robert Devereux, Earl of Essex, whose mansion, Essex House, was here until the developer Nicholas Barbon knocked it down and built the present streets in the 1670s and 1680s. Devereux's bust looks down from the first floor, and the date on it, 1676, is when Barbon built this and the neighbouring houses. The pub was stuccoed in 1844, but in essentials it remains the building that was from the late seventeenth century until 1843 the Grecian Coffee House, the favourite meeting place of Royal Society scientists in the late seventeenth century. A room in St John's Gate, which crosses St John's Lane near Clerkenwell Road, used to be a coffee house run by Richard Hogarth (William's father), perhaps between 1704 and 1714. In 1704 a club met there every day at 4 o'clock in which only Latin was spoken.

The Old Coffee House pub, near Golden Square in Soho, is described in Chapter Six, but quite near it, in Gerrard Street, another Nicholas Barbon street (south of Shaftesbury Avenue), buildings that once housed two interesting coffee houses survive right next to each other. Number 12 Gerrard Street, a late-seventeenth-century house with large Ionic pillars, was once Mills' Coffee House, which entered the historical record in 1702 and left it in 1811. Behind the stuccoed front of 9 Gerrard Street is a house built around 1700 (according to the latest Pevsner guide) or 1758 (according to the *Survey of London*) which was one of the most prominent of the fifty-odd London coffee houses called the Turk's Head. The Turk's Head moved from Greek Street to Gerrard Street around 1750, and it was here, in 1764, that the famous dining club known as the Club, or the Literary Club, was founded by Samuel Johnson and Sir Joshua Reynolds. In April 1773 James Boswell was elected to the Club, and recorded in his diary, 'I hurried to the Turk's Head in Gerrard St, Soho, and was introduced to such a society as can seldom be found: Mr Edmund Burke, Dr Nugent ... Mr [David] Garrick, Dr

[Oliver] Goldsmith.' Other intellectual giants associated with the Club in the 1770s included Edward Gibbon, Adam Smith, Richard Brinsley Sheridan, Thomas Gainsborough and Charles James Fox. Boswell had lodgings at number 22 Gerrard Street in 1775, and Edmund Burke lived at number 37 in the 1780s. The landlord of the Turk's Head died in 1783 (a year before Dr Johnson), and the Club moved elsewhere. From 1825 to 1957 number 9 Gerrard Street was the home of the Westminster General Dispensary, and now, in the main street of London's Chinatown, it is occupied by a gift shop known as the Jensen Trading Company and the New Loon Moon Chinese supermarket. Inevitably, these commercial users have altered the ground-floor rooms, but those on the first floor, probably those used by Dr Johnson's Club, are still intact, with their eighteenth-century deal panelling. As you pass them, remember that this was the meeting place of probably the most talented, versatile and intelligent group of Londoners that ever met together.

In Chapter Three there are brief descriptions of Don Saltero's, 18 Cheyne Walk, Chelsea, and of the Dove Coffee House, now a public house, on Hammersmith Mall.

After a century of decline there was a revival in coffee houses – in the guise of coffee bars – in the 1950s, mainly thanks to Italian caterers who had settled in Soho, Marylebone and Clerkenwell. The Gaggia coffee machine, first made in Italy in 1938, arrived in London in the early 1950s, and made it easy to make espresso and cappuccino coffee well and cheaply. The first of this new generation of Gaggia coffee houses was the Moka espresso bar, at 29 Frith Street, which opened in 1953. The Moka established a smart and modern 'Festival of Britain' style, in which Formica, plastic, lino and leatherette played a prominent part. This style was copied by hundreds of new coffee bars in London and elsewhere in the 1950s. These coffee bars played a vital part in the development of post-war youth culture, with its jazz, skiffle and rock music, radical politics and nuclear disarmament, youth movements (Teddy boys, mods, rockers, beatniks and so on), crime and sex. If 'Swinging London' really existed, it owed its existence, in part, to coffee bars. Since the 1990s the relentless spread of American coffee shops, which can afford much higher rents and sell coffee by the bucket, has driven the independent Italian coffee bar near to extinction, but you can still find them in their natural central London habitat, if you look soon and carefully.

The Moka of 29 Frith Street is gone, but Bar Italia is still at number 22, getting its ground coffee from Angelucci's at 23b. Jimmy's basement restaurant at 23a is in the same style and spirit. Round the corner the 2i's coffee bar (see Chapter Five) used to be at number 59, and the Café Torino was on the corner of Dean Street, but the Algerian Coffee Stores is still there, at number 52. Nearby, in Denman Street, off Shaftesbury Avenue near Piccadilly Circus, the New Piccadilly preserves its 1950s style, with Formica tables and wooden booths. Two streets away, at 18 Brewer Street, the Lina Stores is an Italian delicatessen which evokes the Soho of the 1950s. At the eastern end of Brewer Street, at 101 Wardour Street, is Bar Bruno, an authentic Italian coffee bar, and in Bateman Street, nearby, the Lorelei, another in 1950s style, serves cheap and very good espresso.

In Clerkenwell you can still drink coffee and eat in Scotti's Snack Bar next to the Marx Memorial Library on Clerkenwell Green, or try the Italian cafe and fish shop on Mount Pleasant, the Golden Fry. Near the top of the Farringdon Road, at number 162, the Muratori is a genuine Italian cafe, and if you are further east you should visit the king of Italian cafes, Pellicci's, at 332 Bethnal Green Road (near Bethnal Green Tube), which has been here since 1900 and has looked like this – bright yellow Vitrolite, marquetry panelling and steel lettering – since 1946.

An Islington favourite is S & M's (previously Alfredo's), at 6 Essex Road, near the junction with Upper Street, which was rescued from closure a few years ago. Like Pellicci's, it is English Heritage listed. To avoid disappointment, you should know that S & M stands for sausage and mash. Another favourite of cafe enthusiasts in Islington is Alpino's, at 97 Chapel Market. In Mayfair there is the Chalet, at 81 Grosvenor Street, which combines Swiss and Italian styles, and you might enjoy Gambardella at 47–48 Vanbrugh Park, Greenwich, and L. Rodi, at 16 Blackhorse Lane in Walthamstow. These places are dying out so quickly, like red squirrels under the onslaught of Starbucks' greys, that it is worth visiting them now, before they go the way of Jonathan's, Garraway's and the Turk's Head.

Finally, if you want to find out more about the place of coffee in London's social, cultural and economic life you can visit the Bramah Tea and Coffee Museum, near London Bridge station. It is at 40 Southwark Street, near its junction with Redcross Way, and is open every day. Admission is £4. The museum will show you how to make the best coffee, and also serves very good coffee and afternoon teas. Southwark Street has many fine mid-Victorian office buildings, including the old Hop Exchange (Central Buildings). Nearby, the lovely George Inn on Borough High Street still has its seventeenth-century coffee room.

*

From Pillar to Post

Answers to the numbered questions are on pages 397–401

I'll take you on a West End tour,
With questions that are not too solemn.
So get your pen and walking shoes
And meet your friends at Nelson's Column.

Every answer's plain to see,
So look around and walk quite slowly
And on your way you have to find
The mystery word, which is PINOLI.

Who carved the bronze beheaded King
Who gave his name to Carolina? [1]
Go through the Arch and tell me who
Died in Africa and China. [2]

Upstairs and past the Grand Old Duke,
Through the broad and statued Place.
Who's that glittering on your left? [3]
Which Falcon lost a chilly race? [4]

Cross and turn right in Pall Mall
And soon you take an old arcade.
Who built this little row of shops,
And what's the year that it was made? [5]

Turn right into a kingly street –
Who built the first theatre here? [6]
And what's the tree that guided it
Through its tricentennial year? [7]

Round the front, tell me who founded
The state the US couldn't beat. [8]
Then cross the Market and take Suffolk –
First the Place and then the Street.

Richard Cobden's on your left,
But where's the scene of wild acclaim? [9]
And which painter killed his father
And seems to have his victim's name? [10]

On weekdays go through Hobhouse Court
Which leads you into Whitcomb Street.
If it's shut take Pall Mall East
And Whitcomb till the two paths meet.

Now it's time to name the Digger, [11]
Then watch the ball (the old sign says)?
Identify the comic drinker
Whose whereabouts were known in Fez. [12]

Left on Panton, who's the fellow
Whose weapon was a naked knuckle? [13]
And where's the gilded number seven
Whose customers both drink and chuckle? [14]

Take Oxendon to Coventry,
Then right and left for Wardour Street.
Where's the handsome brick-red bird [15]
And where did gold and finance meet? [16]

Through Gerrard's gates and Chinese arch
Until you find the old Turk's Head.
What wits and scholars gathered there,
With Boswell noting all they said? [17]

Find the metal-beater's house [18]
And name the wit at forty-three, [19]
Then turn back to Wardour Street,
And turn right up to Shaftesbury.

On your way please make a note
Of the man whose goods were curled. [20]
His friends included, as you see,
Two giants of the acting world.

Straight ahead to find St Anne's –
If the garden's open, then go in it.
Three questions for our little quiz –
Answer them and you might win it.

Who left his kingdom to his creditors? [21]
And who's the champion of truth? [22]
Who is buried in the tower,
Creator of a famous sleuth? [23]

North on Wardour, then down Meard Street,
Whose medium was H_2O? [24]
Which house has the highest number, [25]
And when did John Meard build this row? [26]

Left in Dean Street, who's the thinker
Whose words unite the working class? [27]
Now return to Bateman Street –
Where did Orwell drain his glass? [28]

Right on Frith Street, find two people
Who gave us many tuneful treats. [29]
Which pioneer of home enjoyment
Couldn't show his friends repeats? [30]

Left on Compton, left again,
Who's the slowest Greek Street rider? [31]
Where did sixties clubbers go? [32]
And who was London's pot provider? [33]

In Soho Square, who gets the money
When you put it down the chute? [34]
Who did Cibber celebrate? [35]
Who saved the French from Rome's pursuit? [36]

Now take the Row beside St Pat's,
To reach the road where bookworms shop.
Go right and left down Denmark Street,
The London home of jazz and pop.

One door past the diving master
A famous place that has no plaque.
Name the royal-sounding studio
Which made the first Mick Jagger track. [37]

Right on Flitcroft, what's the place that
Paints the scenes for West End shows? [38]
Now take Stacey by the churchyard
And just keep going where it goes.

On the corner of the Avenue,
Whose history started with a chorus? [39]
Now cross and left and go down Mercer.
I need a rhyme – where's my thesaurus?

Seven faces straight ahead –
Which Queen Bee took off their burka? [40]
Now forward into Monmouth Street –
Who used to be a harness worker? [41]

And whose workshop used to ring
With sounds of sawing, carving, chipping? [42]
Now his name means something else,
Not varnishing, but stripping.

You're home and maybe very dry,
So find the pub where Martins meet,
That used to be the Ben Caunt's Head,
And join me for a liquid treat.

CHAPTER THREE

*

LONDON HOUSES

Lindsey House, Lincoln's Inn Fields, in 1761

ALTHOUGH LONDON is a battered and poorly preserved city, there is not a place in England where the development of the English house can be better studied. In Greater London there are dozens of fine old houses, most of which are taken for granted, ignored or almost unknown. Some of them, including Syon House, Hampton Court, Ham House and Kensington Palace, are aristocratic or royal palaces, or what tour companies call stately homes. Others are fine country houses built by rich London merchants or country gentlemen in what is now suburban London. Medieval and Tudor survivors are scattered and rare, but they can be found, and the fact that London is ever-changing, representing not one age of prosperity but many, means that there are plenty of examples from every subsequent period rather than a preponderance from one in particular. Because London has grown in the last three hundred years to absorb many country towns and villages, and hundreds of square miles of open land, Greater London now includes many large and small houses representing, in particular, the desire of rich aristocrats to live in comfort near London or of successful London merchants and financiers to have a place in the country.

There are no ordinary medieval houses left in London, but several great houses still exist, especially in the suburbs. Starting at the top, the Tower of London might be counted as a royal house, and so might what is left of the Palace of Westminster, the London home of medieval kings from Edward the Confessor (died 1065) to Henry VIII. When the palace was destroyed by fire in 1834 its great hall was saved on the orders of Lord Melbourne, who had firefighters concentrate their hoses on its ancient structure. Westminster Hall was originally built by William II (Rufus) in 1097–9, and the lower parts of the walls were kept when Richard II and his master mason Henry Yevele remodelled the hall in the 1390s. The rebuilt hall has the world's biggest surviving medieval hammerbeam roof, and is probably the finest medieval hall in Europe. William built Westminster Hall as a banqueting hall, but its main function from the thirteenth to the nineteenth century was as a centre of royal justice and administration. There can hardly be a building in England that has seen more dramatic events. This is where Edward II abdicated and Richard II was deposed, where Charles I was tried and condemned and Cromwell was made Lord Protector. William Wallace, Sir John Oldcastle, Sir Thomas More, Bishop John Fisher, Anne Boleyn, the Duke of Somerset, the Earl of Essex, Guy Fawkes, the Earl of Strafford, were all tried and condemned here.

The hall can be visited in several ways. When Parliament is sitting there are debates there on Tuesday and Wednesday 9.30 to 2.00, and on Thursday 2.30 to 5.30, which you can sit in on if you arrive early at the St Stephen's Entrance. If you are a UK resident, contact your MP or a member of the Lords to go on a free 75-minute guided tour of Parliament on Monday or Tuesday mornings or Friday afternoons. In the summer break, August and September, you can get the same thing for a fee of about £12 by phoning 0870 906 3773 or waiting at St Stephen's Entrance. For details, see www.parliament.uk.

The other parts of Westminster Palace to survive the fire were the Chapel of St Mary Undercroft, the late-thirteenth-century crypt under St Stephen's Hall, an early Tudor cloister (now offices) and courtyard, which are not easy to visit, and the more accessible Jewel Tower, a personal treasure house built by Henry Yevele for Edward III in 1365. The Jewel Tower stands in a garden next to Abingdon Street, near Victoria Tower (the square tower of the Houses of Parliament) by the wall of the Abbey Garden. It is a three-storey L-shaped tower in ragstone, bearing traces of the walls of the palace grounds, which joined it on two sides. The interior, which you can enter for about £3, has six rooms, with fourteenth-century features and a strongroom created in 1621, when the tower was adapted as a store for parliamentary records. There is a display of ornate and graphic late-eleventh-century stone capitals from William II's Westminster Hall.

Whitehall Palace, the rambling series of buildings and gardens which Henry VIII seized from Cardinal Wolsey in 1529, extended along Whitehall roughly from what is now called Downing Street to the Admiralty and Whitehall Place. Almost the whole palace burned down in 1698, except the Banqueting House, where Inigo Jones's stone was more fire-resistant than the older buildings, and the Tudor wine cellar. Jones built the Banqueting House in 1619–22 for James I, who intended to use it for festivities and ceremonial occasions. The interior of this beautifully proportioned building is decorated with very large paintings by Rubens, who completed them in 1635. Their glorification of kingship, and especially of the reign of Charles I, would have been among the last things the King saw before he stepped out of the window here onto the scaffold in 1649. You can see them at less personal cost: the Banqueting House is open every day but Sunday and costs about £4.50 to visit.

Another remnant of Whitehall Palace is harder, but not impossible, to see. When the Ministry of Defence was built behind the Banqueting House in the 1940s and 1950s some interiors from older buildings on the site were preserved in convenient locations within the new building. The most famous of these is the old Whitehall wine cellar, which dates from 1512–15 and is therefore Wolsey's, not Henry VIII's. To arrange a guided visit to this interesting room you need to contact the Ministry of Defence. They will only accept bookings from groups of 10–20, not individuals, and will require full proof of identity. Their application form is found at http://www.forums.mod.uk/visits/form.htm. Finally, if you continue along Horse Guards Avenue towards the river, you can see Queen Mary's

Steps on the right in Victoria Embankment Gardens, near the Ministry of Defence. These include a corner of the wall of Henry VIII's Whitehall Palace and a rebuilt section of a riverside terrace and steps built by Nicholas Hawksmoor, Wren's assistant, in 1692, six years before the fire. In 1717 the royal party set out from these steps for the river procession at which Handel's Water Music was performed.

The palaces of two medieval churchmen survive. Fulham Palace was the chief residence of the Bishop of London from the eighteenth century to 1973, and is now run by the local council and a trust. Much of the present palace is eighteenth or nineteenth century, but the picturesque west courtyard with a lovely fountain in the middle dates from around 1500, and the great hall is late fifteenth century. The rest of the palace has interesting seventeenth- and eighteenth-century work, including a fine dining room of c. 1750 (Bishop Sherlock's Dining Room), the 1770s–80s east court, and wooden panelling in Bishop Sherlock's Drawing Room which was taken from the Doctors' Commons (near St Paul's) when it was demolished in 1867. The 13-acre grounds were once a very important botanical garden, and there is a herb garden, fine old trees and a stretch of late-medieval brick wall to remind us of their past glory. The very long moat was filled in in 1924. There is a museum in the newer part of the palace, but you can see the older parts in guided tours on the first and third Sundays of each month, costing about £5. The gardens and museum are free and open every day. See www.fulhampalace.org for times and prices.

London's other great ecclesiastical palace, Lambeth Palace (see Chapter One), is older and better preserved but harder to visit, and of Winchester House, near Southwark Cathedral, there is only a ruined fragment of its great hall.

The Archbishops of Canterbury had several houses in the area that is now Greater London. When they were in Middlesex, they lived in Headstone Manor, which is now the oldest timber-framed house in Middlesex, standing in a park between Pinner and Wealdstone, near Headstone Lane station. The house was built in the 1340s, remodelled and enlarged in the 1630s and 1650s, and mostly refaced in brick in 1772. Still, the fourteenth-century open hall and service wing survive, and though the hall is less than half its original size it is a wonderful reminder of the domestic lives of wealthy medieval Londoners, and of the ways in which the houses of the rich developed over the next four hundred years. The moat that surrounded the fourteenth-century house is still there, and two early-sixteenth-century barns in the grounds have been restored for the Harrow Museum. For decades Headstone Manor was under scaffolding, but now it is visible again, and there are guided tours of the house on weekend afternoons between May and October, costing about £2.50. See www.harrowarts.com/museum for details.

Another of the Archbishops' palaces survives in Croydon, between Old Palace Road and Church Street, about 15 minutes from both East and West Croydon stations. Archbishops used this as a halfway house between Canterbury and Lambeth from the thirteenth century until 1780. The surviving buildings include a great hall, built in the 1390s and remodelled fifty years later, with a beautiful and complicated roof, a guardroom or audience chamber of around 1400 and a fifteenth-century chapel, all grouped around two little courtyards. The palace is now the Old Palace School, but there are quite frequent afternoon guided tours of these fascinating buildings, and these are listed at www.friendsofoldpalace.org.

There is a medieval palace in suburban east London, just outside the old London County Council boundary, in Eltham, half a mile from Eltham station. Eltham Palace, now an English Heritage site, was given to the future Edward II by the Bishop of Durham in 1305. Later kings stayed here and added new buildings, many of which are now gone. The main medieval survival is the Great Hall begun by Edward IV in 1475, but there are also some late-medieval walls and gables, the foundations of the chapel built by Henry VIII (who was brought up here) and some early-Tudor royal ap... a medieval moat with a four-arched fifteenth-c... 19 acres of gardens. What makes the palace par...

is the complete makeover it was given by the Courtauld family in the 1930s. Almost the whole house, except the Great Hall, is decorated in the art deco style, making this once-neglected medieval palace probably the best 1930s art deco house in England. It is open Sunday to Wednesday, except in January, for about £8.

The other important remnant of a medieval London house is Crosby Hall, the great hall of Crosby Place, a house built by a rich merchant, Sir John Crosby, in Bishopsgate in the 1460s. The hall was rescued and moved to Chelsea when the site was cleared in 1908, and now has been well restored as the centrepiece of a new Tudor mansion by another rich London merchant, Christopher Moran. It is not open to the public but can be seen from outside in Cheyne Walk or Danvers Street, near Battersea Bridge. The house occupies the site of the garden of Sir Thomas More, whose chapel and monument are a few yards to the east in Chelsea Old Church, restored after extensive war damage but still full of interest.

Some of the most important houses in Greater London date from the sixteenth century. The best, Hampton Court Palace, was built for the mighty Cardinal Wolsey, who presented it to Henry VIII in 1529 in a last-minute attempt to avert his own downfall. Henry VIII, who lived here with five of his wives (consecutively), built the Great Hall, added wings to Wolsey's west facade, and remodelled the Clock Court. The palace remained a favourite royal residence for all the Tudor monarchs, but it was not substantially altered until William III employed Christopher Wren to rebuild the Fountain Court, add a south range to the Clock Court and build an orangery. When you visit Hampton Court today the magnificent west front, built in the old Gothic style, is mainly as Wolsey and his King left it, the Base Court is mainly Wolsey's, and parts of the Great Hall, rebuilt by the King, may reflect Wolsey's work. The kitchens, Chapel Royal, tennis courts, sixteenth-century royal apartments, the astronomical clock and the layout of the grounds date from Henry VIII's reign. Most of the rest of the palace is Wren's work for William and Mary. The palace is open every day, and a full ticket costs £13. The formal gardens can be visited for nothing from October to March.

Outer west London, which is very rich in fine historic houses, has two Tudor mansions reflecting two different classes of wealthy Londoner, the aristocrat with a place near town, and the merchant with a place in the country. The Duke of Somerset acquired the Isleworth estates of a recently dissolved Brigittine convent in 1546, and started building himself a large mansion. When Somerset was executed in 1552 John Dudley, Duke of Northumberland, who had procured his downfall, seized his power in Westminster and his lands in Isleworth. Syon House, the last of the great privately owned mansions in London, is essentially the house these two built in the last years of their lives. The Percys, Earls of Northumberland, took over the house in 1604 but did little to it until Robert Adam was employed to remodel the house in 1761. Adam left the main structure of Syon House much as it was, but his redesign of the most important rooms in the house, the Great Hall, the anteroom, the Dining Room, the Drawing Room and the Great Gallery, turned this into one of the greatest classical houses in England.

The whole exterior was refaced in Bath stone in 1825, and when the Northumberland family's great central London mansion, near Trafalgar Square (also on the site of a convent), was demolished to make way for Northumberland Avenue in 1874 many of its furnishings were brought to Isleworth, and the great lead Percy lion was rescued and placed above the east front of Syon House, where it still makes a fine sight from Kew Gardens or the riverside path. Syon's 40-acre gardens were redesigned by Lancelot 'Capability' Brown while Adam was working on the house, and the gardens still bear the imprint of his work. The beautiful glass and metal Great Conservatory, with its wonderful dome, was built by Charles Fowler (who later designed Covent Garden market) in 1826, predating and inspiring the work of Joseph Paxton on the Crystal Palace. Syon

House is open from 11.00 till 5.00, for a fee of about £8, between March and late October, and the gardens are also open on winter weekends. Its website is www.syonhouse.co.uk.

The other important sixteenth-century house in west London is Osterley Park, which represents London's mercantile wealth just as Syon represents its aristocratic fortunes. It was first built in the 1570s by the richest Elizabethan merchant, Sir Thomas Gresham, and fell into the hands of London's most successful property developer, Nicholas Barbon, in 1683. Then it was bought by the great banker Sir Francis Child, whose grandsons, along with the ubiquitous Robert Adam, completely transformed the house in the 1760s and 1770s. The Entrance Hall, Dining Room, Library, Etruscan Room, Bedchamber, Tapestry Room and Conservatories are Adam's, but the Long Gallery dates from the 1720s, when Child was the owner, and the four refacing turrets and the stables are from Gresham's time. The house is owned by the National Trust and can be visited in the afternoons, for a fee of about £8, from March to October, Wednesday to Sunday, while its eighteenth-century pleasure gardens are open for about £3 for the same season. Osterley Park is open all year and free. Check www.nationaltrust.org for details.

There are other sixteenth-century country houses in suburban London in various states of preservation. Lauderdale House on Highgate Hill was built in the old timber-framed style for a City goldsmith, Richard Bond, in 1582, but only a section in the southeast is Tudor now. The house was converted into a classical mansion in the 1760s, and the whole building was gutted by fires in 1963 and 1968. It is now used as a local authority arts and education centre, and is not very interesting inside. Its beautiful gardens, now part of Waterlow Park, are another matter, and are worth a visit in their own right. Archway is the nearest Tube station.

Sutton House in Hackney was built for a courtier of Henry VIII's, Sir Ralph Sadleir, in 1535. It was later occupied by City merchants and a girls' school, and in the later nineteenth century became a recreational centre for young men, and was restored in the

Arts and Crafts style. Under the ownership of the National Trust the house was vandalized by squatters, but in the 1990s it was restored and opened to the public. The Tudor house was built in diapered brick, and the original brickwork can still be seen in the west wing, the west and east fronts, and the ground-floor window in the rear courtyard. Inside there is a mixture of sixteenth-century and eighteenth-century work, reflecting the history of the house. The panelled Georgian Parlour has part of a Tudor fireplace, and the Tudor Hall has eighteenth-century panelling. The Linenfold Parlour is mostly Tudor, and the largely Edwardian staircase has Jacobean wall paintings. There is a Victorian study on the first floor, but other first-floor rooms, the Great and Little Chambers, have plenty of sixteenth- and seventeenth-century features. Downstairs again, the kitchens and cellars are partly Tudor. Sutton House is at the western end of Homerton High Street, not far from Hackney Central and Hackney Downs railway stations. It is open, for about £3, on Thursday to Sunday afternoons, except in January.

Other Tudor houses have survived here and there in the London suburbs. The old village of Cheam, now part of the borough of Sutton, has Number 1 Whitehall, a well-restored 1500 house with a timber frame, three bays and eighteenth-century weatherboarding. It is an early example of a two-storied house, breaking from the medieval practice of having the downstairs living area open up to the roof. There are seventeenth- and eighteenth-century additions, but inside the structure is original, and it would be hard to find a better or more accessible example of a late-medieval house in London. It also has a lovely garden, interesting exhibitions and good teas. The house is open Wednesday to Sunday afternoons, and all day Saturday, for about £1.50. There are several more old houses in Cheam. Numbers 45–47 the Broadway are seventeenth century, and in Park Lane numbers 7–11 and 25 are good seventeenth-century houses. Old Cottage, on the Broadway, dates from about 1500, though it had to be moved in 1922 when the High Street was widened.

Outlying Sutton has another early-Tudor house, Carew Manor, which is now a school but which can be toured on selected Sunday afternoons in spring and summer. See www.sutton.gov.uk/leisure/heritage/carewmanor.htm for details. Carew Manor is in Church Road, Beddington, on the eastern side of Beddington Park. The River Wandle runs through the park, and you could combine a visit to Carew Manor with a walk along the river. The Great Hall of the manor, with a fine hammerbeam roof, was built around 1500 (perhaps a little earlier), and looks like the one at Eltham. The Carew family were briefly powerful in the sixteenth century, but in the seventeenth and eighteenth centuries they concentrated on their gardens, and some of the fine walls they built for their once-famous orangery can still be seen, along with a dovecote.

On the south-eastern edge of London, in Bexley, is Hall Place, a house built for a merchant and Lord Mayor of London, Sir John Champneys. Since then it has been owned by various Londoners and aristocrats, with the usual spells as a school and in local authority care. The house was built in the 1530s using some carved stonework from recently demolished monasteries, perhaps from Lesnes Abbey, whose excavated remains can be seen about three miles away, near Abbey Wood station. Hall Place is a large house with a big central hall and two projecting wings. The house is mostly chequered grey and white Tudor brick at the front and mid-seventeenth-century red behind. The Great Hall has a fine coved ceiling with mid-sixteenth-century bosses, and a minstrel's gallery which owes as much to its last private owner, Lady Limerick, as to Tudor builders. Much of the rest of the house, especially its south courtyard, was built or altered by Sir Robert Austen in the 1640s, and inside there is a fine seventeenth-century staircase and some good Jacobean plasterwork. In the eighteenth century the house was owned, but not often occupied, by Sir Francis Dashwood, a notorious member of the Hell Fire Club, and today it is in the more mundane but reliable care of Bexley Council and Bexley Heritage Trust, who open it to the public, free of charge, all year round (though not on Sundays and Mondays in the winter). The grounds, laid out in the early twentieth century, are especially fine, with herb and rose gardens, a sunken area, an old walled garden, some famous topiary and the River Cray running through them.

Finally, in the borough of Barking, near Upney station and the Barking bypass, is Eastbury Manor House, built in the 1560s by a City merchant, Clement Sysley. The house was almost in ruins by the 1720s, and was eventually rescued and restored in the 1840s, and saved again when its estate was sold for development in 1918. The house is built of red brick in an H-shape, with wings at each corner and a high wall enclosing the rear courtyard. Despite its troubled history and many alterations the Elizabethan house is still worth visiting, for its fine Tudor exterior, its Great Hall, Painted Room (with interesting seventeenth-century wall paintings) and Long Gallery, its exposed roof, and the servants' quarters, kitchens and spiral staircase in the west wing. Barking and Dagenham Council opens the house for a small fee on Mondays and Tuesdays, and the first two Saturdays of each month.

In central London the best Tudor house is St James's Palace, which Henry VIII built on the site of a leper hospital in the 1530s. The Gatehouse, the Chapel Royal to its right (as you look at it from the corner of Pall Mall and St James's Street) and some of the rooms to the right of the chapel are part of Henry's original building, and much of the rest, including Friary Court, which can be seen from Marlborough Road, is eighteenth or nineteenth century. The palace is the residence of members of the royal family and courtiers, and the only part of it that can be visited is the Chapel Royal, which is open for Sunday services (8.30 and 11.15) between October and Easter. The chapel, including its fine 1540 ceiling, is decorated in the Renaissance style of Henry's day, with the arms of Anne of Cleves and the mottoes of Catherine of Aragon and Anne Boleyn incorporated into the paintwork. The fine musical tradition of the Chapel Royal is traced in Chapter Five.

On old maps of London you can see a succession of palatial

mansions between the Thames and the Strand, belonging to aristocrats or (before the Reformation) eminent churchmen. Nearly all of them were sold to developers in the seventeenth or eighteenth century, leaving only street names to remind us that Northumberland House, York House, Savoy Palace, Arundel House or Essex House once dominated the riverbank. The first of these to go was John of Gaunt's Savoy Palace, which was ruined in the 1381 Peasants' Revolt, rebuilt in 1505 as the Hospital of St John of the Savoy, used for centuries as a refuge or prison for vagrants, a barracks and a military hospital, and eventually cleared away to make room for Waterloo Bridge in 1816–20. Savoy Chapel on Savoy Street (between the hotel and the bridge) is a remnant of the 1505 rebuilding, not of the medieval palace, and was heavily restored after a fire in the 1860s. It is the only pre-Reformation building in this part of town. Arundel House was demolished in 1678 for the development of Howard, Arundel and Norfolk Streets, and Essex House and York House went in the same decade. Somerset House was replaced with the present building, the first London office block, in the 1770s, and Northumberland House, the last survivor, was demolished in 1874 to make way for Northumberland Avenue, a street of grand hotels.

Not much is left of these great houses, except the lion now on the top of Syon House and the 'Roman Baths' in Strand Lane, which may be from Arundel House. The most impressive remnant is the York Watergate, the riverside entrance to York House, the Duke of Buckingham's palace. This was built by Nicholas Stone in 1626, two years before Buckingham, James I's favourite, was assassinated. Buckingham acquired the house from the King's discredited minister Francis Bacon in return for helping him when he was impeached in 1621. When the house was demolished the second Duke, George Villiers, made sure the family's name was comprehensively commemorated in the new roads, which included George Street (now York Buildings), Villiers Street, Duke Street (now John Adam Street), Of Alley (now York Place) and Buckingham Street. You can find the watergate by going into Victoria Embankment Gardens (created when the river was narrowed in the 1860s) from the Embankment, or walking down Buckingham Street from the Strand.

Many ordinary sixteenth-century houses in central London were destroyed when the streets north of the Strand were cleared for the building of the Aldwych around 1900, but there are a few left. Staple Inn on Holborn, near Chancery Lane station, is a famous survivor, though it is not quite as sixteenth century as it looks from the street. The facade of a terrace of timber-framed shops and houses was rescued and restored by Alfred Waterhouse in 1887, reconstructed and strengthened in 1936, and restored again after flying bomb damage in 1944. Enter the quiet courtyard behind the facade (where Dr Samuel Johnson once lodged) to see the 1730s offices (many rebuilt in the 1950s after war damage) and the Hall, which is of 1581 with later alterations. Nevertheless, Staple Inn facade, with its large oriel windows and overhanging upper floors to maximize light and space inside the house, gives a good impression of what a great London street would have looked like in Shakespeare's day.

Staple Inn was once an Inn of Chancery, and the present building was built by the Principal of the Inn, Vincent Engham. The name of the house was probably inherited from an early-fourteenth-century building on the site with an aisle lined with wooden posts, or (in Old English) staples. Another possible explanation of its name is that it stood alongside the Holborn bars, marking the limits of the City of London's jurisdiction. These bars would once have been marked by wooden posts, or staples. The Inns of Chancery prepared law students for entry to the Inns of Court, each being affiliated to a particular one. They lost this function in the eighteenth century and became clubs for lawyers who were not barristers. Most, including Staple Inn, were closed in the nineteenth century, and Staple Inn is now occupied by the Institute of Actuaries. Small parts of others still survive, including Clifford's Inn Passage (Fleet Street) and Clement's Passage and New Inn Passage off Houghton Street (off the Aldwych). The best remnant, along with Staple Inn, is the little early-fifteenth-century hall of Barnard's Inn, which is now owned by the Mercers' Company and used by Gresham College. The hall has been repaired and restored, but its interesting roof (a crown post and collar purlin structure unlike any other in London) and octagonal lantern or smoke vent is original and its linenfold panelling dates from about 1510. In the Council Chamber under the hall there is a chalk and tiling wall which is much older, perhaps even Roman. Barnard's Inn is about 200 metres east of Staple Inn, in an alley off Holborn, and its interior can easily be seen whenever there is a Gresham College public lecture.

A few other timber-framed sixteenth-century houses have managed to escape fire, bombs and the demolition men. The timbered gatehouse of St Bartholomew-the-Great, Smithfield, was built in 1595 on top of the remains of the thirteenth-century west entrance to the demolished nave. Its age was not known until Zeppelin bombs dislodged the tiles that covered it in 1916. Inside the protective walls of the Tower of London a few Tudor and Jacobean buildings survive, especially along the west side and in the southwest corner. The Queen's House, which is actually the home of the head officer of the Tower, was started in 1540. It is like a fine half-timbered manor house, with a great first-floor hall open to the roof. A royal proclamation forbade the building of timber-fronted houses in London in 1605, and though this might have been ignored elsewhere in the City it seems to have been obeyed inside the Tower, where there are two tall 1630s brick houses, just north of the Queen's House. Such houses were once plentiful in the City, but now the only remnant of brick house-building in the sixteenth-century City is in Devonshire Row, off Bishopsgate opposite Liverpool Street, where about 35 metres of red brick wall with stone window survive at the back of the Victorian warehouses at numbers 4–18. This is all that is left of the great house built by the Clerk in Chancery Jasper Fisher between 1567 and 1579, and known, because Fisher could not afford it, as Fisher's Folly. The house was later occupied by the Dukes of Devonshire and then demolished, but for this single wall, by the developer Nicholas Barbon in the 1670s.

Timber-framed houses continued to be built in the early seventeenth century, and several survive in London. There is one on Fleet Street, the Inner Temple gatehouse or Prince Henry's Room, which was built in 1610–11 by John Bennett. The house was once an inn called the Prince's Arms, which may explain the badge of feathers and the initials PH in the plasterwork of the upstairs room. Later, in the 1760s, the house was used by Mrs Salmon's Waxworks, the precursor of Madame Tussaud's, and now it houses a little museum devoted to Samuel Pepys, who was born nearby in Salisbury Court. The house was altered when it was restored by the LCC in 1906, but it is still one of the best pre-Fire houses in central London, and it is open on weekdays, free of charge, between 11.00 and 2.00. About 150 metres to the west, at the eastern end of the Strand, is the Wig and Pen Club, two narrow timbered houses, one of which, number 229, is early seventeenth century, and the other around 1700. Number 229, according to Pevsner, is perhaps 'the oldest ordinary house in Westminster'.

Finally, the transition from timber-framed to brick houses is nicely epitomized by a beautiful house in Cloth Fair, the little road leading east from Smithfield. Number 41–42 is the house of a merchant, built in 1614 or a little after, using a combination of red brick in its main structure and timber-framed two-storey bay windows and weatherboarded gables. The house's neighbours, numbers 39–40 and 43–45, are straightforward eighteenth-century brick houses, and numbers 26–37 are 1980s houses which cleverly mimic the style of number 41–42. One of the finest timber houses in London, the four-storey house built by the City merchant Sir Paul Pindar around 1600 in Bishopsgate, was demolished during the expansion of Liverpool Street station in 1890. Happily, a two-storey section of its facade, a magnificently ornate carved oak bay window, was saved, and can now be seen in the Victoria and Albert Museum.

The museum's British Galleries have a wealth of exhibits illustrating the development of London houses, including some rooms rescued from demolished houses. There is the fine panelled room from the Old Palace, Bromley-by-Bow, which was built in 1606 for a merchant or courtier and demolished in 1894, and the parlour of 11 Henrietta Street, Covent Garden, which was built by and for the architect James Gibbs around 1730 and demolished in 1956.

Timber-framed houses were banned in the City after the Great Fire, but some were built and a few survive. If you go through Middle Temple Gateway, at the western end of Fleet Street, you'll find Middle Temple Lane, the ancient lane that runs through the Temple district down to the river. Numbers 2 and 3, which were built in 1693–4, defied the 1667 Rebuilding Acts with their wooden fronts (now plastered over) and overhanging upper stories. The Hoop and Grapes, numbers 46–47 Aldgate High Street, is another timber-framed building, either built before the Fire or illicitly after it, and in Long Lane, between Smithfield and Barbican Tube station, number 74 is a four-storey timber house, built in the late seventeenth century in defiance of the law.

Houses that followed the 1667 regulations came in four types: those 'of the first sort', with two stories, a cellar and a garret, on by-lanes; 'of the second sort', with an extra storey, on 'streets and lanes of note'; 'of the third sort', with four stories, on six main streets; and large four-storied mansions 'of the fourth sort' where appropriate. Of the post-Fire mansions, only one, the 1667 Deanery of St Paul's, in a walled and gated garden in Dean's Court (between St Paul's Churchyard and Carter Lane), remains. It is now the palace of the Bishop of London. Buildings that follow the rules laid down for houses of the third sort are not uncommon, especially in the areas developed by Nicholas Barbon in the 1670s and 1680s. Walk down Middle Temple Lane from Fleet Street (just east of Temple Bar), look into Pump Court on the left (east), and turn into Essex Court and New Court on the right. All these were built by Barbon in the late 1670s and early 1680s, following a (not *the*) fire. Leave

New Court by the gateway in its north-western corner and enter Devereux Court, another Barbon development of the 1670s (numbers 22, 23 and the Devereux public house survive), and follow it to Essex Street, which has many of Barbon's three-storied red brick houses.

Many three-storied houses of the second sort were built in the few years after the Fire, but only a few remain. The oldest of Barbon's surviving houses are numbers 5 and 6 Crane Court, off Fleet Street, just east of Fetter Lane. These were reconstructed after a fire in 1971, and the front of number 5 is new. But look up to the first-floor front room, if the light is on, to see a beautiful seventeenth-century plaster ceiling. Go down College Hill (off Cannon Street, between Queen Street and Cannon Street station) to see Barbon's 1688 house, number 21, which is through the wonderful carved stone archway of number 22, which was built in the 1670s as part of the Mercers' School. Number 20, which was also part of the school, is on the site of the house of the most famous mercer, and the only medieval Mayor of London whose name is still familiar, Richard Whittington. He was buried in the church next door, St Michael Paternoster Royal, which he had rebuilt in 1409. It was again rebuilt after the Great Fire by Wren, and in 1966–8 it was the last City church to be restored after war damage. Numbers 1–3 Amen Court, a pretty ecclesiastical enclave off Warwick Lane, just west of St Paul's Cathedral, are houses of the second sort, built by Edward Woodroffe in 1671–3 for the Canons of St Paul's. The Stationers' Hall, which forms the southern side of the square, was rebuilt here after the Great Fire, but most of what you can see is eighteenth- and nineteenth-century work, with some post-war rebuilding. The smallest houses, those of the first sort, are nearly all gone, but the three little shops on Cheapside, numbers 124–6, on its corner with Wood Street, built in 1687, give some idea of what they looked like, though there is probably no original material in these houses now.

The best way to see a late-seventeenth-century City house is to pay to go into Dr Samuel Johnson's house in Gough Square, which you can find by turning north off Fleet Street into St Dunstan's Court or Hind Court, near the Old Cheshire Cheese. The four-bayed brick house, which Johnson occupied from 1748 to 1759, has the great attic in which Johnson and his six assistants – seven 'harmless drudges' – compiled his *Dictionary*, and the room in which his beloved wife Hetty died in 1752. It is open every day but Sundays and bank holidays, for about £4.50.

There are several surviving terraces of 1670s–80s houses in Westminster, especially those built by the ubiquitous developer and financier Nicholas Barbon, who decided to pursue a more lucrative career than his Anabaptist father, Praisegod Barebones, whose name was given to the nominated assembly of 1653, the Barebones Parliament. Barbon's surviving work includes Buckingham Street, which runs down from the Strand, a little east of Charing Cross station. Barbon and others built the street in the 1670s on land made available by the demolition of the Duke of Buckingham's house. Numbers 8–12 on the west side of the street are 1670s houses, and numbers 13–14 are late eighteenth century. Number 12 was Samuel Pepys's house from 1679 to 1688, between his release from the Tower of London (on a false charge) and his dismissal from public office after the fall of James II. On the east side, numbers 17, 20 and 21 are 1670s houses. There is an interesting remnant of Barbon's work not far away, in some little streets off Charing Cross Road. Litchfield Street, just south of Cambridge Circus, is a Barbon street, and numbers 25–27 are his houses. Newport Court, a short walk south on the other side of Charing Cross Road, has several houses (numbers 19, 21–24a) built by Barbon when he laid out the street in the 1680s, after the demolition of Newport House. In Holborn, near Russell Square Tube station, there is a good run of Barbon houses, built in the 1680s at the western end of Great Ormond Street as it approaches Queen Square.

*

There are grander seventeenth-century houses all over suburban London. Starting in the west, Ham House, on the Thames between Richmond and Kingston, is one of the largest and best. It was built in an H-shape by the courtier Sir Thomas Vavasour around 1610, and enlarged into a rectangle by William Murray (later Earl of Dysart) in the 1630s, and his son-in-law the Duke of Lauderdale (one of Charles II's ministers) in the 1670s. Around this time the house played an important part in political and court life. Walking through the well-preserved rooms is like taking a course in the development of aristocratic taste in art and interior design. The Great Hall is from the original building, with later amendments, and the staircase next to it is a fine piece of 1630s work, possibly by the joiner Thomas Carter. The North Drawing Room and Long Gallery represent the taste of William Murray in the 1630s, and the South Apartments, especially the Queen's Closet and Antechamber, designed for Charles II's Queen, Catherine of Braganza, reflect Restoration styles and the influence of Inigo Jones and Italian plastering techniques. Other rooms, especially the Queen's Bedroom and the Yellow Satin Bedroom, reflect the fashions of the eighteenth century, but there were no great changes after that. The house is owned by the National Trust, and is open in the afternoons from March till the end of October, from Saturday to Wednesday, for £9. The gardens, restored to their 1670s formality, are open, for £3, all year round.

A sad wartime loss was Holland House, which was badly damaged by incendiaries in September 1940 and largely demolished in the 1950s. Holland House was begun in 1605 as Cope Castle, was enlarged by the Earl of Holland in the 1630s, and became famous as the political and cultural centre of the powerful Fox family (Barons Holland) in the decades around 1800. All the great Whig politicians and intellectuals came here between the 1770s and 1830s, attracted by the style, power and money of Lady Holland's salon: Byron, Macaulay, Sheridan, Sydney Smith, Walter Scott, Canning, Melbourne, Palmerston, and so on. All you can see now are a few scraps of what was once a magnificent Jacobean palace. The biggest remnant is the east wing, which was restored in the 1950s as a youth hostel, but there is also the lower part of the central porch, and surrounding it the lower walls of arcaded galleries, with lively Jacobean ornamentation. Separate from the main structure there are the 1629 gatepiers, and the orangery, which began as stables in the 1630s and became a ballroom in the nineteenth century. The ice house and the formal gardens are interesting, and the wooded grounds, now Holland Park, are among the most delightful in London. The nearest Tube station is Holland Park, and entry is free.

Other west London houses of the same period include Kew Palace (the Dutch House), built as a merchant's country retreat in 1631 in the Dutch style with fine brickwork instead of Tudor wood. There is still some 1630s work inside, but most of it disappeared when the building came into royal hands in the eighteenth century. Kew Palace, which was thoroughly refurbished in the early years of the twenty-first century, is open for a fee (currently £5) to visitors to Kew Gardens (*see* Chapter Ten) between March and October. A little further west, in Brentford, there is a fine red brick house of the same date as Kew Palace, Boston Manor House, which was built in 1623 for Lady Mary Reade, a member of the Gresham family who married into the Spencers of Althorp. It belonged to the Clitherows, a family of London merchants, from 1670 until 1924, when it was sold to Brentford Council. The house has been altered and extended a great deal, and is now converted into flats, but the first-floor drawing room has an exceptional Jacobean ceiling, and this, along with some other fine rooms and a collection of local paintings, is open to the public, without charge, on weekend afternoons from April to October. It is on Boston Manor Road, near its junction with the Great West Road, near Northfields Tube station.

There is a manor house of a similar date but in a purer Jacobean condition on the other side of London, in Charlton, east of

Greenwich. Charlton Manor House was built between 1607 and 1612 for Sir Adam Newton, a tutor to Charles I's son Henry, perhaps by John Thorpe. In 1680 it passed into the hands of an East India merchant and from 1767 to 1924 it was owned by the Maryon-Wilson family, who eventually sold it to the borough of Greenwich. It is a fine three-storey red brick house in an H-shape, with a great hall in the middle and kitchens, a chapel and a parlour in the wings. The building is handsome and ornate, especially the doorway and bay window in the centre of the west side, which, in Pevsner's words, 'suddenly breaks out into the most exuberant and undisciplined ornament in all England'. The two-storied hall, with a gallery and fine ceiling, is one of the first in England to run from front to back of the house, at right angles to the frontage rather than in line with it. The staircase is rich in period decoration, including palm trees and American native headdresses.

The gardens, now mostly public parks and playing fields, contain London's first and oldest mulberry tree, planted at James I's request in 1608. The infamous Charlton Horn Fair was held on the village green in front of the house until the Maryon-Wilsons enclosed the green as part of their front garden in 1829. The fair is held there again now, in late June, but without the drunkenness and sexual misbehaviour that Daniel Defoe denounced in the 1720s. Charlton House is now a community centre and municipal offices, and though this inevitably spoils the historical atmosphere of the house it at least makes it easy (and free) to visit this outstanding Jacobean manor house, except on Sundays. It is a half-mile from Charlton station along Charlton Church Road.

There is an interesting contrast with Charlton House a few miles away in Greenwich, which has one of London's finest early-seventeenth-century houses, Inigo Jones's Queen's House, the first house in England built in the Palladian style. The Queen's House was built for the wives of James I and Charles I, Anne of Denmark and Henrietta Maria, between 1616 and 1637. The structure of Jones's original house was odd in that the front range of rooms,

mainly a cubic hall, drawing room and bedrooms, was only connected with the back range by a first-floor bridge, itself containing
a spacious room, with the Greenwich to Woolwich road below it,
dividing the house in two. In the 1660s two more bridges were
added, but the back and front ranges were still separated at ground-
floor level by the road. The Queen's House is classical simplicity
outside, in great contrast to the Elizabethan and Jacobean fashions
exemplified in Charlton House, but beautifully decorated in French
and Italian styles within. The galleried hall, with a lovely marble
floor and plaster ceiling, and the magical Tulip Staircase to its
east, spiralling up to the roof with (Jones said) a 'vacuum in the
middle', are the most impressive parts of the house, but other
rooms, including the Queen's Bedroom, are also very fine. The house
is part of the National Maritime Museum, and displays works from
the museum's excellent collection of paintings. It is open every day,
free.

While you are in Greenwich you should walk up the hill to see
a house of the next generation, built in 1675–6 by Christopher
Wren and his friend Robert Hooke. This is the house and observatory of the first Astronomer Royal, the disagreeable John Flamsteed.
It is built like a little mock castle, with four living rooms, a basement workshop and an octagonal upper room for Flamsteed's
astronomical instruments. Although the house is part of the Greenwich Observatory complex, it has survived as Flamsteed knew it,
and is furnished and equipped in late-seventeenth-century style. It
also has, in a separate room, London's only public camera obscura,
from which you can still glimpse the beautiful view that the aged
Flamsteed would have seen, the Queen's House and the Royal Naval
Hospital, along with some twentieth-century additions, including
Canary Wharf and the Dome. The observatory is open every day,
free.

The road on the western edge of Greenwich Park, Croom's
Hill, is worth strolling along for its exceptional collection of private
houses, including several dating from the late seventeenth century:

numbers 16–18, 52 and 68. Number 66 dates from the 1630s, and numbers 10–12, built in 1721, can be entered because they are the home of London's (and the world's) only fan museum. It is open Tuesday to Sunday (from 11.00) and costs £4. Go on Tuesday or Sunday and you can have afternoon tea in the Orangery. See www.fan-museum.org for details of special exhibitions. Further along, in Chesterfield Walk, is the Rangers House, which is mentioned later.

Inigo Jones's classical example, especially his work in Westminster (the Banqueting House, the Queen's Chapel at St James's Palace and the Covent Garden Piazza), began to influence other builders in the 1630s. This produced some Jacobean–classical hybrids like Forty Hall, which is on Forty Hill in Enfield, on the northern fringes of London, a short walk from the New River, Jacobean London's new water supply. The house was built in the early 1630s by Sir Nicholas Raynton in a mainly traditional manner, with Jacobean plasterwork, woodwork and fireplaces, but the exterior of the house is in the new classical style. Whether this reflects Jones's influence or later-seventeenth-century rebuilding is unclear. The house was sold by the Parker Bowles family to Enfield Council in 1951, and now houses the Enfield Museum, which is open free of charge from Sunday to Wednesday, 11.00 to 4.00. While you are in Enfield you should walk along its most famous street and one of the best eighteenth-century streets in outer London, Gentleman's Row. This runs alongside the New River (*see* Chapter Eleven) and next to Chase Green, a remnant of Enfield Chase. Many of the houses along here are eighteenth century, or older houses given the fashionable brick-fronted look at that time. Number 17, where Charles and Mary Lamb stayed in 1827, is a late-medieval house concealed by a stucco front. The Lambs also stayed at numbers 87 and 89 Chase Side, another Enfield street with good late-Georgian houses.

There is a mid-seventeenth-century house open to the public in Becontree where, in the middle of a vast council estate, you will find Valence House. This house is an accumulation of rooms and additions of different ages, now occupied by an interesting museum of Essex history and rooms of various periods. The shop is in a timber-framed fifteenth-century structure, the ground-floor service rooms may be Tudor, and the Fanshawe Room, the Period Room and the south-west wing are seventeenth century. The pond in the garden is a remnant of the moat that surrounded the medieval manor house. The house is open free of charge every day but Sunday, and is a modest walk from Chadwell Heath station. A visit could be combined with a look around the LCC Becontree estate, the biggest in interwar Europe, but, as Pevsner warns, 'a tour of Becontree is demanding even for the enthusiast'.

London has several good houses built in the late seventeenth century, including that built for William and Mary by Sir Christopher Wren in the 1690s, Kensington Palace. This is one of London's greatest and most famous houses, a place that every Londoner should visit but most do not. The magnificent state rooms, furnished in the style of William, Anne or the early Georges, are open every day for a fairly large fee (£11.50 in 2006). The wonderful grounds of the palace, Kensington Gardens, are of course freely open to the public, and have been since the 1830s. There is another magnificent Wren set-piece, the Chelsea Royal Hospital, about two miles away. The three courtyards, the Great Hall, the Octagon, Chapel and Museum are open to visitors free of charge, between 10.00 and 12.00 and 2.00 and 4.00 every day, except bank holidays and Sundays between October and March. The whole effect is grand, but inside the hospital is much plainer than the palace, catering as it did (and does) for residents at the other end of the social scale.

To see how a family between these two extremes lived, you might visit Fenton House, a merchant's house in Hampstead Grove, north of Hampstead Tube station. This was built in 1693, and is named after the Baltic merchant who bought it a hundred years later. It is a fine square brick house built plainly in the William and Mary style, with Georgian modernization, especially to the windows, and a beautiful walled garden. The house is owned by the National

Trust, and is open for a fee of about £6 (all day at weekends, and Wednesday to Friday afternoons) between March and October, the usual National Trust season. Burgh House, also in the centre of Hampstead (New End Square and Well Walk), was built ten years after Fenton House, for a Quaker family called Sewell. In the 1720s its owner was Dr William Gibbons, the physician associated with Hampstead Wells, which were nearby. This very fine five-bayed Queen Anne house is now a community centre and Hampstead Museum, and open free of charge, Wednesday to Sunday afternoons. There are often concerts in the Music Room, and part of the garden was laid out by the great garden designer Gertrude Jekyll in 1908.

Another house to visit in Hampstead, interesting for its literary associations rather than its quality as a building, is Keats House (previously two semi-detached houses known as Wentworth Place), where John Keats lived from 1818 to 1819, when the houses were new. Some of Keats's most important poems and letters were written here, and it was here that he fell in love with Fanny Brawne, who lived next door in the larger of the two houses. But this is also where Keats nursed his dying brother Tom and himself began to feel the symptoms of the tuberculosis that would kill him in 1821, when he was 25. In these green and peaceful gardens we are told Keats wrote his 'Ode to a Nightingale', which speaks of a life of weariness and disease, 'where men sit and hear each other groan; / Where palsy shakes a few, sad, last grey hairs, / Where youth grows pale, and spectre-thin, and dies'. The collection here is based on that assembled by his friend Charles Dilke. The house is in Keats Grove, a short walk from the centre of Hampstead and near Hampstead Heath railway station. It is open every afternoon but Monday, and costs about £3.50.

Nearby, on the corner of Willow Road and Downshire Hill, there is a house of a different vintage. Erno Goldfinger, the architect of Trellick Tower, one of London's best 1970s high-rise blocks, settled in London in 1934 and established his reputation by building a terrace of three modern houses with brick and concrete facades in

Willow Walk. Number 2, Goldfinger's own home, is an important and interesting house, with a fine collection of modern paintings and sculpture. It is owned by the National Trust, which offers guided tours at 12.00, 1.00 and 2.00 and unguided visits from 3.00 to 5.00 on Saturdays from March to November, and also on Thursdays and Fridays from April to October, for about £5.

There is a fine house of the William and Mary period on the other side of London, in Woodhayes Road, Wimbledon. The complicated and rambling structure of Southside House reflects its complicated and rambling history, from Stuart origins to Georgian refinements, from extensive war damage to interesting post-war restoration. The house began as a Tudor farmhouse, was rebuilt in the 1680s by Robert Pennington, and has been in the Pennington family ever since. Along the way it has picked up associations with Marie Antoinette, Mrs Hamilton and Axel Munthe, and accumulated a museumful of paintings and other treasures. Unlike many London houses, which have been converted into galleries or community centres, Southside House has the feeling of being lived in by a real (and rather disorganized) family. The garden is as complicated and interesting as the house. Guided tours cost about £5, and take place on Wednesday, Saturday and Sunday afternoons and bank holiday Mondays between mid-April and early October. See www.southsidehouse.com for details.

The fine terraced houses of rich eighteenth-century Londoners still survive in great numbers, because they were well built and suited the needs of successive generations, neither too flimsy to last nor so large that they tempted developers to replace them with more profitable streets. To see some of the best eighteenth-century houses in London, go to Westminster. Queen Anne's Gate, an L-shaped street just to the south of St James's Park and Birdcage Walk, is hard to beat. Those at the western end were built in 1704–5 (therefore not Georgian, but from the reign of Queen Anne, whose statue stands against number 15), and those at the east are mostly 1770s, except for numbers 6–12, which are 1830s. This was a favourite street for politicians, and there are plaques to Lord Palmerston, Lord Haldane (Liberal and Labour Lord Chancellor), Admiral Jacky Fisher and Sir Edward Grey (Foreign Secretary in August 1914). Then cross Victoria Street, take Great Smith Street, turn left into Little Smith Street and go left again to find Great College Street, which was built in 1720 alongside the late-fourteenth-century wall of Westminster Abbey Garden. Numbers 16–19 were built in 1722, and other houses in the street have great interest. The initials on the rainwater heads of numbers 14–15 indicate the names of two Liberal MPs, Walter Runciman and Charles Trevelyan, who were residents in 1905. Follow Barton Street and Cowley Street, two excellent Georgian streets, almost full of 1720s houses in fine condition, into Lord North Street, which is another survivor from the 1720s. This leads to Smith Square, which was laid out in the 1720s and still has the original houses on its north side. The magnificent church in its centre, St John, was built by Thomas Archer in the English baroque style in 1713–28, and restored as a concert hall after serious war damage.

Since January 2006 it has been possible to visit a fine terraced house built around 1730. Number 36 Craven Street, one of the many well-preserved 1730s houses in this street off Northumberland Avenue, was the lodging of Benjamin Franklin between 1757 and 1775, when he was the diplomatic representative of the state of Pennsylvania. Since 1997 it has been restored to its eighteenth-century condition, and it is now open as a Benjamin Franklin museum. Franklin was one of the most interesting and versatile eighteenth-century London residents, a printer, scientist, philosopher and statesman, and the only man to have signed all four of the key documents of American independence. In his laboratory in Craven Street Franklin invented the glass harmonica, bifocal spectacles and the Franklin stove, and in the same house he met William Pitt (Lord Chatham) to try to negotiate a solution to the conflicts that led to the American War of Independence. So this was in effect the first American embassy in Britain, and a key location in the history of science. The house is open to pre-booked visitors from Wednesday to Sunday, 12.00 to 5.00, and a guided visit and the 'historical experience' show cost about £7. Visit http://benjaminfranklin house. org for details.

Some fine early-eighteenth-century houses have survived three centuries of fire, bombing and demolition in the City. One of the best is the 1700 Partners' House in Chiswell Street, near Finsbury Square, on the northern edge of the City. The five central bays of this fine nine-bay house, which was occupied by the brewer Samuel Whitbread in the 1750s, are the original 1700 house. The late-eighteenth-century brewery buildings in Chiswell Street and Milton Street (the old Grub Street) are all that is left of the six-acre Whitbread brewery, which was closed in 1976. In a yard south of Chiswell Street (and off Milton Street) are the 1792 Sugar Room and the huge 1770s Porter Tun Room, a beer storeroom with a timber king-post roof. The brewery is now a set of conference, banqueting and event rooms. If being surrounded by a brewery makes you thirsty, St Paul's Tavern, which occupies a set of mid-eighteenth-century buildings in Chiswell Street, is a good local pub.

The finest City doorcases are those of numbers 1 and 2 Laurence Pountney Hill, off Cannon Street, which were built in 1703, just before more new laws made it harder to indulge in such elaborate and inflammable woodwork. A pair of very fine houses in Queen Street (numbers 27 and 28), just south of Cannon Street, survive, probably from about 1730. There are good examples of later City houses in Devonshire Square, near Houndsditch, where numbers 12 and 13 (Coopers' Hall) represent the best 1740s craftsmanship. Barbon developed this square between 1678 and 1708, and though his houses are gone a little alley here commemorates his name.

About ten minutes' walk away from Devonshire Square you can see eighteenth-century houses which have had a very different history from those in the City or the West End. Go through the late-eighteenth-century East India Company warehouses between Cutler Street and Middlesex Street, which have now been converted into offices, and follow Middlesex Street, Sandys Row, Artillery Passage and Duval Street to reach Spitalfields. A left turn into Commercial Street and a right turn after Hawksmoor's magnificent and newly restored Christ Church brings you to Fournier Street, where most of the houses were built for prosperous Huguenot silk-weavers in the 1720s, with well-lit weaving lofts probably added later. When silk-weaving collapsed in the face of French and Midlands competition in the nineteenth century the houses were subdivided into clothing workshops and fell into disrepair. The arrival of impoverished East European Jews in the 1880s and 1890s confirmed the district's degraded status. A few of the houses are still in a dilapidated condition, but most have been refurbished in recent years, as the area has started to absorb the prosperity of the City, which is only a few hundred metres away. Soon easily visible evidence of the impoverished history of the previous two hundred years will have been almost wiped out.

A walk along Fournier Street, Wilkes Street and Princelet Street will take you past the best of the old houses, and also, if you are interested, into the part of town once prowled by Jack the Ripper and now prowled by Jack the Ripper tours. From Wilkes Street go left into Hanbury Street and right into Commercial Street. Across the road, take Folgate Street and go right into Elder Street, a street of beautiful 1720s houses saved from demolition in 1977 by protesters who occupied the houses as they were being destroyed. As you walk down this street, give thanks for stroppy people. Near here there is a unique way of experiencing life in a weaver's house in eighteenth-century Spitalfields. Dennis Severs House, at 18 Folgate Street, has been recreated as a candlelit and plumbing-free house, in which visitors enter the gloomy and silent world of a struggling family of Huguenot weavers, who always seem to be a room away. It is open on some Sundays and Monday evenings, but you should check the website, www.dennissevershouse.co.uk, for details.

*

The routes suggested in Chapter Four will take you through many good eighteenth-century neighbourhoods. In Mayfair, Bloomsbury, Holborn, Spitalfields, Soho, Marylebone and Westminster, and in suburban (or once-suburban) towns like Wimbledon, Richmond, Highgate, Hampstead, Islington, Chelsea, Clapham and Kennington, you will find well-preserved streets of Georgian houses without much difficulty. Down the social scale survival is much rarer. The houses of the very poorest seventeenth- and eighteenth-century Londoners were not built to last, and they are all gone now, but if you look carefully you can find scattered surviving examples of houses built for ordinary citizens, artisans, shopkeepers and tradesmen, in many parts of London. Most of them are hard to recognize, and often shabby now, perhaps with little shops set into their front rooms (as they might have been from the start) or built over their front gardens. To see some of these modest eighteenth-century houses, go to Kingsland Road, the northern continuation of Bishopsgate and Shoreditch High Street. The Geffrye Museum, about a third of a mile up the road, on the right, occupies a set of almshouses built by the Ironmongers' Company in 1712–14. The museum, whose excellent collection of domestic interiors since 1600 offers one of the best and most enjoyable ways of understanding the history of the London house, is open every day but Monday, free of charge. One of the almshouses has been preserved and restored, and is open on the first Saturday of the month, and alternate Wednesdays, for about £2. Check the website, www.geffrye-museum.org.uk, for details.

Kingsland Road, which runs dead straight from Shoreditch to Stoke Newington, looks rather tatty and unpromising, but on its eastern side, north of the Regent's Canal, there are some modest artisans' houses surviving from the first development of the street in the 1770s and 1780s. Many of the little houses between number 374 and number 438 and between 520 and 566 were built then, though this stretch now looks like any other rather ragged and rundown shopping street. The oldest one, number 436, has a stone panel on its first-floor wall telling us that it was built in 1758 as part of Upsdell's Row, which you can just see from the other side of the road. There are grander four-storied survivors at numbers 318–346, which were built as Kingsland Crescent in 1792 and restored in 1994.

London's grand eighteenth-century houses are too numerous to describe, but not many are accessible to the public. Sometimes houses are open because they once had famous occupants, like Samuel Johnson and George Frederick Handel, whose houses are mentioned elsewhere, while others are art galleries, 'stately homes' or hotels. Perhaps pride of place should go to the Duke of Wellington's house, 'Number One London', Apsley House on Hyde Park Corner. This fine Palladian house was built in the 1770s by the great Robert Adam for Lord Apsley, and enlarged by James Wyatt for Lord Wellesley, Wellington's brother, thirty years later. It has been open to the public since 1853 and owned by the nation since 1947, but the Wellesleys still live in part of the house. What makes Apsley House special is that it still contains the collection of paintings, sculptures and treasures accumulated by Wellington during his 35 years in the house. No other great London mansion has retained such a personal collection assembled by its early occupants. It is open every day but Monday, and costs about £5 to go in.

The Mansion House, near the Bank of England, is the Palladian palace built in the 1740s for the Lord Mayor of London by George Dance the Elder, the City Clerk of Works. The building is still used by the Lord Mayor and his staff, but it is possible for groups of between 15 and 40 to arrange visits to the house, by writing to the Principal Assistant, Mansion House, London EC4N 8BH.

Marlborough House, which was built by Wren for another victorious general, the Duke of Marlborough (and his wife Sarah), in 1709–11, is not so easy to visit. Groups of 10–25 can take guided tours on Tuesday mornings, if they have arranged it in advance, by contacting the Commonwealth Secretariat, which now occupies the house. The email address is www.thecommonwealth.org.

The lower two floors are Wren's, and still largely unchanged, but the top one was added in 1870, to suit the needs of Edward, Prince of Wales (the future Edward VII), who held court here. It is striking that the Marlboroughs had a bigger and better London house than the monarch, who lived across the road in St James's Palace.

Part of the Marlborough fortune was left to the Spencer family, who spent some of it on a magnificent Palladian mansion, Spencer House, on the eastern edge of Green Park. The house was built for John Spencer, the first earl (and father of the more famous Georgiana, Duchess of Devonshire), by John Vardy, between 1756 and 1758, and by James 'Athenian' Stuart between 1758 and 1766. In his designs for the upstairs rooms Stuart pioneered the neoclassical style which would soon become popular among English and European architects. If you walk down St James's Street from Piccadilly and turn right into St James's Place, you will find this grand house, one of London's finest aristocratic palaces, at the end of the cul-de-sac. Since 1985 Spencer House has belonged to Lord Rothschild, who has had it restored to its original condition and restocked with the finest furniture and works of art. You can take a guided tour of this wonderful house on Sundays (except in January and August) for (in 2007) £9.

St James's Place is a good spot for looking at the development of fine London houses. Several of its houses survive from the 1680s and 1690s, when the street was first built. At the eastern end, near St James's Street, numbers 2–4, 6–9 and 40–45 date from 1685, though one or two have been refronted, and at the Green Park end there are original 1690s houses (numbers 14 and 29) and several later eighteenth-century ones, including numbers 10–13, 15 and 28, which was occupied by William Huskisson, the forward-thinking Tory politician who championed the introduction of steam trains and was the first passenger to be killed by one, at the opening of the Liverpool and Manchester line. The little square to the left (walking towards Green Park) is full of 1890s mansion flats, and the one on the right has an interesting mixture: number 18 and the

Stafford Hotel were mansion flats of 1889 and 1899, numbers 21, 22, 24 and 25 were built around 1960 on bombed land, and number 23 is the last large mansion built in the West End. It was constructed in 1930 for one of the few families that could still afford one, the Rothschilds.

∗

Some great London houses can only be seen from the outside. Crewe House on Curzon Street, the fine detached mansion which the Mayfair property developer Edward Shepherd built for himself in the 1740s, is now the gated and guarded Saudi embassy. In the past it has been the headquarters of Tillings the bus company, and the centre of British propaganda in the First World War. Its interiors now are all modern and Arabian. Home House, at 20 Portman Square, is one of the finest Georgian mansions in London. It was built in the 1770s for the wealthy daughter of a Jamaica merchant by James Wyatt and Robert Adam. Once it was the home of the Courtauld Collection and easy to see, but now it has been beautifully restored as an expensive private club, and is difficult to visit unless you are invited by a member. William Kent's finest London house, 44 Berkeley Square, is equally inaccessible without membership of the club that owns it.

Instead, to clear your mind of all this ostentatious luxury and elitism, you could visit the four-storey house which the founder of Methodism, John Wesley, built in 1779 and lived in until his death in 1791. It is at 47 City Road, between Old Street and Finsbury Square, opposite the Bunhill Fields Burial Ground, in which 120,000 London Dissenters are buried. Wesley is buried in his chapel, next to the house, but John Bunyan, Daniel Defoe and William Blake are all in Bunhill Fields, in well-signposted graves, along with Wesley's very influential mother, Susannah, the hymn-writer Isaac Watts and many others. John Wesley's house, which is open every day (not Sunday mornings) free of charge, is now a museum, and its contents include Wesley's exercise machine, his electrical therapy machine

and the bed in which he died. If you walk across Bunhill Fields to
Bunhill Row – where there is a good unpretentious Victorian pub,
the Artillery Arms – you will see housing of a different sort. Dufferin
Court, off Dufferin Street, has a set of houses built for costermongers, with sheds for their barrows. Whitecross Street market
was (and is) at the other end of Dufferin Street, but market traders'
gear would not have fitted into the big Peabody estate built on
Whitecross Street in the 1880s.

*

There is a marvellous late-eighteenth-century house on the northern side of Lincoln's Inn Fields. In 1792 the architect John Soane
bought and rebuilt number 12, and over the next thirty years he
added numbers 13 and 14, and converted the three into a house,
offices and a museum for the vast and eccentric collection of
paintings, architectural drawings, sculptures, antiquities and oddities
which he had previously housed in Pitshanger Manor, Ealing. The
collection is still in Soane's houses, much as he left it, and is open,
free of charge, from Tuesday to Saturday. The interior of number
13 Lincoln's Inn Fields must be one of the most fascinating in
London. Soane used domes, false walls and ceilings, mirrors, hanging arches, colonnades and changes of floor and ceiling level to
create surprise and interest in every room. On the ground floor the
Library, Dining Room and Breakfast Parlour are wonderful, and the
Picture Room has two of William Hogarth's 'modern moral subjects'
series of paintings, *The Election* and *The Rake's Progress*, and three of
London's best Canalettos. In the basement the Monk's Parlour and
Monk's Yard made fun of the fashion for mock medievalism that
Horace Walpole's Strawberry Hill had begun.

Somerset House, on the Strand, where the Courtauld Institute
moved when it left Home House, does not qualify as an eighteenth-
century house because it was intended from the start as accommodation for the Navy Office and other departments. Still, it is a
fine building, and its opening to the public in the 1990s was an

enjoyable addition to London's public spaces. It was built between 1776 and 1801 by Sir William Chambers, in a Palladian style inspired by the work of Inigo Jones, on the site of Protector Somerset's Tudor palace. The magnificent courtyards provide a lovely route from the Strand to Waterloo Bridge, and large sections of the house are open to those visiting the Courtauld and other art collections now housed there.

Another eighteenth-century house accessible as an art gallery is Hertford House, which occupies one side of Manchester Square, north of Oxford Street (near Selfridges). This was built for the Duke of Manchester in 1776, but much altered a hundred years later when Sir Richard Wallace, illegitimate son of the fourth Marquess of Hertford, converted it into a museum for the stupendous art collection assembled (mainly in France in the 1840s and 1850s) by his father. The house and collection, which includes more suits of armour than you could shake a sword at, were left to the nation by Wallace's widow in 1897, and are open every day, free of charge.

If you leave the east side of Manchester Square by Hinde Street, and turn left into Welbeck Street and right to the far end of Queen Anne Street, you will find another of London's finest eighteenth-century mansions, Chandos House. This was built by Robert Adam in 1769–71, for the third Duke of Chandos; became almost derelict in the 1980s; and was rescued and restored to its present fine condition in the 1990s. It is now owned by the Royal Society of Medicine. The house may not be quite as grand as Home House, but its interior decoration, especially its exquisite ceilings, is magnificent. Moreover, the house is accessible to those able to pay for the pleasure of eating, sleeping or meeting in its sumptuous surroundings. See the website, www.rsm.org.uk/chandoshouse for details.

Piccadilly once had two aristocratic palaces, and still has one. Devonshire House, which stood between Stratton Street and Berkeley Street, was demolished in the early 1920s, but Burlington House was protected from destruction (but not mutilation) by the fact that it had been bought by the government in 1854 as a home for various scholarly societies. Its present occupants include the Chemical Society, the Geological Society, the Royal Astronomical Society, the Linnean Society and the Royal Academy of Arts, which occupies the main central block. The original 1660s house (built by Sir John Denham and possibly Hugh May) was extensively remodelled in 1717–20 by Colen Campbell for the third Earl of Burlington, in the Palladian style which they both admired so much. The old house is the one you see ahead of you, five bays wide and two floors high, when you enter the courtyard from Piccadilly. The extra floor and the wings were added in the 1860s and 1880s to make room for all those scholars, along with a range of exhibition rooms and new headquarters for London University at the back, facing Burlington Gardens. The rooms that survive from Burlington and Campbell's day, the John Madejski Fine Rooms, now house the RA's permanent collection, and are open to the public, free of charge, every afternoon except Monday, and all day at weekends. There are free guided tours, too: at 1.00 on Tuesdays to Fridays, and 11.30 on Saturdays. The Saloon, in the centre of the first floor, and the Secretary's Room next to it, are by Campbell and William Kent (whose Saloon ceiling is being restored), and the beautiful Reynolds Room and the General Assembly Room, at the east and west ends of the old house, were remodelled by Samuel Ware in 1815. The main exhibition galleries were mostly built by Sydney Smirke in the 1860s, and the restaurant was added by Norman Shaw in the 1880s.

A few yards from Burlington House, walking towards Piccadilly Circus, is the entrance to the Albany, a fine set of exclusive late-eighteenth-century apartments. They began in 1771–5, when William Chambers built a mansion, set well back from Piccadilly, for Lord Melbourne. The house was sold to the Duke of York (and Albany), and in 1802 converted by Henry Holland into apartments for bachelor gentlemen, with two long rows of apartments in what had been the garden of Melbourne's mansion. You can enter the outer courtyard, but the rest is private. The long covered close along which the rows of three-storied apartments were built, called the Ropewalk, runs right through to Vigo Street, where the development is guarded by two lodges, built by Holland, and a locked black gate. This unusual community has included a large number of distinguished Londoners, including the writers Lord Byron, J.B. Priestley, Aldous Huxley, Terence Rattigan, Isaiah Berlin and Graham Greene, the politicians Lord Brougham, George Canning, Lord Derby and Gladstone, the photographers William Fox Talbot and Lord Snowden, the actor-managers Squire Bancroft and Herbert Beerbohm Tree, and Allen Lane, who began publishing Penguin Books from the Albany in 1936. His achievement is remembered in a slate plaque on Vigo Street. None of these residents would have contributed to the slightly risqué reputation enjoyed by the Albany, but the fact that E.J. Hornung's fictional gentleman cracksman, A.J. Raffles, lived there, might have done so.

Soho, which was mostly built between 1660 and 1740, still has plenty of early-eighteenth-century houses, and a scattering of later-seventeenth-century ones, especially in Meard Street, Beak Street, Berwick Street, Dean Street, Carlisle Street, Frith Street, Gerrard Street and Soho Square. Unlike the Georgian houses of Mayfair, St James's, Marylebone and Bloomsbury, those in Soho were nearly all built for people of modest social standing – artisans, shopkeepers and so forth. The rich deserted Soho in the eighteenth century, and only one fashionable mansion survives, on the corner of Soho Square and Greek Street. The House of St Barnabas, 1 Greek Street, was built in 1746 and first occupied by Richard Beckford, whose vast wealth came from Jamaica sugar plantations. Later it was used by the Westminster Commissioners of Sewers, and it was the first home of the Metropolitan Board of Works from 1855 to 1861. Since then it has been the headquarters of a charity for homeless women, offering dormitory accommodation until 2006. The wonderful plasterwork, panelling and carvings of the staircase and first-floor rooms commissioned by Beckford in the 1750s have survived very well, and can be seen on the first Monday of each month, when the house is open to paying visitors. See www.houseofstbarnabas.org.uk for details.

*

Some of the finest eighteenth-century houses are in the suburbs. To the north, the best is Kenwood House, on the northern edge of Hampstead Heath. This is another James and Robert Adam house, built for the Lord Chief Justice, Lord Mansfield (the judge who declared that slavery in England was illegal), between 1766 and 1774. Some rooms from an existing seventeenth-century house were retained, but most of Kenwood is the work of the Adam brothers, apart from two wings on the north side, which were added in the 1790s. The whole house is interesting, but the best room is the library or Great Room, at the eastern end of the terrace. The house was given to the nation by Lord Iveagh (Edward Guinness, the brewing millionaire) in 1927, and is now run by English Heritage. Kenwood and its excellent collection of paintings are open every day, free of charge.

East London, north and south of the river, was unfashionable in the eighteenth century, and is therefore much less rich in fine Georgian houses than west London. In south-east London there is the Rangers House, on Chesterfield Walk, on the western edge of Greenwich Park. This fine villa built in the 1720s for Vice-Admiral Francis Hosier was occupied by the fourth Earl of Chesterfield, who bombarded his illegitimate son with letters of advice, and whose pretence of patronage was ridiculed by Dr Johnson. 'This man I thought had been a Lord among wits; but, I find, he is only a wit among Lords.' Now the house is owned by English Heritage and contains the wonderful collection of medieval and Renaissance treasures assembled by Sir Julius Wernher, who brought a vast fortune made in South African gold and diamond mining to London in the 1880s. The house is open from Sunday to Wednesday from April to September, and off-season by appointment, and visits cost about £6.

Havering, London's easternmost borough, has some good Georgian houses, including Rainham Hall, a fine 1729 red brick house in the Dutch style, on the Broadway, Rainham. Its first owner was Captain John Harle, a merchant and the owner of Rainham Wharf. The house is now owned by the National Trust, and is open to the public on Saturday afternoons between April and October, for about £2.50. Vanbrugh Castle, the architect Sir John Vanbrugh's medieval-style house on Maze Hill not far south of Maze Hill station, the last survivor of a set of houses he built for his family in Greenwich, is now private apartments, so can be seen but not entered.

✳

Many London suburbs were established country towns or villages before the spreading metropolis engulfed them, and most have retained some vestiges of their pre-suburban existence. Hampstead is only four miles from Charing Cross (much nearer than Greenwich or Richmond) but was protected from rapid nineteenth-century suburban development by its height, which made it a difficult haul for horse omnibuses and trams, and inaccessible to underground trains until electricity replaced steam and tunnels replaced covered trenches in the 1890s. The platforms of the Underground station, probably the starting point for your visit, are the deepest in London, 59 metres below ground level. Thus Hampstead has preserved many of its eighteenth-century streets and houses, giving it a more convincing Georgian village atmosphere than any other London suburb.

A walk around Hampstead, perhaps combined with an exploration of the Heath, one of London's loveliest open spaces, makes an excellent day out. It should include the old streets on either side of Heath Street, which joins Hampstead High Street by the station.

Turn right out of the station and go north (uphill) on Heath Street, which gets more Georgian as you approach the top of the hill, where Whitestone Pond used to refresh horses after their climb.

This very high point was the site of an Armada beacon in 1588. Turn left into Lower Terrace, with the Hampstead Astronomical Observatory on your left, and keep going until you see John Constable's summer residence, number 2, on your right. Go sharp left here into Admiral's Walk, in which the ship-like Admiral's House (1700) was once occupied by the architect George Gilbert Scott. John Galsworthy, author of the Forsyte novels, lived more modestly next door. Cross Hampstead Grove to see Mount Square, one of the many little Georgian squares and alleys in the centre of Hampstead. Turn right down Hampstead Grove, where the late-Victorian illustrator and novelist George du Maurier lived at number 28, and follow it to Fenton House, and then to a large weather-boarded house which was built in 1797 for the painter Sir George Romney and enlarged in 1807 as an assembly room. Clough Williams Ellis, the architect, lived here in the 1930s.

At this point cross to the right to find Mount Vernon, and follow it, going roughly in the same direction as before, until you find Robert Louis Stevenson's house, where you should turn left into Holly Walk, in which number 9 was used in the 1830s as a watch house for the Hampstead police. This pretty lane leads past a nineteenth-century graveyard to St John's church, which was built in the 1740s. John Constable is buried in the south-east corner of the churchyard and the clockmaker John Harrison near the south side of the church. These graves are large and easy to find with the help of the plan near the church.

Turn left into wide and lovely Church Row, Hampstead's oldest street, which has many early-eighteenth-century houses, built just before the Hampstead spa went out of fashion. H.G. Wells and Peter Cook lived at number 17. Turn left at Heath Street, and after a few metres cross it and cut through Oriel Place to the High Street. Bird in Hand Yard, across the road, was the terminus of the omnibus routes between Hampstead and London, and the site of the London Omnibus Company's stables. To its left, take Flask Walk, which has late-Georgian cottages, a nice pub and some fine houses. Continue into Well Walk, the old spa promenade, to see John Constable's house (number 40) and lovely number 46, which is near the site of the Pump Room (*see* Chapter Two). Return to the top of Flask Walk and turn right into New End Square, passing Burgh House and following the right side of the triangle to pass the Old White Bear. The grand 1849 frontage of the workhouse and soup kitchen on your left, now converted into desirable housing, is a reminder of the days when the poor could afford to live in Hampstead, and did so in large numbers. The little theatre on the right is in a converted 1890s hospital morgue, and all around you here are mid-nineteenth-century tenement and workhouse buildings and late-Victorian hospital and school buildings that speak of a Hampstead community that was far removed from the wealth that surrounds us today. Just after the theatre, turn right into cobbled Christchurch Passage to see Hampstead Square (ahead) and Elm Row (left), which have many fine early-eighteenth-century houses, and turn left into Heath Street to return to the station.

*

One of the best ways to explore eighteenth-century London houses is to visit some of west London's riverside towns, especially Chelsea, Chiswick, Richmond and Twickenham. Chelsea, which made the transition from riverside village to London suburb in the later eighteenth century, has a fine collection of Georgian houses, many of which replaced older and greater mansions that once lined the riverfront. Henry VIII had a manor house on the corner of Oakley Street and Cheyne Walk, and his Chancellor, Sir Thomas More, had a mansion, Beaufort House, between King's Road and the river. A picturesque plaque on 28 Beaufort Street commemorates the house, which was demolished in 1766. Its gateway, by Inigo Jones, is now at Chiswick House. The houses that replaced these and other mansions are best preserved on Cheyne Walk, which runs from Chelsea Physic Garden in the east to Cremorne Road and Edith Grove in the west. The houses on the first stretch of Cheyne Walk, east of Oakley Street, were mostly built around 1720. Number 4 was the last home of George Eliot, number 16, which is called Tudor House, was once the home of the Pre-Raphaelite painter and poet Dante Gabriel Rossetti, who had Algernon Charles Swinburne living with him in the 1860s, and number 18 was once a famous coffee house, Don Saltero's. The coffee house seems to have moved here around 1717, and became famous for its museum of curiosities, mostly donated by Sir Hans Sloane, the great collector, who lived nearby. It doubled as a tavern in the nineteenth century and became a private house in the 1860s.

After Oakley Street there are two houses (numbers 38–39) built in the Arts and Crafts style by C.R. Ashbee in the 1890s, when Chelsea was a thriving artistic community, and some older houses, numbers 46–48 (1711) and 62 (1686). Henry James died in Carlyle Mansions, and T.S. Eliot lived there during and after the First World War. After Chelsea Old Church and the 1969 statue of a gold-faced Sir Thomas More, there is a little garden on the site of Jacob Epstein's pre-1914 studios, the relocated Crosby Hall on the corner of Danvers Street, and then Beaufort Street and Battersea Bridge.

West of Beaufort Street there is a terrace of houses outstanding for its age and quality, and for its literary and historical associations. Numbers 91–94 were built in the 1770s in the grounds of Lindsey House, a mansion built in 1674 for Robert Bertie, the Earl of Lindsey. Lindsey House still exists, but is divided now into six houses, numbers 95–100 Cheyne Walk. The 'decadent' artist Charles Conder lived at number 91, the future Mrs Gaskell was born at number 93, Whistler lived at number 96 between 1866 and 1878 (the period in which he famously painted his mother), and the father and son engineers Marc and Isambard Kingdom Brunel lived at number 98. In the smaller houses west of Lindsey House, Hilaire Belloc lived at number 104, the artist Philip Wilson Steer at number 109, and J.W.M. Turner spent his last years (1846–51) as a recluse in his house and studio, numbers 118–119. Sylvia Pankhurst later lived next door, at number 120.

James McNeill Whistler, the American whose paintings contribute so much to our image of Victorian London, and especially the Thames, spent forty years of his life in London, mostly in houses in this part of Chelsea. Before moving to 96 Cheyne Walk he lived at number 101, and when he left number 96 he moved to Tite Street, a little nearer the Royal Hospital, where he owned the White House, number 35, which had been built for him by Edward Godwin (who later turned 34 Tite Street into the House Beautiful for Oscar Wilde). Whistler lost the White House in 1879 when he was bankrupted by the expense of bringing a libel case against the critic John Ruskin, and London lost it when it was demolished in 1968. Whistler later occupied two other houses in Tite Street, numbers 13 and 46, living in acerbic rivalry with his neighbour, Oscar Wilde, at number 34 (which was then number 16). In 1902, not long before his death, Whistler moved back into Cheyne Walk, to number 74.

The eighteenth-century Chelsea house that is easiest to visit is 24 Cheyne Row, in which the historian Thomas Carlyle lived from 1834, when he arrived in London, until his death in 1881. This is the only house open to the public on this famous terrace of Queen Anne houses and is worth visiting even if you do not share the Victorians' exaggerated respect for Carlyle as a sage and prophet. The house has been a museum since 1895 and owned by the National Trust since 1936, and its interior has been preserved as the Carlyles knew it, including the furniture, the gloomy decoration and Carlyle's soundproofed study. Cheyne Row is a turning off Cheyne Walk, west of Oakley Street. The house is open for about £6 between late March (when National Trust members come out of hibernation) and October, Wednesday to Friday afternoons and all day at weekends. Carlyle's unworldly friend Leigh Hunt, the critic and essayist, who lived at number 22 in the 1830s, was the model for the shameless sponger and rather repulsive 'perfect child', Harold Skimpole, in Dickens's *Bleak House.*

*

Leaving aside the older houses with important Georgian additions already mentioned – Osterley and Syon (both substantially remodelled by Robert Adam in the 1760s and 1770s) – the pick of the west London mansions must be Chiswick House, which has a special place in the history of architecture and garden design. The house was built in 1727–9 by Richard Boyle, the third Earl of Burlington, who no longer needed the help of Colen Campbell in realizing his Palladian ideals. It was built as an extension to a Jacobean house, which was demolished in the 1780s, leaving this perfect jewel of a house, one of the finest in London. The house offered very modest accommodation for a man of Burlington's wealth ('too little to live in and too big to hang on a watch chain', as Horace Walpole said), but he intended to use it as a gallery, and a showcase of the Palladian style, which might encourage others to imitate it. Each of the two floors is a square, with sequences of rooms gathered around a domed octagonal hall, or tribune. The rooms still look as Burlington intended, richly decorated by his protégé William Kent, but the Burlington art collection disappeared to Chatsworth when the family left Chiswick in 1892. Now the house is run by English Heritage, and is open, for about £4, between April and October, Wednesday to Sunday.

The wonderful 67 acres of grounds, the work of William Kent, are open all year, free, and are well worth a visit in their own right. Burlington and Kent replaced the earlier formal gardens with 'classical' gardens which looked natural and unplanned, with little buildings to terminate the views along their paths and avenues. There is an obelisk, a deer house, a rustic house, an Ionic temple, an amphitheatre and a Doric column to catch the wanderer's eye. Follow the wide avenue along the west front of the house, go through the Inigo Jones gateway from Sir Thomas More's house in Chelsea, and carry on to reach the Italian Garden and Samuel Ware's interesting and innovative (and now rather tatty) domed conservatory (1813), a model for the work of Joseph Paxton (creator of the Crystal Palace), who was an apprentice here. The stretch of water west of the house is the Bollo Brook, which was enlarged in the 1720s into a river or canal, crossed by a classical bridge. Take the path from the house to the cascade at the Burlington Lane end of the canal, and you will find the elevated terrace walk, round the edge of the wilderness garden, which contrasts enjoyably with the classical and Italian gardens you have just seen. Near the other end of the canal, cross the ornate classical bridge and take the path up to the semicircular space known as an exedra, with the amphitheatre on your right and a wooded area of winding pathways on your left, to reach the house again.

For an interesting contrast, take the Hogarth Lane exit from the grounds of Chiswick House, and turn right towards (but not to) the Hogarth Roundabout, to find the little country house that was occupied by Burlington's bitter critic, William Hogarth, between 1749 and 1764, and by his wife until 1789. Hogarth's house was left derelict for years and badly damaged by wartime bombing, but it has recovered now, and provides a lovely refuge from the noise of the busy road and a touching reminder of the life and work of one of the greatest of London artists and social critics. The pretty walled garden still has a mulberry tree, a relic of the once-important London silk-weaving industry. The house is open every afternoon except Monday, and is free. Hogarth is buried in St Nicholas churchyard, on the river nearby, with an epitaph written by David Garrick, the greatest eighteenth-century actor.

To complete a perfect eighteenth-century day in Chiswick, take one of London's finest walks, along the river to Hammersmith. Take the underpass under Hogarth Roundabout to reach Chiswick Square, which has several 1680s houses, survivors of the massacre when the roundabout was built. To the left, take Church Street, which has some fine Georgian houses and seventeenth-century cottages in Pages Yard, on the right. Once there were two inns in Church Street, serving the beer made in the old Lamb brewery, which is on the left. Lamb Cottage was the Lamb Tap, and the sixteenth-century houses that are now 1 and 2 Church Street, the

Old Burlington, were once the Burlington Arms. The church, St Nicholas, dates back to the twelfth century, but its oldest existing part is the early-fifteenth-century tower. The rest of the church was rebuilt in the 1880s. In the churchyard are the graves of William Hogarth, the landscape and battle-scene painter Philip de Loutherbourg and Lord Burlington's bricklayer Richard Wright.

This was once a highly industrial neighbourhood, with two great breweries and one of late-Victorian London's more important shipyards. Thorneycroft's, which was established on Chiswick Wharf (about 200 metres upstream from Church Street) in 1864, built launches, torpedo boats and destroyers here until it moved to Southampton in 1909. The voyage of one of the last Thorneycroft vessels from Chiswick to the sea is described at the end of H.G. Wells's novel *Tono-Bungay*, which in turn inspired the ending of Vaughan Williams's London Symphony. Ahead of you, at the end of Church Street, is the mid-nineteenth-century causeway that led down to the ferry that had operated from this point since the Middle Ages. Now turn left and go east along Chiswick Mall, which has wonderful eighteenth-century houses, as well as beautiful views of the Thames. In Chiswick Lane, Fuller's Griffin Brewery is a mixture of modern and eighteenth-century buildings. You can tour the buildings, see the brewery in operation and taste the product for about £6, but you must book in advance. The website is www.fullers.co.uk.

Back on Chiswick Mall, look out for Greenash, which was built in 1882 for the shipbuilder Sir John Thorneycroft (who is buried in the churchyard), and wonderful Walpole House. The early-eighteenth-century front hides a Tudor house (with Tudor chimneystacks) with Georgian extensions and interiors and a fine 1720s staircase. It was the home of Charles II's mistress Barbara Villiers, Duchess of Cleveland, who is buried in St Nicholas church. In the 1830s it was an asylum for vagrant girls and in the 1840s a boys' school. William Thackeray was a pupil here, and used the school as a model for Miss Pinkerton's Academy in *Vanity Fair*. This is one of west London's finest houses, and its asking price in 2006 was £8 million.

Your walk then takes you away from the river, along Hammersmith Terrace, where the buildings on the right are the back of a long terrace built around 1750. Number 7, once the home of the painter Philip de Loutherbourg and the engraver Emery Walker (1851–1933), is occasionally open to the public. Walker was a friend of Philip Webb and William Morris, and the house is still decorated and furnished in the Arts and Crafts style. To arrange a visit, go to www.emerywalker.org.uk.

At the late-eighteenth-century Black Lion pub you return to the river, with fine views ahead to Hammersmith. Your walk passes the Old Ship Inn, rebuilt in 1850 but with an early-seventeenth-century entrance round the back, and Linden House, probably built in the 1730s and now a sailing club. Thanks to years of institutional use it is more interesting outside than in. Number 16 Upper Mall, Kelmscott House (built in the 1780s), was William Morris's home from 1878 to 1896, but only the basement and coach house, headquarters of the William Morris Society, are accessible to the public (on Thursday and Saturday afternoons, by appointment). While living here Morris started the Society for the Protection of Ancient Buildings (the first conservation society), founded and led the Socialist League (which met in the coach house) and ran the Kelmscott Press, which was based at number 14. Morris designed his own typefaces and supervised the production of fine editions of his own works and reprints of medieval and classic texts, including the Kelmscott Chaucer. To finish your walk you could have a drink in the Dove, a beautiful but often crowded little pub with seventeenth-century origins, where the poet James Thomson used to take a break on his walks from Richmond (his house is still in Kew Foot Road) to London. It is said (but may not be true) that he wrote the words to 'Rule Britannia' while sitting here. His inspiration might not have been alcoholic, because until 1796, when Fullers bought it, this was the Dove Coffee House.

If you want to find out more about William Morris, philosopher, poet, designer and highly successful industrialist, go to Water House in Forest Road, Walthamstow, the fine 1750s house that was Morris's family home in the 1850s, and which is now the William Morris Gallery. It is open every day except Mondays and most Sundays, free of charge. The gallery illustrates every aspect of Morris's life and work, along with that of other late-Victorian artists and designers, including the Pre-Raphaelites. Behind it, the grounds of the house are now Lloyd Park, whose beauty and utility would have pleased Morris. The website is www.walthamforest.gov.uk/wmg/home.htm.

Richmond is rich in fine eighteenth-century houses, especially on Richmond Hill, with its famous and ever-beautiful view of the Thames across the Terrace Gardens; on some streets off the Hill, especially Ormond Road (near the bridge) and the Vineyard, a street of great variety and interest especially for lovers of almshouses; and others on the two southern sides of the Green. To see some of the best, turn left out of Richmond station, cross the Quadrant and take the alley next to the railway line to reach Little Green. Turn left, passing Frank Matcham's unmissable 1899 theatre, which was once, in an earlier building, managed by the great Edmund Kean. Go ahead, and you will be walking along the south-eastern side of the Green, which has a succession of excellent old houses. Number one is seventeenth century, and most of the rest along here are eighteenth century. Brewer's Lane, off to the left, has eighteenth-century houses and shops. Then, in the far corner, past two good pubs, you will reach Old Palace Terrace, built in 1692, Paved Court of the same decade, and Oak House (1769), Old Palace Place (1700) and Old Friars (1687), which is built on the cellars of a Franciscan friary founded by Henry VII in 1500 and destroyed by his son forty years later. The showpiece of the south-western side is Maids of Honour Row, a terrace of four houses built in 1724 for the attendants of Princess Caroline, soon to be George II's queen. Number 4 was occupied in the 1740s by the Haymarket Theatre manager John Heidegger, and its hall is still decorated with landscapes by his scene-painter.

Further along, the old stone and brick gateway led into the courtyard of Richmond Palace. This had once been Shene Palace, the country home of medieval kings since 1125. Edward III, Henry VII and Elizabeth all died at Shene. Henry VII rebuilt it after a disastrous fire in 1497, and renamed it to match his own title. The palace was mostly demolished in the republican 1650s and the site was redeveloped as housing. All that is visible now of Henry's palace is the gatehouse, some stretches of Tudor brickwork in Old Palace and Palace Gate House on the left of the gateway, and lots of diapered brickwork and filled arches in the Wardrobe, on the left side of Old Palace Yard, through the gate. Trumpeter's House, straight ahead across the courtyard, was built just after 1700, and converted into flats around 1950. Leave Old Palace Yard by the alley marked with bollards and turn left into Old Palace Lane, which has Regency cottages, to reach the river near a well-restored Palladian villa, Asgill House, which was built by Sir Robert Taylor in 1759 for a City merchant banker and Lord Mayor of London, Sir Charles Asgill. The house is not generally open to the public. A walk along the river towards Richmond Bridge, London's only eighteenth-century bridge over the Thames, takes you past a grandiose 1980s riverside office development which hides behind the facades and replicas of fine eighteenth-century houses that were allowed to fall into disrepair in the 1960s and 1970s.

There is a good collection of eighteenth-century houses just across the river from Richmond, in Twickenham. Cross Richmond Bridge, turn left and walk along the riverbank until you see a path into Marble Hill Park, with Marble Hill House standing beautifully in the centre. This was built in 1724–9 for George II's mistress, Henrietta Howard, by Roger Morris, perhaps with advice from Colen Campbell, and certainly under the influence of Inigo Jones's Queen's House in Greenwich. From the outside, the house is a model of what a Palladian villa should look like, and inside the house is decorated and furnished just as it should be. The cubic Great Room has woodcarvings by George I's master-carver, James

Richards, and the main bedchamber has a lovely ceiling. The gardens are a public park, and the house is open between April and October, Wednesday to Sunday, for about £4. Check the website, www.english-heritage.org.uk, for accurate times and prices.

If you leave Marble Hill Park in the far north-west corner you will be next to Montpelier Row, as fine a terrace of early-Georgian (c. 1724) houses as you will find anywhere in outer London. Tennyson lived at number 15 and Walter de la Mare at 30. Chapel Road leads to Orleans Road, which has a gate into Orleans Park, which used to be the grounds of Orleans House until it was demolished in 1927. The Octagon, a beautiful domed garden room built by James Gibbs (architect of St Martin-in-the-Fields) in 1720, survived this misfortune. It is now a municipal art gallery, worth entering to see its dome and the fine early-eighteenth-century plasterwork and sculptures, as well as the temporary exhibitions. It is open every afternoon except Monday, free of charge. A little further west, either along the riverbank or York Road, the Rich- mond Municipal Offices are in York House, a large H-plan house built in the 1650s for Edward Montagu, second Earl of Manchester. The house is much altered, but the gardens are a treat, especially for the spectacular Italian fountain, which was put here by an Indian prince, Sir Ratan Tata, in 1906. Next to York House, to the east, is Syon Road, another very fine Georgian terrace, dated 1721. If you walk down it to the river you will find one of west London's best (and best-located) pubs, the eighteenth-century White Swan Inn.

Twickenham has a fine church, St Mary, mostly rebuilt in 1714–15, with monuments to Alexander Pope (inside) and his nurse, on the outer wall, and a good little museum in a 1720 house on the Embankment, near the river. It also has another great and important house. Take the main road through the town centre and Cross Deep, which passes the site of Pope's house, built around 1720 and demolished ninety years later. All that is left of his house and garden, which used to be where Grotto Road and Pope's Grove meet Cross Deep, is his grotto, a set of artificial caves and tunnels decorated with geological specimens. If you want to see the grotto, you have to contact the head of St James' Boys' School, in Cross Deep, which is built on top of it.

Pope's house, garden and grotto helped to stimulate an interest in picturesque and 'natural' effects in house and garden design, but its influence was small compared with that of Horace Walpole's Strawberry Hill, which is a few minutes away, on Waldegrave Road. Walpole, the Prime Minister's son and a noted writer, gossip and man of wit and taste, bought a fifty-year-old house here in 1749, and spent the next seventeen years turning it into a little Gothic castle, complete with battlements, turrets and buttresses. He formed a 'Committee of Taste', led by himself, to supervise the building, and produced a quirky, charming, irregular house in which romantic notions of the Middle Ages played as great a part as genuine historical research. As the Gothic house was nearing completion, Walpole published *The Castle of Otranto* (1763), which started a fashion for Gothic novels to complement the fashion for Gothic houses. The house is still in good condition, and it is well worth arranging to visit it. Contact St Mary's College, Waldegrave Road (www.smuc.ac.uk), the present occupant. Visits cost about £5, but see www.visitrichmond.co.uk and follow links to 'attractions' and 'historic houses' for up-to-date information. In future, it is hoped that Strawberry Hill will be bought, restored and opened to the public by a local action committee.

Much of the interior design was done by Richard Bentley, and by Walpole's friend John Chute. Their work is a mixture of Gothic fantasy and careful copies of features of medieval buildings in London, York and St Albans. The Library has bookcases copied from Old St Paul's and a chimneypiece based on a tomb in Westminster Abbey; the Gallery has a door copied from St Albans; the Round Room (by Robert Adam) has a ceiling based on the rose window of Old St Paul's; and so on. Every room is interesting, whether you share Walpole's love of the Gothic or not. Walpole's town house, and that of his father, was 5 Arlington Street, off Piccadilly, next to St James's Street.

Finally, you should visit Sir John Soane's country house, Pitshanger Manor, Walpole Park, near Ealing Broadway. Soane bought a City merchant's house here in 1800, and rebuilt it (retaining George Dance's 1760s extension) over the next four years. Externally, Soane's Coade stone copies of classical columns and statues create the illusion of a much bigger and grander house. He sold it and moved his collections to Lincoln's Inn Fields in 1810, but despite eighty years as a public library the house has retained some of Soane's marvellously inventive interiors, and even its lovely gardens, which are now Walpole Park. Soane used some of the devices he used in Lincoln's Inn Fields, including vaults, niches, domes, elaborate ceilings and unusual room sizes and heights, to surprise and delight the visitor. Now Pitshanger Manor is Ealing's main art gallery, and is open to the public, free of charge, every afternoon from Tuesday to Friday, and all day on Saturday. Since the destruction of Soane's Bank of England in the 1920s, Soane's own houses here and in Lincoln's Inn Fields, along with Dulwich Picture Gallery (repaired after the Second World War), the museum and stable block in Chelsea Royal Hospital and three churches (Holy Trinity, Great Portland Street; St Peter, Liverpool Grove, Walworth; and St John, Cambridge Heath Road, Bethnal Green) are the only important Soane buildings in London.

West London has some good nineteenth-century houses open to the public. Gunnersbury House, near Acton Town Tube station, was built in 1835 for Nathan Meyer Rothschild, the City's most powerful banker, by Sydney Smirke. The house is a local museum (especially of pottery and ceramics) and not very atmospheric, but it is open every afternoon all year round, free of charge.

A key work of one of the most influential Victorian architects, Norman Shaw, is accessible in Harrow Weald, on the western edge of the Metropolitan Police District. This is Grim's Dyke, on Harrow

Weald Common, which was built in 1870–2 in the so-called Old English style for the artist Frederick Goodall, and owned by the playwright and librettist W.S. Gilbert between 1890 and 1911. It is now the Grim's Dyke Hotel, which does its best to evoke the Gilbert and Sullivan atmosphere, and it is easy for guests to see the best rooms, including Gilbert's large medieval-style studio, which is now a restaurant. There is another important Victorian mansion, Bentley Priory, less than a mile to the east. This 1760s house was remodelled by Sir John Soane in the 1790s, Victorianized in the 1850s and converted into a hotel in 1885. In the Second World War it was the headquarters of Fighter Command, and it is still occupied by the RAF. Some of the grounds are public, and you can see the handsome building from a distance.

There are two excellent artists' houses on public view in Kensington. The more modest of the two is Linley Sambourne House, 18 Stafford Terrace, just north of High Street Kensington, near the Tube station. Sambourne was a famous *Punch* cartoonist from 1867 to 1909, and after his death his children kept his house much as he left it. The house and its contents were sold to the Greater London Council in 1980, to be opened as a museum. Now it has been fitted out as a typically dark and cluttered Victorian house, and visitors can take guided tours, often led by a costumed actor, on weekends between March and December, for a fee of about £6 (2007). The website, www.rbkc.gov.uk/linleysambourne house, gives details of times and prices.

Leighton House, the home of the artist Lord Leighton, President of the Royal Academy, is 12 Holland Park Road, a sidestreet off Melbury Road, which is itself off Kensington High Street, a quarter-mile west of Sambourne House. Leighton was a richer and more important artist than Sambourne, and his house is more lavish and showy. Leighton House was an important centre for artists and musicians, and a visit offers an insight into their world. Leighton's Arab Hall, with a black marble pool, Persian and Arab tiles, and decorative features by Leighton's friends and contemporaries, is one of London's most extraordinary rooms. The dining room, staircase and studio are also very fine, though they do not convey as strong a sense of the daily life and work of an artist as Sambourne's house does. The house is open every day but Tuesday, for about £3, and you can get a joint ticket for the two artists' houses. For up-to-date details, see www.rbkc.gov.uk/LeightonHouseMuseum.

*

Most of the great Victorian mansions in central London were demolished to make way for offices and hotels in the first half of the twentieth century, when they were no longer needed for the balls, parties and dinners that once filled the London Season. Park Lane, which was once lined with the mansions of the super-rich, is now a street of modern offices, flats and hotels, with a few older houses here and there. Numbers 91–99, between Upper Brook Street and Upper Grosvenor Street, give some impression of what the street looked like in the 1820s, when they were built. The great Jewish philanthropist Sir Moses Montefiore lived at number 99 for sixty years, dying there at the age of 101 in 1884, and Benjamin Disraeli lived for 35 years in number 93. The most impressive house is number 100, Dudley House, one of the two Park Lane mansions (the other is Stanhope House, further south) that remain from the ten there were in 1900. It is a nine-bay house occupied by the Earls of Dudley from 1828 to 1940, and then converted to offices after war damage. When its 125-year lease was for sale in 2005 the asking price was around £40 million, for which the buyer would get 14 reception rooms, 17 bedrooms, a double-height ballroom, a 25-metre picture gallery and the amazing 1850s cast-iron conservatory that dominates the view of the house from Park Lane.

Elsewhere, a few West End mansions survive as government buildings, including two in the precincts of St James' Palace. One of these, Lancaster House, was built for George IV's brother in 1825, and later owned by two extremely wealthy men, the Duke of Sutherland, whose wealth came from land, coal and Highland clearances, and Lord Leverhulme, who made his fortune from soap. It is only open to those attending government functions. The other, Clarence House, was built by John Nash for the Duke of Clarence in 1825–8, and is still in royal possession. One of the easier millionaire's mansions to visit is Dartmouth House, 37 Charles Street, Mayfair, which was remodelled in the 1890s for Lord Revelstoke, of the powerful Baring banking family. It is now the headquarters of the English-Speaking Union, which often holds cultural events at the house, open to non-members, and which has a public restaurant.

The greatest house in London, Buckingham Palace, is also open to the public, in August and September, for £15. The State Apartments on show are the work of John Nash, who rebuilt the palace at shocking expense for George IV in the 1820s, and of the man who took over from him when he was sacked in 1830, Edward Blore. There is an eighteenth-century house hidden behind all this pomp, but it is not on the public route.

CHAPTER FOUR

✳

PLANNED LONDON

Covent Garden piazza in 1744

LONDON IS USUALLY described as an unplanned city which grew haphazardly through the actions of countless landowners and builders who followed building regulations but no overall city plan. This is generally true, but hidden in the unruly jungle of London there are many little planned districts, most of which were built by private landlords in order to make it more desirable to live in their houses. In the nineteenth century housing charities like the Peabody Trust built their owned planned communities, and from the 1890s onward London's local authorities joined in, building 'estates' of houses or flats all over central and suburban London. There are so many of these planned quarters that seeing them all would involve travelling all over London, and visiting places which are of more interest to the sociologist or criminologist than the historically minded sightseer, but others are charming, interesting or historically significant.

Planned developments began as far back as the ninth century, when Alfred the Great, having rescued London (and most of England) from the marauding Danes, set about refortifying and rebuilding the city. We can still see the grid or fishbone pattern of little streets on either side of Cheapside, the main Anglo-Saxon market street, and down to the Thames, laid out under Alfred and his son, Edward the Elder, between 886 and 924. The small right-angled streets also served to divide the city into convenient plots which Alfred granted to his allies and advisers, for building and defence. Some of these old streets have disappeared under redevelopment in recent years, but the City still retains some of its ancient street pattern, and if you walk down Cheapside from St Paul's to the Bank, and into its little sidestreets, Wood Street and Milk Street to the north, Bread Street and Bow Lane to the south, you are following the grid established by Alfred and his immediate successors. There is another Saxon grid, perhaps a little later, with Lombard Street (a Roman road) and Eastcheap as its east–west axes, and Gracechurch Street/Fish Street Hill, Philpot Lane/Botolph Lane and Rood Lane/St Mary at Hill as their north–south connections. Whether you are able to transport yourself back in your imagination to the ninth and tenth centuries as you walk these streets depends on your ability to ignore the traffic and the modern buildings that line them now.

The survival of these Anglo-Saxon street patterns in the City reminds us that when London burned down in the Great Fire of 1666 the grand plans proposed by Christopher Wren, Robert Hooke, John Evelyn and others were rejected, and London was rebuilt on its old street network. If we are looking for planned streets from the seventeenth century, we should not look at the City, but a little to its west, to the suburbs built in the 1630s and after 1660. The centrepiece of each of the earliest western developments, Lincoln's Inn Fields and Covent Garden, was a square or piazza, an idea drawn from the Italian cities which the architect Inigo Jones, who had a hand in both designs, had visited. In the case of Lincoln's Inn Fields, Jones and his client William Newton simply built houses around a huge seven-acre rectangle of land which Newton was not able to build on, partly because of the opposition of his neighbours the Lincoln's Inn lawyers. Covent Garden was a different matter, because here Inigo Jones deliberately imitated the piazzas he had seen in Italy. The ancient Roman forum and the cloistered squares of medieval monasteries might have given Jones (and the Italians) some inspiration, but the model he followed in planning Covent Garden was the Piazza d'Arme in Livorno, on the Tuscan coast. Perhaps he was influenced too by the new (1605) Place des Vosges in Paris, which it is possible his employer, the Earl of Bedford, had seen on his travels. The Earl's mansion, Bedford House, filled the south side of the Covent Garden square, and a new church in the Tuscan style, St Paul's, occupied most of the west side, but for the north and east sides Jones designed externally uniform terraces of houses with arcaded fronts, as he had seen in Italy. Behind Jones's facade these houses were to be constructed by individual builders and leased to wealthy tenants. Jones's design included London's first mews streets, Maiden Lane and Floral Street, for the carriages of the leaseholders.

The Piazza was a paved square, soon used for a market, not a garden for the tenants to share, but in other respects Covent Garden was the prototype for other West End developments for the next two hundred years: terraces round a central square, perhaps with the freeholder's grand mansion on one side, mews streets for servants and horses, a convenient and well-built church, and the leasehold system to give the landlord control over the development and the eventual recovery of the property, while the effort and risk of building and selling were left to others. The original appearance of the Covent Garden Piazza is familiar to us from many seventeenth- and eighteenth-century pictures, but nothing is left of the buildings around the Piazza today except Jones's church, which was restored to its original condition after a fire destroyed the interior in 1795. The arcaded section near the church, in the north-west corner of the Piazza, Bedford Chambers, was built as a copy of the original arcades in 1877, and the new arcades on the Royal Opera House extension are a modern interpretation of Jones's original idea. The market buildings that now dominate the scene were built by Charles Fowler in 1828–30, and preserved when the wholesale fruit and vegetable market moved out in 1974.

Although the square was a foreign idea, English planners and developers made it their own, and it became the favourite device of West End estate developers. Starting at Covent Garden, you could take a pleasant walk to trace the history of the West End square in the seventeenth and eighteenth centuries. Leave Covent Garden by King Street, one of the most interesting streets in the neighbourhood. It was laid out along with Henrietta Street, Russell Street and James Street in the mid-1630s as a way in and out of the Piazza, and still has some good Georgian and Victorian buildings. Best of all, at the start of the road, is number 43, Archer House, which was built for Admiral Russell, the Earl of Orford (a member of the landlord's family), by Thomas Archer in 1716. Much later, in the 1840s, when Archer House was a hotel called the Star, it was taken over by Evans's Song and Supper Rooms, one of the precursors of the London music hall. In 1856 a large music hall was built behind the house, but in 1891 there was another change of use, and number 43 became the National Sporting Club, one of the places where modern boxing was developed.

At the other end of King Street take New Row, another part of Bedford's 1630s plan, with several refronted late-seventeenth-century houses (3–5, 13), and cross St Martin's Lane and Charing Cross Road by taking two alleys (St Martin's Court and Bear Lane) to the corner of Leicester Square. Leicester Square is one of four West End squares built in the 1660s and 1670s, just after the Restoration of Charles II, when the return of royalty, along with the Great Plague of 1665 and the Great Fire of 1666, made living in the new West End very popular. There is nothing left now of Leicester Fields as laid out by Robert Sidney, second Earl of Leicester, in 1670. Leicester House, which stood on the north side of the square, went in 1791, and the gardens were replanned in 1989–92, incorporating the statues or busts of Shakespeare, William Hogarth, Joshua Reynolds, Isaac Newton and surgeon John Hunter, which were erected in 1874 when the Metropolitan Board of Works saved the square from redevelopment. The 1981 statue of Charlie Chaplin was added recently.

In the 1850s theatres began to replace the houses round the square, and now cinemas have replaced the theatres: the black granite Odeon (1937) stands on the site of the Alhambra variety theatre, famous for its Moorish minarets, and the Empire cinema (1927) replaced the Empire Theatre of Varieties, notorious for its high-class

Edwardian prostitutes. There are two more examples here of the lavish buildings produced in the golden age of cinema: the white-glazed Odeon West End, in the south-west corner of the square, and the modernistic beige Warner West End (1938), with reliefs of Sight and Sound (disfigured by billboards), in the north-east, in Cranbourn Street. The grand buildings near this, on either side of Leicester Place, one terracotta the other white baroque, were built in 1897–8 as hotels.

Leave Leicester Square by Panton Street, in its south-western corner, turn left on Haymarket and right along Charles II Street, to reach a much finer example of seventeenth-century town planning, St James's Square. Its developer, Henry Jermyn, Earl of St Albans, had been a close adviser to Henrietta Maria, Charles I's queen, and had raised a fortune for Charles II's cause while he was in exile in France. In return in 1661 and 1662 he was given a 60-year lease to a large part of the fields of St James's, the prime development area in front of the royal palace, bounded by Pall Mall, Piccadilly, Haymarket and St James's Street. In 1670 his lease was extended to 1740, and in 1665 he had obtained the freehold of nearly twelve acres around (but not including) the green space of St James's Square.

Jermyn began building, and selling leases enabling others to build, in 1662, and in the 1670s work on the square and the surrounding streets progressed quickly. Like Inigo Jones in Covent Garden, Jermyn made sure that the individual builders conformed to a uniform plan, so that the square and the streets leading to it were developed to suit the tastes of courtiers, aristocrats and others of the highest quality. None of the houses built by the first leaseholders exists today, but the pattern of streets established by Jermyn, perhaps with the help of royal officials, still survives. There are broad and loyally named streets entering the centre of the north, east and west sides of the square (Charles II Street, Duke of York Street and King Street), but to the south it is only connected to Pall Mall by two short and narrow streets, giving it an air of seclusion. Another part of Jermyn's plan, a local marketplace at the eastern end of Jermyn

Street, disappeared under Regent Street in 1818. The gardens, which are open, were replanned in 1817 by John Nash, who built the little wooden shelter on the south side of the square. The statue of William III on horseback was placed here in 1808.

A walk round St James's Square, the first real square in the new West End, is the best way to get a sense of the wealth and prestige of the families who used to live here. Going anticlockwise from Duke of York Street, you will pass: numbers 9–10, Chatham House, home of three prime ministers (Chatham, Derby and Gladstone); number 11, with a 1770s frontage by Robert Adam; number 12, which was built in 1836 for Earl Lovelace, whose wife Ada (Byron's daughter) worked with the computer pioneer Charles Babbage; number 13 was built in 1735 for Lord Ravensworth and for over a hundred years (1836–1941) was the Windham Club; number 14 was built in 1896 for the London Library, founded in 1841 by Thomas Carlyle; number 15 is Lichfield House, a mansion built in the Athenian style in 1764–6 by James 'Athenian' Stuart. One of the residents of the earlier house on the site of Lichfield House was the courtier Frances Stuart ('La Belle Stuart'), Duchess of Lennox and Richmond (1647–1702), who modelled for Britannia on Charles II's medals and coins.

Numbers 16 and 17 house the East India and Sports Club, built in 1865, number 20 is another Robert Adam house of the 1770s, built for Sir Watkin Williams Wynn, a high-spending man about town, and number 22 is the Army and Navy Club, which moved from Lichfield House into this newly built Venetian Renaissance-style house in 1851. Number 31 occupies the site of Jermyn's own house, which was replaced by Norfolk House, the Duke of Norfolk's sumptuous mansion, in 1748–52. It was demolished in 1937 and replaced with the present house, from which (as the plaque tells you) General Eisenhower masterminded the North Africa and Normandy campaigns of 1942 and 1944. The lavish music room of the old Norfolk House was saved, and has been re-erected in the Victoria and Albert Museum. Number 33 was built by Robert Adam in 1770 for the future Earl of Buckinghamshire and altered by John Soane in 1817 for the Earl of St Germans.

Number 4 was built for the Duke of Kent by the developer Edward Shepherd in 1726–8, and owned by Viscount Astor and his wife Nancy, the first woman to sit in the House of Commons, from 1912 to 1942, when the Free French forces took it over. It passed from the Arts Council to the Naval and Military Club in 1998. Number 5 is Wentworth House, a mansion built for the Earl of Strafford in 1748 by Matthew Brettingham and refaced in the 1850s, and number 7 was rebuilt by Sir Edwin Lutyens for the three Farrer brothers in 1911. Turning right here you will reach Jermyn Street, with its fine old shops and Newton's house, and Sir Christopher Wren's wonderful St James's church, which was commissioned by Jermyn as part of the St James's development in 1676, and restored after terrible war damage 1947–54. You should see two lovely pieces by Grinling Gibbons, the greatest wood carver ever to have worked in England, the font and the altar, and the organ by Renatus Harris, with angelic figures by Gibbons, all made in the 1680s and happily protected from bomb damage.

Go through the church to Piccadilly, cross it and take Swallow Street (a little to the left) into Regent Street. Over the road, take Glasshouse Street and Brewer Street, and go left into John Street, to find Golden Square, which (according to Charles Dickens) is 'not exactly in anybody's way to or from anywhere'. The leaseholder and developer here was Sir William Pulteney, and the square and its approach roads were laid out, probably to Wren's designs, after 1675. The streets that connect it with the rest of Soho, John Street and James Street, enter it at the corners and run along the east and west sides of the square. Most eighteenth-century squares followed this general plan. Soho did not retain its social prestige as St James's and Mayfair did, and Golden Square lost its rich tenants, and their fine houses, in the eighteenth and nineteenth centuries, when (according to Dickens in *Nicholas Nickleby*) it was 'a quarter of the town that has gone down in the world, and taken to letting lodgings'. Many of these lodgers, Dickens said, were foreign musicians, who waited every afternoon under the Opera Colonnade (outside Her Majesty's Theatre, Haymarket) to find work in the West End theatres. In the novel, Ralph Nickleby worked, lived and hanged himself at number 6. There are mostly offices here now, but some houses on the west side (numbers 21, 23 and 24) survive from the original square of the 1680s. The statue in the centre, which Dickens called 'the guardian genius of a little wilderness of shrubs', is George II in a toga, and was originally in Canons, Lord Chandos's mansion in Little Stanmore.

Going north on John Street will take you to a right turn into Beak Street, a nice Soho street with several seventeenth- and eighteenth-century houses (numbers 15–23, 41–43, 65–73, 77–79), some fine shopfronts and two good public houses, the Old Coffee House (which is what it says) and the Sun and 3 Cantons. The Venetian artist Canaletto lived at number 41 from 1746 to 1755. At the end a left and right turn will bring you to St Anne's Court, then left into Dean Street and right into Carlisle Street and Soho Square. This was laid out in open fields in 1677 by Richard Frith, perhaps to plans by the genealogist and statistician Gregory King. It may be the first London square to have had a garden, and the garden today still follows the original plan. The layout is more like St James's Square than Golden Square, with streets entering it at the centre of three sides, and two near the corners of the south side. The buildings around the square are described in Chapter Seven.

If you wanted to follow the West End squares in chronological sequence, you would need to walk west on Oxford Street to see the two early Hanoverian squares just past Oxford Circus – Cavendish Square on the right, down Holles Street, and Hanover Square on the left, down Harewood Place. John Holles, the Duke of Newcastle, bought a St Marylebone estate north of Oxford Street in 1708, and his son-in-law Edward Harley began its development by laying out Cavendish Square and the nearby streets in 1717. He was rather racing ahead of the spread of the West End, and the neighbourhood was still on the edge of town and only half developed when John Rocque mapped it in the 1740s. Now the square is spoiled by an underground car park, but some of the eighteenth-century houses survive, including numbers 17 and 18 (1756), and numbers 11 and 14 (1769–72), on the north side, two rather grand Palladian houses with impressive stone pillars and a connecting bridge added in the 1950s. Number 16, on the Harley Street corner, is the modest house built in the late 1720s for the Duke of Chandos (Handel's patron), in place of the great mansion he had planned before he lost a fortune in the South Sea Bubble stock market crash of 1720. Walk down Henrietta Place to find St Peter, Vere Street, the chapel built by James Gibbs in 1721–4 to serve the new community. If you go inside this lovely chapel you may see the similarity between this and Gibbs's greatest church, St Martin-in-the-Fields, which was finished two years later.

Hanover Square, named after the dynasty that first occupied the English throne in 1714, was laid out in 1713 by the Earl of Scarborough, who owned this north-eastern corner of Mayfair, from Regent Street almost to New Bond Street, and south to include Maddox Street. He was one of the first to develop the fields in the northern half of Mayfair, a little ahead of the Corporation of London, which developed New Bond Street and the land around it after 1716, the wealthy Grosvenor family, whose huge estate occupying the north-western third of Mayfair – from South Molton Street in the east to South Street and the top of Berkeley Square in the south – was built up after 1720, and the Berkeleys, who developed their great square and the streets to its east and west (Bruton Street, Charles Street, Hill Street, and others) from the 1730s to the 1750s. There are four original but altered houses left on Hanover Square (numbers 16, 21, 22 and 24), and a plaque to the statesman Prince Talleyrand, who lived at number 21 in the early 1830s when he was the French ambassador. You get a better feeling for what the area once looked like by walking down St George Street (named in another homage to the Hanoverians), the very wide street running from the southern side of the square, which has good eighteenth-century houses, especially on its west side: numbers 17–13, 10–8 and 5–3. The road passes the estate's new church, St George Hanover Square, built by John James in a mixture of styles borrowed from Wren, Gibbs and Hawksmoor in 1721–5. The oldest feature of the spacious and uncluttered interior was added in 1841 – the lovely 1520s stained glass Tree of Jesse in the east window, from the Carmelite church in Antwerp.

At the end of St George Street turn right into Conduit Street, which was built as part of the City of London's Conduit Mead estate around 1720 (numbers 42, 43, 47 and 48 are the original houses), and continue along Bruton Street, which was developed by the Earl of Berkeley in the 1730s. The course of the Tyburn Brook, which separated the two estates, is followed now by Bruton Lane. Several houses in Bruton Street, especially numbers 21–33 on your right, survive from the original buildings of the 1730s, but the fine house in which the future Queen Elizabeth II was born, number 17, was knocked down in 1937. Bruton Street brings you to the showpiece of the Earl of Berkeley's suburb, Berkeley Square. Unlike the other Mayfair squares, Hanover and Grosvenor, Berkeley Square was not built as the centre of a planned grid of streets, but was fitted into an existing set of streets, which therefore enter the square in an irregular way. The first houses were built round the square in the 1730s and 1740s, and the square itself was landscaped in the 1760s. Like many London squares this is dominated now by modern offices, but the west side has some fine 1740s houses, still with their Georgian railings and lampholders. Numbers 42 to 52 are all good houses, but you might look especially at number 45, where Lord Clive of India died (perhaps deliberately) from an overdose of laudanum in 1774, and number 44, which was built by William Kent in 1742, and is regarded as one of the best terraced houses in London. It is now a gambling club, the Clermont. If you go down Fitzmaurice Place, in the south-west corner of the square, you'll see Lansdowne House, which was built for two prime ministers, Bute and Shelburne, by Robert Adam in the 1760s. The American retail entrepreneur Gordon Selfridge lived here in the 1920s, when he still had his fortune. The house lost its grounds and its front rooms in the 1930s when Fitzmaurice Place was cut through from the square to Curzon Street, but many of its fine rooms, some original and some 1930s replicas, still survive, to be enjoyed by members and guests of the Lansdowne Club, the first West End club to accept men and women on equal terms.

From Berkeley Square you could go south-west, along Charles Street, a well-preserved part of the Berkeley estate, and Chesterfield Street to Shepherd Market, a square which, like Covent Garden, was used for commerce rather than recreation. This was the work of one of Georgian London's busiest builders and planners, Edward Shepherd, who built it on the site of the suppressed May fair in the 1730s. There is a plaque to the May fair in Trebeck Street, in the middle of the market. The earlier two-storied market building was replaced with the present block of shops and houses in 1860.

Alternatively, you could go north on Davies Street and Grosvenor Street towards Grosvenor Square. Davies and Grosvenor Streets are in the south-eastern corner of the grid of streets laid out on the Grosvenor estate (which extends to Oxford Street and Park Lane) between the 1720s and the 1760s. Bourdon House, 2 Davies Street, an extended 1720s town house, was the home of the second Duke of Westminster, the head of the Grosvenors from 1917 to 1953. Turn left into Grosvenor Street, which was built up in the early 1720s. Numbers 52 to 49, on your left, are the original 1720s houses, mostly altered and given an extra floor; number 46 is a palatial Edwardian mansion remodelled for the fabulously wealthy banker Sir Edgar Speyer, one of the financiers of London's electric Tube lines; and number 43 was originally built in 1726 for Bishop Hoadley of Winchester, the most political and polemical bishop of his age. Grosvenor Square was built in 1725–30 as the centrepiece of the Grosvenor estate, using for the first time a plan which made each side of the square look like a single great mansion. All this is gone now, and if the square symbolizes anything today it is American power and the Anglo-American wartime alliance. The only original houses are number 9, in the north-east corner, where the future president John Adams lived as US ambassador in the 1780s, and number 38 (on the south side), which is 1720s behind the Victorian stucco. The Canadian High Commission, numbers 1–3, was the US embassy from the 1930s until the new one took over the whole west side of the square in the late 1950s. The four-acre gardens were replanned in 1947–8 in memory of F.D. Roosevelt, whose statue stands in the square.

To see what the houses here might once have been like, take a walk along Upper Brook Street, which goes west from the north-west corner of the square. It has many excellent houses from the 1730s–1750s, when the street was first developed, and lots of good Victorian and Edwardian additions. For a contrasting street, turn left into Park Lane (a fine run of 1820s houses, including Disraeli's at number 93), and third left into Mount Street. Mount Street was rebuilt by the first Duke of Westminster in the 1880s and 1890s partly in pink terracotta, and in a sort of Flemish Renaissance style. Look out for the Earl of Plymouth's 1896 mansion at number 54 (on the left), and Purdey's gun shop, which has been here on the corner of South Audley Street since 1882, and in London since 1814. Turn right into South Audley Street and first left to see Mount Street Gardens, which were converted from a burial ground under the 1877 Open Spaces Act. Walking through the gardens brings you back to Mount Street, where the Connaught Hotel stands on the corner of Carlos Place. Turn right and continue along Mount Street towards Berkeley Square, passing Allen and Co., a famous and long-established Mayfair butcher, at number 117.

*

On another occasion, you might set off from Lincoln's Inn Fields and trace the development of seventeenth- and eighteenth-century town planning in a different part of town. On the east side of the

Fields there is a gate (only open on weekdays) into Lincoln's Inn. Walking ahead and then right will bring you into one of London's finest, earliest and most forgotten squares, New Square. Henry Searle began building this square in 1680 as a private venture, but two years later the lawyers secured his agreement that it should be used by Lincoln's Inn. The square was finished after Searle's death in 1690 by the developer Nicholas Barbon, whose work can still be found all over this part of town, from Essex Street and the Temple (south of Fleet Street) to Queen Square and Red Lion Square, north of Holborn. The three sides of the square, with matching four-storey houses built as lawyers' chambers, are still perfect and give the best impression you could find of what well-off London must have looked like after the regulated rebuilding after the Fire. Go out as you came in, and leave Lincoln's Inn Fields by one of its little northern exits, Great Turnstile or Little Turnstile. Cross Holborn and take Dane Street into Red Lion Square, which is a part of Nicholas Barbon's development of this area in the 1680s and 1690s. Unlike New Square, Red Lion Square escaped the clutches of the lawyers (of Gray's Inn), but it was badly damaged in the Blitz, and nothing remains here of Barbon's work. The oldest houses are numbers 16–17, older than they look, where Dante Gabriel Rossetti lived and William Morris had offices. Summit House, the striking yellow-tiled art deco house on the corner of Dane Street, was built for the tailor Austin Reed in 1925 on the site of the house once occupied by the watchmaker John Harrison, whose marine chronometers first enabled sailors to establish their longitude.

To get a better impression of Barbon's Holborn, leave the square by Princeton Street, turn right onto Bedford Row, a fine wide street built by Barbon in the 1690s (though the older houses are early eighteenth century), right into Sandland Street and right again into Red Lion Street. This leads directly into Lamb's Conduit Street, another Barbon development, which still has plenty of eighteenth-century houses, some refronted (28–38, 29–37, etc.). The streets to the left and right, Dombey Street and Rugby Street, have interesting eighteenth-century houses, especially numbers 10–16 Rugby Street, built in 1721. From Lamb's Conduit Street turn left into Great Ormond Street, which has some early Barbon houses, numbers 41–61, on the left. Barbon Close, one of only two streets in London to commemorate this prolific developer (the other is Barbon Alley, off Devonshire Square), divides number 50 from number 51. Great Ormond Street brings you to charming Queen Square, which was begun by Barbon in 1686 and which still has a few eighteenth-century houses, including numbers 1, 2, 6, 7, 42 and 43. Since 1913 number 6 has been the headquarters of the Art Workers' Guild, an association founded in 1884 to bring together fine and decorative artists, architects and craftsmen, inspired (but not bound) by the ideas of Norman Shaw and William Morris. In the square itself there is an eighteenth-century pump and a 1775 lead statue of George III's queen, Charlotte. The lovely little eighteenth-century pub here, the Queen's Larder, is named after her.

A pretty alleyway called Cosmo Place (birthplace of Sir John Barbirolli) takes you from the south-western corner of the square to Southampton Row, and crossing this brings you into one of the greatest London estates. The farmland of Bloomsbury passed from the monastery of Charterhouse to Thomas Wriothesley, Earl of Southampton, in the 1530s, and to the Russell family, the Earls and Dukes of Bedford, when the Earl of Southampton died leaving only a daughter (who was married to a Russell) in 1667. This happy accident gave the Russells a vast and valuable tract of development land, stretching from St Giles to the Euston Road, much larger than their Covent Garden estate, further south. Go left (south) on Southampton Row and right into Bloomsbury Place, to reach Bloomsbury Square, the first named square in London.

The Earl of Southampton began selling building leases in his projected square in 1661 (a few years ahead of the Duke of St Albans in St James's), and was one of the first aristocratic landlords to use this highly advantageous system, which brought him a capital gain, a modest rental income and the eventual recovery of his land, together with houses built at the leaseholders' expense. Naturally, leaseholders were not interested in building houses that outlasted their leases, but numbers 9–14 and 17, on the western side of the square, are survivors from the 1660s hidden behind 1860s stucco. The late-Georgian terrace on the north side replaced Southampton House in 1800, and in the garden of the square an 1816 statue of the radical hero Charles James Fox stands on top of a seven-storey underground car park. Southampton pioneered the idea that a development should be like a little town, with a market and cheaper houses in sidestreets. His market was in a street just south of the square, now known as Barter Street.

Great Russell Street, one of London's old country lanes, leads west from Southampton Square. House-building started in this street in 1661–2, and numbers 72–77 date from that time, though John Nash's stucco, added in 1777, makes them look later. Turn right into Bloomsbury Street to reach Bedford Square, the finest and best-preserved of all London squares. This was developed between 1775 and 1783, and the Bedford family made sure that each side of the square would be a coherent and dignified whole, with a grand five-bayed stuccoed house in the centre of each terrace to suggest a great country house. High standards of building materials and personal conduct were specified in the leases. There is plentiful use of that (until recently) mysterious substance, Coade stone.

The houses around the square, which are all still in fine condition, have attracted very many tenants who found distinction in the law, theatre, architecture, literature, science or politics, some of whom are remembered with blue plaques. Number 6 was home to many lord chancellors, including the odious Lord Eldon, and to Leonard Smithers, the publisher of Wilde, Beardsley, Sir Richard Burton and other racy Victorians. Number 48 (previously 47) was the first home, from 1849, of Bedford College, the first women's university college in England, and Robert Owen, industrialist and pioneer of the cooperative movement, did some of his most important writing while staying at number 49 between 1818 and 1820.

Thomas Leverton, who lived at number 13, was the architect of some of the best houses on the square, probably including the finest, number 1. The Gatti family, London's most famous and successful Italian restaurateurs, lived at number 10, the headquarters of the publisher Jonathan Cape were at number 30, and Lady Ottoline Morrell, society hostess and lover (in the physical sense) of Bertrand Russell, lived before the Great War at number 44, which was later the home of ex-Prime Minister Herbert Asquith. Anthony Hope (number 41) wrote *The Prisoner of Zenda*, John Passmore Edwards (number 51) was a Victorian newspaper proprietor and radical philanthropist, Thomas Wakley (number 35) founded the *Lancet*, Sir Edwin Lutyens (number 31) designed New Delhi and the Cenotaph, Edward Fitzgerald (number 19) translated the *Rubaiyat of Omar Khayyam*, Weedon Grossmith (number 1) wrote with his brother George *The Diary of a Nobody*, and Sir Henry Cavendish, who lived and worked at number 11, on the corner of Montague Place, discovered hydrogen and established the density of the earth.

In 1800 the Russells built the biggest square in London, outdoing the Grosvenors. You can reach Russell Square by walking along Montague Place, between the Senate House and the British Museum. The square was designed by Humphrey Repton, who also landscaped Bloomsbury Square, which is just to the south. There are houses built in 1800 on the south and north sides of the square, but only a few houses on the northern part of the west side look as they were when the square was new. Now the Russell Hotel, in the French chateau style of the 1890s, dominates the scene, and the best thing about the square is the large and lovely garden, with a statue of the fifth Duke of Bedford in a toga. To get a sense of what the Bedford estate would have looked like before the coming of the grand hotels and London University, walk down Bedford Place and back up Montague Street, both of which are still lined with good plain terraces built between 1800 and 1810.

By taking Thornhaugh Street in the north-west corner of Russell Square you can find the rest of Bedford's Bloomsbury estate.

Woburn Square, built in 1829 and named after the Bedford country estate, still survives, despite the expansion of London University, but its western neighbour, Torrington Square, is hardly more than a name. The same pattern of development was continued further north in the 1820s, when the great commercial builder Thomas Cubitt took on the job of building on the northern end of the Bedford estate. The outcome was the construction of Gordon Square and Tavistock Square. Both have some houses surviving from the 1820s (36–46 and 55–59 Gordon Square and 16–25 and 27–53 Tavistock Square), and pleasant one-acre gardens, which are both now open to the public. The south-eastern corner of Gordon Square was one of the centres of the Bloomsbury Group. Sir Leslie Stephen's children (including the future Virginia Woolf and Vanessa Bell) lived in number 46 from 1905 to 1907, and the house was John Maynard Keynes's home from 1916 to 1946. Number 50 was a meeting place of the group, and another of its members, Lytton Strachey, lived at number 51.

The residents of these smart houses needed shops, but wanted them tucked away out of sight. If you take Upper Woburn Place from the north-east corner of Tavistock Square and turn right into Woburn Walk and Duke's Road, you will find them, in two beautifully preserved streets of houses and bow-fronted shops built by Cubitt in 1822 in the Grecian style. Then take Burton Street, at the southern end of Duke's Road, and go left into Burton Place. This brings you to Cartwright Gardens, a fine crescent which is the centrepiece of James Burton's development of the Skinners' Company estate in the 1810s. The statue in the gardens is of Major John Cartwright, a great figure in the history of English radicalism between the 1770s and 1824, when he died in a house in what was then Burton Crescent.

*

Cubitt, the greatest London builder of the 1820s–1840s, also undertook the development of two large parts of the Grosvenor estate which we know today as Belgravia and Pimlico, and continued to use squares as the centrepieces of his planned suburbs. The building of Belgrave Square, the centre of Cubitt's new suburb behind (west of) Buckingham Palace Gardens, was taken over in 1825 by a financial syndicate which employed the well-connected George Basevi as its architect and surveyor. Basevi designed four stuccoed villa terraces to go around the three-acre square, following Nash's Regent's Park style by using Corinthian columns, central porticoes and end pavilions to create the illusion that each terrace was a single palace. He signed his name on the portico of number 31. The individual mansions in the four corners (of which three remain) were built by other architects. The square, which still looks magnificent, attracted wealthy and titled residents, and several of their houses are now embassies, including the Spanish and Portuguese in two of the corner mansions, and the Argentine, German and Austrian in the terraces. The beautiful but locked gardens have statues appropriate to the embassies: Simón Bolívar, Columbus, Prince Henry the Navigator of Portugal, and General San Martín, liberator of the Argentine. North-west of the square, Wilton Crescent, built in the late 1820s by Seth Smith, adds an interesting variation to the usual run of squares, though the houses themselves were refaced in stone 1908–12, giving them the look of a Bath crescent. You could take a refreshment break here, by going north up Wilton Place and left into Kinnerton Street, looking into one of the two good pubs here, the Wilton Arms (built in 1826) and the small, cosy and old-fashioned Nag's Head.

To see a little more of Thomas Cubitt's town planning, take Upper Belgrave Street from the east corner of Belgrave Square, and walk down to Eaton Square, taking a look down Eaton Place, his wide and impressive street, as you pass it on your right. Eaton Square is really a long oblong split by a wide central street, but the houses around it are fine examples of Cubitt's (and Seth Smith's) work in the 1830s, 1840s and 1850s. The terraces are stuccoed and beautified with porticoes, columns and colonnades, to create a palatial impression, and they were especially attractive to Conservative politicians in the early twentieth century. Prime Minister Neville Chamberlain lived at number 37, his Foreign Minister Lord Halifax was at number 86, and an earlier Conservative Prime Minister, Stanley Baldwin, lived at number 93. Robert Cecil lived at number 19, Lord Boothby at number 1, and the actress Vivien Leigh at number 54. In the previous century, the great benefactor of the poor Londoner, George Peabody, lived at number 80.

*

It is impossible to do justice to London's hundred or more squares, but there are many others that deserve to be mentioned. When the Portman estate in Marylebone, to the north of the western end of Oxford Street, was developed from the 1760s onwards, its owner, Henry William Portman, grouped his new streets around four squares. The estate was originally huge, at 270 acres, but now, following sales in the nineteenth and twentieth centuries, it is a little over a hundred acres. The best-preserved of the squares, Manchester Square, was built between 1776 and 1788, with terraces on three sides and a mansion for the Duke of Manchester. The mansion was enlarged and rebuilt a hundred years later for Sir Richard Wallace, the Marquess of Hertford, to house his art collection, which is now open to the public free of charge. Most of the rest of the square is well preserved, as are some of the streets off the square, including Duke Street, Manchester Street and Spanish Place. Number 3 Spanish Place was the home of Captain Marryat, the children's adventure writer, and George Grossmith, co-author of *The Diary of a Nobody* and star of many Gilbert and Sullivan operas.

From Manchester Square it is a short walk west to Portman Square, which was developed a little earlier, in 1764, and very uninterestingly rebuilt since the 1920s. Its best survivor is Home

House (*see* Chapter Three). The other Portman squares, Montagu and Bryanston, are a little to the north-west, along Gloucester Place and George Street. Both are long, narrow, leafy and quiet. They are late Georgian, completed around 1820, and Montagu Square is especially pleasant and well preserved, with a lovely mixture of brick and partly stuccoed houses along its two long terraces. Bryanston Square has not survived quite so well, but its peaceful late-Georgian atmosphere is much the same. Further north, across the Marylebone Road, is Dorset Square, which was laid out in the 1820s and still has most of its original terraces. It was the laying out of Dorset Square that forced Thomas Lord to move his Marylebone Cricket Club, the MCC, which had played there since 1767, further north into St John's Wood, to the cricket ground still known as Lord's. As is the case with nearly forty West End and west London squares, the Portman estate squares are locked.

From Portman Square walk a little to the west along Berkeley Street and cross Edgware Road into the early-nineteenth-century suburb known then as Tyburnia, after the stream that ran through it. It was developed in the 1820s and 1830s by the Grand Junction Canal Company on land owned by the Bishop of London, according to the plans of the Bishop's surveyor, S.P. Cockerell. The triangle of land between Edgware Road and Bayswater Road is a district of squares and crescents, as neatly planned as anything done in London up to the 1830s. But twentieth-century flats and underground car parks have spoiled the scale and interest of much of the area, and Oxford and Cambridge Squares, bracketed by Norfolk and Hyde Park Crescents, look better on the map now than on the ground. Only Connaught Square, very near Marble Arch, is in something like its original 1820s condition, with four terraces of modest handsome houses, stucco below and brick above, and a leafy private garden. Hyde Park Square, reached by walking west along Connaught Street, is in the more grandiose 1840s style, showing the influence of John Nash, with columns and more extensive stucco. Only the northern side survives, and this joins cleverly to Gloucester

1. A turret of the Roman fort at Noble Street. The wall of the fort (built around 120 AD) was strengthened and incorporated into the City wall when this was built around 200 AD, and the meeting of the two walls can be seen here.

2. The twelfth-century round nave of the Temple Church, with its Purbeck marble columns and its effigies of early medieval knights, before they were damaged in the Blitz.

3. The Guildhall has been the centre of City government for 800 years, and state trials, including those of Lady Jane Grey and Thomas Cranmer, were held here. This is the second or third hall, built in 1411–30 by John Croxton. A lithograph by Thomas Shotter Boys, 1842.

4. Number 9 Gerrard Street, on the right, was once the Turk's Head Coffee House, where Samuel Johnson and Joshua Reynolds founded their famous Literary Club in 1764.

5. An aerial view of Ranelagh Gardens, Chelsea, with the huge Rotunda, in the year of their opening, 1742. The gardens closed in 1803 and now form part of the grounds of the Royal Hospital. Engraving by W. Jones.

6. The Crystal Palace in 1896, midway between its move from Hyde Park to Sydenham and its destruction by fire in 1936. The two towers supplied water for its many fountains.

7. Staple Inn, Holborn, central London's only Elizabethan terrace, in 1911. The façade still looks almost the same, despite war damage.

8. Lord Burlington's Chiswick House and gardens as they looked in the 1750s. The canal and cascade in the foreground were created by William Kent from the waters of Bollo Brook.

9. Dudley House, one of the last of Park Lane's dozen aristocratic mansions, photographed in 1896. It was built for Lord Dudley in 1828, and the cast-iron conservatory was added in the 1850s. In 1912 it was sold for £10,000.

10. Regent Street Quadrant, the showpiece of John Nash's route between Carlton House Terrace and Regent's Park. The buildings were replaced in the 1920s, but the grand curve, following the boundary between Mayfair and Soho, survives. Engraved by John Woods in 1838.

11. Cumberland Terrace, built in 1826 by James Thomson, the grandest part of
Nash's plan for Regent's Park. Engraved by John Woods in 1838,
and still looking magnificent today.

12. Two early eighteenth-century houses in Brook Street, Mayfair.
Handel lived at number 25, on the right, from 1723 to 1759,
and Jimi Hendrix lived next door in 1968–9.

13. A music party in a London house in 1736, drawn by Marcellus Laroon.

14. The Royal Albert Hall, opened in 1871, London's oldest and biggest concert hall. Photographed in 1896.

15. The George Inn, Borough High Street, the last of London's galleried inns. The George was built after the Southwark fire of 1676, and is now owned by the National Trust.

16. 'A tavern of dropsical appearance.' The early eighteenth-century Grapes Inn, on the Limehouse riverfront, as described in Dickens' *Our Mutual Friend*.

17. The Hop Exchange (now Central Buildings) was built in 1866 to serve the Southwark hop trade. It lost its two top stories in a fire in 1920, but its exchange hall is still impressive.

Square, which was built in a similar style at around the same time, but which has been rebuilt on all but its southern side.

＊

Although no other form of planned development was as popular as the square, other devices were often used. Thomas Neale, who developed an area between Covent Garden and St Giles in the 1690s, chose a radiating set of seven streets, all meeting at a central point where a pillar with six sundials stood at the intersection. Since the pillar itself was also a sundial the district was called Seven Dials, and kept the name after 1773, when the pillar was removed. Now there is a new one (reinstated in 1989), which you can see by taking Earlham Street from Cambridge Circus, or walking north on St Martin's Lane. The fact that the district quickly became a notorious slum quarter may suggest that a radial plan is less attractive to the wealthy than a square, but it is more likely that Seven Dials was dragged down by the social decline of this part of town as wealth and title moved westward after 1660.

An alternative plan was devised by the Adam brothers, William, James and Robert, for a riverside development in 1768. The brothers, of whom Robert was by far the most important, leased the land (from the Duke of St Albans) which had once been occupied by Durham House, on the river downstream of what is now the new Hungerford Bridge. Robert Adam chose to model his new development on Diocletian's palace in Split, on the Dalmatian coast, which he had written about in 1764. He raised the sloping riverbank (in the days before the Victoria Embankment) by constructing an arcaded terrace, the arches of which would be rented as warehouses, he hoped, by the government. On this terrace Adam built a rectangular block of 24 fine four-storey houses, with eleven (the Royal Terrace) facing the river, ten facing the other way onto John Adam Street, and three at the sides. The houses were in dark brick, beautifully ornamented with thin pilasters and mouldings in the shape of ribbons and branches. The whole scheme was called the Adelphi, from the Greek for 'brothers'. Financially it was a failure, because the government did not rent the warehouses and the riverside wharf was half a metre too low, and to avoid bankruptcy Adam had to raffle the houses, selling 4,370 tickets at £50 each. But the Adelphi was an architectural success, introducing the idea of embanking the riverside and giving a West End showcase to a new decorative style. Beauty is no defence against philistinism, and the main Adelphi block was first mutilated and then destroyed. In 1872 it was covered in stucco and in 1936 it was demolished to make way for a huge Portland stone block called the New Adelphi, which may have a pleasantly art deco appearance for those who do not know what was destroyed to make room for it.

You can still see something of the Adam brothers' great development if you go down Adam Street, off the Strand. The first part of the street, on your left, is part of the original Adelphi. Richard Arkwright, the pioneer of industrialized spinning, lived at number 8, and number 7, with its white pilasters, floral decoration, iron balconies and Adam coat of arms, is a beautiful reminder of what was lost in 1936. Turn right into John Adam Street, where the first half of the northern side is still almost as the brothers built it in 1771–4. The house on the first corner was once the Adam Tavern, but all these houses now belong to the Royal Society of Arts, whose main building, number 8, is fronted in stone like a Greek temple. To see inside this large and interesting house, you should visit it on an open day, the morning of the first Sunday each month, except January. The upstairs rooms and the Tavern Room are the best, and the underground rooms and vaults are in the catacombs on which the Adelphi was built. You can see more of these supporting vaults by walking past Robert Street, which has three Adam houses (numbers 1–3) with a string of distinguished residents, and turning down York Street to find, on your left, Lower Robert Street. If you walk down this rather uninviting tunnel you will see Adam's original vaulting above you, and emerge on Savoy Place, below the destroyed Adelphi Terrace.

Despite this loss, Adam left his mark in many other parts of London. One of his last pieces of work was Fitzroy Square, the centrepiece of Lord Southampton's new estate, just south of the New Road (Euston Road). Adam designed the well-preserved east side of the square, which was built in Portland stone just after his death in 1792, and the south side, which was restored after being damaged in the Blitz. The other two sides were built in the 1820s, when stucco replaced stone, creating an especially harmonious and attractive square. Robert Cecil, the future Prime Minister Lord Salisbury, lived at number 21, but the important house is number 29, George Bernard Shaw's home in the 1890s, where Virginia Stephen (later Virginia Woolf) lived between 1907 and the Great War, having moved from the Stephen family home in Gordon Square. This move meant that the avant-garde intellectual evenings involving the Stephens' circle of friends (John Maynard Keynes, E.M. Forster, Roger Fry, Lytton Strachey and others) moved too, and Fitzroy Square became the birthplace of the Bloomsbury Group.

The square's rather bombastic statue of General Francisco de Miranda, 'the Precursor of Latin American independence', is a reminder that this neighbourhood (and London as a whole) was a centre of the early-nineteenth-century movement to free Latin America from Spanish and Portuguese rule. Nearby, at 58 Grafton Way (which runs across the south side of the square), is the 1790s Adam house occupied by Miranda from 1802 to 1810, which was a meeting place for others working for independence – Simón Bolívar, Bernardo O'Higgins (who has a house and statue in Richmond), Andrés Bello, Luis López Méndez and many others. Miranda House is now owned by the Venezuelan embassy and used as a cultural centre and museum.

Another piece of Robert Adam town planning, begun in the mid-1770s, just after the Adelphi, was Portland Place, the widest street in eighteenth-century London. Like the Adelphi, the whole composition was ruined in the twentieth century when most of Adam's palatial terraces (except those between New Cavendish Street and Weymouth Street) were replaced with hotels, offices and flats.

You could visit Portland Place as part of a walk following the work of the architect and planner who left the most enduring mark on the shape of London, John Nash. In 1806 Nash was appointed architect to the Office of Woods and Forests, which managed the Crown Estate. Five years later the lease on the Crown-owned fields known as Marylebone Park came to an end, and Nash was involved in plans to turn the fields into a royal park or pleasure ground, encircled by fine houses. There was already an outline plan for a great new street connecting the new park with the Prince Regent's London house, Carlton House, on Pall Mall, in order to tempt wealthy tenants to take houses north of the New (Euston) Road. Nash presented an ambitious plan for an aristocratic garden suburb in a wooded park, with a picturesque canal and a grand memorial or tomb for national heroes, and a magnificent new road ending in a large circus where it met the Euston Road. Nash was in favour with the Prince Regent (perhaps because of a secret arrangement between Nash, Nash's young wife and the lusty Prince), and his plan was accepted and to a large extent carried out. The Regent became George IV in 1820, and until his death in 1830 Nash could spend public money fairly freely to beautify the West End to suit his and his patron's tastes.

Some elements of Nash's plan were abandoned, including the memorial, the circus (half of which became Park Crescent) and many of the villas in the park, but others were added as the plan developed. Eventually the Nash scheme stretched from the top of Regent's Park to Buckingham Palace, St James's Park, Trafalgar Square and part of the Strand. If you want to feel the size of Nash's grand plan under your feet, and see some of the views as he intended them to be seen, take a walk from Trafalgar Square, along Regent Street and Portland Place up to Regent's Park.

Trafalgar Square was formed in the 1820s by moving the Royal Mews, demolishing old houses in front of St Martin-in-the-Fields and extending Pall Mall east to meet the new Duncannon Street and make a straighter route between Pall Mall and the Strand. Canada

House was built (for the Royal College of Physicians) in the 1820s, the National Gallery in the 1830s, and Nelson's Column (the second-highest in London) in 1839–43. The most interesting thing in the square is the statue of Charles I (London's first bronze equestrian statue), which was made by Hubert Le Sueur around 1630, hidden during the Cromwellian period and re-erected in 1675, exactly where the last of Edward I's Eleanor Crosses (or Charing Cross) stood until parliamentary troops destroyed it in 1647. It stands on the island created by the intersection of Cockspur Street, Whitehall and the Strand, the main road junction before the formation of the square.

Take the Mall and go through Admiralty Arch, which was built in 1908–11, when the Mall was widened as an imperial route between the refaced Buckingham Palace and Trafalgar Square, all to the designs of Aston Webb. Much of what you see around you here is the work of John Nash. Buckingham Palace, at the far end of the Mall, was enlarged from Buckingham House by Nash in the 1820s, as the monarch's chief London home, replacing St James's Palace in that role. It was built at vast expense, both to the public purse and to Nash's reputation, and was completed by the much more economical Edward Blore in the 1830s and 1840s. The present front is Aston Webb's, but much of what you see when you pay to go inside is Nash's work. On your left, St James's Park, which was landscaped for Charles II in the formal Versailles style in the 1660s, was redesigned by Nash in 1827–8. He chose the informal 'picturesque' style which prefers surprises to grand vistas, and turned Charles II's canal into a natural-looking lake with a wooded island. On your right is Carlton House Terrace, which was designed by John Nash to replace Carlton House, which the Prince Regent demolished in 1827. Nash's plan was for terraces all around St James's Park, but George IV's death in 1830 ended his favoured status, and only two terraces were built. Take a look at some of the distinguished institutions that occupy the terraces today: in the first (east) block, the British Academy at number 10, the Institute of Contemporary Arts at number 12, the Crown Estates Office at numbers 13–16, and in the west block the Royal Society at numbers 6–9 (bearing some signs of Albert Speer's remodelling when this was the German embassy in the 1930s) and the Turf Club at number 5.

Climb the steps between the two terraced blocks up to Waterloo Place, which was meant to be the grand finale of Nash's north–south route. Its centrepiece, the Duke of York's Column, erected in the early 1830s, does more than justice to the far from heroic Frederick, the 'Grand Old Duke of York', George III's son and commander-in-chief of the British army during the Napoleonic Wars. What impresses here are the two splendid clubs, stuccoed and painted to look like Portland stone. The United Services Club (now the Institute of Directors) on the right (east) side was built by Nash in 1826–8 in the Roman style, and Victorianized by Decimus Burton in the 1850s. Burton also built the club on the left, the Athenaeum, in 1827–30, in a Greek style, with a gilt Pallas Athene to represent the wisdom and learning expected of (though not always achieved by) its members. Ahead, you have a direct view of the lower part of Regent Street, the beginning of Nash's great route to Regent's Park. As you walk towards it, take a look at the collection of statues of Victorian and Edwardian heroes, mostly soldiers or explorers, that has been gathered in Waterloo Place. There is a good monument on the left to Sir John Franklin, whose expedition to find the North-west Passage perished in 1847 because of starvation, lead poisoning and his incompetent leadership, and further on Captain Scott, who led his men to their deaths in Antarctica in 1915, is commemorated in a statue by his widow.

Nash's Regent Street was not greatly admired by later Victorians and Edwardians, and most of his buildings were replaced by larger ones that provided more shop and office space between 1905 and 1928. So you pass several Edwardian and 1920s banks and offices, and one of the earlier grand London cinemas, the Plaza (Frank Verity, 1925; closed in 2002), on your way up to Piccadilly Circus. This is where Nash's street met Piccadilly (but not Shaftesbury Avenue, which only arrived in the 1880s) and swung round in a westward curve so that it could reach Swallow Street, the straight route to the north, in the cheapest and most interesting way possible. Nash also wanted to follow (and strengthen) the borderline between Soho and Mayfair, using the cheaper land of Soho, but making sure by the quality of the building that Regent Street would be Mayfair's shopping street, not Soho's. The colonnade which lined this section of Regent Street, the Quadrant, was removed in 1848, partly because it attracted prostitutes, and Nash's fine buildings were replaced by the present ones, which give Regent Street grandeur where it once had grace and spaciousness. Norman Shaw's Piccadilly Hotel, which fills the space between Regent Street and Piccadilly just after Air Street (on the left), got the ball rolling in 1905–8. Opposite it, on the right, is the Café Royal, which retained some of its old features from the days of Oscar Wilde and the Decadents when it was rebuilt in 1923–8. The new Quadrant was built in the 1920s by Reginald Blomfield, the architect of the Menin Gate and many other war memorials in France, Belgium and London, and the replacement of individual buildings further up the street was supervised for the Crown by John Murray to ensure a degree of harmony and consistency. Even Liberty's, a wildly interesting building in Great Marlborough Street, presents a restrained classical front to Regent Street.

Cross Oxford Street, where Nash's Circus was replaced by the present four matching quadrants in 1913–25, and follow the rest of Regent Street until it joins Langham Place, which swings round to the left to meet Robert Adam's stately Portland Place. Nash's All Souls (much used by the BBC) stands on this curve, giving a pleasant conclusion to the views from north and south. Nash's effect is spoiled, though, by two large ugly buildings on the same curve, the mid-Victorian Langham Hotel, on the left, and the 1930s Broadcasting House, on the right. The best things about the latter building, apart from the programmes it produces, are the Eric Gill sculptures that decorate the exterior. At the far end of Portland Place is Park Crescent, the southern half of Nash's planned circus.

This was built in 1812, and completed by the construction of Park Square about ten years later. The summer house in Park Square is really a ventilating shaft for the Jubilee Line, erected in 1976, and number 18, on the left, was once the entrance to a primitive pre-cinematic illuminated picture show called the Diorama, which operated here from 1823 to 1851, when it became a Baptist chapel. The house now forms part of the headquarters of the Prince's Trust, but it still has 'Diorama' in large letters at the top of the building, and if you look through the window you will see that the house is even now arranged like a theatre.

Beyond Park Square is Regent's Park, which is surrounded by Nash's palatial terraces, which were all given names taken from the royal family's many titles. These were designed by Nash and built in the 1820s by various builders, including Nash (Sussex Place, Gloucester Gate) and James Burton and his son Decimus. Most have been restored or rebuilt as offices or institutions behind their beautiful stucco facades since the Second World War, in which several were damaged. Luckily for Londoners, the Crown Estate decided not to fill the park with 56 villas, as Nash originally intended. Of the eight that were built, all but one (Grove House, now Nuffield Lodge, near the mosque) have been radically altered or rebuilt.

A three-mile walk around the whole Outer Circle might be rather long and tedious, but you could see some of the finest terraces by walking briefly to the west (left) to see Ulster Terrace and York Terrace (with a view of Marylebone's lovely parish church, St John, built in 1813 by Thomas Hardwick), and then following the left bank of the boating lake to get a view of Decimus Burton's Cornwall Terrace and Clarence Terrace, and Nash's magnificent Sussex Place, with unusual oriental domes on the bay windows. In the next row, the magnificently classical Hanover Terrace, H.G. Wells lived and died at number 13, and Ralph Vaughan Williams at number 10. Just past the children's boating pond, with a view of the London Central Mosque on your left, turn right and cross two bridges. Go straight along this path until you reach the Broad Walk, near the southern corner of London Zoo, which has occupied this part of the park since 1826. The south entrance to the zoo is a short distance up Broad Walk to the left or, if you are interested, you could take the diagonal north-easterly path up to Gloucester Gate, to see two neighbourhoods of smaller houses, Park Villages East and West, laid out by Nash in 1824 to provide cheap but picturesque housing for the poorer residents of his new suburb. Park Village West, reached by turning right down Albany Street and taking the first left, is a U-shaped sidestreet of stuccoed Italianate villas, with number 12 outshining the rest, and Park Village East, which is almost straight ahead when you come out of Gloucester Gate, is a road full of pretty Nash villas, decorated with white trellising. This is the beginning of the idea that London suburbs could be built like model villages, an innovation which led to Bedford Park and Hampstead Garden Suburb.

If you prefer, you could turn right on Broad Walk and walk south until it crosses Chester Road. Away to your left as you walk this stretch is James Thomson's very fine Cumberland Terrace (1826), perhaps the best of the Regent's Park terraces, and the long and handsome Chester Terrace. A right turn into Chester Road brings you to the Inner Circle, all that was ever built of Nash's inner circus, and without his proposed national memorial. From 1839 to 1932 the Inner Circle was leased to the Royal Botanical Society, but since 1932 it has been occupied by the Open Air Theatre and Queen Mary's Rose Garden, the prettiest part of the park. When you have wandered these winding paths, over land raised by dumping earth excavated from the boating lake, find your way to York Bridge, between Regent's College and the tennis courts, to get back to the noisy realities of the Marylebone Road, and a choice of Tube stations, Regent's Park to the left and Baker Street to the right.

*

The old borough of Finsbury, the district south of Pentonville Road and east of King's Cross Road/Farringdon Road, has several interesting estates built by early-nineteenth-century landowners, as well as some pioneering post-war council estates. Walking from the northern end of King's Cross Road (near the station), go straight ahead into Vernon Road where the main road curves to the left, and you will find yourself in Percy Circus, which was built on this hilly site by the New River Company in 1842. Lenin lived at number 16 when he visited London in 1905. Go straight across into Prideaux Place, which brings you to Wharton Street, which was built about 1830 by William Joseph Booth for the Lloyd Baker family, which owned the land ahead of you from the seventeenth century until 1975. The centre of the Lloyd Baker estate is Lloyd Square, just to the left, and Lloyd Baker Street, which runs along the south of the square. The street and square are lined with small but handsome semi-detached brick villas, built in or soon after 1825. Granville Square, built between Wharton Street and Lloyd Baker Street in 1842, was Riceyman Square in Arnold Bennett's 1923 novel, *Riceyman Steps*. The steps of the title go down to King's Cross Road.

From Lloyd Square, go east across Amwell Street into River Street, which brings you to Myddleton Square. This is the middle of the New River estate, which was built by William Mylne, surveyor of the New River Company, in the 1820s. The square is named after Sir Hugh Myddleton, who in 1612 founded the company that dug the New River, which brought water from springs in Amwell and Chadwell, in Hertfordshire, to Clerkenwell. Myddleton Square (1827) is still a beautiful (though a little neglected) late-Georgian square, perhaps the best in Islington, despite war damage. Jabez Bunting, who led the Methodists after Wesley's death, lived at number 30 from 1833 to 1858, and the socialist MP Fenner Brockway, campaigner against capital punishment, lived at number 60. The enclosed reservoir in Claremont Square, a short walk north up Amwell Street (which has some nice old shops, especially number 42), was an open pond, the Upper Pond, until 1852, receiving pumped water from New River Head, the other side of Myddleton Square. This particular piece of London's growth was immortalized in a famous cartoon of 1829, *The March of Bricks and Mortar*, by the illustrator George Cruikshank, who lived at 71 Amwell Street between 1824 and 1849. The Spa Green and Priory Green estates, which are mentioned later in this chapter, are both nearby, and the watery connections of this fascinating area are discussed in Chapter Eleven.

*

London had to wait another eighty years or so for another piece of municipal town planning nearly as bold as Nash's Regent Street. The Aldwych and Kingsway, which the London County Council laid out between 1900 and 1907, cut through a fascinating (or revolting, depending on your point of view) tangle of old streets north of the Strand, and carved out a wide avenue from the Strand to Holborn, dividing the legal quarter to the east from Covent Garden and the Bedford estate to the west, just as Regent Street separated Soho from Mayfair. Between 1905 and the 1920s the new streets were lined with impressive offices and public buildings, most of which are still there today. Kingsway was built with an underpass to take electric trams, which seemed to be the transport of the future, and with the Holborn to Aldwych branch of the new Piccadilly line underneath it. This line was closed during the Second World War, when it was used to store the Elgin Marbles, and closed for good in 1994. It is still often used as a film set. The original Strand station, now dingy and abandoned, is on the corner of the Strand and Surrey Street.

A walk along the Aldwych and Kingsway is a walk into the new world of the early twentieth century, motorized, electrified, spacious and steel-framed, though often dressed in the grandiose imperial fashions that were so popular in Edwardian England. London's first major steel-framed building was the Ritz Hotel on Piccadilly, built in 1906, but the first Aldwych and Kingsway buildings were only a year or two behind it. Steel frames and electric or hydraulic lifts enabled builders to construct very tall buildings, as in New York, but the London Building Act of 1894 had set a limit of 80 feet (24 metres) on buildings on the widest streets, plus two stories in the roof, giving a total permitted height of about 30 metres. The introduction of steel frames after the Act did not result in an increase in these height limits, which reflected concern over fire safety, the right to light and the appearance of the town. European cities were not keen to reproduce the dark canyons created by the skyscrapers of Manhattan, and so Kingsway, modern in most other respects, was not built very high. Theses rules remained in force until after 1945, with the 64-metre steel-framed tower of London University's Senate House (started in 1932), between Malet Street and Russell Square, the only major exception. But this is well off the road, and the upper floors were used for books, not people.

Starting from Lancaster Place and Wellington Street, the first building on your left is Inveresk House, built for the right-wing *Morning Post,* which was absorbed by the *Daily Telegraph* in 1937. It is two stories and a dome higher than it was when it was built in 1906–7, and is well-carved granite on a steel frame. Then, on the left, are the Novello Theatre, previously the Strand (renamed in honour of Ivor Novello, who lived above the theatre), the Waldorf Hotel, whose Palm Court brings a touch of Paris to London, and the Aldwych Theatre. Both the theatres are by W.G.R. Sprague, who built eight of London's present theatres. Across the road, on the southern curve of the Aldwych, is India House, which has been the home of the Indian High Commission since its completion in 1930, and the impressive entrance to Bush House, built in the bold classical style favoured by American architects and their clients in the 1920s. Bush House was built for Irving T. Bush as an Anglo-American trade centre, and the figures in the arch symbolize England and America. The inscription 'To the friendship of English-speaking peoples' over the doorway recalls this Anglo-American enterprise, rather than the ethos of the BBC's multilingual World Service, which took a lease on Bush House in 1940 and moves out in 2008.

Past Bush House, on the far (eastern) corner of the segment created by the Aldwych and the Strand, is Australia House, built between 1913 and 1918 for the Australian High Commission. It is the oldest Australian diplomatic mission and London's oldest continuously occupied foreign mission. The walk up Kingsway takes you past a succession of office buildings with royal and imperial names – Imperial House, York House, Alexandra House, Victory House, Windsor House – built between 1912 and 1920 mostly by Trehearne and Norman, the architects' firm that won most of the work along here. The statues on Africa House, near the northern end of the east side, represent British images of Africa in the early 1920s, with Africans working and hunting under Britannia's supervision. There are two interesting buildings on the west side of Kingsway: the handsome baroque church of Holy Trinity (1910), now disused, and the Gallagher Building at numbers 61–63, which was built in 1911 for Kodak by Sir John Burnet, who was also partly responsible for Selfridges. This is one of the very few pre-1914 office buildings in London which abandoned decorative Victorian features and declared the modernity of their steel-framed construction in the simplicity of their external shape. Other examples are Blackfriars House (F. Troup, 1913) on New Bridge Street (near Tudor Street) and Holland House (H.P. Berlage, 1914), at 1–4 and 32 Bury Street, between Houndsditch and Leadenhall Street.

Some of the 'garden suburb' ideas tried out by Nash in and around Regent's Park were applied in a new development in Chiswick in the late 1870s. Jonathan Carr owned a large estate near Turnham Green, which the arrival of the London and South-Western Railway (now the District Underground Line) in 1869 turned into prime suburban development land. In 1875 Carr employed the architect and designer Edward Godwin to begin the development, but two years later the great Norman Shaw became the estate architect, until he passed the job on to his assistant E.J. May in 1880.

The plan of Bedford Park was that there should be no apparent plan – no squares, no formal crescents and hardly any right-angled corners. Most of the streets bend and turn in apparently casual ways, giving the impression they are old village lanes. The houses maintain the same illusion, looking more like country cottages than suburban terraces and semis, in styles that are picturesque variations on the Queen Anne theme favoured by Shaw. By 1883, when Carr's near-bankruptcy brought the work to an end, there were nearly five hundred houses covering 113 acres. The carefully planned rusticity of Bedford Park gave it a reputation as an arty and aesthetic suburb, and it was often depicted (notably in G.K. Chesterton's *The Man Who was Thursday*) as a colony of artists and intellectuals, a second Chelsea. About twenty houses were built with artists' studios, and others were added later. For instance, at number 14 South Parade, which runs along the north side of Turnham Green, the architect Charles Voysey built a house with a top-floor studio for the artist J.W. Forster in 1891.

Bedford Park was threatened with redevelopment in the 1960s, but the listing of 356 houses in 1967, the year in which Conservation Areas were first introduced, saved it from further damage. Now Bedford Park looks and feels like a true garden suburb, probably the best in London, and a walk around its leafy streets is delightful. A few paces north from Turnham Green station will take you to two of the key buildings of the suburb, both built by Shaw, the church and the pub. The Tabard Inn and the (former) Bedford Park Stores (with big bay windows) are on the right, in Bath Road, and the church of St Michael and All Angels, Shaw's interesting blend of medieval, Tudor, Wren, Georgian and Arts and Crafts features, is opposite. The interior of the church is large and striking, with green-painted pews and woodwork and good Arts and Crafts stained glass. Walk a little way up the Avenue, which has some houses (numbers 1 and 2) built by Godwin before Norman Shaw took over as architect, and Shaw's first semis, numbers 20–22. The best streets, mostly given names drawn from Shaw's favourite Queen Anne period, are to either side of the Avenue: Newton Grove, Queen Anne's Grove, Marlborough Crescent and the Orchard to its left (west), and Blenheim Road (with the Yeats family's house at number 3), Queen Anne's Gardens, Woodstock Road, Priory Avenue, Rupert Road and Addison Grove to its right.

The ideas pioneered by Nash and developed by Carr and Shaw were applied on a more ambitious scale in Hampstead Garden Suburb, much of which was built between 1907 and 1914. The visionary who inspired the suburb was Henrietta Barnett, wife of the slum clergyman Canon Samuel Barnett. She was guided by the notion that people of all classes could live in harmony and good health in a suburb which combined the best qualities of urban and rural life, and by the ideas of Ebenezer Howard, whose book, *Garden Cities of Tomorrow*, was published in 1902. Hampstead Garden Suburb was not a self-sufficient town, as Howard advocated, but Barnett borrowed some of Howard's social and planning ideas, and used the architect and planner of Letchworth Garden City, Raymond Unwin, to do the same job in Hampstead. Unwin's firm, Parker and Unwin, was responsible for laying out about 350 acres of Hampstead Garden Suburb between 1907 and 1914, and for the design of very many of the houses. Like Bedford Park, the Hampstead layout used curved roads and irregular junctions, preserved or planted plenty of trees, and tried to make a new suburban development feel like a long-established country town. Unlike most suburban developers, Unwin preserved large pieces of woodland, made liberal use of footpaths, closes and culs-de-sac, and built houses at a maximum density of eight per acre, giving each one a garden. Later on, Unwin became a great advocate of the Green Belt, but at this stage gobbling up farmland for suburban development did not seem to bother him.

Barnett's hope was that rich, middling and poor would live together in Hampstead Garden Suburb. The first section of the development, on 243 acres bought from Eton College, between Finchley Road, Temple Fortune Lane, Bigwood Road, Addison Way and the northern limit of Hampstead Heath, was built as an artisans' quarter, with plenty of smaller houses designed to appeal to well-off working men. High prices, poor transport, lack of shops and local jobs kept the working classes away and prevented Hampstead Garden Suburb from becoming an all-class community, but it was a great experiment in town planning, influential in Britain and around the world. In addition, it was (and is) a showcase for some of the best domestic architecture in Edwardian London, much of it by Parker and Unwin, but also by Sir Edwin Lutyens, Sir Guy Dawber, and M.H. Baillie Scott and dozens of others.

Golders Green Underground station, which dates like the Suburb from 1907, is the most convenient starting point for a walk round the older parts of Hampstead Garden Suburb. Hoop Lane, a right turn off Finchley Road, takes you uphill between the cemetery and the crematorium to Meadway Gate and on to Meadway, a pleasant and varied road with especially interesting houses in the closes that run off it. A left turn into Heathgate brings you to Central Square, large, informal and grassy, which was designed in 1907–8 by Edwin Lutyens to provide a social and cultural focus for the Suburb. Lutyens's church, St Jude (named after Samuel Barnett's church in Whitechapel), combines Gothic, Byzantine and baroque elements in an original and impressive way, especially from the outside. The other buildings on the square are the Free Church, the Friends' (Quakers') Meeting House and the Institute. The west side, where Lutyens's memorial to Henrietta Barnett stands, was meant to look towards the medieval church of St Mary, Harrow-on-the-Hill, which helped to inspire Barnett's conception of a garden suburb, but now trees obscure the view. The square's success as a social centre, especially for those elusive artisans, was gravely limited by its lack of shops, pubs, cafes, bus stops, or any other everyday utilities.

To see more of Hampstead Garden Suburb take the path from the west side of Central Square (between the two churches) to Hampstead Way (the second road you reach), and turn right to follow Hampstead Way up to the Finchley Road. Look especially at numbers 136–138, and at numbers 140–142, Foundation Cottages (1907), which were the first houses built in the suburb by Parker and Unwin. Asmuns Place, on your right as you approach Finchley Road, has a green that was planned as a skittle alley, and the first tree planted by Henrietta Barnett. The corner of Finchley Road and Hampstead Way was planned by Unwin as the main entrance to the Suburb, and the buildings on the main road (Arcade House, Temple Fortune House) are part of his scheme. Buses in the Finchley Road take you back to your starting point, or you could turn left on Finchley Road, then left again down Temple Fortune Lane, which has interesting little squares and crescents, to return to Meadway Gate and Hoop Lane on foot.

From the 1630s until the 1860s, most planned developments were intended for the rich or comfortably-off, though, as in the case of Seven Dials, they sometimes fell into the hands of the poor. From the 1850s and 1860s, however, some charitable, private and local authority developers built well-planned neighbourhoods for tenants who could only pay a few shillings a week. The best-known of the private housing developments for the poor are the tenement blocks built by the Peabody Trust, the Improved Industrial Dwellings Company, the Metropolitan Association for Improving the Dwellings of the Industrial Classes, the Artisans', Labourers' and General Dwellings Company, the Guinness Trust and the Rothschilds' Four Per Cent Dwellings Company. These are mostly in the centre of London, replacing slums that were demolished to make way for them, and they are still a familiar sight in Covent Garden, Shoreditch, Clerkenwell, Westminster and elsewhere. The earliest surviving block of charity flats is in Streatham Street, between Great Russell Street and New Oxford Street, a solid brick building with a flat roof built by the Society for Improving the Condition of the Labouring Classes in 1849.

The housing charities occasionally tried something more adventurous than tenement blocks, and pioneered the first working-class cottage estates. The Artisans', Labourers' and General Dwellings Company built the first, the Shaftesbury Park Estate, between Lavender Hill and the railway line running north-east out of Clapham Junction. The estate, which anticipated similar council estates by twenty-five years, was built to the designs of Robert Austin in the later 1870s, and consisted of 1,135 cottages, a block of flats, a board school, thirty shops and no public houses, between Grayshott Road and Tyneham Road, north of Lavender Hill, between Clapham Junction and Wandsworth Road stations. The houses vary in size and appearance, with Gothic details, but they are of interest mainly for the lesson they tried to teach to other builders of cheap housing – that the poor did not have to be piled on top of each other.

There is a bigger and more ambitious charity housing estate for the working classes in West Kilburn, in the corner between Harrow Road and Kilburn Lane. The Artisans', Labourers' and General Dwellings Company built the Queen's Park estate between 1874 and 1885, employing Robert Austin and Rowland Plumbe to design and build over 2,000 houses on a 76-acre estate. They built brick terraces with a few Gothic touches, and named some of their streets a little unimaginatively, with First Avenue and Sixth Avenue marking the eastern and western limits of the estate. Some of the terraces have been rebuilt or refaced, but the Meeting Hall on the corner of Third Avenue is still there, and the streets still have the feeling of a self-contained Victorian world. If you visit this district, you might take a look at the primary school in Droop Street, on the edge of the estate. This was originally a board school, designed, as so many were, by E.R. Robson. Its special distinction is that in 1882 the old boys of Droop Street School formed the team that a few years later became one of London's first professional football clubs, Queen's Park Rangers.

The 1890 Housing of the Working Classes Act made it possible for London's new county government, the London County Council, to build its own houses or flats on slum clearance land in central or suburban London. This power, in the hands of a council that saw rehousing as part of its mission, helped to change the face of London and the lives of thousands of Londoners. London boroughs, which were given new names and powers in 1899, built estates of their own, but the biggest contributor to this enterprise was the LCC. Council planners and architects adopted some of the ideas of the housing charities, especially the design of their blocks of flats, but they built on a larger scale, and some of their architects were inspired by a more enlightened vision of what sort of housing the working classes might be offered. Some of these early council estates are well planned and ambitious, and worth seeing not for their beauty but for the historic contribution they made to the development of social policy and social life, and to the changing appearance of London.

The first large LCC estate, and one of the most influential, replaced the slums and backstreets of the Old Nichol, Shoreditch, in the 1890s. The planners of the new estate tried to do better than replacing the old grid of slum streets with a new grid of functional tenement blocks, and instead built their rather handsome five-storey blocks along seven roads radiating from Arnold Circus, which was built on the rubble of the demolished rookery. The bandstand on the top of the mound is now rarely used, but once would have been a focus for weekend entertainment. The LCC architects drew their inspiration from the Arts and Crafts movement and Norman Shaw's expensive mansion flats in South Kensington, rather than the spartan Peabody blocks. Although the estate is now not especially beautiful or well kept, it is easy and interesting to visit. Walk north on Bishopsgate and Shoreditch High Street from Liverpool Street station, or take a Tube to Shoreditch, turn left into Sclater Street and right into Club Row, a lively market street, to reach Arnold Circus. Walking up Club Row takes you past Redchurch Street, which still has some of the qualities (though not the abject poverty and high infant mortality) that made this neighbourhood a successful candidate for demolition, and Old Nichol Street, which gave the district its name. It also has a handsome and interesting old pub, the Owl and the Pussycat, previously the Crown, which is a 1760s public house impressively refronted in nineteenth-century stucco.

Walking around the circus, you can see how the LCC architects improved on previous charity housing styles. Compare the two earliest blocks, Walton House and Henley House, built in 1894 in charity style by Rowland Plumbe, between Montclare Street (off Rochelle Street) and Swanfield Street, with the much more handsome Cookham House, built on the west side of Montclare Street just three years later. The blocks built by the LCC's Charles Winmill – Sonning, Culham, Taplow and Sunbury – to the north of Rochelle Street between 1894 and 1897 are also fine examples of the new LCC style. Sunbury has a row of two-storied workshops, to make sure some of the tenants had space to pursue their crafts. The estate was well supplied with elementary schools, and there were two on the circus, Rochelle Primary (1879), now converted into housing, and Virginia Primary (1875). Both were the work of the London School Board's most prolific school architect, E.R. Robson, whose work can be found all over London. Some of the blocks around the circus, Chertsey House, Hurley House and Sandford House, built by R. Minton Taylor in 1895–6, represent the best of the LCC's working-class housing. These were well-designed, well-built blocks, mostly with individual toilets and sculleries and shared laundry rooms, but since they were not subsidized until after 1918, only relatively well-off working-class tenants could afford to live in them, and the slum-dwellers who had lost their homes when the Nichol was pulled down had to look elsewhere. By 1900 the 23 blocks of the Boundary Street Estate had 5,300 residents, but very few of these had lived in the Old Nichol, or Jago.

The old parish vestries were also not incapable of providing cheap housing for the local poor. In Ingestre Place, Soho, an L-shaped road off Broadwick Street, there is an impressive four-storied block called St James's Dwellings, which was built in 1886 by St James's vestry for working-class women, with window boxes to encourage a little 'window gardening'. But local authorities were much more active after the vestries were amalgamated into 28 larger boroughs in 1899. One of the boroughs that pioneered its own housing estates was Battersea, inspired by the advocacy of its radical councillor and MP John Burns. The first borough estate in London is the Latchmere Road estate in Battersea, only a short walk from the privately built Shaftesbury Park Estate described a few paragraphs ago. It was built in 1903 on a corner of land between Battersea Park Road, Latchmere Road and the railway line between Clapham Junction and Battersea Park. Battersea built its 300 two-storey cottage flats in terraces along a grid of roads with names that reflected the spirit in which they were constructed, Reform Street and Freedom Street, or to commemorate the radicals who had inspired the enterprise: Burns Street after John Burns and Odger Street after the socialist, trade unionist and shoemaker George Odger. The little brick houses may be nothing much to look at, but they all had a garden and the use of a good-sized recreation ground, and they remind us of the efforts being made at the turn of the century to bring comfort and self-respect to the lives of poorer Londoners.

*

If Boundary Street marked the start of council housing in London, establishing a model that was followed in London and other great cities for the next fifty years, the model for the post-1945 decades was a famous mixed-development estate (high- and low-rise dwellings), known as Alton East and Alton West, or the Roehampton estate, in the space between Richmond Park and Roehampton Lane. These estates were developed by the LCC's Architects' Department in the early 1950s as modern solutions to the age-old problem of London's housing shortage, and became the most admired and imitated of LCC estates. Alton East, the earlier and smaller estate, was begun in 1952 on Scandinavian lines, with a mixture of maisonettes, terraces and high square 'point' blocks in brick-clad concrete with eleven stories and four flats to a floor. Alton West, begun in 1954, was inspired by Le Corbusier's Unité d'Habitation in Marseilles which had been finished in 1952, and is a larger and more influential estate. Danebury Avenue, which runs north-west from Roehampton Lane to the Roehampton Gate of Richmond Park, is the spine of the estate, and a walk along it will take you past the most important features of the development. Passing shops, schools and maisonettes, you come to a set of point blocks, and then to the outstanding feature of the estate, the five concrete slab blocks set into the hillside of a large green space called Downshire Fields. The two-storey squares on the frontage represent the shape of the maisonettes into which the blocks are divided. When these slabs were built in 1954–6 it was decided at the highest level that they should not sit on the hilltop facing full on to Richmond Park, creating a massive concrete wall, but should be set into the slope, showing their narrow sides to the park. You can appreciate this dramatic effect from the terrace of Mount Clare, the 1770s mansion on a hill to the west of Danebury Avenue. The house is now owned by Roehampton University but is open by appointment. Whether you enjoy the view or not you should remember that Alton West, and especially these five blocks, inspired architects and local authorities in London and elsewhere to aim for a similar effect in dozens of other high-rise estates built in the 1960s.

If you have a taste for modern housing estates, and want to look at those that set new standards of height, organization or design, visit the Spa Green estate in Finsbury, in the triangle formed by the junction of Rosebery Avenue and St John Street. This estate was planned in the 1930s, to replace demolished slums, by Tecton, the practice led by the greatest British modernist architect, Berthold

Lubetkin (who was born in Georgia but took UK nationality in 1939), and built between 1946 and 1950 by the new firm of Lubetkin and Skinner. The estate consists of two eight-storey blocks and one four-storey one, which is curved. Finsbury chose Lubetkin because he knew how to bring potentially charmless slabs of municipal housing to life by the use of balconies, curves and patterns of brick and ironwork. He also devoted great attention to practical improvements that would make life in his blocks easier and more pleasant for the council's tenants: aerofoil roofs designed for the fast drying of laundry, scientifically designed kitchens, soundproofing between flats, a refuse-disposal system to eliminate dustbins, and bedrooms facing onto a landscaped garden. The estate is now rather run down, but is worth a visit, perhaps as part of a walk between the Lloyd Baker and New River estates, which are nearby. There are two more Lubetkin estates in Finsbury worth visiting if you are interested in the development of modern housing. Bevin Court, a single eight-storey Y-shaped block on Holford Place, north of Percy Circus, was built in 1952–5 and has a terrific central staircase which is described in the Pevsner and Cherry guide to north London as 'one of the most exciting twentieth-century spatial experiences in London'. And across Pentonville Road, between Calshot and Rodney Streets, there is the bigger Priory Green estate, which was planned by Lubetkin before the war, and built between 1947 and 1957, more cheaply than Spa Green and without its excellent facilities. It is now owned by the Peabody Trust, which has used a lottery grant to revitalize the estate.

Lubetkin gave up architecture in the late 1950s. The best of his earlier work in London includes the penguin enclosure at London Zoo (1934), Finsbury Health Centre (1938) in Pine Street (at the junction of Farringdon Road and Rosebery Avenue), and Highpoint 1 and 2, on North Hill (near Highgate Tube station), two blocks of flats which have been regarded ever since their construction in 1938 as modernist masterpieces, in the spirit of Le Corbusier.

*

Lawyers, Printers and Monks

Question 42 is impossible to answer at weekends and public holidays.

Somerset House, the Navy Office,
Was built when London was a port.
We'll meet by George's fishy statue,
Which dominates the Fountain Court.

This walk goes eastward to the City
All around the Street of Ink.
The verses tell you where to wander,
What to answer, where to drink.

Reach and go right on the Strand
And date the street lamp just near here. [1]
Who act Sancte et Sapienter
According to their sloganeer? [2]

Going east, who'd read your fortune
And tell you what the stars ordain? [3]
And where would you wait for ever,
For that Piccadilly train? [4]

In Surrey Street where did Marcus
Wash his grimy hands and face? [5]
Forward now towards the river,
And turn left into Temple Place.

The old green shelter here is meant for
What specific breed of men? [6]
And what is this IISS place, [7]
Where you must take a left again?

Take Arundel to find Maltravers
Which brings you out on Water Lane.
Take a plucky little alley
To Milford, then go right again.

In the gardens at the bottom,
Why's that maiden never blotto? [8]
And, turning back, the ship-topped house,
Has what worthy traders' motto? [9]

This little place is quite a beauty,
A house Lord Astor used to own.
The style is old – Elizabethan –
But who's that on the mobile phone? [10]

Climb the steps to Essex Street,
And by the pub that thinks it's best,
Take Devereux, and find a tavern,
Where you could have a moment's rest.

The Devereux was once named what? [11]
And who's the redhead looking down? [12]
After him, which speculator
Built this part of London Town? [13]

Ahead, the George, which once sold coffee,
Claims Johnson used this as his digs.
Your task here is a simple one –
Enumerate the golden pigs. [14]

In the middle of the Strand here,
What colour car is in the gents? [15]
And who's the woman linked to Johnson,
That man of mighty common sense? [16]

A few steps east and say which creature
Rests between two Chinese men. [17]
This shop's been selling tea and coffee
Since . . . you have to tell me when. [18]

Whose symbol is a golden beehive? [19]
What did wig and pen escape? [20]
Which bank was the first in Fleet Street? [21]
Templars take which ovine shape? [22]

Who never lived at seventeen? [23]
Who first fixed your clutch and throttle? [24]
Past that lawyer looking out,
Who traded at the Golden Bottle? [25]

Cross the road where sturdy clubmen
Beat the hours in Dunstan's tower.
Which Napoleon conquered Fleet Street [26]
And what man makes all fishes cower? [27]

Who stands here with orb and sceptre,
Forced from Ludgate to decamp? [28]
And, in Red Lion Court, your next street,
What's the slogan of the lamp? [29]

Pemberton Row and then Gough Square,
The place where Johnson used to lodge.
You know his name, you've seen his statue,
But tell me, who on earth was Hodge? [30]

By Boswell's clock return to Fleet Street,
And name the pub within whose gates
Goldsmith had a drink with Reynolds
And Dowson used to rhyme with Yeats. [31]

Cross Fleet Street once again and tell me
Tipperary's claim to fame. [32]
And who made sixty-seven tick? [33]
Two men whose interests were the same.

Go east and turn down Salisbury Court –
Which old diarist lived here, please? [34]
Across from him what started out
That meant the death of many trees? [35]

Take the passage of St Bride's,
And at the far end of this alley,
Write down on your answer sheet
The name of Henry's long-gone palais. [36]

Skirt around the printers' church,
And come to Fleet Street once again.
What humpy joker started here, [37]
And who first fed Sir Chris's men? [38]

Cross the circus, pass the station,
Turn before you reach the dome
Down Pageantmaster on your right –
What tonsured preachers called this home? [39]

Crossing over Andrew's Hill
Your next puzzle's very near:
Where did all those well-dressed monarchs
Store their clothes and other gear? [40]

Down the hill that you just passed,
Then Ireland Yard (the Cockpit's there) –
Name the ruin on your right [41]
And walk straight on through Playhouse Square.

Briefly detour to your right,
A horny gate in Blackfriars Lane.
Peep inside the chemists' court –
Who'd relieve your pupils' strain? [42]

Now turn back and go downhill
Making for the Thameslink line.
Underneath the railway bridge
You'll find a pub of strange design.

Inside this dark and monkish place
The old back room's the place to go.
You can check your answers now,
In surroundings art nouveau.

*

CHAPTER FIVE

MUSICAL LONDON

William Hogarth, *An Enraged Musician*, 1741

As THE CAPITAL CITY of a 'land without music' (Oscar Schmitz's unkind description of England in 1914), London has a remarkably rich musical past and present. Perhaps London has not produced as many great composers as some European cities, but as a place in which music has been performed, enjoyed and inspired it has few rivals.

For centuries London has been a city hungry for music, a capital in which the best European composers and performers could be sure of a loud and lucrative welcome. Many of its greatest composers, like many of its best painters and writers, were immigrants, either from Europe or the rest of Britain, but several of these, like Handel, J.C. Bach (the 'London Bach'), Vaughan Williams, Gustav Holst and Ivor Novello, became real Londoners rather than occasional visitors. Others regarded a visit to London as a stepping stone to international stardom, the triumphant culmination of a great career or a good way to fill their pockets. Of native Londoners, Henry Purcell is the outstanding figure, but we could also include William Byrd, William Boyce, John Dowland (perhaps born in Westminster), Thomas Arne, Samuel Coleridge-Taylor, Sir Arthur Sullivan and a good collection of twentieth-century composers – Peter Warlock, Sir Michael Tippett, Constant Lambert, Noël Coward, George Butterworth, Sir Arnold Bax, Gerald Finzi and Lionel Bart. As for musicians, conductors, instrument makers, concert promoters, bandmasters, organists, singers and music publishers, they were drawn to London and its vast audience in their thousands. Ever since the 1670s, when it staged Europe's first commercial concerts, London has been an unrivalled centre of orchestral performances, and today it sustains more large professional orchestras than any other city in the world.

The most important focus for musicians and composers in Tudor and Stuart London was the royal court, and in particular the choir of the Chapel Royal, which sang in St James's Palace, Hampton Court and elsewhere. The Chapel Royal choir was founded by Henry VIII, and sustained by his three children, Edward VI, Mary I and Elizabeth. To maintain its high quality, the best singers, composers and organists were employed by the Crown. Thomas Tallis worked there as chorister and organist for over forty years (1543–85), composing hymns, liturgical music and pieces for state occasions. William Byrd joined Tallis as organist and chorister in the 1570s, and was in turn replaced by John Bull around 1592. Westminster Abbey shared many of the Chapel Royal's choristers, and some musicians had jobs in both. Orlando Gibbons, the leading court musician of James I's day, was choirmaster and organist with both choirs, until his sudden death in 1625. Under Charles II John Blow sang in the Chapel Royal and Westminster Abbey choirs, and was organist for both, until he gave the posts up in 1679 to his brilliant pupil, Henry Purcell. Purcell made his career in the Chapel Royal, Westminster Abbey and the royal court, composing religious music for the King's worship and masques for his entertainment. His career was short, but he lived long enough to see the focus of musical activity shift from the court to the theatre, especially after the accession of William and Mary in 1689. Purcell's operas were staged in the 1690s at London's only licensed theatre, the Theatre Royal Drury Lane, and his early death in 1695 created a hiatus in the history of native English opera which lasted until 1951, when Britten's *Peter Grimes* was staged.

Several of the places associated with the history of music in Tudor and Stuart London still exist. Westminster Abbey is still a great centre of church music and contains the tombs of several

English musicians. In the north aisle, the left side of the abbey as you enter it, you will find the stones marking the graves of Ralph Vaughan Williams (on your right as you enter the aisle), and of Henry Purcell and his wife (further along on the right). Just past this, near a window commemorating the engineers George and Robert Stephenson, there are memorials to John Blow, who is buried here, and Orlando Gibbons and William Walton, who are not. Continue round to the south transept, 'Poets' Corner', and you will see the grave of Handel, and a statue by Roubiliac showing the composer at work. Roubiliac took Handel's face from his death mask. In the middle of the south walk of the cloisters there are paving stones marking the graves of two European musicians who settled in London, the violinist Johann Salomon, who persuaded Haydn to come to London in the 1790s, and the composer, pianist and piano maker Muzio Clementi. In the west walk of the cloisters, near memorials to Westminster Abbey organists and choristers, there is a little black marble tablet marking the grave of the composer, violinist and concert organizer John Banister, a man of particular importance in the history of music in London.

The Chapel Royal in St James's Palace, one of the places in which the royal choir performed, was altered by Sir Robert Smirke in the 1830s, but its marvellous ceiling, with the arms and mottoes of Catherine of Aragon, Anne Boleyn and Anne of Cleves, is still intact. Members of the public are welcome to attend services at the Chapel Royal on most Sundays, and might well hear music written by Tallis, Byrd, Gibbons or Purcell in the golden age of English music, sung by the six men and ten children of the Chapel Royal choir. Service times (usually 11.15 every Sunday, from the first Sunday in October to Easter Sunday) can be found on the royal family's website, www.royal.gov.uk, following links to royal residences, Chapel Royal and services, or in *The Times* on Saturday. From Easter Sunday to the end of July, services are held in Inigo Jones's Queen's Chapel in Marlborough Road, right next to the palace.

Some City churches still have late-seventeenth-century organs which were played by Restoration musicians. Organs made by the great organ maker Renatus Harris (1652–1724), who lived in Wine Office Court (off Fleet Street), still survive in St Vedast, on the corner of Fetter Lane and Cheapside, St Andrew Undershaft, St Clement Eastcheap, St Sepulchre, and (in part) St Michael Cornhill. The last of these was played by Purcell, and regularly by William Boyce, who was organist at St Michael for over thirty years (1736–68). In 1685 the organs of Harris and his rival Bernard 'Father' Smith (1628–1708) were tested against each other in the Temple church, with Henry Purcell and John Blow playing the two instruments. In a close contest the Inner Templars judged for Harris and the Middle Templars for Smith, with Judge Jeffreys' casting vote going to Smith. In retrospect this is hardly a recommendation. The Temple church has another place in musical history because it was here, in 1927, that one of the most popular church choir recordings of all time, including Ernest Lough's solo of Mendelssohn's 'Oh for the Wings of a Dove', was recorded. There are 1680s Smith organ cases in St Peter Cornhill, St Mary Woolnoth, and a very fine one in St Katherine Cree. In the interesting church of St Magnus the Martyr, in Lower Thames Street, there is a fine organ built in 1712 by Abraham Jordan, the first with a swell pedal. All these organs have been rebuilt from time to time, and only the cases are as their original makers made them. The organ in St Paul's Cathedral still has some pipes by Bernard Smith in a case by Wren and Grinling Gibbons, but has often been altered and restored.

John Banister's career, like Purcell's, reflected the growing opportunities open to musicians and composers in Restoration London. Banister was employed as the leader of the King's band of violinists between 1664 and 1667, and he used the royal band in his second career, as a composer and performer with the King's Company in the Theatre Royal, on the corner of Bridges Street (now Catherine Street) and Russell Street, near Covent Garden. In 1672 Banister discovered an entirely new way of making a living. He found a large room in Whitefriars (the street just to the east of the Temple, between the Strand and the river), fitted it out with a curtained stage and chairs and tables, like an alehouse, and started to organize four o'clock afternoon concerts, to which listeners were admitted for a shilling. For this fee, customers could drink and smoke as much as they liked. The first concert was probably held early in 1673. Banister's 'Musick School', where Europe's first public commercial concerts were held, was near the back gate of the Temple, probably in the road now called Tudor Street, but then called Whitefriars. At the end of 1675 Banister moved his concerts to Chandos Street (now Chandos Place), Covent Garden, and in 1676 they moved to Essex Buildings, near Essex Street and St Clement Danes church, where Fleet Street meets the Strand.

When Banister died in 1679 his place as London's only concert promoter was taken by Thomas Britton, a small-coal (slack) merchant and book dealer with a shop on the corner of Jerusalem Passage and Aylesbury Street, a few yards from Clerkenwell Green. Britton used a long, narrow and low loft above his shop (reached by a difficult outside staircase) to put on concerts, and these became fashionable in spite of their unpromising location. The fact that Britton had made influential friends (including Robert Harley, Earl of Oxford) through his book dealing helped to get his concerts established. Britton's performers included Handel and J.C. Pepusch, who played Britton's excellent harpsichord. Britton held these concerts for nearly forty years, at first free of charge and later for a ten shillings (50p) subscription. He continued to sell coal and books, and to dress in the plain blue smock of his trade, and his funeral in 1714 was attended by 'a great concourse of people'. He was buried in the churchyard of his local church, St James Clerkenwell, and is commemorated by a green plaque on the site of his coal shop and upstairs concert room. To pursue the musical theme in this district, you could take a drink in the Crown Tavern, on Clerkenwell Green, which used to be a music hall, the Apollo Concert Room.

By the time of Britton's death there were several concert rooms in London, and the city had become a favoured destination for foreign musicians who wanted to find a paying audience. Handel, who moved to London from Hanover in 1712, was London's greatest catch, but there were many others, including the Prussian composer Johann Christoph Pepusch (1704) and the Flemish composer Jean-Baptiste Loeillet. One of the main concert rooms around 1700 was in York Buildings, the set of streets built in the 1680s by Nicholas Barbon on the site of the demolished York House, now to the east of Charing Cross station. Villiers Street, right next to the station, seems to be the most likely location of the concert room. There was a second concert room in Covent Garden, the Vendu, an auction room on the corner of Charles Street (now Wellington Street) and York Street (now the eastern end of Tavistock Street). To add to these, early-eighteenth-century London had several amateur musical societies or gentlemen's clubs based in public houses. The Academy of Ancient Music, founded in 1726, met in the best room of the Crown and Anchor Tavern on the corner of Arundel Street and the Strand (near St Clement Danes church), and two others, both founded in the 1720s, met in the Swan Tavern in Cornhill and the Castle Tavern in Paternoster Row, near Panyer Alley.

Handel was the giant figure in London's musical life between 1712 and 1759, and we can find his footprints all over the city. In 1711, even before he had decided to move permanently to London, Handel had performed for Queen Anne in St James's Palace and directed his own opera, *Rinaldo*, from the harpsichord in the Queen's Theatre, Haymarket. In 1713 Handel's music was played in St Paul's to celebrate the Treaty of Utrecht, and probably in 1715, definitely in 1717, his *Water Music* was played for a royal party on the Thames.

Handel was happy to accept royal and aristocratic patronage, but what most attracted him to London was the possibility of making a good living writing for the commercial stage. For most of his career he composed, conducted and performed his operas in the theatre in the Haymarket which had been opened in 1705 by Sir John Vanbrugh and which was known as the Queen's or the King's Theatre, depending on who occupied the throne. This theatre was generally used for opera, and was often known as the Opera House, or Italian Opera House. It burned down (as most London theatres did at one time or another) in 1876, but Her Majesty's Theatre (built in 1897 by Herbert Beerbohm Tree) now occupies part of its site, which ran from Charles II Street almost to Pall Mall.

There was another theatre on Lincoln's Inn Fields – converted from a tennis court in 1661 by Sir William Davenant and the first in England with a proscenium arch. For two years, after a fire destroyed the Drury Lane Theatre in 1672, it was the only licensed theatre in London. In 1728, under the management of John Rich, the theatre had an enormous success with *The Beggar's Opera*, a musical play about London low life, with John Gay's lyrics set to popular melodies, including folk tunes and London street songs, probably arranged by Pepusch. A few years later Rich abandoned the decaying theatre and built another in Bow Street, the forerunner of the present Covent Garden Opera House. Handel, whose work was everywhere, used the Lincoln's Inn Fields Theatre from 1739 to 1741, but it was little used after that and had several non-musical careers until it was finally demolished in 1848. Its site, in the middle of the north side of Portugal Street, is now occupied by the rear of the Royal College of Surgeons.

The Covent Garden Theatre in Bow Street was opened in December 1732, and staged plays as well as operas until 1849, just before the present Royal Opera House was built. In 1735 Handel, who had lost the King's Theatre to a rival opera company, started staging his new operas there. In the 1740s he used Covent Garden for his annual oratorio season, and this was where the first London performance of the *Messiah* (premiered in Dublin) took place in 1743. Handel also used the other main London theatres of his day, the Theatre Royal Drury Lane and the Little Theatre in Haymarket, built almost opposite the King's Theatre in 1720. It was rebuilt by

John Nash in 1830, and survives as the Theatre Royal Haymarket today. Handel was a favourite in Vauxhall Gardens, and a statue by Roubiliac of him playing the lyre with a cherub at his feet was erected there in 1738. Life-sized marble statues of non-royal figures were very rare at this time, and this one created a stir and made Roubiliac's reputation. When the gardens closed it was placed in the entrance of Novello's music publishers in Soho, and since 1964 has been in the Victoria and Albert Museum. And finally, Handel's famous *Music for the Royal Fireworks*, written to celebrate the Peace of Aix-la-Chapelle of 1748, was performed in Green Park in April 1749. The house that Handel lived and worked in from 1723 to 1759, number 25 Brook Street, still exists, and its upper floors were opened as a Handel museum in 2001. Just along the road is St George's Hanover Square, newly built in Handel's day, in which Handel was a regular worshipper. The museum extends into number 23, where the rock singer and guitarist Jimi Hendrix had a flat in 1968–9, the years of the Jimi Hendrix Experience. Like Handel, Hendrix chose Brook Street because it was close to the main music venues of his day.

Handel's patron in 1717–18 was James Brydges, later Duke of Chandos, who embezzled a fortune when he was paymaster-general of the forces and built himself a mansion, Canons, in Little Stanmore, near Edgware. Handel lived there as Brydges' kapellmeister for some of this time, and two of his early dramatic works, *Acis and Galatea* and *Esther*, were probably performed there. Eleven of his anthems were performed at the church of St Lawrence Whitchurch, which Chandos had completely rebuilt in 1715. Canons was demolished when Chandos lost his fortune, leaving the present park, Canons Park (and the grounds of the North London Collegiate School), but the church is still in fine shape and worth a visit if you are at Canon's Park station, near the end of the Jubilee Line. Inside, there is a dramatic baroque interior covered in paintings of biblical scenes, with an organ case and the Chandos mausoleum carved by Grinling Gibbons.

John Gay, the poet and playwright whose musical play, *The Beggar's Opera*, had such an impact on the history of opera in eighteenth-century London, ending the vogue for Italian opera and starting a fashion for English ballad operas, lived in a London house that still survives. Although Gay made a fortune, he spent much of his time rent-free with aristocratic patrons. In 1721 he spent the summer with Lord Burlington in Chiswick House, and in 1722–3 he had lodgings in Burlington House, on Piccadilly. Shortly afterwards he found fresh protectors in the Duke and Duchess of Queensberry, who moved into their new house in Burlington Gardens (behind Burlington House) in 1723 or 1724. From 1730 Gay lived with the Queensberrys in London or in the country, and when he died in their London house in December 1732 the Queensberrys arranged for him to be buried in Westminster Abbey. Queensberry House, now 7 Burlington Gardens, was enlarged in the 1780s, and altered to suit the needs of its later owners, the Bank of Scotland, but it retains its eighteenth-century exterior and some original first-floor rooms including the great staircase, a part of the Great Drawing Room, and two anterooms.

Most native composers were overshadowed by imported ones, but one of those who made an important contribution to national life was Thomas Arne, whose birthplace still stands at 31 King Street, which runs west from Covent Garden piazza. This was the Crown and Cushion, the home and workshop of his father, the upholsterer and theatre servant Thomas Arne. Thomas Arne (junior) spent his life writing songs for pleasure gardens and the London theatres, especially those in the Covent Garden area. The houses he occupied were all around here, in Great Queen Street, Lincoln's Inn Fields, the Strand, Drury Lane, Bow Street and Covent Garden piazza. He was baptized in St Paul's Covent Garden in 1710 and buried in its churchyard, near his father, in 1778. Arne wrote or arranged several songs which are still sung today (including the familiar tunes for Shakespeare's songs 'Where the Bee Sucks', 'Blow, Blow Thou Winter Wind' and 'Under the Greenwood Tree'), and two which have a unique place in British national life, 'Rule Britannia' and 'God Save the King'. 'Rule Britannia' was first performed in 1740, and Arne (a Catholic) led the singing of his version of 'God Bless Our Noble King' at Drury Lane Theatre in September 1745, when the Jacobite rising seemed to threaten the English monarchy and 'confound their politics, frustrate their knavish tricks' really meant something.

The main concert hall in Handel and Arne's London was Hickford's Room, which was attached to Mr Hickford's dancing school in Panton Street, off the Haymarket, from 1714 to about 1738. Around that time John Hickford opened a new concert room behind number 41 Brewer Street, the road just south of Golden Square, Soho. The new Hickford's Room was the only important West End concert hall of the 1740s and 1750s, a regular stop for people in London for the Season and an important venue for the work of Handel, Thomas Arne and others. On 13 May 1765 nine-year-old Mozart gave a concert with his sister, including pieces of his own composition. According to a later advertisement, the concert room was 'large and finely proportioned, viz. 50 Feet long, 27 Feet 6 Inches wide, and 22 Feet high to the top of the Cove and Ceiling'. The Hickford family ran the concert hall until 1787, but it was overshadowed by four rival halls in the 1760s and 1770s. In the 1790s the hall was used for various concerts and assemblies, and later the building was used by schools, clubs and dancing academies. It was demolished in 1934 to make way for an annexe for the Regent Palace Hotel.

Mozart and his family stayed in London for fifteen months from April 1764, and he studied there with J.C. Bach, who had an important influence on his development. His first lodgings were with a barber at 19 Cecil Court, between St Martin's Lane and Castle Street (now Charing Cross Road), then the family moved to a staymaker's house at 15 Thrift Street (now 21 Frith Street) near Soho Square, where a plaque marks the site of the demolished house. To make money, Leopold Mozart invited the public in to put his son to the test by 'giving him anything to play at Sight, or any Music without Bass, which he will write upon the Spot'. But Leopold became ill, and they all moved to the village of Chelsea in August 1764 to speed his recovery. In the house in Chelsea, 180 Ebury Street (then known as Five Fields Row), Mozart composed his first two symphonies and many other early pieces – known as the London or Chelsea Sketchbook. The house had fine views and a lovely garden, and was only a short walk from Buckingham House, where the Mozarts visited King George III three times, and near one of London's most popular music venues, Ranelagh Gardens. Mozart performed a charity concert of his own music at Ranelagh on 29 June 1764. The house is still standing at the southern end of Ebury Street, and there is a statue of the young Mozart in nearby Orange Square, where Ebury Street joins Pimlico Road. Later, when Leopold's health had improved, the family moved to a tavern in Cornhill, the Swan and Hoop, which long ago disappeared under offices.

The new and larger concert halls which supplanted Hickford's Rooms in the 1760s were Mrs Cornelys' Rooms in Carlile House on Soho Square (where St Patrick's church now stands), and Almack's Assembly Rooms, which were about halfway along the south side of King Street, off St James's Street. J.C. Bach (J.S. Bach's son), who settled in London in 1762, began the world's first series of subscription concerts in Carlile House in 1765. Ruined by competition from newer and better concert halls, Carlile House closed in the early 1780s and was demolished in 1791. In 1772 the Pantheon was built on the south side of Oxford Street, a little west of Poland Street (near Oxford Circus), for masquerades, assemblies and concerts. It was fashionable for less than twenty years. Rebuilt after a fire in 1792, it was later converted into a shopping bazaar which was demolished in 1937 to make way for a large Marks and Spencer store. More important and successful than all these were the Hanover Square Rooms, which opened in 1774 with a concert by J.C. Bach and the viola player Abel, on the south-east corner of the square, on the north side of Hanover Street. These were London's most important concert rooms for a hundred years, the place where the greatest resident and visiting musicians and composers would usually play. For most of the nineteenth century the Hanover Square Rooms attracted the greatest musicians in the world, including Liszt, Rubinstein, Wagner and Clara Schumann. The opening of St James's Hall Piccadilly, a large concert hall with excellent acoustics, in 1858 and of the Royal Albert Hall in 1871 diminished the Hanover Square Rooms' popularity, and they were sold to a social club in 1875 and demolished in 1900.

With three good concert halls, several opera houses and musical theatres (including Sadler's Wells, opened in 1765), late-eighteenth-century London enjoyed a golden age of musical entertainment. Going to professional orchestral concerts at the Pantheon, Hanover Square Rooms and Almack's, and to the Italian opera at the King's Theatre, Haymarket, became one of the essential pleasures of the London Season. The long visits to London of the great Joseph Haydn in 1791–2 and 1794–5 marked the high point of this rage for music. In March 1791 Haydn began a series of twelve concerts at Hanover Square with the German violinist Johann Salomon, who had arranged the visit. The next year, between February and May, he played the first of his series of twelve London symphonies, from the 93rd through to the 98th, and in February–March 1794 and February–May 1795 he introduced the rest, from the 99th to the 104th, persuading even George III to enjoy something other than Handel. With Haydn writing and performing a dozen of his finest symphonies in the city, London seemed to be at the centre of the musical world. Its combination of aristocratic and middle-class wealth, of fashion and numbers, gave musicians and composers opportunities for every kind of moneymaking, from patronage and subscription concerts to private performances, music lessons, sheet music sales, instrument promotions and individual benefit performances.

A new concert room was opened in 1806, in a converted house on the north corner of Little Argyll Street and King Street, which followed the route of today's Regent Street. Its first name, the Fashionable Institution, was soon replaced with a less pretentious one, the Argyll Rooms, but the hall was not successful until 1813, when it was chosen by a newly formed society of professional musicians (led by Salomon and Muzio Clementi), the Philharmonic Society, as its main concert hall. The old Argyll Rooms were rebuilt in a much finer form by John Nash in 1819–20 when King Street was replaced by Regent Street, and remained one of London's smartest concert halls until they burnt down in 1830. The society moved to the Hanover Square Rooms, and still survives as the Royal Philharmonic Society, the second-oldest music society in the world. Before their destruction the Argyll Rooms witnessed the London debut of the 12-year-old Franz Liszt in 1824, staged the British premiere in 1825 of Beethoven's Ninth (Choral) Symphony, which was commissioned by the Philharmonic Society, and hosted Mendelssohn's first London concert in 1829. It was here, in 1820, that Ludwig Spohr became the first person to conduct an orchestra in England with a baton. The Argyll Rooms were not rebuilt after the fire, and the Dickins & Jones building now occupies the whole of its Regent Street–Little Argyll Street site.

After 1830 the Hanover Square Rooms were restored to their prime position, with their only important rival being Exeter Hall, which was built on the Strand in 1831, opposite the present site of the Savoy. Exeter Hall was used by the Sacred Harmonic Society and specialized in religious music. Mendelssohn conducted his own oratorios there in 1837 and 1847. The hall was demolished in 1907 and had stopped staging concerts long before that. The primacy of the Hanover Square Rooms was finally ended in 1858, when St James's Hall was opened on the north side of Piccadilly (and the west side of Regent Street), just west of Air Street. Dickens gave some of his famous readings in St James's Hall in the 1860s, and in the 1870s and 1880s it was London's main concert hall, despite the opening of the Royal Albert Hall in 1871. Edvard Grieg had a stupendous debut there in 1888, and Tchaikovsky, Dvořák,

Liszt and Paderewski all performed there when they visited London. The only problems with the hall were the smell of cooking from the ground-floor restaurants, and the sound of the Moore and Burgess Minstrels who usually performed in one of the two smaller concert halls below. St James's Hall needed expensive repairs, and it had lost its position as London's best concert hall when the Queen's Hall was opened in 1893 and the Bechstein (now Wigmore) Hall in 1901. So it was demolished in 1905 and replaced by Norman Shaw's Piccadilly Hotel, which is now called Le Meridien, Piccadilly.

*

Queen's Hall, which stood on the southern corner of Langham Place and Riding House Street (opposite All Souls) until it was destroyed by bombing in May 1941, was London's most popular concert hall for nearly fifty years. Its guiding genius was Henry Wood, the conductor of the Queen's Hall Orchestra from 1895 until 1927. Wood started the summer promenade concerts in 1895, picking up a tradition started in Ranelagh and Vauxhall Gardens, offering a mixture of popular ballads and classical pieces. In 1904 Wood accidentally prompted the creation of an important new London orchestra. Breaking established practice, he insisted that the members of the Queen's Hall Orchestra attend his rehearsals, instead of sending deputies. Forty-six players resigned, and a group of them formed a new self-governing orchestra, the London Symphony Orchestra, the oldest of London's five major symphony orchestras.

Wood's promenade concerts needed financial support, and they were saved from closure first in 1902 by a German-born banker, Sir Edgar Speyer, and then, when Speyer was expelled from England during the First World War, by the music publishers Chappell's. When Chappell's withdrew in 1927 the BBC stepped in to support the Proms, but the Queen's Hall Orchestra, which Wood had conducted for thirty years, ceased to exist. In 1941 the Proms moved to the Royal Albert Hall, where Wood's bust is still displayed, and his *Fantasia on British Sea Songs* still played, every summer at the great musical festival he created, sustained and conducted for nearly fifty years. Wood's house, marked with a blue plaque, is 4 Elsworthy Road, on the north-western edge of Primrose Hill.

Wood's ashes were buried in the church of St Sepulchre, where his father had sung and where Wood played the organ. St Sepulchre (on the corner of Giltspur Street and Holborn Viaduct) is known as the musicians' church, mainly because it has a chapel dedicated to St Cecilia, whose saint's day is celebrated here every year on 22 November by the choirs of St Paul's, Westminster Abbey and the Chapel Royal. Wood's tomb and a spectacular memorial window are here, and so is the organ casing of the Renatus Harris organ upon which Handel, Mendelssohn and the young Henry Wood all played. The church also displays the bell which played the last music that condemned men and women taken from Newgate to Tyburn ever heard (*see* Chapter Eight).

There are two Victorian concert halls in modern central London: the Royal Albert Hall, which opened in 1871, and the Wigmore Hall, which opened in 1901. The contrasts between the two could hardly be greater. Wigmore Hall is small (540 seats), unpretentious, acoustically excellent and devoted exclusively to classical music. It was built by T.E. Collcutt, the architect of the Savoy Hotel, for the German piano-maker Carl Bechstein, who needed a place to showcase his pianos. It was seized, auctioned and renamed in the First World War. Saint-Saëns, Prokoviev, Britten, Hindemith and Poulenc all performed in Wigmore Hall. Wigmore Street is north of and parallel to Oxford Street, and the hall is near Wimpole Street. Bechstein's piano showrooms, also by Collcutt, are next door at number 40, but the building has been altered inside.

The Royal Albert Hall is a vast and ostentatious domed amphitheatre, able to hold over 8,000 people. It was and is used for shows, dances and sporting events as well as the Proms and other concerts. Its echo, now reduced by various acoustic devices, used to give the attentive listener two performances for the price of one. In its neighbourhood there are several interesting musical sites. The Royal College of Music, Sir Arthur Blomfield's red brick building of the 1890s, is on Prince Consort Street, immediately south of the Albert Hall, and the building occupied by the Royal College of Organists between 1904 and 1990, with unusual and attractive plasterwork, is just to its west. The RCM has a Museum of Instruments (from 1480 to the present), which is open to the public, free of charge, on Tuesdays to Fridays, 2.00 to 4.00. East of the Albert Hall, on Albert Hall Mansions, Norman Shaw's pioneering red brick mansion block of 1879, a plaque commemorates Sir Malcolm Sargent, a dominant figure in London's musical life from the 1930s to the 1950s. While you are here you could walk down Hyde Park Gate, a little street running south off Kensington Road, just to the west of the Royal Albert Hall. There are plaques here marking the homes of Sir Winston Churchill (who died at number 28 in 1965), the Boer War hero and founder of the Boy Scouts Lord (Robert) Baden-Powell (number 9), the sculptor Sir Jacob Epstein (18) and Sir Leslie Stephen (22), the first editor of the *Dictionary of National Biography* and thus the historian's great benefactor.

If any twentieth-century figure had more influence on London's musical life than Henry Wood it was Thomas Beecham, the man most responsible for London's wealth of top-class symphony orchestras. Beecham arrived in London to study music around 1900, and within a decade, and still in his twenties, he had formed two high-quality orchestras. The fact that his father, a manufacturing chemist, had enough money to buy the Covent Garden estate (including the Opera House and the Theatre Royal Drury Lane) from the Duke of Bedford in 1916 eased Beecham's path, but Beecham was a musical entrepreneur of unusual skill and energy. In 1932, having failed to gain a permanent position with the two established London orchestras, the LSO and the BBC Symphony Orchestra (founded in 1930 under Adrian Boult), Beecham formed a new orchestra (his third), the London Philharmonic, which was probably the best in Europe, and based it in the Queen's Hall. In October 1945 London got a fourth permanent orchestra when Walter Legge of EMI formed the Philharmonia, primarily as a recording orchestra. Beecham conducted the Philharmonia's inaugural concert, but he now had no permanent orchestra of his own. To remedy this he created another orchestra, the Royal Philharmonic. This meant that London had five major orchestras, two of which had been created by Beecham: the LSO, the BBC Symphony, the LPO, the Philharmonia and the RPO. The RPO is now resident at the Cadogan Hall, behind Sloane Square, the Philharmonia and the LPO are based at the Royal Festival Hall, and the LSO is now the resident orchestra in the Barbican Centre.

As well as the big five, London has many smaller chamber orchestras, including the London Chamber Orchestra (founded in 1921 and resident at St John Smith Square), the London Symphonietta, the Academy of St Martin-in-the-Fields (founded in 1958 and resident in its church on Trafalgar Square) and the London Mozart Players (founded in 1949). No great city has as many permanent commercial orchestras as London. Their survival is made possible by the size of concert audiences, the patronage of the BBC and the strength of London's recording industry.

Before the coming of recording and broadcasting, most Victorian Londoners heard their music in music halls, either in central London or the suburbs. The first large-scale music hall (as opposed to a public house with singing) was Charles Morton's Canterbury, which opened in 1852. In late-Victorian London there were over a hundred music halls, as well as variety theatres and suburban 'Empires' which offered very similar entertainment. Changing tastes, especially the rise of the cinema, undermined the popular appeal of music hall, and nearly all of the London halls were demolished or converted into theatres or cinemas in the early twentieth century. Of those that survived the 1930s, some were destroyed in the

Blitz, and the last disappeared in the 1950s and 1960s. The Royal Holborn (the Holborn Empire), the last true West End music hall, was destroyed by bombing in 1941 and the Canterbury only lasted a few months longer. The Holborn was on the corner of Holborn and Little Turnstile, and the Canterbury on Westminster Bridge Road between Upper Marsh and Carlisle Lane. Collins Music Hall in Islington burned down in 1958, and the Metropolitan Music Hall on Edgware Road, one of the oldest, was demolished in 1963. It was on the west side of Edgware Road, just north of Harrow Road, opposite Bell Street.

One of London's last surviving music halls, Wilton's, opened in 1858 and closed in 1884, when the building was taken over by Methodist missionaries. They sold it as a rag warehouse in 1956, and it was saved from destruction in the 1960s by John Betjeman and others. Now a trust is struggling to keep Wilton's alive, staging plays and operas rather than music hall shows, and giving guided tours. So you can look around a real Victorian music hall with a surprisingly fine interior, and at the same time contribute something to its survival. You can find out about tours and shows by going to www.wiltons.org.uk or phoning 020 7702 9555. Wilton's is in Graces Alley, off Ensign Street, near Wellclose Square, a short walk from Tower Hill or Aldgate East Tube stations.

Another east London music hall has survived, in what is left of the old village of Hoxton. Hoxton Hall is at 130a Hoxton Street, a few streets away from the Geffrye Almshouses. It is better seen from a little alley, Wilks Place. The music hall was established in 1863 and became McDonald's Music Hall in 1866. The hall was closed for most of the 1870s, because of licensing difficulties and perhaps competition from the much bigger and more successful Britannia Theatre. In 1879 it was bought by the Blue Ribbon Temperance Mission, a Quaker organization. The Quaker Bedford Institute continued to use the hall for services, but in 1976 they gave control of it to a group interested in restoring it as a youth theatre and community arts centre. To see what is happening there, visit www.hoxtonhall.co.uk. This area is rich in theatrical associations. The Britannia Saloon was rebuilt as the 4,000-seat Britannia Theatre in 1858, and this was one of the most important popular theatres in north-east London until it was converted into a cinema in the Great War. It was destroyed by bombing in 1940. Its site is on the west side of Hoxton Street, between Fanshawe Street and Myrtle Street, where there is a plaque. Two other plaques on this short stretch of Hoxton Street commemorate the discovery of the Gunpowder Plot and Pollock's Toy Theatre Museum, which was also destroyed in the Blitz.

If you walk south on Hoxton Street and cross Old Street you will find Curtain Street, which is the birthplace of the Elizabethan theatre. On your left, on the corner of New Inn Yard, Richard Burbage built The Theatre in 1576, in the grounds of the demolished Holywell Priory. This was the playhouse dismantled and carried across London in 1597, and re-erected on Bankside as the Globe. A little further south, roughly on the corner of Hewett Street, is the site of the second of London's purpose-built theatres, the Curtain, which was here from 1577 at least until the late 1620s, and possibly until 1642. Shakespeare acted at the Curtain, and it is quite likely that *Henry V* and *Romeo and Juliet* had their first performances there and that it was therefore the famous 'wooden O' mentioned in the opening speech of *Henry V*. Nothing now commemorates this historic spot. Curtain Street, Great Eastern Street, and the other messy and interesting streets around here were the centre of London's cheap furniture industry in the later nineteenth century, and there are several reminders of this in the warehouses and workshops that survive in the neighbourhood.

The great variety theatres that were built in London between 1885 and 1914 offered entertainment rather like that of music halls, but in a twice-nightly programme rather than a whole evening of 'turns', and without the free and easy eating and drinking that was usual in music halls. Their architecture, seating and sense of occasion were drawn from the theatre, not (as with true music halls) the public house. Several of these theatres of varieties still exist, offering plays or musicals and occasional variety shows. The London Pavilion, built on Piccadilly Circus in 1885, was the first really big West End music hall theatre. The owners bribed Metropolitan Board of Works officials to get the site, and built it in four months, using electric light to work at night. It was reconstructed in 1934 and again in 1986, so only the exterior looks Victorian. The London Hippodrome, between Charing Cross Road and Leicester Square, was built by Frank Matcham in 1898–1900 as a floodable circus which could stage water shows. Its interior was rebuilt in the 1950s, and its present owners use it as a nightclub, casino, conference centre and circus. Its lavish exterior is worth lingering over. Nearby, on Cambridge Circus, the Palace Theatre is in much better shape. It was built as a grand opera house by Richard D'Oyly Carte in 1888–91 (from his Gilbert and Sullivan profits), and still looks like this, both inside and out. It became a music hall in 1892, and switched to musicals, its current speciality, in the 1920s. The London Palladium, on Argyll Street, near Oxford Circus, is also in good hands. It was built as the Corinthian Bazaar and Exhibition Rooms in 1867, with great wine cellars beneath, and was used as a circus for about forty years, until Frank Matcham converted it into a music hall or theatre of varieties in 1909. It now stages lavish musicals, with an occasional variety show.

The Coliseum, in St Martin's Lane, looks like a true theatre of varieties. It was built by Matcham in 1902 for Oswald Stoll as a 'People's Palace of Entertainment and Art', and it has been the home of the English National Opera since 1968. If you go to an opera there, look around and enjoy the newly restored Frank Matcham interior. The Victoria Palace Theatre, opposite Victoria Station, was built on the site of the Royal Standard Music Hall, perhaps reusing part of the old building, by Matcham in 1911. It operated for twenty years as a music hall, but switched to revue, then to straight theatre, in the 1930s. Its production of Noel Gay's *Me and My Gal* was one of the last great pre-war hits, and featured one of the most famous London song and dance tunes, 'The Lambeth Walk', which was used as a morale-booster during the Second World War. Between 1947 and 1962 the Victoria Palace was almost monopolized by the Crazy Gang, a song and comedy act in the old music hall tradition, and in the 1970s it was the home of the Black and White Minstrels. It now stages musicals. Finally, the Lyceum on Wellington Street and the Strand, which has a fine 1834 exterior, was reconstructed internally as a music hall or variety theatre by Bertie Crewe in 1904. For most of the next 35 years, under the control of the Melville brothers, it staged very light musical comedies and pantomimes. The outbreak of war in 1939 saved it from demolition, and in 1951 it became a Mecca ballroom. In 1996, surprisingly, it was restored as a musical theatre, so now you can see Crewe's lavish interior once again, doing what it was designed to do.

Away from central London, the Old Vic, on the corner of Waterloo Road and the New Cut, was a music hall in the 1870s and a temperance music hall from 1880 almost to the Great War. It was built as the Royal Coburg Theatre in 1818, and still has a late-Georgian exterior, but its interior has been rebuilt several times. Its great days as a Shakespearean theatre lasted from 1914 to 1976, when the National Theatre moved to the South Bank. Now it stages straight plays with an occasional pantomime.

Early in the twentieth century Frank Matcham built huge suburban variety theatres, all called Empires, for the Oswald Stoll organization in Hackney, Shepherd's Bush, Chiswick, Finsbury Park and Wood Green. Most were demolished in the early 1960s, but two, the Shepherd's Bush and Hackney Empires, still exist, and both are still places of entertainment. The Shepherd's Bush Empire (built on Shepherd's Bush Green in 1903) survived as a BBC recording theatre from 1953 to 1994, and is now a successful popular music venue. Best of all, the Hackney Empire, which lived through the dangerous 1960s and 1970s as a bingo hall, was reopened as a theatre in 1986 and has now been restored to the condition it was in when Marie Lloyd topped the bill. The Hackney Empire was built in 1901, baroque terracotta without and marble and rococo plasterwork within. To see what it has to offer now, go to www.hackneyempire.co.uk, where you will also find out about tours of the theatre on the first Saturday morning of each month.

East London has another fine Victorian theatre with strong musical traditions and a Matcham connection. The Theatre Royal, Stratford East, on Salway Road, near Stratford station and shopping centre, was built by James Buckle for the actor-manager Charles Dillon in 1883, and restored and refitted by Matcham in 1902, when electric lighting was installed. Beaten by the cinema, the theatre closed in 1926, reopening briefly from time to time over the next 25 years. Its revival began in 1953, when Joan Littlewood's Theatre Workshop Company, founded in the idealistic days after the Second World War, leased the theatre. Littlewood's most celebrated musical success was *Oh What a Lovely War!* (1963). In the late 1960s the company saved the theatre from demolition – the town planners' answer to every problem in those days – and it was beautifully restored in the 1990s, returning the auditorium, foyer and bar to their old Edwardian splendour. The theatre has adapted its output to reflect the changing nature of the local community, and is still going strong. Its productions are listed on its website, www.stratfordeast.org.uk.

There was another chain of suburban variety theatres in Edwardian London, the United Variety Syndicate. A single survivor of its chain of theatres still stands on Tottenham High Road, at numbers 421–7. This was the Tottenham Palace Theatre, built by Oswald Wylson in 1908, a cinema from 1922 to 1968 and a bingo hall for the next thirty years. Now it has been converted into an evangelical church, the Palace Cathedral, but though its theatre stalls are gone its baroque exterior and elaborately plastered interior still remind us of its original purpose and the possibility of a return to it.

If one parent of modern popular music was the music hall, another was the musical theatre. So if we are looking for the birthplace of modern popular music in London, the Savoy Theatre on the Strand, where most of the great Gilbert and Sullivan light operas were staged in the 1880s, is a good candidate. The Savoy operas laid the foundations for the musicals that played such an important part in the development of popular music in England and America in the twentieth century, and were admired and emulated by the great American popular composers. The theatre was built in 1881 with the profits from the early Gilbert and Sullivan operettas, but shifted its emphasis to straight plays after 1903. It was reconstructed in 1929 and again after a fire in 1990, so a visitor today will find it hard to recapture the spirit of the 1880s. For somewhere that still summons up the spirit of the late-Victorian and Edwardian musical theatre, it might be better to go to the Lyric Theatre on Shaftesbury Avenue (near Piccadilly Circus), which has not changed much since C.J. Phipps (the architect of the Savoy Theatre) built it in 1888. This was the theatre that staged the most successful late-Victorian musical comedy, Leslie Stuart's *Floradora*, followed by Oscar Straus's *The Chocolate Soldier*, making the transition from operetta to musical.

For the coming of the jazz age, the Hammersmith Palais de Danse (230 Shepherd's Bush Road, demolished in 2007), at which the Original Dixieland Jazz Band performed from October 1919, was a symbolic location, though this pioneering jazz band also performed at the Palladium in Argyll Street, and gave its first performance, and therefore London's first jazz show, at the Hippodrome in Charing Cross Road in April 1919. Marion Cook's Southern Syncopated Orchestra, which played at the Royal Albert Hall and many other places in London, was equally influential. Travelling with them, the clarinettist Sidney Bechet saw and bought a soprano saxophone in J.R. Lafleur's music shop at 147 Wardour Street and transformed his career. In the 1930s and 1940s all the great American stars – Duke Ellington, Fats Waller, Louis Armstrong, Count Basie – appeared at the Palladium. Other places in London with strong associations with the jazz age include the

Streatham Locarno ballroom (156–160 Streatham Hill, now Caesar's nightclub), which opened in 1929, the Savoy Hotel and the Café de Paris at 3 Coventry Street, near Piccadilly Circus. The Café de Paris opened in 1924 and became a favourite with London high society, a place where you might meet the Prince of Wales or Cole Porter. It was hit by two huge landmines on 8 March 1941, and 80 customers and performers were killed. It is in business again now, a cabaret and restaurant open to the public on Saturday nights.

If London has an equivalent to New York's Tin Pan Alley (28th Street) it must be Denmark Street and the nearby stretch of Charing Cross Road. Francis Day and Hunter, the music publisher, moved to Charing Cross Road in 1897, and in 1911 the prolific songwriter and publisher Lawrence Wright started a business in the basement of 8 Denmark Street. After the Great War he moved to 19 Denmark Street, Wright House, from which he published the *Melody Maker*, mainly to promote songs written by Horatio Nicholls (his own nom de plume) and the American jazz standards whose English rights he owned. Rose Morris, which still sells instruments and music at number 11, moved here in 1919. The leading music magazine of the rock and roll age, the *New Musical Express*, was also started in Denmark Street, in 1952. In the 1960s the street became the centre of the new popular music, and its basement recording studios helped start the careers of several famous bands. In 1964 the Rolling Stones recorded their first two albums in Regent Sounds Studio, at number 4, and another independent studio important to rock musicians, Tin Pan Alley (TPA) Studios, still operates from number 22. The early careers of David Bowie, Elton John, the Kinks, the Small Faces, Bob Marley, the Sex Pistols (who rehearsed behind number 6) and dozens of other 1960s and 1970s stars centred on Denmark Street, and the street's Giaconda Café (which was at number 9) was a leading social centre and recruiting ground for musicians. Denmark Street still has a good concentration of shops selling music and musical instruments, especially guitars, as well as recording studios. To listen to live music here, you might try 12 Bar Club (www.12barclub.com)

in Denmark Place (parallel to Denmark Street), a folk/popular music club in a late-seventeenth-century cellar. Denmark Street was laid out in 1687, and numbers 5–7, 9 and 10 date from this time.

London has been a major recording centre for a century. In 1908 the Gramophone Company built a large factory and studio at Hayes in Middlesex. This was greatly extended after 1931, when the company amalgamated with Columbia to form EMI. That same year EMI opened its new recording studios at 3 Abbey Road, near St John's Wood Underground station, which were used over the next seventy years by some of the world's greatest classical and popular artists. Edward Elgar, Yehudi Menuhin, Artur Schnabel, Thomas Beecham, Paul Robeson, Noël Coward, Fred Astaire, Fats Waller, Glenn Miller, Janet Baker and Cliff Richard all recorded here, and in the 1960s Abbey Road was the studio from which George Martin produced all the Beatles' hits. In their golden year, 1963, 15 of the 19 UK number one singles came from Abbey Road's Studio 2, and six years later the cover of the Beatles' last album made its zebra crossing the most famous in England. The studios are still considered among the best in the world.

There are studios with an impressive list of historic rock recordings all over London. Olympic Studios in Barnes, still at 117 Church Road, are where the Rolling Stones recorded their albums between 1967 and 1972, Led Zeppelin recorded albums between 1968 and 1975, and Jimi Hendrix made his ground-breaking *Are You Experienced?* in 1966/7. Eric Clapton recorded here in the 1970s, Morrissey and Queen in the 1980s, Oasis in the 1990s, Coldplay, Arctic Monkeys and the Kaiser Chiefs in the 2000s. The Beatles used the studios sometimes in the 1960s, but more important for them was Trident Studio (now the Sound Studio) in St Anne's Court, between Dean Street and Wardour Street, where 'Hey Jude' was recorded in 1968.

Beatles fans can visit several important sites that relate to the group's life and work in London between 1963 and 1969, all within walking distance of each other. Starting at Marble Arch, it is a short walk to 57 Green Street, two blocks south of Oxford Street. This is where all four Beatles lived in a fourth-floor flat, their first London home, from autumn 1963 to spring 1964. You could walk north up Quebec Street or Portman Street to Montagu Square, where Ringo Starr lived in a ground-floor flat at number 34, in 1965. Later he lent it to Jimi Hendrix and to John Lennon, who was caught with drugs during a police raid here in 1968. Walk east along George Street and New Cavendish Street to Wimpole Street, where Paul McCartney lived with Jane Asher's family at number 57 in 1964–5. This is where Lennon and McCartney wrote 'I Want to Hold Your Hand', 'Eleanor Rigby' and 'Yesterday'. Walk back to Oxford Circus to find Argyll Street, the first right turn as you walk east on Oxford Street. The London Palladium, on 13 October 1963, was where Beatlemania was born (or named), when crowds of fans mobbed the group after a televised Sunday night performance. Next door, in Sutherland House, was the office that the Beatles' manager, Brian Epstein, moved into (from 13 Monmouth Street) in 1964. Now walk down Regent Street and turn right into New Burlington Street and left into Savile Row. On 30 January 1969 the Beatles gave their last public show (including their famous performance of 'Get Back') on the roof of the Apple headquarters at 3 Savile Row, a house once bought for Lady Hamilton by Lord Nelson. The Savile Row rooftop concert can be seen at the end of the film *Let It Be.*

*

The most important performance venues in the history of London popular music in the mid- and late twentieth century were not concert halls, but clubs. Most of these were ephemeral places, closed by bankruptcy, drug raids, changing fashions or moves to larger premises. The Embassy Club, which opened at 6–8 Old Bond Street in 1924, was one of the first London nightclubs. Its resident band-leader for much of the 1920s and 1930s was Bert Ambrose. There were dozens of jazz clubs in Soho from the 1920s to the 1950s, and a few survived into the rock and roll age, or even to the present day, by changing the music they offered, moving from jazz to skiffle, then on to rhythm and blues and rock and roll.

One of the leading jazz clubs of the 1920s, the Bag O'Nails, at 9 Kingley Street, between Regent Street and Carnaby Street, survived to host the Beatles and to give the Jimi Hendrix Experience their first big break in 1966. It is now a members' club called Miranda's. Round the corner in Old Compton Street the 2i's coffee bar, where the first English rock stars, Tommy Steele and Adam Faith, were discovered, used to be at number 59, which has a green plaque to prove it. Of the many other jazz and rock clubs in and around Wardour Street and Dean Street perhaps the most important was the Marquee, a jazz club that began at 165 Oxford Street (under the Academy cinema) and moved to a warehouse at 90 Wardour Street in 1964. Many of the great names in rock music, including the Rolling Stones, The Who, David Bowie, Manfred Mann, the Cream, the Sex Pistols, the Clash and the Police, made early appearances there, and often continued to play at the Marquee when they were famous, despite its sticky floor and unsavoury smells. Although the Marquee name is still used by a London music club, the real Marquee closed in 1988, and the building was converted into shops and housing by Soho Lofts in the 1990s.

Another important location in the history of skiffle, blues, rock and pop music in the 1950s and 1960s was the Roundhouse pub on the south corner of Wardour Street and Brewer Street, where musicians like Alexis Korner and Cyril Davies started moving from skiffle, the home-grown fashion, to American-influenced blues in the later 1950s. It is now a bar, but its old name, carved in stone, is still visible. At 100 Oxford Street, at the northern end of Wardour Street, another club managed to surf the different waves of musical taste even more successfully. The 100 Club was started as Mack's, a jazz club, in 1942, and was known as the Humphrey Lyttelton Club from 1956, when it was the centre of the trad jazz boom (Acker Bilk, Kenny Ball and the rest). It switched its name and allegiance to rock and roll in the 1960s. In 1976 it hosted London's first punk

festival, and accommodated every successive musical fashion there-
after, while still keeping a tapping foot in the jazz camp.

In 1959, when most London jazz clubs were about to be
overwhelmed by the popularity of blues, skiffle and rock and roll,
Ronnie Scott and Pete King opened a club that would keep jazz
alive in central London. Ronnie Scott's first club was at 39 Gerrard
Street, in a house built in 1737. The easing of restrictions on
the employment of American musicians in 1961 helped the club
to thrive, and in 1965 it moved to a fine late-Georgian house at
47 Frith Street, its present home.

Although Soho has been the home of London popular music
from jazz to punk and beyond, the suburbs of west and south-west
London can claim to have played an important part in the history
of rock and roll. In the 1960s Pete Townshend, Ronnie Wood
and Freddie Mercury, later of The Who, Rolling Stones and Queen
respectively, and David Bowie were students at Ealing Art College,
which is now part of Thames Valley University, in St Mary's
Road, Ealing. In April 1962 in his Ealing Jazz Club in the basement
of 42a Ealing Broadway, Alexis Korner introduced Mick Jagger to
Ronnie Wood and Brian Jones, a meeting which led to the formation
of the Rolling Stones a few months later. This is also where The
Who, who were based in Ealing, played as the Detours, and where
such future stars as Rod Stewart and Paul Jones honed their skills.
The club still exists, as the Red Room, but it is not what it was.
The first gig of the newly formed Rolling Stones, in February 1963,
was in a new club opposite Richmond station, the Crawdaddy Club
in the Station Hotel. The popularity of the Rolling Stones forced
the Crawdaddy to move to a bigger room in Richmond Athletic
Ground, and in April 1963 the group also started performing in
a jazz club in Twickenham, the Eel Pie Island Hotel, which had a
good pre-war dance floor. Other west London groups, including
The Who and the Yardbirds (from Kingston), played on Eel Pie
Island, along with Rod Stewart, David Bowie, Paul Jones and the
influential Long John Baldry, but the club closed in 1967 and

the hotel burned down in 1971. The Station Hotel in Richmond is now the Bull, and a very far cry from what it was in the early 1960s.

The best musical instrument collection in London today is in the rather out-of-the-way Horniman Museum in south London, at 100 London Road, Forest Hill (part of the South Circular Road), near Forest Hill station. It is open every day, admission is free, and it has over 7,000 musical instruments. The Horniman Museum has many attractions, but if it seems too far, there are two good musical collections in South Kensington. The Victoria and Albert Museum has many musical instruments in its huge collections, and the Royal College of Music in Prince Consort Road (near the Albert Hall) has a collection of over 800. It is part of the College's Centre for Performance History, which can be visited free of charge from Tuesday to Friday, between 2.00 and 4.30. The website is www.cph.rcm.ac.uk. Those interested in mechanical instruments, which were such an important part of London's street life in the eighteenth and nineteenth centuries, should take a trip to the Musical Museum in Kew Bridge Road, Brentford. The museum has everything from musical boxes to the Mighty Wurlitzer, which can be heard in action in its concert hall. It is open every day but Monday and costs about £7, but you should check its website, www.musicalmuseum.co.uk, for details of times and prices. The museum is near Kew Bridge station, the Kew Steam Museum and (over the bridge) Kew Gardens.

Like other great cities, London has been celebrated or remembered in many pieces of music. Joseph Haydn's twelve London symphonies (numbers 93–104) were written here between 1791 and 1795, but they are named only for their place of composition. The music of Handel, especially that composed for great London occasions (the *Water Music* and *Music for the Royal Fireworks*), and the songs of Thomas Arne, especially his patriotic songs for the theatre, evoke the spirit of eighteenth-century London more powerfully. The songs written by William Boyce, Arne, Handel and J.C. Bach for performance at Vauxhall Gardens, which are available on CD, are true London pieces. Best of all, John Gay's immensely popular ballad opera *The Beggar's Opera*, packed with traditional urban and rustic melodies dealing with themes of organized crime, corruption and philandering, captures the boisterous atmosphere of London in the 1720s.

Some Victorian and Edwardian music hall songs give a strong sense of the city that produced them: Vesta Tilley's 'Burlington Bertie' (words and music William Hargreaves, 1915), Marie Lloyd's 'My Old Man' and the coster songs written and performed by Albert Chevalier ('My Old Dutch', 'Knocked 'em in the Old Kent Road' and ''Appy 'Ampstead') and Gus Elen ('If It Wasn't for the Houses in Between' and 'It's a Great Big Shame'). Several twentieth-century composers have written about London, beginning with Ralph Vaughan Williams' *London Symphony* (1913), which refers to the noise and hurry of London, the atmosphere of a Bloomsbury square and Westminster Embankment, and a voyage down the river. Albert Ketélbey, a popular composer of atmospheric pieces, wrote a *Cockney Suite* in 1924, with an effective finale on ''Appy 'Ampstead'. Eric Coates, who worked in London from the 1900s to the 1950s, produced something similar, the *London Suite*, in 1932. Its third movement, the 'Knightsbridge March', became famous as the signature tune of the long-running programme *In Town Tonight*. The songs of Ivor Novello and Noël Coward evoke the upper-class world of interwar London as effectively as music hall songs evoke an earlier working-class world.

There are many twentieth-century popular songs with a London setting, from Gershwin's 'A Foggy Day', Manning Sherwin and Eric Maschwitz's 'A Nightingale Sang in Berkeley Square' and Sandy Wilson's 'A Room in Bloomsbury', to the Smiths' 'London', the Pogues' 'A Rainy Night in Soho', and 'Waterloo Sunset', written by Ray Davies and recorded by the Kinks in 1968 ('Dirty old river . . .'), which does a good job of describing a melancholy riverside atmosphere, and the great pleasure of watching the sun setting from Waterloo Bridge. Perhaps there is no really great London song, the equal of Rodgers and Hart's 'Manhattan', but many would say that the best twentieth-century song really about Londoners and their city is Noël Coward's 'London Pride', which was written in 1941, when a quarter of the City had been destroyed and Londoners deserved to have songs sung in their praise. The tune is based on the London lavender sellers' cry, 'Won't you buy my sweet blooming lavender', and the words capture the moment when London stood on the front line against Nazism: 'In our city darkened now, street and square and crescent, / We can feel our living past in our shadowed present, / ... Grey city, stubbornly implanted, taken so for granted for a thousand years. / Stay, city, smokily enchanted, cradle of our memories and hopes and fears.'

There is a good collection of London songs sung by Catherine Bott, called *London Pride* (Hyperion CDA67457), which includes some enjoyable rarities.

CHAPTER SIX

LONDON PUBS

The George and Vulture

ALTHOUGH LONDON has changed out of all recognition over the centuries, a few institutions have maintained a continuity of existence, purpose and even appearance for a millennium. Two of the city's most enduring institutions, the church and the drinking house, might be seen as rivals and opposites, but in their different ways both have served the needs of Londoners for a thousand years or more. London's churches have managed to retain rather more of their ancient fabric, but its public houses have kept more of their customers, and a greater part of their central role in London society.

The earliest substantial description of London, in the prologue to William FitzStephen's *Life of St Thomas Becket*, written around 1173, mentions London's drinking houses and the early history of binge drinking. He talks of the wine for sale in ships and vintners' cellars, and makes only one significant criticism of the city: 'the only plagues of London are the immoderate drinking of fools and the frequency of fires'. The two evils seem to have been connected, because a City order of about 1190 closed all unlicensed alehouses except those made of stone, because of the danger of fire. In 1309, despite such restrictions, there were said to be 354 taverns (generally selling wine) and about 1,330 aleshops and brewhouses (making and selling beer) in London, a city of about 60,000 or so. About seventy years later, it was into one of these alehouses that Gluttony, representing one of the seven deadly sins in William Langland's *Piers the Ploughman*, was lured by Betty the ale-wife while on his way to confession. Inside he found as varied a fictional gathering as that assembled by Langland's contemporary Geoffrey Chaucer in the

Tabard Inn, at the start of their pilgrimage to Canterbury. Gluttony was welcomed by Cissie the shoemaker, Wat the gamekeeper and his wife, Tim the tinker, Hick the hackneyman, Hugh the haber-dasher, Clarice the whore of Cock Lane, the parish clerk, Davy the ditcher, Peacock the Flemish wench, Father Peter of Prie-Dieu Abbey, Rose the pewterer, Griffiths the Welshman, a Cheapside scavenger, a fiddler, and a company of apprentices, tradesmen and auctioneers.

During the Middle Ages the brewer-retailer tended to give way to the alehouse keeper who bought beer from a larger local brewer, a process which was encouraged by the introduction after about 1400 of the German and Flemish practice of using hops rather than spices to flavour and preserve beer. With this more stable and long-lived product it was no longer so advantageous to brew and sell from the same building. In most other respects, the London alehouse seems to have been much as it was in Langland's day, a simple meeting place for ordinary Londoners who wanted to drink, eat, talk, gamble, do business and relax.

In the sixteenth century London's population grew very rapidly, and it seems that the number of inns, taverns and alehouses increased to keep pace with the growth in demand. Some riverside beer houses are marked on the Braun and Hogenberg map of London published in 1572. Visitors to Elizabethan London were amazed at the concentration of drinking houses, and a survey in 1657 found 924 licensed alehouses within the City. This impressive figure would probably double if we added all the inns, taverns and unlicensed alehouses in Cromwellian London.

In the late seventeenth and eighteenth centuries simple medieval and Tudor alehouses were generally replaced by more elaborate brick buildings (meeting post-Fire building regulations), which often had stabling for the growing number of stagecoaches linking London with the provinces. Some new pubs occupied small medieval sites, but most were larger, with more rooms, so that customers who had once drunk in the landlord's kitchen could now, if they chose, drink in his parlour instead. Modern eighteenth-century public houses had a cellar for storing drink and a bar for serving it, and rooms upstairs for games, lodging or club meetings. Rents were higher, and in London from the 1750s only larger public houses, rented at £12 a year at least, could sell spirits. The rise of big commercial brewers (Fullers, Trumans, Whitbread, Barclays and others) in the later eighteenth century turned most publicans from brewers into retailers, sometimes tied to one supplier. Social and religious pressures made it difficult for small and unlicensed drinking houses to survive, and this combination of commercial, social and political changes tended to drive the labourer who kept a small alehouse as a sideline out of business, replacing him (or her) with full-time innkeepers who made a substantial livelihood from the trade. Simple alehouses of the medieval or Tudor type hardly exist in London now, though a few, like the Seven Stars in Carey Street, retain something of their pre-Hanoverian simplicity.

Some of the biggest and most important early-nineteenth-century drinking places were coaching inns that drew their prosperity from the long-distance coaching trade. They used to appear regularly on Christmas cards and are familiar to us now from the novels of Dickens, who wrote as most of them were disappearing, victims of the rise of the railway and the railway hotel. Coaching inns were especially common on the main roads out of London: Piccadilly, Oxford Street, Bishopsgate, Aldgate, Borough High Street, and so on. Still, side alleys on these main streets have names that recall the inns that once occupied them, and on eighteenth- and nineteenth-century maps you can see many more. By Aldgate, where passengers took coaches to Essex, you can still find Mitre Street, Saracen's Head Yard and Hartshorn Alley, all named after vanished inns. Nothing illustrates the prevalence and disappearance of coaching inns better than a walk down Borough High Street, which has a long succession of inn yards on its eastern side, mostly now empty. White Hart Yard was the scene of one of the most celebrated fictional meetings, between Pickwick and Sam Weller, and Talbot Yard, a few metres further on, was the scene of an even greater meeting, of the pilgrims who were about to set off for Canterbury, telling tales as they went. In between these two is the George, London's last remaining galleried coaching inn, which was rebuilt after the Southwark fire of 1676. Even this is only half of what it used to be, thanks to the demolition of its northern part by the Great Northern Railway company in 1889. It is now owned and run by the National Trust.

The popularity of gin in eighteenth-century London led to the rise of hundreds of gin and spirit shops, which generally did not offer the home comforts available in taverns and inns. Despite the powerful campaign against gin drinking in the 1730s and 1740s the taste for gin was still strong in the early nineteenth century, and in the 1810s London had hundreds of simple single-roomed dram shops. In the 1820s and 1830s some gin sellers began building larger and more luxurious premises, taking advantage of new developments in gas lighting and plate glass, and imitating similar developments in shop design. Critics called these places gin palaces, but they sold wine and beer as well as spirits, and set a standard in design and comfort for other drink sellers to follow. The early gin palaces seem to have been pretty modest places, but compared to what they replaced they were bright and lavish. Dickens, in *Sketches by Boz* (1836), described a gin palace in the St Giles rookery:

All is light and brilliancy ... the gay building with the fantastically ornamented parapet, the illuminated clock, the plate-glass windows surrounded by stucco rosettes, and its profusion of gas-lights in richly gilt burners, is perfectly dazzling when contrasted with the darkness and dirt we have just left. The interior is even gayer than the exterior. A bar of French-polished mahogany, elegantly carved, extends the whole width of the place; and there are two side-aisles of great casks ... Beyond the bar is a lofty and spacious saloon, full of the same enticing vessels, with a gallery running round it, equally well furnished.

LONDON PUBS

The style of these new premises influenced the design of many later Victorian public houses, and Victorian pubs with plenty of cut glass, mirrors and bright lights are often called gin palaces, even though their trade was mainly in beer or wine. Many of these ornate public houses survive in London, along with a huge number of less elaborate local pubs. Most of London's more ostentatious public houses were built or rebuilt in the later 1890s, when the Conservative electoral victory of 1895 relieved the drink trade from the threat of temperance legislation, which always seemed likely under Liberal governments. This pub-building boom ended in a wave of bankruptcies after 1899, but enough 1890s public houses survive in London to remind us of the splendour of late-Victorian pub design.

The new Arts and Crafts decorative style influenced pub design in the 1890s and 1900s, with tiles and mosaics replacing the glass and mirrors of the gin palace style. London still has a few of these art nouveau pubs, notably the Black Friar, the Coal Hole in the Strand, and the Fox and Anchor, Charterhouse Street (now re-opened). A feature of Victorian pubs, beginning in the 1850s, was the division of the drinking area into many small bars the size of railway compartments. It was common by the 1870s for a public bar to be separated from several private bars by wood and glass partitions. By the 1890s there were pubs in London with about ten compartments, or boxes, but then the fashion changed, and by the 1950s there were hardly any of these subdivided pubs left in London. The Barley Mow in Dorset Street, the oldest pub in Marylebone (1791), still has some subdivisions, and so do the Argyll near Oxford Circus, the Prince Alfred in Formosa Street, and the Windsor Castle in Campden Hill Road, near Notting Hill Gate Tube station, a popular and unpretentious pub that dates from 1835.

*

There are no medieval alehouses left in London today, although several pubs can trace the origins of their name and location back to the Middle Ages. All those within the area destroyed in the Great

Fire of 1666 (80 per cent of the walled City) are gone (though perhaps rebuilt), and many others were demolished or rebuilt, especially in the nineteenth century. Therefore London's oldest surviving public houses are to be found in what were the sixteenth-century suburbs.

There is a good concentration of very old pubs, with sixteenth- and seventeenth-century buildings, on the Wapping and Shadwell riverside, which was part of the working port of London from the sixteenth century to the twentieth. A walk from Tower Bridge along the river in front of St Katharine's Dock brings you to Wapping High Street, which was once a canyon of warehouses, many of which are now converted into smart flats and studios. Wapping High Street suffered great damage in the Blitz, and most of its western end is occupied by modern blocks of flats. You cross the Hermitage Wharf entrance to London Docks, and then the Wapping entrance, before coming to Wapping Old Stairs, a narrow way down to the river. This is where pirates (including Captain Kidd) and other seafaring wrongdoers were hanged, and where the notorious hanging judge, George Jeffreys, was captured as he tried to escape dressed as a sailor during the Revolution of November 1688.

Nearby, at 62 Wapping High Street, standing on its original narrow sixteenth-century plot, is the Town Of Ramsgate, one of the thirty-odd pubs that used to cater for the thirsty sailors and dockers of the street. The pub is of uncertain age, but its dark interior takes you back to the days when Captain Bligh and Fletcher Christian had a last drink here before the *Bounty* set sail, and convicts bound for Australia were held in the basement. Continue along Wapping High Street, passing the Edwardian river police station, which is on the spot where the Marine Police office was founded in 1798 to protect the ships and goods of West India merchants. Wapping railway station is built above the entrance to the world's first underwater tunnel (*see* Chapter Ten). Continue east on Wapping High Street until the road goes left at New Crane Place and its converted 1880s warehouses. Here, turn right into Wapping Wall, lined with converted mid- and late-Victorian warehouses, until you get to Pelican Wharf and Pelican Stairs. Here is probably London's oldest public house, the Prospect of Whitby. The facade is nine-teenth century, and the oldest feature, its panelling, is eighteenth century, but the pub occupies a small sixteenth-century plot, and may well date from about 1520. It was called the Devil's Tavern until the eighteenth century, when it was rebuilt following a fire and renamed after a ship moored nearby.

If you fancy a third East End riverside pub, keep walking east along Wapping Wall, and north when it becomes Glamis Road. Turn right into the Highway, along the northern side of King Edward VII Memorial Park, until it is crossed by Butcher Row and Narrow Street. Turn right into the latter, a riverside street lined with converted warehouses. The road crosses the entrance to the Lime-house Basin, the start of the Regent's Canal (heading for the Grand Union Canal and the Midlands) and the Limehouse Cut (from the River Lea). Ropemakers' Fields, on the left, is a reminder of a vanished riverside industry. After this there is a lovely row of old houses, starting at number 78 with the early-eighteenth-century Grapes public house, and ending with a very well-preserved late-seventeenth-century house which is now a pleasant East End pub called Booty's Bar. Booty's Bar is not as old as its premises, but the Grapes (previously the Bunch of Grapes) has been serving riverside workers of one class or another since about 1720, when it was built on the site of an earlier pub. Most old public houses claim a connection with Charles Dickens, but the Grapes' claim is stronger than most. Dickens knew this pub well, and based the pub in *Our Mutual Friend*, the Six Jolly Fellowship Porters, 'a tavern of dropsical appearance ... long settled down into a state of hale infirmity', partly on it. It is claimed that Dickens wrote part of *Great Expecta-tions*, which drew upon his knowledge of this part of London, in an upstairs room of the Grapes. The place has been smartened up since

Dickens's day, and the customers are not quite as rough as they used to be, but the Grapes still has an enjoyably Dickensian atmosphere.

To get back to central London from here continue east along Limehouse Causeway until you reach Westferry station, on the Docklands Light Railway, and take a train to Bank or Tower Gateway, to join the Tube system. Alternatively, walk back (west) along Narrow Street to its end, turn right into Butcher Row, and right again into Cable Street, to reach Stepney East station, which has trains into Fenchurch Street.

*

The City of London does not have many really old pubs, perhaps because it has been subjected to the forces of change and destruction (fire, bombing and commercial and civic development) more than any other part of London. The most famous of its old inns are gone. The fabled Mermaid Tavern was on Cheapside, between Bread Street and Friday Street, which now stops at Cannon Street but used to continue north to Cheapside. A Victorian fantasy was that all the Jacobean greats – Shakespeare, Ben Jonson, John Donne, Inigo Jones, Christopher Marlowe and other 'heroes and witts of that time' (John Aubrey, *Brief Lives*) – used to meet here in a weekly club, the Friday Street Club, started by Sir Walter Raleigh. The reality is less exciting, but Ben Jonson certainly used to drink here, along with the playwright Francis Beaumont, and probably with Beaumont's close friend and collaborator John Fletcher. Beaumont's famous verse letter to Jonson, written around 1605, recalled their convivial meetings there:

> In this warm shine
> I lie, and dream of your full Mermaid wine.
> . . . What things have we seen
> Done at the Mermaid! heard words that have been
> So nimble, and so full of subtile flame,

> As if that every one from whence they came
> Had meant to put his whole wit in a jest,
> And had resolved to live a fool the rest
> Of his dull life . . .

It is not improbable that Shakespeare was one of the wits who gathered there, but there is no proof that he was.

Another Mermaid drinking society, the Fraternitie of Sireniacal Gentlemen, was formed in 1610, and it is likely that Ben Jonson, Inigo Jones and John Donne were among the courtiers, lawyers and politicians in the group. They were just as likely to have met in the equally popular Mitre Tavern, which was just across Cheapside in Wood Street. Samuel Pepys spent a jolly evening at the Mitre, 'a house of the greatest note in London', in September 1660, defending 'the ladies' from the kisses of his drunken friend Luellin, but not of course from his own. Six years later it was destroyed in the Great Fire, along with all the other Cheapside taverns. There was another Mitre Tavern, equally famous for its literary connections, in Fleet Street, opposite Chancery Lane. This is where Samuel Johnson and James Boswell first consolidated their friendship in June 1763, having met for the first time in Mr Davies's Russell Street bookshop (the building is still there) a month earlier. At the end of their evening at the Mitre Johnson said to Boswell, 'Give me your hand. I have taken a liking to you . . . Sir, I am glad we have met. I hope we shall pass many evenings and mornings too together.' Later, they planned their tour of the Hebrides in the Fleet Street Mitre. The tavern closed in 1788 and was demolished in 1829, when Hoare's bank was extended eastwards.

The scientists of the Royal Society used to meet informally in the Fleet Street Mitre, but they moved after its closure to the Crown and Anchor, another tavern that played an important part in London's social and cultural life. This stood on the corner of Arundel Street at the eastern end of the Strand and had one of eighteenth-century London's largest public meeting rooms. This was where the

Academy of Ancient Music held its concerts and where, in February 1732, Handel's (and England's) first English oratorio, *Esther*, was given its first public performance. The radicals of the London Corresponding Society met here in the 1790s, and Chartists in the 1830s. In 1823 2,000 people turned up to the first meeting of the London Mechanics' Institute here, under the leadership of Francis Place and George Birkbeck. It was a favourite with scientists and intellectuals. The Royal Society of Arts held its dinners here; the Royal Medical Society held its early meetings here after 1800; it was the first home of the Royal Pharmaceutical Society in 1841. The Crown and Anchor burned down in 1854, and was rebuilt as the Temple Club.

Most of the best surviving City pubs are on the fringes of the City, rather than in the old walled area. On the eastern fringes, you might try the Hoop and Grapes, at 47 Aldgate High Street, a part of the City that escaped the Great Fire. Numbers 46 and 47 are probably the City's (though not London's) last surviving pre-Fire houses, built with timber frames that were illegal in new buildings after 1666. The exterior of the Hoop and Grapes has some eighteenth-century features, and the whole rickety structure was strengthened in the 1980s (just as well in view of the traffic that roars past it today), but inside the staircases and wooden panelling look seventeenth century. The pub itself is not so old, though. It was a private house at the time of the Fire, and only went public in the nineteenth century.

A much older pub, though in a slightly younger building, is the Old Dr Butler's Head, in Mason's Avenue, off Basinghall Street just to the east of the Guildhall. The pub is named after Dr William Butler, an eccentric physician who attended James I's son Prince Henry (the supposed occupant of Prince Henry's Room in Fleet Street) during his last illness in 1612. A medicinal drink apparently developed by him, Dr Butler's Ale, was popular in the seventeenth century, and is said to have been sold in several taverns associated with or owned by him, of which this one is the last survivor.

Perhaps the pub and the makers of the ale simply took Dr Butler's name, hoping to benefit from his great reputation as a healer. The Old Dr Butler's Head was founded before the Great Fire (probably 1610) and rebuilt after it. The place has been restored several times, and the present building is mostly early nineteenth century, but Bradley and Pevsner suspect that the ground floor still has some late-seventeenth-century features. This is a good old-fashioned (and overcrowded) City pub, which serves excellent (though not medicinal) beer and solid sandwiches by gaslight, and chops and steak and kidney puddings upstairs. The alley is dominated by a long run of ugly 1920s mock-Tudor offices.

There are several good Victorian pubs in the City with interesting connections or in historic buildings, which are enjoyable to visit if you are in the neighbourhood. Most of them are closed at weekends, and very busy when City workers are let out of their offices. There is a cluster of good pubs around Cornhill and Leadenhall, just east of the Bank. Pride of place goes to the Jamaica Wine House, hidden away in St Michael's Alley, a tiny passage behind St Michael's church on Cornhill. Since the Jamaica has a distinguished history as a coffee house, I have described it in Chapter Two. The Counting House, which is on Cornhill a few metres from the Jamaica Wine House, is one of the many new London pubs in converted bank buildings, but this is a very good one, and the vast interior of the old NatWest banking hall, with its Tuscan columns, shining brass and panelling in alabaster and mahogany, is a fine place to sit. Nearby, the Lamb Tavern occupies a magnificent site in Leadenhall Market, in Sir Horace Jones's 1880s glass and iron market buildings, and has an excellent tile picture, made in 1889, of Wren explaining his plans for the Monument in 1671. Turn left (south) on Gracechurch Street, which is just to the west of Leadenhall Market, and just before you reach Eastcheap you'll see Talbot Court on your left. Hidden down here is the Ship, a good Victorian pub that still occupies its own courtyard, as so many used to do before the railways killed the coaching inns.

Now find Cannon Street, which begins near the Monument Tube station, and follow it west until you come to Martin Lane, which has one of London's oldest wine bars, the Old Wine Shades. Although its claim to date from 1663 seems implausible, the house it occupies was built soon after the Fire, and the front dates from around 1800. Thread your way west through little alleys to find Bush Lane, where you will find an unspoiled early-Victorian pub, the Bell. Carry on along Cannon Street and turn right into Bow Lane (one of King Alfred's new streets), to find the Old Watling, a good pub that dates from around 1700 but which lost its front in the Blitz and got a new one in 1947. A few metres up Bow Lane, behind fine eighteenth-century wrought-iron gates, there is William- son's Tavern, in Groveland Court, which was rebuilt in the early 1930s but which has been a public house since 1739. Back to Cannon Street, and walk west until you reach the approach to the Millennium Bridge. A left turn brings you to Knightrider Street and another old City pub, which at present is called the Centre Page but was once, and for hundreds of years, the Horn Tavern. The Horn Tavern claims to have pre-Great Fire origins, and certainly existed in the early eighteenth century, when it appears on John Rocque's map of London. Masonic lodge meetings were held there from the 1750s to the 1830s, and it became a coffee house for a few years in the 1830s. Dickens mentioned it in *Household Words*, as a watering hole used by Mr Pickwick's friends when they visited him in the Fleet prison. But the building was replaced between 1973 and 1985, and though some features of the old pub were preserved within the new building the general feeling is modern.

For a pub that feels older, continue along Knightrider Street, go right into Godliman Street and left into Carter Lane. A short way along, you will find the Rising Sun, an unpretentious 1840s pub fronted by fine Tuscan columns. Go left down St Andrew's Hill for the Cockpit, a lovely 1860s pub which claims to have once been what its name suggests. Its bar, with an unusually high ceiling and a gallery halfway up the wall, has the look of a cockpit, but cockfighting was illegal by the time this pub was built. Now you are near the Black Friar and the pubs at the eastern end of Fleet Street, which will be mentioned later.

*

There is a much richer selection of old and very old pubs just to the west of the City, and especially in the Fleet Street and Holborn area, which was thickly settled by the early seventeenth century and mostly survived the Great Fire. We could start at Smithfield, which was already a busy market and fair district in the twelfth century, and one of London's first suburbs. Cloth Fair, the narrow medieval street between Smithfield and Aldersgate, has two nice pubs. The Rising Sun is a good, simple 1890s pub, open at weekends, and the Hand and Shears (in Middle Street, Cloth Fair's eastern extension) is a well-preserved 1830s pub, named after the Lord Mayor's ceremony that always opened Bartholomew Fair in August. It is said that there has been an alehouse on this site since the twelfth century. Go through the quaintly named Back Passage between Cloth Fair and Charterhouse Street, and turn left to go behind the meat market. Here, at 115 Charterhouse Street, you'll find a lovely art nouveau pub of the 1890s (a good decade for new pubs), the Fox and Anchor. The exterior is decorated with fine Doulton tiles, and inside there is a long bar and lots of little snugs. The pub was very well restored in the 1990s, and re-opened after a brief closure in 2008.

If you continue west on Charterhouse Street you will cross the River Fleet (buried under Farringdon Road) and come to Ely Place on your right. Take it, and turn left into tiny Ely Court. Here you will find another contender for the London's oldest pub title, the Old Mitre Tavern. This is not Dr Johnson's Mitre Tavern, or Shakespeare's, but a pub originally established in 1547 for the benefit of the staff of the Bishop of Ely's palace, which was here until 1772. The Old Mitre was demolished and rebuilt in the 1770s, and is still an unspoilt eighteenth-century pub, with the remains of an old cherry tree at the corner of the bar. Set into the wall outside there is a stone mitre from the gatehouse of the medieval bishop's palace.

Through Ely Court, turn left on Hatton Garden and right onto Holborn. Go west, passing the magnificent late-Victorian Gothic Prudential Building on your right and Staple Inn, a famous and carefully preserved mid-sixteenth-century terrace of shops and houses, on your left. On the right, just before Red Lion Street, you will find the Cittie of Yorke (previously Henekey's Tavern), which claims to have been an inn since 1430. The pub has been rebuilt more than once, and the present frontage dates from 1923. But the huge and very atmospheric interior feels almost medieval, and is mostly nineteenth century, with some seventeenth- and eighteenth-century features. It is possible that it was at one time the Gray's Inn Coffee House, which existed from the 1770s to the 1850s, at 20 Holborn.

The Old Red Lion, at 72 High Holborn, has been modernized once too often, so those in search of old pubs should cross High Holborn, go a little east, and turn into Great Turnstile, a little alley leading into Lincoln's Inn Fields. Walking straight ahead brings you to Searle Street, and then Carey Street, in which you will find a pub that seems little changed since the seventeenth century. The Seven Stars celebrated its four-hundredth birthday in 2002, but Pevsner and Bradley spoil the party by saying that despite its wooden frontage it can be no older than New Square (just behind it), which was built in the 1680s. Still, for someone who wants to forget that we live in modern times there can be no better place to have a drink than this simple and quiet place, with its slow ceiling fans and film posters for fifty-year-old courtroom dramas.

Now go to the western end of Carey Street and take Grange Court and Clements Inn, streets that survived the devastation of this area first by the construction of the Law Courts in the 1870s and then the building of Kingsway and the Aldwych in the 1900s. This brings you to the western end of Fleet Street, right next to the statue of that great tavern specialist Samuel Johnson. Fleet Street might have lost all the newspaper offices that made it famous, but it still has some very good pubs. Starting at this western end, cross the road and find Devereux Court, a lane that leads into Essex Court and Fountain Court, in Middle Temple. The pub here, the Devereux, is named after Robert Devereux, Earl of Essex, whose mansion, Essex House, was here until the developer Nicholas Barbon knocked it down and built the present streets in the 1670s and 1680s. Devereux's bust looks down from the first floor, and the date on it, 1676, is when Barbon built this and the neighbouring houses. The pub was stuccoed in 1844, but in essentials it remains the building that was from the late seventeenth century until 1843 the Grecian Coffee House, the favourite meeting place of Royal Society scientists in the days of Hooke, Halley and Newton.

Crossing Fleet Street again, you might like to look into the Old Bank of England, a new pub in a magnificent old building, the 1888 Law Courts branch of the Bank of England. Better to keep going east until you get to one of London's oldest and most famous pubs, Ye Olde Cheshire Cheese, in Wine Office Court. Dr Johnson lived very nearby in Gough Square and Bolt Court for most of his London life, and it is not unlikely that he used the Cheshire Cheese from time to time, though the Mitre Tavern on Fleet Street was his favourite. Ye Olde Cheshire Cheese has plenty of other literary and historical associations, and it is a genuinely old and atmospheric pub. It is a sixteenth-century pub occupying a refronted late-seventeenth-century building, with older vaulted cellars and a dark, rambling and complicated interior which lives up to its 'Ye Olde' image as well as any pub in London. In the 1890s it was the meeting place for an important and interesting literary group, the Rhymers' Club. The founder and most famous member of this mainly Irish poetry group was W.B. Yeats, but others included Ernest Rhys (later the editor of Everyman books), Richard Le Gallienne, Ernest Dowson and John Davidson. If you go upstairs in the Olde Cheshire Cheese, you might picture this Bohemian group, smoking clay pipes and drinking ale, in their loose ties, knee breeches and Inverness capes, reading out their poems often sitting (according to Yeats) in 'gloomy silence'.

There is another seventeenth-century pub in Fleet Street, but one that makes less of a song and dance about its antiquity. The Old Bell Tavern, at 96 Fleet Street, just west of Ludgate Circus, occupies a house probably built around 1670 by Christopher Wren as lodgings for the masons working on St Bride's church. When the masons were gone there were printers to cater for, and the Old Bell has been selling drink here for about three hundred years. The building was refronted in 1897, but behind this late-Victorian facade there is a pub built and in business since the reign of Charles II. And almost next door to the Old Bell is another interesting, though not ancient, pub, the Punch Tavern. In 1841, when this was the Crown and Sugarloaf, a group of journalists and writers (Henry Mayhew, Douglas Jerrold and Mark Lemon) met here and founded the humorous magazine *Punch*. When this had become the most successful magazine in Victorian England, the pub was renamed to commemorate this historic meeting. The present building was erected in the 1890s, and recent refurbishment has preserved its late-Victorian appearance, its lovely skylight and its *Punch* mementoes. The Tipperary, at number 66 Fleet Street, which claims to be London's first Irish pub, occupies a building just as old as the Olde Cheshire Cheese or the Old Bell, even though the pub's interior was designed in the 1890s. The house was built by the City bricklayer Peter Mills in 1667–8, and its toplit central staircase is typical of the period.

There are some good examples of well-preserved Victorian pubs in the Holborn area. The Viaduct Tavern (126 Newgate Street), built when the viaduct was opened in 1869, still looks like a late-Victorian pub. Its Burne-Jones-style paintings may not appeal to you, but its 1899 interior, cut glass, gilded mirrors and all, still looks very fine. A further point of interest is that the pub's cellars were once cells of Newgate Prison, which stood over the road until 1902, when it was replaced by the Old Bailey. A short walk down Old Bailey and across Ludgate Hill into Pageantmaster Court, Ludgate Broadway and Blackfriars Lane (passing the lovely Apothecaries' Hall on your left) will bring you to an even finer late-Victorian pub, the Black Friar. The Blackfriars were the powerful Dominican order, whose priory was on this site until the 1530s. The Black Friar was built next to the railway in 1873, but it owes its fame to its transformation by members of the Arts and Crafts movement in 1905. The mosaics, enamel, metalwork and carved reliefs outside hardly prepare you for the extravagant art nouveau splendours inside.

The architect H. Fuller Clark, along with sculptors Henry Poole and Frederick Callcott, created a fantasy world of Merrie England scenes in copper, wood, marble and mosaic. Copper monks are depicted at work, play and prayer, fetching water, gathering grapes and apples, cutting corn, playing the cello. In 1917–21 Poole and Clark created a Grotto behind the main bar, which is even wittier and more unrestrained than the work of 1905. Here the monks' antics are wilder (even on the light fittings), and their supposed philosophy is encapsulated in a series of mottoes: 'Finery is foolery', 'Industry is all', 'Wisdom is rare', and so on. It is like a chapel, a secular comment (the architectural historian Andrew Saint suggests) on the side-chapels of Westminster Cathedral, which were built in similar materials and in similar Byzantine style at the same time.

*

To find some of the best Victorian pubs with a gin palace feel (as well as some older ones) you should take a walk in the West End, starting where the West End started, in Covent Garden. The oldest and most interesting public house in Covent Garden is the Lamb and Flag, in Rose Street, at the junction of Floral Street and Garrick Street. The building was nicely refaced in 1958, but it is essentially a house built around 1688 which has been a pub ever since. It has two small and crowded bars, and an old staircase leading up to the well-preserved first floor. Bare-knuckle boxing matches used to be held in the back room (the Bucket of Blood), or in the front yard. The Lamb and Flag is therefore second only to the Ring in Blackfriars Road (near the Cut and Southwark Tube station) in its association with the history of boxing. Rose Street was not a lucky place for Restoration satirists. Samuel Butler, author of *Hudibras*, died in poverty here in 1680, and a few months earlier the poet and playwright John Dryden, one of the wittiest of the coffee house wits of Charles II's day, was badly beaten by the henchmen of someone he had poked fun at, probably the Earl of Rochester. Another contender for London pub with the strongest boxing connections would be the Tom Cribb, at 36 Panton Street, between Leicester Square and Haymarket. The pub is named after its ex-landlord, the bare-knuckle boxer Tom Cribb, who became British champion in 1809 and retired undefeated in 1828. He became landlord of this eighteenth-century pub, then called the Union Arms, around 1812 and ran it until gambling debts forced him to give it up in 1839. He died in 1848, apparently throwing a feeble punch and saying, 'The action's still there but the steam's all gone.' His house is marked with an English Heritage blue plaque, and the pub provides further information on Cribb's life.

A short walk down Long Acre or Garrick Street (or, better still, along Goodwin's Court, off Bedfordbury) brings you into St Martin's Lane, the old lane between the two churches 'in the Fields', St Martin and St Giles. Number 90 St Martin's Lane is the Salisbury, one of the very best of the many pubs built in London in the boom of the 1890s. A pub called the Salisbury Stores stood here in the mid-nineteenth century, but it was swept away when this mansion block was built in 1892. The new restaurant was reopened as a pub in 1898, and fitted out in a magnificently lavish style, with cut, engraved and frosted glass, mirrors, mahogany, spectacular art nouveau electric lights with nymphs and flowers, and leather seats (nearly always occupied) in little alcoves. It is named after Lord

Salisbury, who owned the land until 1892 and was Prime Minister in 1898.

If you like the Salisbury style there are several other public houses in the West End which will suit you. Cut through Cecil Court to Charing Cross Road, turn right, and after Cambridge Circus go left on Old Compton Street and right on Frith Street (rich in eighteenth-century houses), to find the Dog and Duck on the corner with Bateman Street. This is a crowded little pub, fitted out in 1897 (by Francis Chambers) with floor-to-ceiling tiles and glittering mirrors to win customers as the big brewers battled for business in the 1890s. Shiny surfaces were easy to keep clean in those smoky days, too. When it is too crowded downstairs, there is another bar on the first floor. Moving on, you could follow some nice old Soho streets – Meard Street (where the Pitcher and Piano occupies a 1730s house with nineteenth-century stuccoed front), Peter Street, Ingestre Place and Silver Place, to Beak Street, which has plenty of seventeenth- and eighteenth-century houses and shops. Canaletto lived in number 41 in the 1740s and 1750s, conveniently near the Canaletto Coffee Bar, and John Wilkes the gunmaker (not the demagogue) traded at number 79. Number 49, on the corner of Beak Street and Marshall Street, is the Old Coffee House, an eighteenth-century coffee house which became a pub, and was refitted as a 'temperance tavern' in 1894. Inside, it is cluttered with stuffed animals, old prints and assorted historical mementoes, and the drinker might well think himself back in Boswell's day, straining to catch the *bons mots* coming from the wits on the next table. Nearby, on the corner of Great Pulteney Street, is the oddly named Sun and 13 Cantons, built in 1882 by Henry Cotton, who avoided choosing between the prevalent Gothic and Queen Anne styles by mixing them together in a peculiar hybrid style which you may find interesting.

From Beak Street, follow Carnaby Street north to Great Marlborough Street, and go left to find Argyll Street. Here, a few metres from Oxford Circus, you'll find one of London's best historic pubs, the Argyll Arms, an eighteenth-century establishment rebuilt in 1868, when the London Palladium was built over the road. Its interior was redesigned in 1895, with screens dividing the front bar into three areas, to create (as the Victorians thought) a more orderly and sober atmosphere. This unfashionable division, which has been removed from most other Victorian pubs, has been retained here, giving us an unusually well-preserved interior, and (in Pevsner and Bradley's words) 'a maze of mahogany and engraved mirrors under a Lincrusta ceiling'. There is a big saloon bar at the back and a spacious bar at the top of the big mahogany staircase. So, by walking a few metres from Oxford Circus, you can travel back a hundred years, to the days of the late-Victorian gin palace.

*

The part of Marylebone north of Oxford Street and east of Oxford Circus is now generally called Fitzrovia. The compilers of the latest *Oxford English Dictionary* found the first written reference to Fitzrovia in the *Times Literary Supplement* of January 1958, which described the neighbourhood as 'a world of outsiders, down-and-outs, drunks, sensualists, homosexuals and eccentrics'. But in his *Memoirs of the Forties* (1965) Julian Maclaren-Ross, the writer and drinker who epitomized the Bohemian literary figures who wasted their time, money and livers in this part of London in the 1940s and 1950s, recalled that J. Meary Tambimuttu, editor of *Poetry London*, warned him about the danger of catching 'Sohoitis' in 'Fitzrovia' in 1943. '"If you get Sohoitis," Tambi said very seriously, "you will stay there always day and night and get no work done ever. You have been warned."'

Fitzrovia was not named after Fitzroy Square but after the Fitzroy Tavern, on the corner of Charlotte Street and Percy Street, which had been a meeting place for composers (Constant Lambert, Peter Warlock) and artists (Augustus John, Jacob Epstein, Nina Hamnett) in the 1920s and 1930s, and attracted poets and novelists, including Malcolm Lowry, Roy Campbell, Lawrence Durrell, George Orwell, Dylan Thomas and Julian Maclaren-Ross, in the years before, during and after the Second World War. The present pub is not especially atmospheric, but the essence of this often aimless intellectual world is captured in the interwar volumes of Anthony Powell's *A Dance to the Music of Time*, in which Maclaren-Ross appears as the poet X. Trapnel. The Fitzroy Tavern drinkers also favoured several other pubs in the neighbourhood of Charlotte Street. The Wheatsheaf, at 25 Rathbone Place (the southern continuation of Charlotte Street), was popular with young writers, especially those interested in surrealism, in the later 1930s, and a group of them, including Orwell, Dylan Thomas, Edwin Muir and Humphrey Jennings, were briefly known as the Wheatsheaf writers. Turn back to Rathbone Street to find the Marquess of Granby, which stayed open later than other pubs in the area because it was in Marylebone rather than St Pancras, and thus won the custom of Orwell, Thomas and others.

The Fitzrovia pub that best retains the spirit of the 1930s and 1940s is the Newman Arms, a plain little pub with a very popular upstairs pie room, which once served working-class customers but now has the usual businessmen. Orwell is thought to have used the Newman Arms as his model for the working-class pubs described in Chapter 5 of *Keep the Aspidistra Flying* ('a filthy, smoky room, low-ceilinged, with a sawdusted floor and plain deal tables ringed by generations of beer-pots') and Chapter 8 of *1984* ('a dingy little pub' at the end of a steeply sloping alley), but it has been spruced up since Orwell's day. The lovely alleyway alongside the pub, Newman Passage, was the scene of a murder in Michael Powell's controversial film *Peeping Tom*. Another pub on Rathbone Street (number 47) which might appeal to the historically minded is the Duke of York, a small plain late-eighteenth-century pub which has resisted the lure of the plasma screen and the gourmet menu. Finally, on the corner of Windmill Street and Tottenham Court Road is the beautiful Rising Sun, the delicate Gothic masterpiece of Treadwell and Martin, leading pub architects of the 1890s. Before you go in, take a look at the art nouveau foliage and rising suns on the painted exterior. When it was built it might have served local furniture industry workers, but now it is popular with students.

*

Mayfair has a few interesting old pubs, and many rather expensive ones. Starting at Oxford Circus, stroll down Regent Street and turn right into Conduit Street. After crossing New Bond Street you will enter Bruton Street, whose northern side has plenty of houses that date from the construction of the street in the 1730s. Turn right at once into the mews, Bruton Place, where a lovely little pub called the Guinea claims a history that goes back to 1423. The present building has some seventeenth-century features but mostly dates from the early nineteenth century, when it used to serve employees of the Berkeley estate. The bar is small, dark and simple, with brass fans, simple wooden benches and old prints, and the steak and kidney pies served in the upstairs restaurant are national prizewinners. If you take Bruton Place west to Berkeley Square and go anticlockwise round the square you will find Hill Street, a road which still has many of the fine houses built in the late 1740s when the Berkeley estate was first developed. Walk along it a few metres, and you will find the Coach and Horses, a decent public house in a 1740s house stuccoed in 1850. A right turn into Hay's Mews brings you to Farm Street, which has only one original 1740s building, the Punch Bowl public house. Outside, the Punch Bowl's age is obscured by mid-Victorian stucco, but inside it still feels like a simple country pub. The traditional partition between the public and saloon bars has been removed, but there is nice etched glass, and the food and drink are well priced, considering the area.

To finish this public house tour in St James's, return to Berkeley Square and leave by Berkeley Street, in its south-east corner. Go left along Piccadilly, cross it and cut through to Jermyn Street by one of the two pretty early-twentieth-century arcades to either side of

Fortnum and Mason, and go left on Jermyn Street until you come to Duke of York Street, opposite St James's church. Here you will find one of St James's two Red Lion public houses. This one was built in 1821 and refaced fifty years later. Inside it is a wonderland of mid-Victorian sparkling mirrors, cut and bevelled glass, ornate tiles and polished mahogany. The old partitions are gone, but the pub still seems small, intimate and, most of the time, crowded. You can find the other Red Lion by walking on to St James's Square and leaving it by King Street, on its west side. Just before you get to St James's Street, turn left into Crown Passage, the only place in St James's that feels at all working class. At its far end is the Red Lion, which claims to be 'London's last village pub' and to have the second-oldest beer licence in the West End. The Red Lion is said to be four hundred years old, but its building is no older than the rest of the eighteenth-century shops and houses in Crown Passage. Its bar is no longer partitioned, but it is small, simple and old fashioned, and the narrow stairs lead up to an intimate dining room, which fills up on the last Saturday in January with 'Cavaliers' commemorating the execution of Charles I.

At the end of Crown Passage, turn left into Pall Mall, which takes you to Trafalgar Square. Your walk could end here, but you could continue down Whitehall, where there are some good late-Victorian pubs. The Old Shades, at 37 Whitehall, is a nice pub built by Treadwell and Martin, masters of late-Victorian Gothic, in 1898. Further south, where Whitehall turns into Parliament Street, there is another Red Lion, built by another prolific pair of pub architects, Shoebridge and Rising, in 1896. It has a well-preserved etched-glass and mahogany interior, and is popular with the political classes. Nearby, in Bridge Street and Canon Row, St Stephen's Tavern, a famous political drinking place built around 1870, has recently been refurbished and reopened after nearly 15 years closed. Its rich Gothic Revival style matches that of Pugin's Houses of Parliament, across the road.

On the other hand, if you are walking towards the new

Hungerford Bridge and Waterloo station, go down Villiers Street, a right turn off the Strand just past Charing Cross railway station, to find a particularly old and interesting drinking place, Gordon's Wine Bar. Gordon's, at 47 Villiers Street, sells wine, port and sherry, as well as cheese and other food, in a wine cellar which is dark, sooty, cosy and very old. This is probably London's oldest wine bar, and began in 1890, when Rudyard Kipling was living next door.

*

Some of the best of the 1890s pubs were in the outer suburbs, which were growing so fast at the end of the century. One of the best of them is the Salisbury, on Green Lanes (called Grand Parade in this stretch) near its junction with St Anne's Road, near Harringay or Turnpike Lane station. All the sidestreets along here are named after heroes, and the pub is named after the hero of the 1895 general election. Everything is good about this pub, but its lavish and well-restored late-Victorian architecture and interior design are what would bring you out here to see it. The wonderful art nouveau mirrors were probably the work of Cakebread Robey, a firm that is still supplying materials to the building trade. The Salisbury was designed and built in 1899 by a builder and brickmaker, John Hill, who was responsible for many of the houses in this part of London. Hill built a second pub about a mile to the west, in Crouch End, where he was also a leading developer. This was the Queen's Hotel, which was built between 1899 and 1902 in Tottenham Lane, near Crouch End Broadway. This pub is now more 'gastronomic' than the Salisbury, but they are clearly from the same stable: a prominent corner site, a grand cupola, Cakebread Robey coloured glass, art nouveau fittings, excellent joinery and several spacious bars.

Other good 1890s suburban pubs that might repay a visit include the Elgin in Ladbroke Grove (near Westbourne Park Road), which has fine late-Victorian glass and tilework, the Assembly House in Kentish Town Road, near Kentish Town station, which was rebuilt in 1898 in an extravagant style, with an interior rich in fine ironwork, mahogany and cut glass, and the Boleyn, at the corner of Barking Road and Green Street, near West Ham's Upton Park football stadium, which was built in 1898 in a baroque style, with the usual cut-glass mirrors and screens and a lovely toplit billiard – now pool – room. In south London, one of the best pubs in this same 1890s style is the King's Head (1896) at 84 Upper Tooting Road, south of Tooting Bec station. Its architect, William Brutton, built or altered at least 65 London pubs between 1891 and 1904 (especially in the mid-1890s), and this is the best of his surviving work. The Prince Alfred in Formosa Street, Paddington, near Warwick Avenue Tube station, has been spoiled by unsympathetic refurbishment, but it still looks beautiful from the outside with its delicate curved windows, etched glass and slim cast-iron pillars, and its interior, with many screens and divisions, is still interesting. It is an 1860s pub (named after Victoria's second son) redesigned around 1898.

CHAPTER SEVEN

✳

SHOPS AND MARKETS

A cookshop near St Martin's Lane

ALMOST FROM THE year of its creation London has been a city of shops and markets. Excavations of the first Roman forum, destroyed by Boudicca in AD 60, revealed what appeared to be a row of shops, and the earliest description of London, by the Roman historian Tacitus, called it 'an important centre for businessmen and merchandise'. In Anglo-Saxon London there were little shops along Cheapside (*ceap* is the Old English word for market) and its side roads, which were named after the commodities once sold in each street: Honey Lane, Milk Street, Ironmonger Lane, Bread Street, Wood Street and so on. Around 1300 there were probably about four hundred shops on Cheapside, London's busiest street, along with many more sites for mobile traders. Some of these shops were stone-built, but most were little wooden huts or lean-tos in which the front shutter folded down to make a shop counter during business hours. There are still plenty of kiosks like this selling papers, sweets and souvenirs in London today, though not in Cheapside.

Until the nineteenth century, London's main shopping centre was in the City of London, especially around St Paul's and along Cheapside, and along Fleet Street and the Strand. In Elizabethan London Cheapside was renowned for its unbroken rows of jewellers and goldsmiths, but in the seventeenth century shops selling everyday wares started to take over. There is still a little row of seventeenth-century shops, built after the Great Fire on the corner of Wood Street, which recalls Cheapside's retailing past. At the western end of Cheapside, in the middle of the City, the Royal Exchange, which was built by Sir Thomas Gresham in the 1560s (and rebuilt after the Great Fire and another fire in 1838), was an early shopping precinct, with lock-up shops selling books, medicines, jewellery, cloth, tablewares and so on. Lloyd's, the insurance market, moved into the Royal Exchange in 1774, and for most of the following two centuries financial institutions occupied the buildings. Since 2001, though, the Royal Exchange has been a shopping centre again, the home of jewellers, tailors and luxury retailers.

The westward movement of retailing was begun by the construction in 1609 of the Earl of Salisbury's New Exchange, a double row of stone shops, at the western end of the Strand between the present numbers 54 and 64. These did not really thrive until after Charles II's Restoration in 1660, when fashionable London took a decisive step westward. Eighteenth-century visitors to London singled out the Strand and Fleet Street, along with Cheapside and Cornhill, as London's greatest shopping streets, and we can still see evidence of the spread of smart shops into St James's Street, Jermyn Street and the Haymarket in the 1750s. Bond Street was built up between 1684 and the 1720s, and was well established as a centre of fashionable shopping and promenading by the 1750s. Oxford Street was developed between 1680 and 1750, but was mainly residential, and not very smart, until the building of Regent Street as a great shopping street between 1813 and 1820 connected it more closely with the fashionable West End. Its great days began with the development of department stores later in the nineteenth century.

In the past, much of London's retailing was done from baskets, barrows, street stalls or in covered markets. A charter of around 1000 referred to farmers and their wives selling hens, eggs and dairy produce from baskets or hampers in London, and a fifteenth-century poem, 'London Lickpenny', took its readers on a tour of London's street markets. In Westminster Flemish merchants tried to sell the narrator felt hats and spectacles; at Charing Cross he was offered bread, ale, wine and ribs of beef; in Cheapside they were selling fine cloth, cotton and thread; in Cannon Street he could buy cod, mackerel and hot sheep's feet; in Eastcheap there were pewter pots and 'many a pie'; and in Cornhill there were old clothes and stolen goods. The descendants of these medieval street sellers are still in business today, though you will not find many of them in the City's sober streets. But there is still a flower seller near the steps of St Mary-le-Bow, Cheapside, just as there has been for hundreds of years.

There were two covered markets in medieval London, one of which is still in operation today. The Stocks Market, which was founded in the thirteenth century and specialized in meat and fish, was demolished in 1737 to make way for the Mansion House, the Lord Mayor's official residence, on Walbrook Street, opposite the Bank of England. Leadenhall Market, founded in 1445 with help from Richard Whittington's will as a general market for meat, fish, groceries, wool and leather, is the survivor. Its massive walls helped stop the Great Fire, and the rebuilt market was not replaced with the present cast-iron buildings until 1881. In recent years sellers of fish and fruit have deserted the market, making way for bars and coffee shops, but the market, which sits on top of the site of the Roman forum, is a reminder of the central place of retailing in City life.

Another of London's great medieval markets, Smithfield, also survives, and has kept faith with its ancient purpose more steadily than Leadenhall. Smithfield Market sold horses, cattle, sheep and pigs from the twelfth century until 1855, when the market in live animals was closed, to be replaced in 1868 by the Central Meat Market there today. The old Smithfield sold more than animals: Cloth Fair, running from the north-east corner of West Smithfield, is a reminder of the old cloth trade. Some of the houses on it (especially numbers 41 and 42) and the little alleys off it retain some of the appearance of the old market quarter. The real work of the market is done by 8.00 a.m., but later in the day you can walk along the avenues of Horace Jones's fine brick and iron building, watching the last of the morning's market activity. If you fancy buying some meat from London's ancient butchery quarter after the market is shut, Hart's and the other butchers' shops in the surrounding streets are excellent. The market buildings have been extended several times, most recently in 1961–3 when the concrete poultry market was built, and the Edwardian Central Cold Storage building, on Charterhouse Street, is particularly impressive. There has often been talk of closing and moving the market, as has happened with Covent Garden and Billingsgate, but it has recently been refurbished, and the buildings are in a City of London conservation area. London's oldest wholesale market is not completely safe, because when Crossrail comes to Farringdon station there is likely to be pressure for the redevelopment of some of the land occupied by the huge market buildings.

The other two great wholesale markets have moved to more spacious and unromantic suburban sites. Billingsgate Market was located on the riverside east of London Bridge from about the year 1000, when it was first mentioned in a royal ordinance, but did not become a specialist fish market till 1698. It closed in 1982, but reopened on a 13-acre site between West India Quay and Aspen Way, near Poplar station on the Docklands Light Railway and not far from Canary Wharf on the Jubilee Line. Although it is a wholesale market, the biggest inland fish market in the country, members of the public are not excluded. It is open Tuesday to Saturday, 5.00 to 8.30 in the morning. Covent Garden Market moved to a 56-acre site between Nine Elms Lane and Wandsworth Road, west of Vauxhall station, in 1974. It sells fruit, vegetables, flowers and some other foods wholesale from Monday to Friday 3.00 to 11.00 a.m., Saturday 4.00 to 10.00 a.m., but only to traders.

There have been street markets in London since the earliest times, and despite occasional hostility from the authorities and the development of many other ways to buy goods, including fixed shops, covered arcades, department stores, chain stores, supermarkets and online shopping, markets are still going strong, sometimes many centuries after their first foundation. Four thriving markets in London's suburban town centres – Romford (Wednesdays, Fridays and Saturdays), Kingston (Monday–Saturday), Woolwich (Monday–Saturday) and Bromley (Thursdays) – got their first licences in the thirteenth century, and began as markets for local farm produce. In central London there are several markets with medieval roots. Borough Market is descended from a market sited in the thirteenth century on London Bridge, and then in Borough High Street. When it was suppressed in 1754 for obstructing the High Street, it was reopened in its present site south-west of Southwark Cathedral, Rochester Yard. It prospered as a wholesale (especially root) vegetable market, and in the 1850s was rehoused in its present glass and iron buildings. It was given a grand art deco entrance on Borough High Street in 1932, and the magnificent cast-iron south portico of the Covent Garden Floral Hall was moved to Borough Market in 2004, when the Royal Opera House was extended. The wholesale market operates early on weekday mornings, but on Fridays and Saturdays there is a retail market, mostly selling interesting cooked food to local workers and visitors enjoying the social and cultural revival of Bankside.

Covent Garden itself was one of London's most important street markets in the seventeenth and eighteenth centuries, when the fashionable Italian piazza designed for the Bedford family by Inigo Jones was taken over by fruit and vegetable sellers with carts, stalls and baskets. By the early nineteenth century the open market had become too congested and disorderly, the haunt of homeless and dishonest boys, and the Bedfords employed Charles Fowler to build a market house to bring order and dignity to the piazza. Fowler's structure is still much as he designed it (and William Cubitt built it) in 1828–30, except for the roofs, which were added in 1875 and 1888. There were shops selling herbs and flowers all along the middle passage of the central range of buildings, and underneath were storage vaults, which have been opened up to create new shopping areas. Other market buildings were added over the following eighty years, as Covent Garden grew into London's main wholesale market for fruit, vegetables and flowers. The Flower Market (1871–87) is now the London Transport Museum, and the Jubilee Hall, built in 1904 for the sale of foreign flowers, was saved from redevelopment in the 1970s and now houses a general market. The lovely iron and glass Floral Hall in Bow Street was built by Edward Middleton Barry, the architect of the Royal Opera House next door, in 1859, for Frederick Gye, in a style and materials reminiscent of the Crystal Palace. The market was hit by the opening of the nearby Flower Market in 1887, and the Floral Hall went over to dealing in foreign fruit, under Bedford's ownership. A fire destroyed part of the Floral Hall in 1956, and the extension of the Opera House in the 1990s left it reduced and structurally altered, but at least preserved and useful.

Spitalfields Market, east London's seventeenth-century wholesale fruit and vegetable market (licensed in 1682), moved out to Leyton in 1991, leaving its 1880s iron and glass hall between Bishopsgate and Commercial Street empty and in danger of demolition. After a local campaign a compromise was reached which allowed part of the covered market square to be used by stalls selling food, crafts and collectibles. The market is open every day, but shuts early (3.00) on a Sunday.

There are several other very old street markets within a short walk of Liverpool Street station, and a determined bargain hunter could take them all in on one visit. Leaving Spitalfields Market by the Commercial Street exit, walk down Hanbury Street and turn left into Brick Lane, which has been an important market street since the eighteenth century, when Essex farmers sold their produce here. Now, as well as food, the stalls on Brick Lane, Sclater Street and Cheshire Street (to the north) sell clothes, furniture, books, electrical goods, tools, collectibles and almost everything else, but only on Sundays between 8.00 and 2.00. If you walk further north along Brick Lane, and continue on Swanfield Road, you will find an attractive Sunday market in Columbia Road, which specializes in plants, shrubs, flowers and trees. A little further east, opposite the Royal London Hospital in Whitechapel Road, Whitechapel Market sells eastern specialities, especially food, spices and clothes, every day but Sunday, from 8.00 to 6.00.

London's most famous street market is in Middlesex Street, which runs between Bishopsgate (near Liverpool Street station) and Aldgate High Street. Petticoat Lane, the old and still the popular name for Middlesex Street, became the favourite market for old-clothes dealers in the sixteenth century, after they had been evicted first from London Bridge and then from Cornhill. The great London historian John Stow, writing around 1600, had plenty to say about the growth of housing along Petticoat Lane (which he called Hog Lane), but he did not refer to clothes dealers. Probably its colonization by the clothes trade was not completed until the Huguenot silk weavers (French Protestant refugees) settled in Spitalfields in the 1690s, and the early Jewish settlers established themselves nearby, at the eastern end of the City. The Petticoat Lane market had its greatest days after the 1880s, when East European Jews started to settle in Whitechapel in very large numbers. By the end of the century it was one of the great sights of London, the new Cheapside. The character of Petticoat Lane has changed as Bengalis have replaced Jews in the past forty years, and as tourists and day trippers have joined local shoppers in its crowded streets, but it is still well worth a visit on a Sunday morning. On other mornings there are stalls in a few streets, but the whole market is only there on Sundays, between 9.00 and 2.00. Try the sidestreets, Strype Street, Wentworth Street, Goulston Street and Cutler Street, for different specialities.

Those looking for a street market which has not been turned into a tourist attraction or a middle-class antiques market might go to Dalston, where there is a very thriving street market in Ridley Road, between Kingsland High Street and Dalston Lane. There is not a better way to experience the rich variety of cultures and nationalities in north London, and the goods on sale, especially food, are cheap and interesting. It is open Monday to Wednesday 9.00 to 3.00, Thursday morning and all day Friday and Saturday. The Silverlink railway from Richmond to Woolwich stops at Dalston Kingsland station. On a different occasion you could take the Victoria Line or mainline rail to Walthamstow Central, which stands at the eastern end of Walthamstow High Street. The 450-stall market runs the whole length of the High Street, making it perhaps the longest street market in Britain, though Portobello Road seems to be just as long. There have been costermongers here since the 1880s, when Walthamstow first became a suburb of London, and now it sells clothes, household goods, leather goods, food and bargains of all sorts. It is open every day but Sunday, from 9.00 till 4.00 (5.00 on Saturdays). Other things to see in Walthamstow are described in Chapter One.

There are some enjoyable remnants of London's old markets in the City and West End. One of the oldest is Leather Lane, a little road running north from Holborn just to the west of Holborn Circus. Leather Lane's name has nothing to do with what it sells. It began in the thirteenth century as Louerone Lane, which was corrupted by 1600 into Lither Lane, and by 1740 into Leather Lane. It has had a street market since the eighteenth century, and survived several Victorian attempts to get rid of it as a nuisance and an anachronism. Today the small market sells food, clothes and household goods to local office workers, and is active on weekdays between about 11.00 and 3.00. There is a similar weekday lunch-time market further east, on the other side of Smithfield Market, in Whitecross Street, which runs south from Old Street. Whitecross Street was a very large and busy Sunday market in the nineteenth century, and its origins are probably medieval, but it went into a decline in the late twentieth century and is now a fairly small affair. The local authority, Islington, is trying to revive the market by improving trading facilities, and perhaps it will bounce back.

The busiest street market in the West End is in Berwick Street, which runs through the middle of Soho from Oxford Street almost to Shaftesbury Avenue. There has been trading here since the eighteenth century, but the police only recognized it as a market street, legitimizing its obstruction of traffic, in 1906. Now the street is full of stalls between Broadwick Street and Peter Street, every day but Sunday, mostly selling fruit and vegetables, with a few selling clothes and household goods. Finally, you might call in on Strutton Ground, a lively little market in a sidestreet off Victoria Street, near St James's Park Tube station. The market is busy on Mondays and Saturdays, and provides a lovely contrast with the modern commercial streets around it, a fascinating remnant of the days when this part of Westminster was very poor, and when Old Pye Street (running south from Strutton Ground) was a notorious slum, or rookery.

Islington has two contrasting markets, one representing the old London of foodstuffs and cheap basic provisions, the other the new London of luxury and fashion. Chapel Market, a sidestreet off Liverpool Road a few metres from the Angel Islington Tube station, is a mid-Victorian market which still sells food and cheap general goods every day except Mondays. It is busiest from Friday to Sunday. In contrast Camden Passage, on the other side of Upper Street, only began in 1960, and sells antiques, furniture, paintings, books and bric-a-brac to a more middle-class clientele on Wednesdays and Saturdays. The old houses in Camden Passage and Camden Walk, at its northern end, were built in the 1760s, when the area was first developed by Thomas Rosoman, the manager of Sadler's Wells theatre. The Passage leads up to Islington Green, which also has a few of Rosoman's houses and some interesting remnants of London's cultural history. Number 75, with the dome, was once the Electric Cinema, opened in 1909, and the still thriving Screen on the Green, founded as the Picture Theatre in 1911, is one of London's oldest cinemas. Until the 1950s Collins Music Hall, one of the longest-lasting Victorian halls, stood on the far side of the Green, on the site now occupied by Waterstone's bookshop. It was already closed when it burned down in 1958.

Camden Passage, confusingly, is not in Camden Town, a district which now has some of London's busiest and best markets. The market at Camden Lock (where Camden High Street becomes Chalk Farm Road and crosses Regent's Canal) only opened in 1972, but now it is one of London's busiest and most interesting, especially for those looking for clothes, craft goods, pictures, books, antiques and cooked food. It is open every day but is busiest on Saturdays. Camden Lock is one of several markets in this little area, between Camden Town and Chalk Farm Tube stations. There is a Friday-to-Sunday market along Regent's Canal, between Kentish Town Road and Camden High Street; a very large and interesting market in a converted horse hospital, the Stables Market, on the western side of Chalk Farm Road; an older and more traditional street market in Inverness Street; and Camden Market, for clothes, jewellery and crafts, in Buck Street. A walk north from Camden Town station, along Camden High Street and Chalk Farm Road, will bring you to all these markets, starting with Inverness Street on your left and Camden Market on your right, then the cobbled courtyards of Camden Lock and the canal market on your right and left, then the Stables Market connected with Camden Lock, on your left. The canal and stable buildings are worth seeing, whether or not you are interested in buying old prints, ethnic clothes or a head massage. The prosperity of these Camden markets shows that Londoners still, after a thousand years, like buying things on the street, even if what they buy, and what they spend, have changed almost beyond recognition.

In west London Camden's rival is the set of markets centred on Portobello Road, which runs north–south alongside Kensington Park Road. Portobello began as a Saturday market in the 1860s, and Saturday is still the day to see the market at its fullest and best. Since the 1920s, thanks to pressure from jobless war veterans, it has operated as a fruit and vegetable market during the week, also selling household goods and cooked food. In general the southern section of Portobello Road (and its sidestreets) between Lonsdale Road, Westbourne Grove and Chepstow Villas has most of the best stalls and off-street covered markets selling antiques, works of art, books and collectibles; the central section concentrates on fruit and vegetables; and the northern part is scruffier and cheaper, with lots of stalls selling new and second-hand clothes, leather jackets, and so on. The market's official website, www.portobelloroad.co.uk, tells you how to find dealers in everything from advertising memorabilia to woodworking tools, and a walk (or slow shuffle) from Ladbroke Grove Underground station in the north to Notting Hill station in the south will take you past most of them.

There are more mundane local markets in other parts of suburban west London. In Shepherd's Bush there has been a market next to the railway line between Goldhawk Road and Uxbridge Road since the nineteenth century. Now it mainly serves the Irish and Afro-Caribbean populations, selling food and household goods, and is open every day except Monday and Thursday. A short walk away, in North End Road, Fulham (south of Lillie Road), there is a lively Monday–Saturday market, mostly selling food to the local population.

*

South London does not have a street market as famous as Petticoat Lane or Portobello Road, but it keeps the old spirit of street trading alive in several fascinating markets. My father's favourite in the 1950s and 1960s was East Lane, a big working-class market in East Street and nearby streets running east from Walworth Road about half a mile from the Elephant and Castle. East Lane operates every day but Monday, and it is at its biggest and best on Sunday mornings. It sells fruit and foodstuffs, but its strength is in clothes, household goods, bric-a-brac, plants and junk. Unlike its bigger rivals north of the river East Lane does not attract crowds of tourists, but those in search of what is left of old working-class London might visit it one Sunday. The market started in 1880, and was in its early years when one of Lambeth's greatest sons, Charlie Chaplin, was growing up in the neighbourhood. He was born in 1889 on the corner of East Street, at 277 Walworth Road, but his family was always on the move, and his other recorded (and blue-plaqued) houses are nearly a mile away in Kennington, at 287 Kennington Road and 39 Methley Street.

Another old Lambeth favourite, the Cut and Lower Marsh, just south of Waterloo Station, is not what it used to be in its Victorian heyday. The growth of traffic in the Cut in the 1960s limited the market to Lower Marsh, and even this has few stalls now. There is a better market in Bermondsey, where Bermondsey Square, the site of the ancient abbey, has been the site of the New Caledonian Market since 1949. The Old Caledonian Market developed alongside the cattle market established on Copenhagen Fields, Islington, when Smithfield cattle market was closed down in 1855. This vast assortment of stalls, barrows and baskets closed down in the Second World War, but reopened across the river as a major specialist antiques market. Its opening day is Friday, starting at dawn and finishing by noon.

Further south, Brixton Market is one of London's liveliest and most thriving. Stalls selling raw and cooked food (especially Caribbean specialities and meat and fish), new and old clothes, jewellery, bric-a-brac, craft and household goods have spread into the streets, covered markets and arcades near the Tube and railway stations, Electric Avenue, Brixton Station Road, Market Row, Brixton Village and Tunstall Road, and Granville and Station Arcades. Atlantic Road, where the market began in the early 1880s, has had few stalls since the market was moved to nearby streets in 1921. The market was transformed in its atmosphere, merchandise and customers when Brixton became a favourite area for Caribbean settlers in the 1950s and 1960s, and is now an excellent place for enjoying the new multicultural London, even if you do not want to buy anything. Opening hours vary, but the market is generally open Monday to Saturday.

If markets usually reflect the nature of their host community, then it is not surprising that the market in middle-class Greenwich is a world away from that in working-class Brixton. Greenwich Market has been licensed since 1700 and on its present site since 1831, but it is no longer the general market it was in the nineteenth century, or the fruit and vegetable market it was in the 1960s. Now its stalls sell the sort of thing you might find in Camden Lock or Portobello Road, but on a smaller scale – antiques and twentieth-century relics, crafts, food, books, jewellery, music, furniture and so on. There are several markets in Greenwich, but the main covered market is inside the square of handsome streets, including Nelson Road and Greenwich Church Street, which were built in the centre of Greenwich in 1829. The market is open from Thursday to Sunday, 9.30 (7.30 on Thursday and Friday) to 5.30. When you tire of bargain hunting, you are a few metres away from the last surviving tea clipper, the *Cutty Sark* (damaged by fire in 2007), the National Maritime Museum, Greenwich Park, the Royal Naval Hospital, the Greenwich Observatory and Inigo Jones's Queen's House, which is part of the museum. These are described in Chapters Three and Ten.

*

The open market predated the covered shop, but shops are not newcomers to the London street. There were 139 shops on London Bridge in 1358 according to rental records, and shops have been a feature of London life for many centuries. In general, they were started in the front rooms of houses or workshops. Old London shops were much smaller than they are today, with smaller window-panes and gloomier interiors. The plate-glass window, so important for enticing customers into modern shops, was not readily available until the mid-nineteenth century, so large windows had to be constructed from many small panes.

There are chance survivors of this old world of retailing scattered around London, though very few sell what they sold in the eighteenth century. The Old Curiosity Shop in Portsmouth Street, near the south-west corner of Lincoln's Inn Fields, a remnant of the demolished Clare Market, is generally regarded as London's oldest shop, but there is no evidence that it was a shop in the seventeenth century, when it was built, or that it acquired its present name until after Dickens's novel had been published in 1841. At present it sells shoes rather than curiosities. The single-room shops on the ground floor of Staple Inn, which was built in the 1580s, when Holborn was an important shopping street, can claim a longer ancestry, though this building has been reconstructed several times, and the oldest shopfront here, on number 3, is early nineteenth century. To find a shop that is still selling its original product in its original building we have to go to the eastern end of the Strand, number 216, where R. Twining & Co. have been dealing in tea, coffee and other drinks from this site since 1706, and from this building (allowing for the usual alterations) since 1787. The pretty 1787 shopfront, with a golden lion and two Chinese (not Indian) tea merchants, is said to be London's narrowest, but the shop is long and quite big inside. Until a few years ago there was a tobacconist in the Haymarket, Fribourg & Treyer, which had been in business since 1751. Fribourg & Treyer ceased to trade from 34 Haymarket some years ago, but the shopfront, with two bow windows glazed with small panes, and fanlights and the old tobacconist's insignia, is the oldest in London, and some of the interior fittings are eighteenth century too.

Not far away, at the Pall Mall end of St James's Street, there are two old shops still selling what they sold when George III lived in St James's Palace. Lock's, at number 6, has been supplying hats to the London gentry from this shop since 1765, and its present shopfront dates from the 1810s. The house itself is late seventeenth century with an eighteenth-century brick front. Lock's made hats for Wellington and Napoleon, and Nelson was wearing one of their hats when he was fatally wounded on the *Victory* in 1805. Lock's made the first bowler hat in 1850, and supplied Oscar Wilde and Charlie Chaplin with their bowlers. A selection of their old stock can be seen through the windows of the shop. A few doors along, next to Pickering Place, is Berry Brothers and Rudd, which has been selling wine here since 1698. The hanging coffee mill sign is a reminder that for their first hundred years they also sold coffee and tea to the many coffee houses that lined the streets of St James's. The house was rebuilt by William Pickering in 1731, and the oldest part of the present shopfront dates from around 1800. Inside, there are coffee scales on which distinguished customers from the Prince Regent and the Duke of Wellington to Laurence Olivier have been weighed, and under the shop, extending across the surrounding streets, are vast and ancient cellars, the largest of their kind in London, in which part of Berry Brothers' stock is stored.

Lobb, the shoemaker at number 9, seems like an upstart next to these two veterans, though it has been trading in St James's Street since the 1890s. There are several other very long-established retailers in St James's Street, though they have not occupied their present shops for so long. The pharmacist D.R. Harris and Co., which only moved into 29 St James's Street in 1963, first opened at number 11 in 1790. The fine interior of the shop is Victorian. Robert Lewis, London's oldest cigar and tobacco shop, has been trading at 19 St James's Street since the 1840s, but started out in Long Acre in 1787. Justerini and Brooks (J & B), the wine merchant at number 61, began trading in London in 1749, and the barber Truefitt and Hill, at number 71, has been cutting Londoners' hair in various shops since 1805. William Evans has been selling guns in clubland since 1883, but only moved to 69a St James's Street when their Pall Mall shop was bombed out in 1944.

There are remnants of London's eighteenth- and nineteenth-century shopping world all over central London. James Smith and Sons' umbrella shop on the corner of New Oxford Street and Shaftesbury Avenue is a famous survivor. They have been making and selling umbrellas, sword-sticks, riding crops, whips, Malacca canes and shooting sticks in London since 1830, and here since 1867. The shop is in one of the houses built when New Oxford Street was driven through St Giles in the 1840s, and the beautiful brass, mahogany and plate-glass shopfront dates from the 1870s. The inside is a treat, and a Smith walking cane or umbrella might help you take advantage of the rest of this book. There is another excellent umbrella shop, in a totally different style, at 118 London Wall, near the Moorgate corner. T. Fox and Co. has been trading in the City since 1868, and their building is late Georgian (1830s), but their shopfront was designed in the modern style in 1937 in stainless steel and Vitrolite, the glassy black material used in the slightly earlier Daily Express building on Fleet Street. The interior is in the same 1930s style.

Out by themselves in Artillery Lane, Spitalfields, just where it meets Artillery Passage (near Bishopsgate), there are two lovely shops, built in the 1760s for two silk merchants, Nicholas Jourdain and Francis Rybot. Number 56 with two curved windows, a fashionable door and fanlight and impressive Doric columns, is one of London's finest Georgian shops, and number 58, refronted in the early nineteenth century, is simpler but still handsome. The interior of number 56 is also very fine, but since the shop is shut you cannot see it. When Samuel Johnson told Oliver Goldsmith in 1773 that a walk from Charing Cross to Whitechapel would take him past 'the greatest series of shops in the world', perhaps he had these two shops, among others, in mind. Walking in the opposite direction (west), there are a few fine old shops (no longer in use) in the City, recalling the days when this was London's main shopping centre. Number 43 Eastcheap, near St Margaret Pattens church, has a fine 1830s shop window between two classical doorways, and in Laurence Pountney Lane, off the eastern end of Cannon Street, number 9 has a good late-eighteenth-century shopfront on a seventeenth-century house. An alley on the right joins Laurence Pountney Lane to Laurence Pountney Hill, in one of those little hidden City squares that Dickens praised in Chapter 37 of *Nicholas Nickleby*, contrasting them with the 'aristocratic gravity' of the Mayfair squares: 'The city square has no enclosure, save the lamp-post in the middle: and no grass, but the weeds which spring up round its base. It is a quiet, little-frequented, retired spot, favourable to melancholy and contemplation, and appointments of long-waiting.' Bow Lane, between Cannon Street and Cheapside, is still a real shopping street, and some of its shops (numbers 6–8 and number 54) have late-Victorian fronts.

The walk along Fleet Street and the Strand, the old route between the City and Westminster, is enjoyable now for its public buildings, churches, offices, hotels, theatres, banks and pubs, its very rich historical connections and its side alleys, rather than for its shops, old or new. Fleet Street, once a great shopping artery, has a late-eighteenth-century shopfront on the side of the Cheshire Cheese pub (number 145), facing 1 Wine Office Court, and another in Middle Temple Lane, just before Temple Bar and the Twinings shop mentioned earlier. Hoare's, roughly opposite the Fleet Street corner of Chancery Lane, is one of London's oldest and best bank buildings. Hoare's was established here in 1690, at the very beginning of specialist banking in England. This fine building in Bath stone was built in 1830, and involved the demolition of the Mitre Tavern, Dr Johnson's favourite drinking place. Its restrained domestic style contrasts very greatly, inside and out, with the ostentatious designs favoured by later-nineteenth-century bankers. Sir Arthur Blomfield's Fleet Street branch of the Bank of England (1886–8), on the other side of the street (now a pub) by the Law Courts, makes the contrast clear.

The Strand, another famous shopping street, lost the interesting old shops at its eastern end a hundred years ago, when Wych Street and Holywell Street, famous for their rickety old houses and second-hand bookshops, were demolished to make way for the Aldwych development in 1900. West of Waterloo Bridge, there is the fine Savoy Tailors' Guild shop next to the Savoy Hotel, which started selling suits to gentlemen on a cash-only basis in 1903. After the

Savoy, the shops at numbers 77–86 occupy the Strand front of what used to be the Hotel Cecil, which was Europe's biggest hotel when it opened in 1885. Its developer, Jabez Balfour, was a fraudster who later spent ten years in prison. Across the street, numbers 409–10, the impressive building with Corinthian columns next to the Adelphi Theatre, was built in 1886 as the Adelphi Theatre Restaurant by the Gatti brothers, the owners of several theatres and restaurants. It is now an amusement arcade. Numbers 399–400, now a very ugly building occupied by Stanley Gibbons the stamp dealer, was the site of one of London's most famous restaurants, Romano's. It was opened as the Café Vaudeville in 1899 by Romano, a head waiter at the Café Royal, and became immensely popular with theatrical and music hall people, and Bohemian London in general. Its popularity declined after the Great War, and it took a direct hit in the Blitz.

A right turn into Wellington Street, opposite Waterloo Bridge, takes you past the lovely Lyceum Theatre, and Penhaligon's the perfumier, which has been here since 1870. And in Tavistock Street, on the left, is London's oldest theatrical costumier, Charles Fox's, which has been supplying make-up to the Lyceum and Drury Lane theatres since 1878. Fox's still has its designs for the wigs made for Sir Henry Irving and Ellen Terry in the 1880s and 1890s when Irving ran the Lyceum and Terry was his leading lady. Now (and perhaps then) part of its trade involves supplying cosmetics and teaching make-up skills to transvestites. A walk along Henrietta Street and Chandos Street, a right turn into Bedfordbury, and a left turn into a well-hidden gaslit alley, Goodwin's Court, take you to one of the best-preserved rows of eighteenth-century shops (now offices) in London. The houses in Goodwin's Court were probably built in the 1690s, but the bowed shopfronts on numbers 1–8 are late eighteenth century.

*

18. Lock & Co, hatters, one of the oldest shops in St James's Street. Lock's invented the bowler hat, and supplied bowlers to Oscar Wilde and Charlie Chaplin.

19. London's oldest shop, Twinings, has been selling tea and coffee from this site in the Strand since 1706, and from this very narrow building since 1787.

20. Burlington Arcade, London's longest and best-known covered shopping street, built by Lord George Cavendish between 1818 and 1819. It is one of four arcades in this neighbourhood.

21. Leadenhall Market in 1897. There has been a provisions market here since the late fourteenth century, and this glass and iron building, the work of Horace Jones, dates from 1881.

22. New Scotland Yard, the headquarters of the Metropolitan Police from 1890 to the 1960s. Norman Shaw's new style, with projecting turrets and stone bands in red brickwork, was much imitated.

23. Troops and spectators at the execution of the Jacobite Lord Lovat, the last person to be beheaded on Tower Hill, in 1747.

24. 'A pleasant place indeed . . . So shady!' Fountain Court, in the Temple, where John Westlock courted Ruth Pinch in Dickens' *Martin Chuzzlewit*. Photographed in 1896.

25. Nicholas Barbon's Buckingham Street, leading from the Strand to the York Watergate. Samuel Pepys lived at number 12 in the 1680s, and Dickens lodged at number 15 in 1834. David Copperfield had 'a compact set of chambers' here, thanks to Mrs Trotwood. Drawn by Arthur Moreland in 1931.

26. St Martin-in-the-Fields and Charles I's statue, engraved by John Woods in 1838. On the church steps David Copperfield met Mr Peggoty, searching for little Emily.

27. The courtyard of Apothecaries' Hall, on Blackfriars Lane. The hall was built just after the Great Fire of 1666, on land once occupied by the Blackfriars monastery and Blackfriars playhouse.

28. *Left*. Paddington Station in 1896. Isambard Kingdom Brunel built the station between 1850 and 1854, as the London terminus of the Great Western Railway, under the influence of Paxton's new Crystal Palace. Brunel's iron columns were replaced with steel ones in 1922.

29. *Below, left*. Greenwich Observatory in 1896. The centrepiece, Flamsteed House, was built for the first Astronomer Royal by Wren and Robert Hooke in 1675–6. The time ball on the turret falls at exactly one p.m., for the benefit of ships on the Thames.

30. *Below*. Little Venice, where the Regent's (or the Grand Union) Canal meets the Paddington Basin near Paddington Station. Robert Browning suggested the name, which is more convincing to those who have not seen the original.

31. The twelfth-century Clattern Bridge crossing the Hogsmill river in Kingston. The bridge is one of the oldest in Britain, and the Hogsmill (at Ewell) was the stream depicted in Sir John Millais' painting *Ophelia* (1851–2).

32. The River Lea at Tottenham Mills, about 300 metres east of Tottenham Hale station. Engraved by John Henshall in 1838, two years before the Great Eastern Railway disturbed Tottenham's rustic tranquility.

Those interested in fine old shopfronts might take a short walk around the streets near Soho Square. In the square itself there is a nice bow-fronted shop at number 13, dating from 1768, another of 1766, with Doric columns, at number 37, and a fine mid-nineteenth-century shop at number 38, across Carlile Street. Numbers 4–6 were Trotter's Bazaar, mentioned below. Take a walk around and across the square to see C.G. Cibber's rather weathered contemporary statue of Charles II, standing in front of an electricity substation disguised as a Tudor arbour in the garden, the imposing front of Crosse and Blackwell's old pickle factory at number 20, and the House of St Barnabas on the corner of Greek Street (1744–57), the finest eighteenth-century house in Soho. Then leave the square by Carlile Street (which has some good seventeenth- and eighteenth-century houses) to find Dean Street, a few metres away.

Ahead of you, on the left, is number 88 Dean Street, Rippon Stationer and Newsagent, a house and shop of 1791, with two very charming bay display windows, each divided into ten panes of glass. The decorative detail is classical, and the paint-encrusted brown panels over the two windows have unusual shell-like rococo, or *rocaille*, decoration. It is still a newsagent's. Go left on Dean Street, which has plenty of houses surviving from the street's rebuilding in the 1730s and one or two from the 1690s, when the street was first built. Most of the houses from numbers 76 to 80 and 86–90 were built in the 1730s, and opposite them are numbers 26–28 (1734) and 29 (1692). Karl Marx and his family (and maid) lived in debt and discomfort in two rooms on the top floor of number 28 (now part of the restaurant Quo Vadis) in 1850–6 (the plaque is wrong). Two of Marx's babies and his consumptive eight-year-old son Edgar died in Dean Street. At around this point turn briefly into Meard Street, which is named after John Meard, the carpenter who built this street between 1722 and 1733. Numbers 9 and 13 Meard Street have good old shop windows. Most of the houses here, including the whole south side of the street, were built by

Meard, and so was 68 Dean Street, Meard's own house, and its neighbours.

Turn left into Old Compton Street, Soho's busiest shopping street, and a centre of Soho's French community in the eighteenth and nineteenth centuries. Patisserie Valerie, which moved here when its original Frith Street cafe was bombed in the Blitz, tastily preserves the French culinary tradition. Then return to Soho Square along Frith Street, which still has plenty of fine houses dating from the early eighteenth century, and a few (numbers 60–62, opposite the essayist William Hazlitt's) that survive from the 1680s, when the street was first built. At number 15, built in 1733, there is an impressive Gothick shopfront, probably inserted by a book-binder in 1816, which is a rarity in London. The widest bay, topped with cast-iron tracery, was the original shop window.

For refreshment you might try the Dog and Duck pub on the corner of Bateman Street, which has a lovely 1890s mirrored and tiled interior. And as you walk along Frith Street you might notice the houses of some of its famous ex-residents, including John Logie Baird, who gave the first demonstration of television to members of the Royal Institution in his attic laboratory at number 22 in January 1926, Mozart, who lived at number 20 (rebuilt) in 1764–5, and Hazlitt, who spent his last years in poverty and pain in a room in number 6, and died there in 1830 with Charles Lamb at his bedside. Hazlitt was buried in the churchyard of St Anne's church, near the southern end of Wardour Street. Only the tower survived the Blitz, and on the west side of this tower you will find Hazlitt's much-eroded headstone, under a memorial to the King of Corsica, who 'died immediately after leaving the King's Bench Prison', having 'registered his Kingdom of Corsica for the use of his creditors'. Hazlitt's large tomb is in the churchyard, with this epitaph: 'A man of true moral courage who sacrificed profit and present fame to principle'. A little further (south) down Wardour Street, across Shaftesbury Avenue, there is a very fine shop (with an excellent clock) at numbers 41–43, which was built for the theatrical wigmaker Willy Clarkson in 1904–5. His fame in the theatrical world is shown by the names of those who laid the first and last stones – Sarah Bernhardt and Sir Henry Irving. Clarkson's wigs were not always convincing. Dr Crippen and his mistress were wearing them when they were recognized and caught in 1910.

Greek Street, which is parallel with Frith and Dean Streets, has some interesting and important shops. Numbers 12–13, which were built in 1684 and stuccoed in the twentieth century, were used between 1774 and 1795 as the London showrooms of Josiah Wedgwood, the greatest pottery manufacturer of the Industrial Revolution. This was the beginning of a new phenomenon, the association of mass production with sophisticated commercial marketing. Wedgwood began making his fine pottery in Staffordshire factories in the 1760s, and soon saw the need to win rich and fashion-setting customers in London, especially members of the aristocracy and royalty, in order to stimulate imitative middle-class demand. To achieve this he opened London showrooms, first in Charles Street, now Carlos Place, off Grosvenor Square, in 1765, then in Great Newport Street, in 1768, and then in Greek Street in 1774. Wedgwood took over this bigger showroom to put the thousand-piece 'Frog' dinner service, made for Catherine the Great of Russia, on public display. Next door, number 14, another stuccoed late-seventeenth-century house, was the headquarters of an early working men's club, the St James and Soho Club, from 1864, and over the road at L'Escargot the original restaurateur Monsieur Gaudin has been riding a snail for over a hundred years. Further along, there are four early-nineteenth-century shopfronts, at numbers 17, 18, 20 and 21.

*

Sometimes, developers built large buildings to provide accommodation for a collection of individual shops. The Royal Exchange and the New Exchange in the Strand were two early examples, and London has several others. Ten St James Street, on the corner of

King Street, was built in 1830–2 by James Pennethorne as the St James' Bazaar, and the building still exists, though it has been altered and heightened since then. There was another bazaar on Soho Square, where John Trotter, an army contractor, converted his warehouse (numbers 4–6) into a covered market in 1816 to give employment to people (especially young women) thrown out of work by the post-war slump. Trotter's Bazaar, two floors of stalls and counters, was a great success despite competition from the Pantheon in Oxford Street, which was converted into a bazaar in 1834. Trotter's lasted until 1889, when the building was taken over by the publishers A. and C. Black. The building still exists, unlike the Pantheon, which was demolished to make way for the Oxford Circus branch of Marks and Spencer in the 1930s.

Another Regency innovation, the shopping arcade, had a greater impact on the London shopping scene. The idea of a covered private street lined with shops, where the well-off could spend time and money without spoiling their shoes in dust or mud, was inspired by the example of classical Greece and Rome, and by the arcaded piazzas of Renaissance Italy. The Place des Vosges in Paris, built between 1605 and 1612, and Covent Garden piazza, built in the 1630s, had shops protected by arcades, and Thomas Gresham's original Royal Exchange, built in 1568, had an open courtyard surrounded by arcaded booths or shops. We can see what the Covent Garden arcades looked like because part of the original arcading on the north side was rebuilt in replica in 1877–9. Other covered exchanges or shopping centres were built in seventeenth-century London on either side of the Strand, but are now gone. Perhaps the immediate model for London's Regency arcades was the Jardins du Palais Royal, a large Italian-style arcaded quadrangle built in the 1780s and still largely intact. Over thirty arcades were built in Paris in the 1790s and 1800s, and their social, aesthetic and commercial advantages were greatly appreciated by English visitors to the city from 1814 onwards.

London's first arcaded covered shopping street was the Royal

Opera Arcade, between Pall Mall and Charles II Street, which was built as part of John Nash's Regent Street scheme between 1815 and 1817. It was built by Nash and George Repton behind the 1813 Royal Opera House in the Haymarket, which is now Her Majesty's Theatre, rebuilt in a grand style for Herbert Beerbohm Tree in the 1890s. The arcade is about 3.5 metres wide, and has 18 shops in 18 square bays, all on the same side of the street and each lit by a circular skylight, and by lamps for evening shoppers. The arcade survived two rebuildings of the theatre and the construction in the late 1950s of New Zealand House, on the east side of the arcade. When you are here, remember this neighbourhood's special place in London's theatrical history. There has been a theatre here ever since Sir John Vanbrugh built the Haymarket Theatre in 1704, and in London only Drury Lane has a longer continuous history of theatrical activity.

Although the West End needed new shops, there was not an arcade craze on the Parisian scale. Only four arcades, the Burlington on Piccadilly, the Lowther and the New Exeter, both on the Strand, and the Halkin Arcade in Belgravia, were built in London between 1817 and 1875, and only the first and last of these still exist. The Burlington Arcade was built by Lord George Cavendish between 1818 and 1819 as a shopping street linking Piccadilly and Burlington Gardens, alongside Burlington House (now the Royal Academy). It soon became a fashionable promenade, and its shops still attract wealthy and fastidious customers. England's longest, richest and most famous arcade is lined with 72 beautiful and highly polished two- and three-storey Regency shops, which look more or less as they did in 1819, although some have increased the size of their window panes. The T-shaped Halkin Arcade, a thriving and handsome enclave of shops, cafes and offices, was built in 1830 between West Halkin Street, Motcomb Street, Lowndes Street and Kinnerton Street, near the west corner of Belgrave Square.

The popularity of the arcade did not disappear with the coming of the department store after the 1860s. The Royal Arcade was built between Albemarle Street and Old Bond Street in 1879, and two arcades were built in Kensington, the Brompton Arcade of 1890 and the Park Mansions Arcade of 1910. The Metropolitan Railway built the Metropolitan Arcade between Liverpool Street and Broad Street in 1911, when the switch from steam to electric power made it possible to build over the tracks. When Bush House was built as a trade centre between the Aldwych and the Strand in the 1920s it included an arcade of eight shops on the Strand side, which is still in use. The Quadrant Arcade was built on Regent Street in 1920 and Prince's Arcade on Piccadilly in 1930, and three were built between the world wars in once-fashionable Brixton – Market Row and the Reliance Arcade in 1925 and the Granville Arcade in 1937. The Brixton arcades are now part of Brixton Market, as far removed from the Burlington Arcade in price and spirit as one could imagine.

There is a variation on the covered arcade in Holborn, between Southampton Row and Vernon Place, the southern side of Blooms-bury Square. This is Sicilian Avenue, London's first open-air pedes-trian shopping street. It was built by the Bedford estate between 1906 and 1910, when slum clearance and the new Aldwych/ Kingsway scheme made smart shopping developments profitable in this neighbourhood. Robert Worley's design included a classical screen at each end to establish the Bedford estate's right of way, black and white marble paving, little bow-fronted shops with flower beds between big Corinthian columns, fancy shopfronts in Doulton terracotta and turreted offices above.

When you come out of the Burlington Arcade into Piccadilly, cross the road and choose one of the two arcades linking Picca-dilly with Jermyn Street. To your right is the Piccadilly Arcade, built in 1910 as part of an office development. The pretty shops are neo-Regency, and the lighting, from the start, was electric, not, as in earlier arcades, natural light through skylights. Emerging by the new statue of Beau Brummel, a local boy (from Chesterfield Street, Mayfair) and a hero of the fashion industry, turn left into Jermyn

Street. Just past Fortnum and Mason, you can turn left again along the Prince's Arcade, the last arcade built in the West End. Then take a look around Fortnum and Mason, London's grandest and most expensive department store. Charles Fortnum's grocery shop has been on this site since 1773, and John Mason joined the partnership in 1817. Fortnum and Mason supplied the royal family, local West End clubs and military and geographical expeditions, including Wellington's officers and Scott's expedition to the South Pole. The present shop dates from 1926–8, and now sells gifts and flowers as well as groceries and its famous hampers.

Return to Jermyn Street, which has some old and interesting shops. Floris, at number 89, has been selling (and until the 1960s making) perfume in Jermyn Street since 1730, in a house that was about fifty years old when they first moved in. The shopfront is mid-nineteenth century, and the interior evokes the spirit of the Great Exhibition of 1851. The two houses next door to Floris, numbers 87 and 88, were once the homes of Isaac Newton. He lived in a house on the site of the present number 87, the one with the plaque, from 1700 to 1709, but number 88, his home from 1696 to 1700, is still standing, but plaqueless. A few doors along, Paxton and Whitfield, number 93, have been selling cheese here since 1835, in a stuccoed 1670s house with a fine Victorian shopfront. They are said to be London's best cheesemongers. Harvie and Hudson, the shirtmakers at number 97, have kept their lovely tiled and arcaded Victorian shopfront, though the house itself was rebuilt in 1910, and numbers 20, 21 and 113 are good late-nineteenth-century shops.

In offering the convenience of shopping for a variety of goods under one roof, arcades were the predecessor of the department store. Once again Paris, not London, was the birthplace of department stores, but it was in late-Victorian and Edwardian London, the world's biggest and richest city by far, that department stores reached their greatest heights. By 1914 there were about twenty in central and suburban London, depending on how a few borderline cases are classified. There has been a severe reduction in the number of great department stores in London over the past few decades, but when the stores have closed down the buildings have sometimes survived.

Some of the great department stores had their origins in small draper's or grocer's shops early in the nineteenth century. Harrods started as a small Knightsbridge grocery shop in 1849, and its neighbour Harvey Nichols as a linen drapers on the corner of Knightsbridge and Sloane Street in 1813. These shops took several decades to develop into what we would recognize as department stores, and the first London shop to achieve this status was William Whiteley of Bayswater. Whiteley made the transition from haberdasher to 'Universal Provider' very quickly, between 1863 and 1871, and his rapid rise was resented by other Bayswater traders, who might have been responsible for the fact that his shops burnt down so often. Like most early department stores, Whiteley's grew by the gradual aggregation of neighbouring shops into a ramshackle and unplanned whole. The building of purpose-built superstores generally took place in the Edwardian decade, between 1901 and 1911. Whiteley's moved from Westbourne Grove into its grand new store on Queensway in 1911, and out of it seventy years later, when Selfridges (which bought Whiteley's in 1927) decided that Bayswater could no longer support its own great store.

Having given up being a department store, Whiteley's reopened in 1989 as a gigantic arcade, or covered shopping mall, with a multiplex cinema, restaurants, film studios and a branch of Marks and Spencer. Some of the best features of the old Whiteley's, including the two impressive galleried and glass-domed courts, one with a fine double staircase, and the 1920s plasterwork in the top-floor restaurant, have been retained. Other stores to close and reopen as multi-store bazaars include Swan and Edgar's on Piccadilly Circus, between Piccadilly and Regent Street. This is an impressive pile in the French baroque style, built by Sir Reginald Blomfield between 1910 and 1920, but its interior was rebuilt in 1985.

Some other ex-department stores have not been so lucky. Gamages, stranded in Holborn when shoppers moved west, closed in 1972 and was demolished, and the first purpose-built department store, Bon Marché of Brixton, shut in 1975, when Brixton had lost its middle-class customers, and is now used by smaller retailers. Shoolbred's, the great furniture department store in Tottenham Court Road, is gone, leaving only Maples and Heal's, a fine steel-framed shop built at the start of the First World War, to represent the once-powerful Tottenham Court Road furniture trade. Notice the depictions of woodworking tools that decorate the Heal's frontage, the cleverly curved display windows and the well-made staircase. The Civil Service Stores burned down in 1982, though part of the building survives at numbers 423–427 the Strand.

Several of the great Edwardian department stores remain, both in the West End and the suburbs. Harrods, which was rebuilt in grand style on 4.5 acres of Knightsbridge between 1894 and 1912, is still a great London institution and landmark, worth a visit whether or not you want to shop. The familiar Brompton Road exterior, two stories of windows topped with four stories of red Doulton terracotta and a dome, is in the baroque style of the Second Empire (inspired by the rebuilding of Paris in the 1850s and 1860s, especially the Opéra Garnier), and the rear block on Basil Street was built in the Beaux Arts style in 1929–30. Inside, Harrods retains many of its lavish Edwardian decorative features. The 1902–3 Doulton tiling in the Meat Hall is wonderful, and the tiles and plasterwork in the Food Hall are as delicious as the food on sale there. The interior was remodelled and restored in the 1980s by its new owner, Mohamed Al Fayed, and some of the results are spectacular. The black granite perfumery department is impressive, the Egyptian Hall (with its escalator hall) is extraordinary, and the memorial to Diana and Dodi is very odd.

A short walk through Hans Place and Cadogan Square brings you to Sloane Square and a store built in an entirely different style. Peter Jones has been trading on this site since 1877, and was taken over by John Lewis in 1906. This was the store in which John Spedan Lewis first introduced his profit-sharing staff partnership system in 1920. Lewis rebuilt the store in the 1930s to the designs of William Crabtree, whose inspiration was the work of the German architect Erich Mendelsohn. If Harrods in terracotta looks like an opera house, Peter Jones in functional steel and glass resembles a handsome office block. Its curtain wall (non-load-bearing on a steel frame) was one of the first in England. Inside the store is impressive, with a fine central atrium and a lovely spiral staircase which makes climbing the stairs a pleasure.

There was another concentration of department stores in Kensington High Street, where John Barker, a Whiteley's manager, opened his own draper's shop in 1870. Like his old boss, he gradually expanded along the street until in 1895 he had 60 departments and 1,500 staff. In 1927, when Barker's owned the whole block between King Street and Young Street, they started building the store that now dominates this part of Kensington High Street. The big vertical windows in a steel frame are reminiscent of Selfridges, but here the steel is encased in plain stone piers rather than Ionic columns, and the mood is art deco rather than classical. The interior was remodelled in 1985–8, and now the building is occupied by a shopping mall and offices. Next to Barker's, going west, was Derry and Toms, which started in the 1860s and was taken over by Barker's in 1920. Barker's built the present dull classical building, which lacks the bold style of its own store. The House of Fraser, which bought Barker's and Derry and Toms in 1957, closed Derry and Toms in 1973 and Barker's in 2006. What Derry and Toms had, and still has, is a lovely 1.5-acre roof garden, laid out by Ralph Hancock in 1936–8, which includes Spanish, Tudor and English woodland gardens, fountains, streams, palm trees and lakes with exotic birds. After Derry and Toms closed the building was taken over by Biba, the 'swinging sixties' women's clothes store, which in turn gave way to Marks and Spencer, BHS and other retailers. The gardens are now owned by Sir Richard Branson and can be visited when they are not in use for private events. The website www.roofgardens.com gives details of ways to visit the gardens.

∗

A walk along Oxford Street, Britain's busiest shopping street, is an interesting way to examine the development of London retailing. Almost every building in this 1.25-mile street was built as a shop or public house, and the buildings that survive represent almost every sort of shop since the early nineteenth century, though most of them are now occupied by very modern and often transient shops. Walk on the southern side, from the eastern end, looking across the road, and turn back on the other side when you have passed Selfridges.

Starting at the Tottenham Court Road junction, the first building of interest is the Tottenham pub, which claims to have been on this spot since 1824, though until 1894 it was called the Flying Horse. It is the only survivor of the nineteen pubs a determined drinker could have visited in Oxford Street in the 1890s. The building is 1790s with a 1900 frontage, and the fine art nouveau interior is full of painted mirrors and ceilings. The pub was rebuilt in 1892 by the Baker brothers, the greatest pub owners of the time, who employed the firm of Jones and Firmin to paint the mirrors and F. de Jong and Company to do the panels depicting the seasons. The Tottenham used to serve drinks to the customers of one of London's greatest music halls, Charles Morton's Oxford Music Hall, which was built in 1861, rebuilt in 1892 and demolished in 1926. Its site at number 14 is now occupied by a large 1920s building faced with white faience (glazed porcelain), which used to be a 2,500-seat Lyons Corner House restaurant and is now a Virgin (or Zavvi) entertainment store, with a reconstructed interior. Walking west, you cross Rathbone Place, which has a street sign (Rathbones

Place) dating back to 1718, when the area was first developed. After Berners Street is the old Bourne and Hollingsworth department store (numbers 116–132), built in the mid-1920s on a site laboriously assembled between 1902 and 1920 from over thirty smaller shops. Its monumental Greek-style exterior survives, but after Bourne and Hollingsworth closed in 1983 it was gutted for a new shopping mall, the Plaza, which was replanned in 1996 and looks like the inside of a Hollywood spaceship. Michael Rizzello's sculpture of a girl with ribbons, on the front of the building, was placed there in 1997.

Mappin House, the old Mappin and Webb building at number 156–162, was built for the jeweller's by J.J. Joas in 1906–8, an early steel-framed building faced with white marble, and fine Doric columns dividing large plate-glass windows. After Winsley Street, at numbers 164–182, was another famous old store, Waring and Gillow, which used to supply furniture to the best West End clubs and hotels. The palatial shop was built in 1901–6, and the architect Frank Atkinson was helped by advice from the great Norman Shaw. The general style (in the words of Nikolaus Pevsner) is 'riotous Hampton Court Baroque' in orange brick, granite and Portland stone. Look at the carved ships' prows, cornucopias and rainwater heads. Robert Gillow had made and sold furniture on Oxford Street since the 1760s, and went into partnership with the Waring family, more recent Oxford Street arrivals, in 1897. The shop was reconstructed as shops and offices in 1977. Next door (numbers 184–190) was a basic Lyons cafe of 1959, and from Great Portland Street to Oxford Circus there is the grandiose pillared building, with enormous barrel-vaulted arches over the doors, which was the department store Peter Robinson, and which is now (2007) Topshop. Peter Robinson's story is typical of many West End department stores. It started here as a draper's in 1833, and gradually acquired enough of its neighbours to enable it to build a great store occupying a whole block or island site. This store was built in the early 1920s, using an arrangement of windows and columns copied from Lord and Taylor's store on Fifth Avenue, New York. There was another Peter Robinson's on Regent Street, which specialized in mourning wear, and was thus known as Black Peter Robinson's.

After Oxford Circus, the north side of Oxford Street is dominated by several big department stores. First, after the huge London College of Fashion and British Home Stores building (1962–3), is the John Lewis department store, the central store of a thriving suburban and national chain based on staff partnership principles first introduced in the 1920s. John Lewis, a buyer for Peter Robinson, started trading as an independent draper at what is now 286 Oxford Street in 1864, and by 1895 he had a three-storey department store with 150 staff. The big Oxford Street store that his son, John Spedan Lewis, started building in 1936 was badly damaged by bombing in 1940 and rebuilt in 1958–60. Barbara Hepworth's *Winged Figure* was added a year later. The Cavendish Square side of the building is pre-war. Next to John Lewis there is the 1935–7 D.H. Evans department store, which replaced their earlier store of 1909. D.H. Evans began here as a draper's in 1879, and now trades as part of the voracious House of Fraser chain. Then Debenham's externally severe but internally interesting department store, built in 1968–71 to replace Sir Horace Jones's old Marshall and Snelgrove store, which had stood here since 1870. Like John Lewis and House of Fraser, Debenham's has built up a chain of department stores by taking over suburban and provincial retailers.

Then comes Stratford Place, a 1770s terraced street that ends in a little square and the mansion of the owner of the street, Edward Stratford, Earl of Aldborough. Stratford House (later Derby House and now the Oriental Club) was built in the Robert Adam style, with impressive Ionic columns and sculptures of *Fame* and *Mars*. The three-storey wings were built by Lord Derby in 1908–9. The entrance to Stratford Place was once gated and guarded, and one of the lodges or guard-boxes remains, with a Coade stone lion on its top. It is easy to miss in the bustle of Oxford Street. Next, at numbers 362–366, H & M occupies yet another old Lyons restaurant, built during the Great War with a handsome white faience exterior.

Selfridges, which occupies the whole block between Duke Street and Orchard Street, represents the arrival of American retailing methods in London before the Great War. Gordon Selfridge came to London from Chicago, where he had managed the retail department of Marshall Fields, in 1906, and decided that a department store did not need to grow over decades, as other London stores had, but could be created at a stroke. So the first part of his great new store, the nine eastern bays and seven bays on Duke Street, was built between 1907 and 1909. The building was designed by several American and British architects and engineers, and the huge plate-glass windows and cast-iron panels between the partly exposed piers of the steel frame gave the building an unusually modern appearance for its time, despite the gigantic Ionic columns. The store was organized on American lines, displaying its goods in uncluttered and artistic window displays and offering its customers the freedom to browse without being bothered by floorwalkers. The western end of Selfridges was built between 1920 and 1924, and the central section, with its bronze and Portland stone statue, the *Queen of Time*, was started in 1926, when the last of the Victorian shops on the site had been acquired. Many of the decorative features of the original shop, including the bronze work on the great revolving doors, still survive. The large plaque in the pavement praising Gordon Selfridge's achievement was placed there in 1930, when the whole store was finished.

In the 1920s Gordon Selfridge's success enabled him to buy up Whiteley's and several suburban department stores, but after his wife's death in 1918 he had started spending his fortune on actresses and gambling, and was finally (in 1941) forced to give up his interest in the business. By the time he died in Putney in 1947 all his fortune was spent. The collection of suburban stores that Selfridge had accumulated, including Bon Marché in Brixton, John

Barnes in Hampstead, Jones Brothers in Holloway and Pratt's of Streatham, was sold to John Lewis, and all have now closed down.

*

Now cross to the northern (Selfridges) side of the road and walk back towards Oxford Circus. Look across the street to the impressive red brick building at numbers 407–413, a remnant of a planned rebuilding of this part of Oxford Street by the Grosvenor estate (the landlords of this stretch of the street) in French Second Empire style. It was designed by the Grosvenor estate architect, Thomas Cundy III, in 1864 and built eight years later. Numbers 385–397 were also the work of Grosvenor estate architects, this time in the late 1880s, in the Loire chateau style, with rather fine red brick crests and badges. After Gilbert Street, West One Shopping Centre numbers 375–383, around Bond Street Tube station – is a new shopping mall, not converted from older buildings as most of the West End malls are. At this point, spotting the angular Hog in the Pound pub, you might enjoy a brief diversion down South Molton Street, which leaves Oxford Street at an acute angle, following the course of the Tyburn brook. This is a fine pedestrianized shopping street, with many good eighteenth-century houses converted into interesting or expensive shops. The great trade unionist and Labour politician Ernest Bevin lived in a flat on the left (number 34), and on the right there is a run of fine eighteenth-century houses, numbers 14–26. The visionary poet and artist William Blake lived in obscurity with his wife Catherine on the second floor of number 17 from 1804 to 1820. Several other shops and houses in the street are worth a look.

Returning to Oxford Street, numbers 363–367 were built for HMV in the new modernist style in 1938–9, faced in black granite, and with glass bricks and small windows to transmit light but not sound. HMV's first shop was opened here by Edward Elgar in 1921, and in 1962 the Beatles cut a 78 rpm demo disc at the recording studio here which led to their first long-term contract with EMI. HMV moved out in 2000, and the shop's fine spiral staircase was removed at the same time. The white-tiled building at number 311, now Waterstone's, was the headquarters and chief shop of Woolworth's in London, built in 1924, next door to the nicely decorated 1890 Noah's Ark public house (number 313), now closed, which looks like an opera house with its false balcony and gesticulating classical figures. Behind the dull red brick frontage of numbers 275–279 there is a hall built as a rink in the ice-skating craze of 1875 and converted six years later into the Salvation Army's first West End hall, which it still is.

After Oxford Circus, on either side of Argyll Street, are two early Tube stations, the first a Bakerloo Line station of 1905–6 by Leslie Green, with arcades of deep red glazing known as sang-de-boeuf (beef blood), the second a Central London Railway station of 1899, designed by Harry Measures in light brown terracotta. These two stations were products of the great electric underground railway boom of 1899–1907. The lovely Argyll Arms is only a few steps away, in Argyll Street. Numbers 169–173 Oxford Street are the black granite Marks and Spencer, built in 1937–8 on the site of the vast and famous eighteenth-century assembly room known as the Pantheon. Number 145 is an early-nineteenth-century house, the oldest plain brick house on the street, and numbers 105–109 were built in 1887 as a hatter's shop, Henry Heath's, with terracotta beavers on the gables in reference to the beaver fur used in making felt hats, and HH, the hatter's initials. Heath's Victorian hat factory is still on Hollen Street, at the back of the shop, but no longer making hats. Numbers 73–89 were built in polished grey granite for a furniture dealers, Drage's, in 1929, with decorative waves and zigzags on pink metal panels that refer to the Paris Exhibition of 1925. After Soho Street there are a few pre-1914 shops, and then numbers 37–39, now Waterstone's, which were built in 1909–10 as the Cinematograph, the first purpose-built cinema in the West End. Finally there is a terracotta Underground station built (also by

Harry Measures) when the Central London Railway, the 'Tuppenny tube', opened in 1899/1900 to compete with the omnibus services that ran along Oxford Street and Bayswater Road.

In their heyday the West End's great department stores formed a T-shape, with Oxford Street as its top, and Regent Street as its tail. From Oxford Circus, designed in four matching quadrants in 1911 and built between 1913 and 1925, walk south on the left (east) side of Regent Street. The first big building, numbers 224–244, was (until 2006) Dickins and Jones, built just after the First World War. Thomas Dickins, a linen draper, moved here from Oxford Street in 1835, and his sons, in partnership with John Jones, gradually expanded into gifts and household goods. Harrods bought them out in 1914, and the store was bought by the House of Fraser group in 1959. The interior has been much remodelled, but the 1994 circular atrium is a handsome feature, worth looking in for. As you come out look over the road at numbers 235–241 (between Hanover Street and Maddox Street), which were built in 1898 to display Angelus player-pianos. The whole building is decorated with the arms of cities in Venetian mosaic, and topped with a copper dome in the French style.

Next to the Dickins and Jones building is one of the West End's special treats, Liberty's department store. The neo-classical Regent Street frontage, built in 1926, is interesting enough, with its huge frieze (one of London's largest sculptures) representing England's imperial trade and carved figures looking down from the parapet, but the Great Marlborough Street building is in a class of its own. This was built in the timber-framed Tudor style in 1922–3, under the influence of the Arts and Crafts movement and post-war nostalgia, using timbers from the last two wooden warships, HMS *Hindustan* and HMS *Impregnable*. The pegged timbers, the hand-made roof tiles, the twisted brick chimneys, the leaded and stained-glass windows, the chiselled Portland stone, the St George and the Dragon clock, the Mayflower weathervane, the carved bargeboards, are all fine examples of 1920s Arts and Crafts workmanship, and the interior, with cloth-draped oak galleries arranged around three skylit wells, forerunners of the atriums used in John Lewis, Peter Jones and Dickins and Jones, is a fine sight, even for those who do not like shopping. The goods for sale are distinctive too. Arthur Liberty began trading here in 1875, and his interest in eastern silks, carvings and furniture is still reflected in Liberty's stock. Nearby, still on the east side of the street, is the world's biggest toy shop, Hamley's. Hamley's started in Holborn in 1760, opened a Regent Street branch in 1881, and moved into its present seven storeys at 188–196 Regent Street a hundred years later.

An alternative route out of Oxford Street takes you down New and Old Bond Streets, which have some of the West End's finest and most expensive shops. Old Bond Street was laid out by Sir Thomas Bond and other speculators in 1684, on land made available by the demolition of Clarendon House on Piccadilly. The northern extension of the street up to Oxford Street, which ran through the City of London's Conduit Mead estate, was built in the early eighteenth century, mainly after 1720. As the Mayfair neighbour-hood became richer and more fashionable in the early eighteenth century, Bond Street established itself as a centre for luxury shop-ping, a position it has held ever since. As a parade of wealth, con-spicuous consumption and famous retailing names it is hard to beat.

As you walk down New Bond Street from Oxford Street you might notice number 103, Nelson's house in 1798, on the right (west) side, and a nice variety of 1890s and 1900s shopfronts, numbers 76–64, on the left. After Maddox Street, on the left, Sothebys is one of a set of early-eighteenth-century houses (31, 32 and 34–36), and Sekhmet's head, over the door, dates from 1320 BC. On the right, numbers 135–137, now Wempe to Daniel Swarovski, have an interesting history. They were built in 1876 as the Grosvenor Gallery for Sir Coutts Lindsay, who showed artists (including Whistler) who were too avant-garde for the Royal Academy. In the late 1880s Sebastian de Ferranti pioneered com-mercial electricity generation (to supply the West End) in the basement. In 1904 the gallery was converted into a 500-seat concert hall, the Aeolian Hall, and in 1941 it became a BBC studio. There are other impressive galleries nearby. Partridge's, at 144–146, was built just before the Great War, and the Fine Art Society, number 148, was built in 1875 and remodelled five years later by E.W. Godwin, Oscar Wilde's interior designer.

After Grafton Street and Clifford Street the most striking shops are Asprey's on the right (west), and Bentley and Skinner, number 8, an 1850s shopfront, on the left. Asprey's occupies three 1770s houses which were fitted with large plate-glass windows in the 1860s and in the early twentieth century, as the shop expanded. After Burlington Gardens Old Bond Street begins on the left with number 24, Ferragamo, an unusual 1920s building which claims London's only carillon (a set of bells that can be played by hand or machine), and Chatila (number 22), an ornate Renaissance shopfront in granite and Doulton earthenware, built around 1905. On the right, Tiffany's arcaded 1865 shopfront is made from Cornish serpentine stone; the Royal Arcade, 18 tall shops with 1930s curved windows, was built in 1879, and Agnew's gallery, numbers 42–43, was built in 1876–8 in the new Queen Anne style. This brings you back to Piccadilly and the shops of Jermyn Street, St James's Street and the Piccadilly arcades.

CHAPTER EIGHT

✳

CRIMINAL LONDON

A bawdy house riot in 1749

As Britain's biggest city, and the biggest city in the world for over two hundred years, London was bound to acquire – and probably to deserve – a reputation as the nation's centre of crime. Big cities offer more tempting targets for thieves – more shops, banks, businesses, rich citizens with bulging pockets and well-stocked houses. London offered the best opportunities for hiding, enjoying or selling what you had stolen, and for turning crime into a business. Even in the fifteenth century the popular ballad 'London Lickpenny' joked that a visitor to London, having lost his hood to a thief in a Westminster crowd, saw it for sale on a stall in the City in Cornhill, 'where is much stolen gere'. The vulnerability of the gullible or inexperienced visitor to the skills of the London pick-pocket, footpad or cheat has been a stock theme of poems, plays, novels and advice manuals from the Middle Ages to modern times, and it is probably true that crime has been more professionalized and specialized in the capital than elsewhere in the country. Eighteenth- or nineteenth-century London thieves had the services of houses of resort, or flash houses, where they were sure of a friendly welcome, located in criminal districts known as Alsatias or rookeries, where the arm of the law did not reach, and of professional receivers who would buy and resell their stolen goods. Jonathan Wild was the most notorious of these early receivers, until he was forced into early retirement by the hangman in 1725.

London has had its fair share of notorious or spectacular murders, and probably more than its fair share (in relation to its population) of business swindles, prostitutes and political crimes. Those out for the blood of princes and politicians were most likely to find them in London or Westminster, and plotters or protesters wanting to blow up Parliament, kill the cabinet or bring their grievances to the attention of their governors were most likely to focus their efforts on the royal and political capital. London has a tradition of riot, rebellion and peaceful protest stretching back at least to 1066, when William the Conqueror had to build three castles 'against the fickleness of the vast and fierce populace'. One of these castles, and therefore one of the earliest surviving measures taken against crime and disorder, was the Tower of London. Another survivor, about 850 years older, is the Roman wall, which was repaired and maintained to ensure London's security from crime and rebellion until the seventeenth century. London's apparent criminality, and the danger to any ruler of losing control of the capital, meant that it nearly always took the lead in the development of the instruments and institutions of law and order. London had many places of public execution and dozens of prisons of every size and type, and in the eighteenth and nineteenth centuries it was the place in which professional (as opposed to unpaid communal) policing first developed in England.

Many of the districts once notorious for crime have changed beyond recognition, and the houses, pubs, shops and brothels which gave shelter and comfort to criminals are very unlikely to have escaped 150 years of slum clearance and urban improvement, which often had the secondary intention of getting rid of the most criminal quarters. Still, the determined London explorer can find scraps of the old rookeries, now no longer dangerous, and even one or two notorious locations and criminal backstreets that have escaped the demolition ball. A few remnants of London's old prisons can be found, and some of the most famous places of execution are still there, unused for 150 years or more. Some of the most famous places in the history of policing, Bow Street and Scotland Yard, are in London, and the most famous address in detective fiction is there too, in a way. And those who are interested in London's terrific radical past can stand where Wat Tyler's peasants, Sir Thomas Wyatt's Protestants, John

Wilkes's radicals, Lord George Gordon's anti-Catholics, Arthur This-tlewood's Cato Street conspirators or Feargus O'Connor's Chartists met, and follow their routes into central London.

*

London's earliest criminal districts, oddly enough, were in its monastic precincts. In the Middle Ages wanted criminals could take temporary refuge in any church or seek permanent shelter in two monasteries, Westminster Abbey and St Martin-le-Grand, living on their estates with impunity unless the King was extremely keen to arrest them. The Dissolution of the Monasteries in 1539 did not completely abolish this peculiar privilege, although it seems to have ended St Martin-le-Grand's history as a thieves' kitchen. Westminster remained a sanctuary town until James I abolished sanctuary for felons in 1623. Even after that some notorious ex-monastic districts still enjoyed a degree of protection from the City and the Crown, as much from their impenetrable topography as from any specific legal privileges. The most famous of these sanctuaries was Alsatia, the old Whitefriars monastic territory south of Fleet Street, between the Temple and Dorset Street, but there were many others. When the remaining sanctuaries were abolished in 1697 and 1723 the acts mentioned ten places, including Salisbury Court (near Whitefriars), the Savoy (off the Strand) and Baldwin's Gardens (between Leather Lane and Gray's Inn Road). The biggest concentration of sanctuaries was in Southwark, especially in riverside districts under the authority of the Bishop of Winchester: Deadman's Place (now the eastern end of Park Street, running from Bankside to Redcross Way), the Clink and Montague Close (on the river, just to the west of Southwark Cathedral) and the Mint, which centred on Mint Street, which ran from Borough High Street almost to Southwark Bridge Road. Its eastern end is now called Marshalsea Street. The liberty of the Mint, which lasted until 1723, was especially popular with debtors, who could avoid debtors' prison (including the nearby Marshalsea) by staying within its limits.

The abolition of the sanctuaries did not leave criminals with no hiding place. As London grew in area and population slum neighbourhoods developed which were virtually impenetrable to the forces of law and order, such as they were. Alsatia and the Mint kept a little of their lawless reputations, but the neighbourhood feared above all others in the later eighteenth century was the Irish quarter between St Giles High Street and Great Russell Street. This was St Giles, the first and greatest rookery (as the Victorians called it), a fearsome place until the construction of New Oxford Street in 1847 and Shaftesbury Avenue in 1886 split it into easily controlled pieces. This was the place depicted in William Hogarth's famous engraving attacking the gin craze, *Gin Lane*, in 1751. The slum dwellers remained after New Oxford Street was built, squashed more tightly than ever into rooms in Dyott Street and Earnshaw Street, but the Victorians gradually replaced most of the slums with schools, chapels and model dwellings. In fact, Streatham Street (between New Oxford Street and Great Russell Street) has London's oldest surviving block of working-class flats, Parnell House, which was built in 1849 by the Society for Improving the Condition of the Labouring Classes. The inscription on the building, 'Model Dwellings for Families', sums up the intentions of the society pretty well. The block is now owned by the Peabody Trust.

A walk around St Giles today is safer and simpler than it would have been in Charles Dickens's day, but also a good deal duller. Of the 35 streets, courts and alleys there used to be between Tottenham Court Road and Museum Street, there are now only fifteen. The main buildings in the remaining streets of St Giles are those built to replace the slums of the old rookery. Yet there is still a gloomy and impoverished atmosphere in Dyott Street and Bainbridge Street, considering their closeness to Oxford Street, Covent Garden and the British Museum. Walk a little south down Monmouth Street (a left fork off Shaftesbury Avenue) to Seven Dials, which was an extension of the Victorian rookery, and the atmosphere changes. The streets radiating from Seven Dials, from which Dickens could conjure 'prodigies of wickedness', now share the lively prosperity of Covent Garden. The other eighteenth-century rookery was St Katharine's, the fascinating area of courts and alleys to the east of the Tower. But this was all swept away, along with the medieval hospital, for the creation of St Katharine's Dock in 1825.

The destruction of St Giles did not mean the end of rookeries. In 1852, when Thomas Beames published his survey *Rookeries of London*, he identified six, including Saffron Hill, Jacob's Island, the Ratcliffe Highway, Berwick Street (Soho) and Pye Street, in Westminster. As the working-class suburbs grew in the later nineteenth century, especially in the East End, the number and size of these feared criminal quarters grew. The Old Nichol (*see* Chapter Four) was a rookery, so was the area just south of Christ Church, Spitalfields, around Flower and Dean Street. Charles Booth's poverty map, published in 1889, picks out London's poorest and most criminal streets, and shows that as well as the expected concentration in the East End, streets that now seem dull or prosperous were once seen as dangerous or depraved. Walk down the Colonnade behind Russell Square Tube station, or Parker Street and Macklin Street in the corner of High Holborn and Kingsway, or Eagle Street, between High Holborn and Red Lion Square, or Tabard Street in Southwark, parallel to Great Dover Street, and imagine them as places where policemen always went in twos.

The most interesting ex-rookeries to visit today are probably Spitalfields and Whitechapel, because many of the streets are well preserved, and not yet completely gentrified. The connection with the Whitechapel murders of August–November 1888 (the so-called Jack the Ripper killings) and the evidence of three waves of foreign settlement give the walk an added interest. As in all the ex-rookeries the efforts of those in authority to tame the neighbourhood with roads, schools, police stations, workhouses, chapels and charities have left a more enduring mark than the beggars, fences and prostitutes that once lived there. The worse the rookery, in general, the more comprehensive its destruction.

Saffron Hill, which runs on the side of the Fleet Valley, alongside Farringdon Road, between Charterhouse Street and Clerkenwell Road, was the rookery used by Dickens in 1837 as the location of Fagin's hideaway in *Oliver Twist*. There is not much today to remind us of Saffron Hill's fearsome reputation, or of its importance as a centre of Italian settlement in the nineteenth century. The upper reaches of the stinking Fleet were covered by Farringdon Road in the 1850s, and new roads were cut through the slums: Holborn Viaduct in 1869, Clerkenwell Road in 1878 and Rosebery Avenue in 1890.

You can still follow most of the route that Oliver took, led by the Artful Dodger, from the Angel Islington into Saffron Hill, which was so carefully described by Dickens. They started after 11.00 in the evening on St John Street, and turned right down a little street running south-west from Sadler's Wells Theatre, now lost under Rosebery Avenue. A left turn into Garnault Place brings you to Exmouth Street (now Exmouth Market), which Oliver and the Dodger followed to its junction with Coppice Row, which is now Farringdon Road. In Exmouth Market, past the impressive steel-framed church of the Holy Redeemer (1887) and next to a tattoo parlour, England's greatest pantomime clown, Joseph Grimaldi, lived at number 56 between 1818 and 1828. Turn left, and about 200 metres down Farringdon Road there is a right turn down a nameless alley, exactly opposite Bowling Green Lane. Take this alley and then go left into Crawford Passage. This crosses Ray Street, which was once Hockley-in-the-Hole, almost next to the Coach and Horses, which occupies the site of a once-famous bear garden. Over the road is the northern end of Little Saffron Hill (now Herbal Hill), the way into the rookery, which Oliver and the Dodger now entered. This was Oliver's first impression of Saffron Hill:

> A dirtier or more wretched place he had never seen. The street was very narrow and muddy, and the air was impregnated

with filthy odours ... Covered ways and yards, which here and there diverged from the main street, disclosed little knots of houses, where drunken men and women were positively wallowing in filth; and from several of the door-ways, great ill-looking fellows were cautiously emerging, bound, to all appearance, on no very well-disposed or harmless errands.

Oliver and his new friend walked the length of Saffron Hill until they reached its southern extension, Field Lane, 'the emporium of petty larceny: visited at early morning, and setting-in of dusk, by silent merchants, who traffic in dark back-parlours'. Field Lane is gone, but the inoffensive northern part of Shoe Lane, a little to the right across Charterhouse Street, roughly follows its course. In a dark passage near Field Lane, roughly where steps now take you up from Saffron Hill to Charterhouse Street, they found Fagin's hide-away, full of trainee pickpockets.

Field Lane had a long history of infamy. Among the 450 criminal cases involving this street in the Old Bailey records between 1684 and 1834 (oldbaileyonline.org) there is the case of Margaret Clap, the rather well-named keeper of a 'molly-house', who was indicted for keeping a house of resort (not quite a brothel) for homosexuals 'in which she procur'd and encourag'd Persons to commit Sodomy' in December 1725. Mrs Clap was pilloried in the nearby Smithfield Market in 1726, and was treated so roughly by the merciless crowd that she fell off the pillory, fainted several times and had convulsions. Mrs Clap's arrest was the result of a crackdown in the 1710s and 1720s organized by the Society for the Reformation of Manners on homosexual rendezvous. This drive led to some tragic personal misfortunes but provided lots of interesting detail about London's gay subculture. A trial in 1717 revealed the information that 'many Leud & Scandalous Persons, frequently held unlawful Meetings and wicked Conversation in the Dusk of the Evening near the Royal Exchange, Leaden-Hall-Market, Moorfields,

White-Chappel, and several obscure Places', and other prosecutions mentioned homosexual activity in St James's Park.

*

Dickens set Bill Sikes's last stand in a south London riverside rookery, 200 metres east of Tower Bridge (then unbuilt) and next to an inlet called Saviour's Dock, the mouth of the lost River Neckinger. This was Jacob's Island, 'the filthiest, the strangest, the most extraordinary of the many localities that are hidden in London, wholly unknown, even by name, to the great mass of its inhabitants'. Jacob's Island was particularly mysterious because it was surrounded by a wide ditch which had to be crossed by rickety wooden bridges, and it is not surprising that it was one of the worst centres of cholera in the epidemic of 1849. After this the ditches were drained and built over, but the district was still described as 'repellent' in the *Victoria County History of Surrey* in 1912. Not many reminders of this horrible place remain, except the pattern of its streets and the mills and warehouses that swept Jacob's Island into oblivion in and after the 1860s. Many of these are gone now, and the survivors have been converted into offices and luxury apartments. A walk east from the south side of Tower Bridge, along Shad Thames, across the bridge over St Saviour's Dock and along Bermondsey Wall West, returning by Jacob Street, Mill Street, Dock Head and Queen Elizabeth Street, might give you some sense of how one London has been laid on top of another: the slum of Jacob's Island replaced by an industrial landscape of mills and warehouses which have been replaced in turn by smart shops, offices and flats. If you stand on the bridge over the dock, which gives very fine views up and down the river to the City and Canary Wharf, and look back to the grimy waters of the dock and the few unconverted warehouses on its banks you might glimpse for a moment the squalid world with which Dickens terrified his Victorian readers.

*

Until the introduction of professional policing in 1829, the authorities' most effective response to crime was punishment. This took various forms, from fines and whipping or public humiliation in the pillory, to imprisonment, exile or execution. Much of this punishment was public and often took place in the neighbourhood where the crime had been committed. So there were pillories, gallows and gibbets (for the display of corpses) scattered around London, sometimes in places still identifiable today, and new ones could be erected for particular criminals. The Temple Bar, where Middle Temple Lane meets Fleet Street, was a favourite spot. This is where Lodowicke Muggleton, founder of the Muggletonians, was pilloried for three days in 1677, and where Daniel Defoe was pilloried in 1702. There were pillories in Cheapside and Cornhill, in the City, and a famous and often-used one at Charing Cross, near the statue of Charles I on the triangular island at the top of Whitehall. This is where the printers Edmund Curll and Richard Nutt were pilloried for seditious libel in 1726 and 1754, and where the radical lawyer John Frost was rescued from the pillory by a friendly crowd in 1793.

Those who had offended the King or his ministers, perhaps convicted by Star Chamber, were likely to get their punishment in Old Palace Yard, the open space just to the east of Westminster Abbey, in front of what is now the Victoria Tower of the Houses of Parliament. This is where the radicals John Lilburne, William Prynne and Peter Bales were pilloried and had their ears cut off in 1637, and where Titus Oates, the perjurer and inventor of the Popish Plot, was pilloried and cruelly pelted in May 1685. Oates did his own personal tour of the London pillories, since he was confined to five different ones every year, as well as being whipped from Aldgate to Newgate and Newgate to Tyburn (Marble Arch), a fair distance even if you are not being whipped. Some offenders were pilloried near the scenes of their crimes, perhaps to excite maximum public interest. Charles Hitchen, City thief-taker and Under-Marshal of the City of London, was convicted of sodomy in April 1727 and sentenced to six months in prison and an hour in the pillory 'at Katherine-Street

End in the Strand, near the Place where he made his vicious Attacks upon young Youths'. Catherine Street no longer meets the Strand (because of the Aldwych), but the pillory would have been roughly at the western end of the Strand frontage of Somerset House. Hitchen was rescued from the crowd more dead than alive. The crowd was no kinder to Elizabeth 'Mother' Needham, who kept a brothel in Park Place, a (now) smart cul-de-sac about halfway up St James's Street, and was pilloried 'over against Park Place' on 30 April 1731. She died three days later. In the 1720s there was a pillory 'against the Monument, on Fish Street Hill' and another at 'Chancery Lane End, in Fleet St'. So it seems that almost wherever you walk in old London, from Stepney to Hyde Park, and especially at important road junctions, you walk past a place of rough and simple punishment.

Executions, of which there were many thousands in the seventeenth and eighteenth centuries, could also be carried out in places chosen for their deterrent value near the culprit's home or crime, but there were a few well-established places of execution which are easy to find today. The method and place of execution depended on status, and perhaps the nature of one's crime. A few (only seven in all) whom the monarch wanted to dispatch without public knowledge or participation were beheaded inside the Tower of London, on Tower Green. This is where Edward IV's brother George, Duke of Clarence, was executed in 1478, probably on Edward's orders, by drowning in a butt of malmsey wine, and where their brother Richard executed William, Lord Hastings, in 1483, in preparation for his seizure of the throne. Henry VIII had his second wife, Anne Boleyn, beheaded on Tower Green in May 1536, and his fifth, Katherine Howard, in February 1542, along with her friend Jane Boleyn. Lady Jane Grey, 16-year-old claimant to the throne, was beheaded here in February 1554, and Elizabeth's favourite, the Earl of Essex, died here in 1601. The victims were generally buried in or outside the church of St Peter ad Vincula, which stands to the north of the scaffold. The church was rebuilt in 1520, and must have been one of the last things these unlucky souls saw. The Tower was also the scene of many murders, including that of two kings, Henry VI in 1471, and the young Edward V (along with his brother Richard), probably by their uncle, Richard III.

There was a busier execution spot outside the Tower, on Tower Hill, which was first used as a place of execution in 1381 by the leaders of the Peasants' Revolt, and later by Richard II and his opponents the Lords Appellant. The execution spot, at the western end of Trinity Square Gardens, is marked now with a little fence and a list of the most famous of the 125 who were beheaded there, starting with Simon Sudbury, Archbishop of Canterbury, who was dragged from the Tower by rebels in 1381 and beheaded, along with the King's Treasurer, Sir Robert Hales. Sudbury's head was displayed on London Bridge with his archbishop's hat nailed onto it. Sudbury's execution happened while Wat Tyler was meeting the King, and his own end, at Smithfield. The last to die here were four Scottish leaders of the 1745 Jacobite rebellion to restore Charles Stuart to the throne. The block on which these four were beheaded is still kept in the Tower. In between, this was the spot where Sir Thomas More, John Fisher, Thomas Cromwell, William Laud, the Earl of Strafford, the Duke of Monmouth and many others lost their heads. A little to the west, in Great Tower Street, there is a pub called the Hung, Drawn and Quartered, but there is no particular connection between the pub and the Tower Hill executions other than the name.

Other places might be chosen for high-profile executions. Anthony Babington and his friends, who had plotted the assassination of Elizabeth, were hung, drawn and quartered in Lincoln's Inn Fields, where they used to meet, in 1586, and Lord Russell, the leader of the Rye House Plot against Charles II, was beheaded there in 1683. After the Gunpowder Plot of 1605, Guy Fawkes and three other plotters were hung, drawn and quartered in Old Palace Yard (east of Westminster Abbey), and the other four met the same unpleasant end in St Paul's Churchyard. Sir Walter Raleigh was beheaded in Old Palace Yard in 1618, and buried in St Margaret's church nearby. Until a few years ago his jaunty statue stood not far away, in front of the Ministry of Defence, but it has now been moved to the old Royal Naval College in Greenwich. And the most momentous beheading of them all, that of Charles I in January 1649, took place in Whitehall, on a scaffold erected outside the windows of his own Banqueting House. His head is still there, but in bronze. Eight regicides, those who had signed Charles I's death warrant, were hung, drawn and quartered in 1660 at Charing Cross, on the spot now occupied by the King's equestrian statue at the northern end of Whitehall.

The regular execution spot for south London was Kennington Common, the remnant of which is now called Kennington Park. The gallows were on the land opposite the Oval Tube station, where St Mark's church was built in 1822. This is where several of Bonnie Prince Charlie's supporters were executed in 1745, the notorious highwayman Mathias Keys was hanged in 1751, and the man sometimes called the last of the true highwaymen, Jerry Abershaw, the scourge of Putney Bottom, was hanged in 1795. In the 1790s a new prison, Horsemonger Lane jail, was built, and hangings took place on its roof, giving a fine view to the Southwark crowd, whose conduct so disgusted Charles Dickens in 1849. The prison was on the south side of Horsemonger Lane (now Harper Road) between Newington Causeway and Bath Terrace. It was closed in 1878 and demolished in 1945, and its site is now the recreation ground (the 'jail playground') on the corner of Bath Terrace, behind the 1921 Sessions House.

The most important centre for state executions in the Middle Ages and the sixteenth century was West Smithfield, the marketplace and fairground just outside the north-western corner of the City walls. Smithfield is one of those places, along with Cheapside, Westminster Abbey, the Tower, Trafalgar Square, the Strand and Whitehall, which seem to embody the history of London, or at least a substantial section of it. In 1196 William FitzOsbert was hanged here for satanism, and in 1305 William Wallace, the Scottish patriot and rebel, was hung, drawn and quartered, and his body and his head placed on London

Bridge. There is a memorial to Wallace on the wall of St Bartholomew's Hospital, on the south-eastern edge of Smithfield. This is close to the usual execution place, which was near the entrance to the church of St Bartholomew-the-Great, where there was a group of elm trees. It was at Smithfield in 1381 that the leader of the Peasants' Revolt against the poll tax, Wat Tyler, was assaulted by William Walworth, Mayor of London, during his negotiations with Richard II. Tyler was badly wounded and took refuge in the hospital, but he was dragged out and executed. His followers were persuaded by the young King to march back to Clerkenwell Green, where they were later surrounded by royal troops and forced to surrender.

Smithfield was the place where heretics and those who refused to accept the religion of the monarch were usually put to death. The Lollard William Sawtre was killed here in 1401, 'bound, standing upright, to a post set in a barrel with blazing wood all around, and thus reduced to ashes', and John Badby, another Lollard, was burned here in 1410, as was Joan Boughton in 1494. Since nobody carries a torch for the Lollards these days, there is no memorial at Smithfield to these courageous martyrs, whose ideas were the precursors of those of the sixteenth-century Protestants. In the 1530s Catholics who refused to recognize Henry VIII as head of the Church were hung, drawn and quartered as traitors, and Protestants who wanted to push change too far were burned as heretics. This is what happened on 30 July 1540, when three Catholics and three Protestants died here together, each in the way that fitted their crime. And on 30 July 1546 the Protestant Anne Askew was burned with three others, all Protestants. Many of the almost three hundred Protestants killed by Mary Tudor between 1553 and 1558 were burned at Smithfield, and are commemorated on the wall of the hospital. The first to die, John Rogers, 'washed his hands in the flame, as though it had been in cold water' and died courageously in front of his wife and eleven children. Smithfield burnings were rarer under Elizabeth, and the first heretics to be burned there were two Dutch Anabaptists in 1575.

Elizabeth preferred another medieval execution site, Tyburn, which is where Edmund Campion and two fellow Catholics were hung, drawn and quartered in 1581. Tyburn was a fair distance outside medieval or Elizabethan London, where Bayswater Road (Tyburn Street) met the Edgware Road, near the present Marble Arch. John Rocque's map of London in the 1740s marks the Tyburn gallows in the middle of the road at this junction, and the place 'Where soldiers are Shot' on the parkland just to its south. There is a plaque on the Marble Arch traffic island, but the miserable spot where thousands of men, women and children (especially men) died between 1196 and 1783, often for fairly trivial offences, was a little further west. A permanent gallows with three tall posts in a triangle connected by three nine-foot beams, enough for 24 simultaneous hangings, was erected at Tyburn in 1571. The 'Tyburn Tree' was only used to its full capacity once, in 1649, but the condemned were rarely hanged alone. Famous lives that ended at Tyburn include Roger Mortimer, Edward II's favourite and the virtual ruler of England in the 1320s (1330), Sir Nicholas Brembre, Mayor of London (1388), Perkin Warbeck, who conspired to replace Henry VII as king (1499), the Benedictine nun Elizabeth Barton, the 'Maid of Kent' (1534), John Houghton, Prior of the Charterhouse, with two Carthusian monks (1535), Roderigo Lopez, Elizabeth's physician and a model for Shylock (1594), Claude Duval, highwayman (1670), Robert Hubert, who falsely confessed to starting the Great Fire of London (1666), Oliver Plunket, Catholic Archbishop of Armagh (1681), Jack Sheppard, thief and jailbreaker (1724), Jonathan Wild, receiver and informer (1725), and Dr William Dodd, forger (1777).

The two-mile road from Newgate, London's main prison, to Tyburn, taken by so many condemned criminals for about six hundred years, must be London's saddest journey. From 1605 to about 1800 the condemned man or woman's last day started at midnight with 'twelve solemn towles [tolls] with double strokes' on a handbell, rung by the bellman of St Sepulchre, the church nearest to Newgate. The present church, on the corner of Holborn Viaduct and Giltspur Street, was built by Sir Hugh Popham in the mid-fifteenth century, gutted but not destroyed in the Great Fire and restored by the parish (not by Wren) in 1667–71, and given various Gothic features in the eighteenth century. It is known now as the musicians' church, but its associations with the penal system are just as strong. It was joined to Newgate by a tunnel, and was across the road from the Giltspur Street compter (a local jail), which was next to the Viaduct Tavern. When the church is open, on Tuesdays and Thursdays 12.00–2.00, and Wednesdays 11.00–3.00, you will see the handbell and a copy of the verse that the bellman had to read. In the morning the prisoners were taken in an open cart (or dragged on a hurdle, if they were traitors) from Newgate to St Sepulchre, where the great bell ('of Old Bailey') tolled mournfully in the fifteenth-century tower and the bell-man delivered this solemn exhortation: 'You that are condemned to die, Repent with lamentable tears; Ask mercy of the Lord, For the salvation of your souls.'

The procession, which would include friends and enemies of the condemned and crowds enjoying a day out, as well as the City Marshal and enough constables and 'javelin men' to keep order, then followed Snow Hill down into the Fleet Valley (there was no Holborn Viaduct until 1869), climbed Holborn Hill into Holborn, then went along High Holborn and St Giles High Street, which joined Oxford Street (or the Tyburn Road) at the Tottenham Court Road junction. The condemned could eat and drink at several inns along the route and often arrived at Tyburn completely drunk, making the execution itself a less edifying spectacle than it was meant to be. The inns most often mentioned were the George, roughly opposite Red Lion Street in High Holborn, and the Bowl Inn in St Giles High Street, to the west of St Giles church. The final drink was usually taken in the Mason's Arms, at the corner of Seymour Place and Berkeley Street, a little to the north of the Tyburn gallows. The charming old Mason's Arms pub is still there today, and thriving despite the loss of this particular part of its business.

In 1783 the authorities decided the procession was too unruly and the Tyburn gallows were an obstacle to suburban development, and moved them to the large space outside the rebuilt Newgate Prison, in Old Bailey. The new gallows, which were near the great black iron gates close to the Newgate Street end of the Central Criminal Court, had a trapdoor and a drop, so that (when it worked properly) criminals would die from a broken neck rather than slow strangulation. The last burning (of a woman, Christian Murphy, for coining) took place here in 1789, and the last beheadings (of five Cato Street conspirators) were in 1820, in both cases only after the victims had already been killed by hanging or strangulation. The last public hanging took place here in 1868, when the Irish Fenian (militant Republican) Michael Barrett was hanged for killing 15 people when he blew a hole in the wall of Clerkenwell House of Detention. Hangings were terribly popular, and the huge crowds could be dangerous. In 1807 the crowd stampeded, killing 28 people.

Some of the buildings that formed part of London's system of repression and control, its courthouses and prisons, are still in existence and easy to visit. A great Norman court, Westminster Hall (*see* Chapter Three), and a mighty prison, the Tower of London, can both be visited. The Tower of London was not built as a jail, but its great strength made it useful for holding important state prisoners. The first of these, and the first to escape, was Ranulf Flambard, Bishop of Durham, who was held there by Henry I. In August 1100 Henry arrested Flambard and put him in the White Tower, but a rope was smuggled in to the Bishop in a flagon of wine, and using the wine to intoxicate the guards and the rope to climb down the walls, Flambard escaped, rode to the coast and fled to Normandy. The list of later prisoners reads like a *Who's Who* of great royal and political figures, including King John II of France, King John Balliol of Scotland, William Wallace, Henry VI, Edward V (one of the murdered princes), Thomas More, Anne Boleyn, the future Elizabeth I, Sir Walter Raleigh, the Duke of Monmouth, Arthur Thistlewood and the Cato Street conspirators, Roger Casement and Rudolf Hess. If you visit the Tower, remember to look at the information on prisoners in the Bloody Tower (where Raleigh was held) and Beauchamp Tower, which has moving and interesting inscriptions carved by sixteenth- and seventeenth-century prisoners, many of whose minds were concentrated by their expectation of execution. The carving done by the Dudley family, the Duke of Northumberland and his four sons, who were brought here in 1553 for trying to put Lady Jane Grey on the throne, is especially interesting, and so is that of Philip Howard, Earl of Arundel, done in 1587. Three of the four Dudley brothers were set free, but Howard died in captivity in 1595.

Although imprisonment was not a mainstay of the English penal system until the nineteenth century, there were dozens of prisons in pre-Victorian London. All except the Tower are gone now, replaced by rebuilt and reformed nineteenth-century prisons. The City of London had dozens of prisons, compters (local or sheriff's jails) and lock-ups in medieval and early-modern times. There were important prisons in Ludgate and Newgate, on the western stretch of the City walls. Medieval Ludgate was used for debtors, clergy and freemen of the City, Newgate for common criminals. Ludgate was demolished with the City walls in 1760, and all that is left of it is a plaque on the church of St Martin-within-Ludgate, on Ludgate Hill, and some statues rescued from the old gate and placed in the tiny churchyard of St Dunstan-in-the-West, on Fleet Street, near Fetter Lane. When the gates of the churchyard are closed you can see the fine statue of Queen Elizabeth I, which dates from 1586 (the oldest outdoor statue in London), and when they are open you can look into the porch underneath Elizabeth to see very battered statues of King Lud and his two sons, also from the old gate.

Newgate was wholly or partly rebuilt several times, in the 1420s, the 1660s and the 1770s, when the City walls had been demolished. The new prison, a masterpiece of intimidating and windowless baroque stonework by George Dance, was torched by the Gordon rioters in 1780, but repaired and used for another 120 years. It was a notoriously overcrowded and corrupt place, and became the

focus of the efforts of penal reformers like Elizabeth Fry. It was
demolished in 1902, when the site was needed for the enlarged and
rebuilt Central Criminal Court, or Old Bailey, which had stood
alongside the old prison since the 1530s. Some of Dance's rusticated
Newgate stonework was reused in the outer walls of the new courthouse, and the Viaduct Tavern on Newgate Street has remnants of
Newgate cells in its cellar. You can visit the public galleries of the
Central Criminal Court when the courts are sitting, between 10.00
and 1.00 and 2.00 and 5.00, as long as you have no big bags, small
children, cameras or recording equipment. Alternatively, you can see
some of the doors and gates from Dance's Newgate, with a reconstructed cell, in the Museum of London. Even better, the museum has
rescued a wooden cell from a local jail in Wellclose Square, between
Cable Street and The Highway (Ratcliffe Highway), east of the
Tower. The names scratched on the pine panels give as strong a
flavour of the realities of pre-Victorian imprisonment as the novels
of Dickens.

Some of London's most important prisons were situated just
outside the City's western border, along the Fleet Valley, which starts
at Blackfriars Bridge and follows the route now taken by Farringdon
Road. A walk up the valley from Blackfriars Bridge is a good way
to see several important places in the history of London's law enforcement. Ahead of you, in New Bridge Street, is the site of Henry VIII's
Bridewell Palace, which was built in 1515–20 on the west bank of
the Fleet near its meeting with the Thames, and became a City prison
and workhouse, especially for prostitutes and vagrants, in the 1550s.
It was rebuilt after the Great Fire, and continued as a prison until
1855, when its inmates were transferred to Holloway and its buildings, after a few years, demolished. It was set back from New Bridge
Street, between Tudor Street and Bride Lane, where office buildings
occupy the site. Nothing is left of the Bridewell except its name,
which came to be used for all prisons for petty offenders, and its
early-nineteenth-century gatehouse, which survives as number 14
New Bridge Street. The head in the centre of this handsome Tuscan-

pillared building is Edward VI, whose deathbed gift to the City turned Bridewell from a palace into a jail.

The Fleet prison, the first purpose-built jail in London, operated from before 1170 until its closure in 1842, and thus did longer service than any other London prison except Newgate and the Tower. It was destroyed in the Peasants' Revolt of 1381, the Great Fire and the Gordon Riots of 1780, but rebuilt each time because of its great value as an all-purpose prison for heretics, enemies of the state, debtors and common criminals. John Donne the poet and clergyman was held here in 1602, and so was the Leveller John Lilburne in 1638. William Penn was a debtor here from 1707 to 1709, and the pornographer John Cleland, also in the Fleet for debt, wrote the *Memoirs of a Woman of Pleasure*, or *Fanny Hill*, here in 1748. The Fleet was demolished in 1846, and nothing now remains of the old buildings. You can find the site, now occupied by Caroone House, by crossing Ludgate Circus and walking a few metres up Farringdon Street. Two turnings on the right, Old Seacoal Lane and Fleet Lane (once notorious for prostitutes), follow the shape of the prison grounds.

If you follow Fleet Lane to Old Bailey you will be standing right opposite the site of Newgate and very near its execution place. Turn left onto Old Bailey and cross Newgate Street, and St Sepulchre is on your left and the site of the Giltspur Street Compter is marked next to the Viaduct Tavern. Continue up Giltspur Street, passing a rebuilt eighteenth-century watch house on your left and the fat golden boy on the corner of Cock Lane, with its interesting but perhaps inaccurate information about the dealings between body-snatchers and St Bartholomew's Hospital surgeons, and bear right on Smithfield to see the memorials to William Wallace and the Protestant martyrs. Then go through Smithfield Market, and take St John Street, bearing left into St John's Lane, following the route taken by the peasants of 1381 as they returned to Clerkenwell Green after the murder of Wat Tyler. If you go under the early-sixteenth-century gatehouse of St John's Priory, and across Clerkenwell Road into

St John's Square, you will see the outline of the round nave of the priory church, which Tyler's men had destroyed, on the roadway. Through Jerusalem Passage, passing the marked site of Thomas Britton's shop and concert room, turn left to reach Clerkenwell Green, one of the open spaces where rebels and protesters often assembled before marching down to London. Chartists (radical campaigners for the vote) met and marched from here in 1848, and unemployed workers and socialists did the same on 'Bloody Sunday', 13 November 1887. This is where Dickens had the Artful Dodger teaching Oliver Twist how to pick a pocket (or two), and where Oliver was chased and arrested.

Number 37a, an early-eighteenth-century Welsh charity school, was the printing house of London's first socialist party, the Social Democratic Federation, from 1892 to 1922, where Lenin worked on a revolutionary magazine, *Iskra*, in 1902–3. Now it is the Marx Memorial Library, and still has the room where Lenin worked. The library is open to visitors from Monday to Thursday between 1.00 and 2.00, and to readers those four afternoons and Saturday mornings. Its website is www.marxlibrary.net. The sort of repressive state power that Marx rejected is well represented opposite, in the former Middlesex Sessions House, built in 1779–82, used until 1920, and now a Masonic centre. There is a bar now in the old basement cells. For many of the thousands of prisoners who stood trial here, a quick glance at the reliefs (by Nollekens) depicting *Justice* and *Mercy* must have been their last contact with these two virtues.

Those who were awaiting trial in the Middlesex Sessions House might have found themselves lodged in the Clerkenwell House of Detention, which was only a short walk away. Follow Clerkenwell Close (which follows the western edge of St Mary's Nunnery), starting from the Crown public house ('and Apollo concert rooms'), and turn right into Sans Walk. Sir Hugh Myddleton School (now Kingsway Place), on your left, was built on the cellars of the Clerkenwell House of Detention. The cells are still there, and for some years in the 1990s were open to the paying public. It was a wall of this prison that Michael Barrett, the last man to be hanged in public in England, blew up in 1867, with dramatic results. The event is commemorated in St James' church, which was built around 1790 on the site of the choir of the nunnery.

Nearby, on the other (west) side of Farringdon Street, Cold Bath Fields Prison stood on the site of the present Mount Pleasant Sorting Office from 1794 until 1877. The River Fleet, which flowed openly along the line now followed by Phoenix Place, marked the western edge of the prison grounds. In the early nineteenth century it was one of London's more important jails, but like most of the others it was riddled with corruption. A reforming governor, George Laval Chesterton, took control in 1829, and found that 'widespread defilement... polluted every hole and corner of the Augean stable'. Despite Chesterton's efforts, Cold Bath Fields was an old-fashioned structure which could not impose on its 1,600 prisoners the solitary confinement regime which was the fashion in the mid-nineteenth century. So when local prisons were taken under central government control in 1877 it was closed, and twelve years later the site was cleared for the sorting office.

Many rebels and radicals were held in Cold Bath Fields Prison, but the most famous prisoner, in his day, was John Williams, a 27-year-old Irish sailor, who hanged himself in his cell on 27 December 1811. Williams was awaiting trial for the brutal murder of two families – five adults, a boy and a baby – in the Ratcliffe Highway (the road between the Tower of London and Shadwell) earlier in December. Until the Whitechapel killings of 1888 this was London's most sensational murder case, and the crowd was furious at being cheated of watching Williams (who had not been tried or convicted) hang at Newgate. Instead, on New Year's Eve 1811 his corpse was dragged on a sloping cart from Ship Alley along Ratcliffe Highway, stopping at the scenes of his supposed crimes, then up Cannon Street Road (or the New Road) to its junction with Cable Street, where it was pierced through with a stake and dumped in a hole, as suicides used to be. The bones were dug up and taken as souvenirs about a hundred years later.

Many of the street names around the Ratcliffe Highway were changed in the 1930s, and the whole area was altered dramatically by the Blitz and post-war redevelopment, but it is not hard to find the places where this famous multiple murder happened. Ratcliffe Highway, now called The Highway, begins where East Smithfield ends, about 400 metres east of the Tower of London. The events took place in the area around the News International building, between Virginia Street and Hawksmoor's church of St George-in-the-East. The first murders were committed in a shop at 29 Ratcliffe Highway, on the south side just east of Artichoke Hill, where there is now a car showroom, and the second in the King's Arms public house, at 81 New Gravel Lane, now Garnet Street, which runs down to New Crane Stairs. The King's Arms pub was demolished when the London Dock was extended in the 1830s, and the shop was destroyed in the Blitz in 1940. The Thames Police Office on Wapping High Street, by Wapping New Stairs, from which John Harriott investigated the crime in 1811, is still the headquarters of the river police, but the building there now dates from 1907. It has been the centre of river policing since 1798, when the Marine Police was first established, by Harriott and Patrick Colquhoun, with money supplied by the West India merchants whose goods they were to protect. Harriott himself committed suicide in the police office in January 1817, because of the pain of advanced cancer, but his body did not suffer Williams's ignominious fate.

At the time of the murders this area was being transformed by the construction of the London Dock, by the engineer John Rennie and the surveyor Daniel Alexander. The first dock was built between 1801 and 1805, but new basins were added, spreading east to Shadwell, over the next fifty years. The original London Dock was south of Pennington Street, where News International's vast printing works now occupies much of its site. The only water that was retained when this dock was filled in in the 1970s is a pretty ornamental canal along which you can walk from Wapping Lane to St Katharine's Dock. Despite many recent demolitions, you can still see some fine dockside buildings around here. On the corner of Pennington Street and Wapping Lane there is an impressive section of Alexander's New Tobacco Warehouse, which was built in 1811–14 all around Tobacco Dock, and there are good Victorian warehouses (converted to flats, offices and workshops) at the eastern end of Wapping High Street, at New Crane Wharf, and along Wapping Wall, where Great Jubilee Wharf, Metropolitan Wharf and Pelican Wharf allow you only brief glimpses of the river. The walk along here leads you conveniently past the Prospect of Whitby (*see* Chapter Six), and to the Shadwell Basin, which was built between 1828 and 1858, and is now used for community leisure purposes.

Those of a ghoulish disposition might enjoy finding the scenes of some other London murders. The most famous, the Jack the Ripper killings, have been done to death, but looking for some of the places where the unfortunate victims were discovered takes you to some interesting corners of the old East End, and allows you to visit the Whitechapel rookeries. Most of the murder scenes have changed their names, and some bear no resemblance to the squalid backstreets in which the killer did his work, but some still have a Victorian atmosphere. Starting at Aldgate East Underground station, walk a short way to the east on Whitechapel High Street and turn left into a cobbled alley now called Gunthorpe Street but once known as George Yard. Near the far end of this road on the right, in George's Yard Buildings (now gone), a prostitute, Martha Turner or Tabram, was found dead with multiple stab wounds on 6 August 1888, perhaps the first victim of the Whitechapel killer. The building roughly opposite this site is Toynbee Hall, which was founded by Canon Samuel Barnett in 1884 as a way of bringing university graduates into mutually beneficial contact with the poor of the East End.

A little to the right of the end of Gunthorpe Street is Thrawl

Street, which used to be (along with Flower and Dean Walk) a notorious rookery. Mary Anne Nichols, generally said to be the first victim of Jack the Ripper, lived here in 1888. Like most rookeries, the area was comprehensively rebuilt, first by slum clearance and housing charity model dwellings in the 1880s and 1890s, then by an enlightened housing association in the 1980s. Go a little way down Thrawl Street, turn left into Flower and Dean Walk, and go straight on (in Thrawl Street again) to reach Commercial Street. Turn right and walk north on Commercial Street, which was cut through the area in the 1840s and 1850s, passing Christ Church, another Hawksmoor masterpiece, now looking marvellous again, and Fournier Street. Turn right into Puma Court and left into Wilkes Street, which has fine Huguenot houses of the 1720s (restored after war damage), which brings you to Hanbury Street. In the backyard of number 29, across the road and a little to the right, now covered by brewery buildings, the body of Annie Chapman, the second (or perhaps third) Ripper victim, was found on 8 September 1888. Some of the houses on the street are the ones that were here in the 1880s, though their social level has changed.

Now turn round and return to Commercial Street, and cross over towards Spitalfields Market. Between the left side of the market (as you face it) and the multistorey car park, the unnamed service road is Duval Street, which was once Dorset Street, a road of pubs, lodging houses and many Jack the Ripper associations. About halfway down on the right was an alley next to number 26, which led to 13 Miller's Court where the very badly mutilated body of Mary Jane Kelly was found in her room on 9 November 1888. She was the last recognized Ripper victim, and the only one not broken down by age, drink, poverty and hard work.

Duval Street is a dead end, so take White's Row, the next street along (south), to reach Crispin Street. Turn left and go south on Crispin Street as it changes into Bell Lane and Goulston Street. On the left as you cross Wentworth Street are Wentworth Street Model Dwellings, which were brand new in 1888. In the doorway of num-

bers 108–119 Jack the Ripper (or somebody else) chalked an enig-
matic message after his double murder on 30 September which
seemed to implicate 'the Jewes' (thousands of whom had settled in
these streets in the 1880s) in the killings. It was wiped away on the
orders of the Metropolitan Police Commissioner before it could cause
any harm. The double murder took place in two locations. Elizabeth
Stride was found in Berners Street (now Henriques Street), a right
turn off Commercial Road (not Commercial Street), walking east from
Aldgate East Tube station. This is rather a distance, and the street
has completely changed, so it is better to continue down Goulston
Street to Whitechapel High Street, and turn right to reach Aldgate
High Street. A little way along, on the right, is Mitre Street, which
takes you to Mitre Square, the site of the only Ripper killing to take
place in the City of London. This was the murder of Catherine
Eddowes, the second victim of 30 September, whose corpse was
found in the south-west corner of the square, horribly mutilated in
the face and body.

Of course, the East End has been the scene of many serious
crimes, though none were as dramatic as the 1888 killings. A close
rival might be the Siege of Sidney Street, an anarchist outrage of
1911. This involved the burglary of a jeweller's shop on 10 December 1910 by four Latvian anarchists, which led to a gun battle in
which four policemen and one of the Latvians were killed. The
shop was at 119 Houndsditch, near Cutler Street and Goring Street.
On 2 January the police discovered that two of the three survivors
were hiding in 100 Sidney Street, and next day the famous siege
began, involving Scots Guards and the young Home Secretary, Winston Churchill. Eventually the house caught fire and burned down,
killing two more of the Latvians. Their supposed leader, 'Peter the
Painter', was not in the house and was never captured. Sidney Street
runs north–south from Whitechapel Road to Commercial Road quite
near Whitechapel Underground station. It has all been rebuilt as the
Sidney Street estate, part of Stepney's post-war reconstruction, a
1950s mixture of houses, maisonettes and tower blocks. One of these

blocks, at the southern end of the street, is called Siege House, but there are no other reminders of the drama of January 1911. Number 100 Sidney Street was on the east side, about halfway down, near Sidney Square.

As you walk back up Sidney Street towards Whitechapel Underground station you could look at two more criminal sites. Opposite Sidney Street, at 337 Whitechapel Road, is the Blind Beggar, an otherwise ordinary public house famous because Ronnie Kray, one of the notorious Kray twins, shot dead George Cornell of the rival Richardson gang there on 8 March 1966. Another two years of gang warfare and several murders followed before the twins were jailed for life. Going left (west) towards the station, you could turn right into Brady Street and left into Durward Street, which used to be Buck's Row. On 31 August 1888 the body of prostitute Mary Anne ('Polly') Nichols was found on the pavement on the right (north) side of the street, by an old wooden gateway, just before the old School Board school.

*

There are crime scenes all over central and suburban London, but most of them are of little interest today. The otherwise nondescript London addresses made famous by their association with a great crime or scandal have mostly disappeared. Number 10 Rillington Place, the house in a cul-de-sac near where Westway now crosses Ladbroke Grove, where the necrophiliac John Christie murdered seven women and hid their bodies between 1938 and 1953, no longer exists. And 39 Hilldrop Crescent, the house in which Dr Crippen poisoned and buried his wife in 1910, was destroyed in the Blitz, though the street is still there, at the junction of Camden Road and Brecknock Road, a short walk from Holloway Prison.

Two murderers who used a bath to get rid of their victims have surviving homes in London. George John Smith, the 'brides in the bath' killer, drowned his third victim at 14 Waterlow Road (previously Bismarck Road), Highgate, in 1914, and in 1944 John

Haigh dissolved the bodies of three women in baths of prussic acid in the basement of 79 Gloucester Road, opposite the Tube station. A notorious Victorian poisoning case centred on the Priory, 225 Bedford Hill, a big Gothic house on the western edge of Tooting Common. This was where Charles Bravo died in 1876 from antimony poisoning, probably at the hands of his wife Florence, whose first husband had died in the same way. Her probable accomplice (though neither was tried) was her lover and neighbour, Dr James Gully. Three years later Kate Wilson, a servant at 9 Park Road, Richmond Hill, chose a simpler way of killing Julia Thomas, who had just dismissed her. After throwing her down the stairs, she dismembered and boiled down the body, offered the 'dripping' to the Hole in the Wall, still the local pub, and dumped the remains from two west London bridges – Richmond for the body, Hammersmith for the head.

Disappointingly, Sweeney Todd, the 'demon barber of Fleet Street', who is said to have cut his customers' throats and sent their bodies along to his mistress's pie shop for baking and sale, is an entirely fictional creation. The gruesome tale first appeared in 'penny dreadfuls' and melodramas in the 1840s, and has been the basis of several films and a Stephen Sondheim musical since then. Mrs Lovatt's pie shop is meant to have been in Bell Yard, off Fleet Street by the eastern end of the Law Courts, and the Old Bank of England public house on that corner claims to be built over vaults and tunnels that linked the barber's with the pie shop. The fact that the pub, which occupies the magnificent 1888 premises of the Law Courts branch of the Bank of England, still sells 'finger sandwiches' is mildly disturbing.

Number 19 Cleveland Street, which became notorious in 1889 as a gay brothel where aristocrats and members of the royal family had sex with post boys, has now been consumed by Middlesex Hospital, but a few houses of sexual ill repute are still standing in London. Number 76 Sloane Street was the home of the leading Liberal politician Sir Charles Dilke, who allegedly enjoyed a three-in-a-bed affair there with Virginia Crawford and Fanny Gray, the discovery of which in 1886 ended his ministerial career. Dilke's house is next door to the Cadogan Hotel, where Oscar Wilde was arrested in room 120 (now room 118) in April 1895.

You can trace Wilde's story from the rooms he took in 1883 at 9 Carlos Place (previously Charles Street), near Grosvenor Square, to the fashionable Chelsea house, 34 (previously 16) Tite Street, where he lived with his family and wrote all his greatest works, from 1884 to 1895. You can eat or drink in his usual haunt, the Café Royal at 68 Regent Street near Piccadilly Circus (rebuilt but still atmospheric), and eat in his favourite restaurant, Kettner's, on the corner of Romilly Street and Greek Street. Kettner's, Soho's oldest restaurant, was founded in 1868 and some of its rooms still have a fin de siècle look, even though it is hard to imagine Oscar Wilde enjoying a Kettner's cheeseburger. St James's Theatre in King Street, St James's, which staged *Lady Windermere's Fan* in 1892 and *The Importance of Being Earnest* in 1895, was demolished in 1957, but the Theatre Royal Haymarket, which staged *A Woman of No Importance* in 1893 and *An Ideal Husband* in 1895, is still in fine condition, though its auditorium was reconstructed in 1905. A green plaque at the back of the theatre commemorates its association with Wilde. You can follow him to the Savoy Hotel in the Strand, where he stayed so indiscreetly with his lover, Lord Alfred Douglas, and to the rooms he took at 10–11 St James's Place (off St James's Street), where he met the young men who later gave evidence against him. His descent took him through Bow Street Police Station, the Old Bailey, Pentonville and Wandsworth Prisons, to Clapham Junction railway station, where Wilde, on his way to Reading Gaol, had to stand, handcuffed and in prison uniform, while a crowd jeered and spat at him. Finally, you might visit the memorial to Wilde opposite Charing Cross station, Maggi Hambling's green granite sarcophagus with Wilde's bronze head emerging from it, and the lines from *Lady Windermere's Fan*: 'We are all in the gutter but some of us are looking at the stars.'

Mayfair and St James's are the places to find the homes of the mistresses and courtesans that were once so important a part of aristocratic and royal life. Charles II's mistress Nell Gwynne lived in Pall Mall, next to Schomberg House, and though her house no longer exists a plaque records its location. The actress and courtesan Mary Robinson, 'Perdita', mistress to the future Prince Regent and Charles James Fox, lived at the south end of Cork Street (at the northern end of the Burlington Arcade) in the 1780s, and at 14 St James's Place in the 1790s, when her star had waned. Lola Montez, an Irish dancer and courtesan with royal lovers all over Europe, lived at 27 Half Moon Street (off Piccadilly, near Shepherd Market) in 1848–9, until a bigamy scandal forced her to leave the country. Harriette Wilson, mistress to Byron, Wellington and the future Lord Melbourne in the early nineteenth century, lived at 16 Trevor Square, Knightsbridge, in the 1820s. When she threatened to include Wellington in her alarmingly indiscreet *Memoirs* (published in 1825) he sent her a famous note: 'Publish and be damned.' The famous courtesan Catherine Walters, or 'Skittles', who had affairs with various aristocrats, the poet Wilfred Scawen Blunt and the future Edward VII, lived at 15 South Street, near its junction with Park Street and Park Lane, from 1872 to 1920. This was conveniently near Hyde Park, her shop window.

The geographical pattern of illicit sexual life in London has always been far more complicated than the existence of a red light district, whether on Bankside in the Middle Ages and the sixteenth century, Covent Garden in the seventeenth and eighteenth centuries, the Strand and Haymarket (among many others) in the nineteenth century, and Shepherd Market and Soho in the twentieth. Most brothels and prostitutes met local demand and therefore were as widely spread as grocery shops or dairies. In medieval and Tudor London there were four Love Lanes and three Maiden Lanes, which might have been named after the women who solicited on them, just as other streets were named after more respectable trades. John Stow, London's first real historian, says that at least one Love Lane was 'so called of wantons'. Gropecuntelane, a lost lane near Cheapside, is much less ambiguous. Medieval Oxford, Northampton and Wells had lanes with the same name.

Bankside, the southern bank of the Thames between the present Blackfriars and London Bridges, was the most notorious red light district in the sixteenth and early seventeenth centuries, when brothels and playhouses stood side by side, and prostitutes looked for customers in the Globe and Rose. After the Restoration of Charles II in 1660 and in the eighteenth century London's theatre district moved to Covent Garden and the Haymarket, and both these districts also became well-known centres of prostitution. The Haymarket was one of James Boswell's hunting grounds in the 1760s, and Covent Garden, according to Sir John Fielding, chief magistrate of Bow Street in the 1750s, was 'the great square of Venus'. Naturally, this is where John Cleland had his fictional prostitute, Fanny Hill, take an apartment in the 1740s. The area was so full of prostitutes that an enterprising enthusiast, Samuel Derrick, produced an annual guide to them, *Harris's List of Covent Garden Ladies*, which was published between 1757 and 1795. The area covered by the guide included Soho, which was not so clearly divided from Covent Garden as it became after the construction of Charing Cross Road in the 1880s. We learn from James Boswell's *London Journal* (covering his visit of 1762–3) that prostitutes could be picked up in almost any part of London and enjoyed in a nearby secluded spot. His most daring 'engagement' took place on the new Westminster Bridge: 'The whim of doing it there with the Thames rolling below us amused me very much.' The bridge was replaced with the present one in 1854–62, so it is not possible, even if it were advisable, to re-create Boswell's feat.

In the nineteenth century prostitutes were plentiful in almost every London district, and some of the most scandalous concentrations of open prostitution were in such smart West End streets as Haymarket, Piccadilly and the Strand, and in the big music halls in Leicester Square. In the twentieth century Soho established itself as the main centre of the London sex industry, but no doubt prostitution is still as widespread as the demand for it.

*

Rebellious Londoners have always needed somewhere to gather before marching on the City, Westminster, or some other centre of wealth or power. In north London, Cold Bath Fields, Spa Fields and Clerkenwell Green were favourite places of assembly well into the nineteenth century, when they almost disappeared under the spreading city.

If you take Clerkenwell Close north from Clerkenwell Green, following it round to the right, through the little square and into Rosoman Street, and then go left into Exmouth Market, the land on your left was Spa Fields, where protesters and rioters used to assemble. Spa Fields Open Space, all that is left of the Fields, does not look like a radical hot spot today, but this was the site of the famous Spa Fields Riots of December 1816, in which post-war distress, a demand for the vote and the agitation of the followers of Thomas Spence, the Spenceans, attracted a crowd of a few thousand to hear Henry 'Orator' Hunt calling for the reform of Parliament. About two hundred men then marched to Smithfield, the Royal Exchange and the Tower of London, plundering gun shops on the way and presenting a real threat (though they did not know it) to the security of the Tower.

Sometimes demonstrations and even riots did not seem enough. The 1816 riots sparked repressive government measures, and encouraged the Spenceans, led by Arthur Thistlewood and egged on by a government spy, George Edwards, to plot something bigger, the assassination of the cabinet. They were betrayed by the spy, and when twelve Bow Street Runners raided the plotters' loft on 23 February 1820 Thistlewood killed an officer with his sword. By a miracle the little house in whose hayloft they planned their doomed insurrection, 1a Cato Street, has survived nearly two hundred years of redevelopment and is now a listed building. You can find it by walking up Edgware Road from Marble Arch, turning right into Harrowby Street and going left under an arch into Cato Street. Oddly, Harrowby Street (which is a quite well-preserved eighteenth-century street) is named after the family of Lord Harrowby, whose house in Grosvenor Square was the conspirators' target, and Castlereagh Street, a cul-de-sac right next to it, is named after another of their targets, the Foreign Secretary. Tricked and trapped, Arthur Thistlewood and his friends were the last people in England to be beheaded.

Campaigning for the vote was a more promising way forward. Close to Spa Fields, on the western side of Farringdon Road, near Rosebery Avenue, is the Mount Pleasant Sorting Office, which stands on the site of Cold Bath Fields, the scene of a mass demonstration for the vote, a free press and other outrageous things on 13 May 1833, after the passing of the disappointing 1832 Electoral Reform Act. This time the dispersal of the crowd was in the hands of the new (1829) Metropolitan Police, and a rather aggressive police baton charge ended in the fatal stabbing of a constable, Robert Culley.

In the eighteenth century an open space in south London, St George's Fields, provided the venue for some of London's most famous riots. St George's Fields occupied the then huge undeveloped space between Borough High Street, Union Street and The Cut, Kennington Lane and Kennington Road. St George the Martyr church, after which they were named, marks the eastern edge of the Fields; St George's Circus is roughly their middle; and Geraldine Harmsworth Park, the grounds of the Imperial War Museum, is all that is left of them today. In the eighteenth century the fields were home to the Dog and Duck tea gardens, on the site of the present War Museum, and to Apollo Gardens, a little further north (near Morley Street). They were also the scene of two of the century's most famous outbreaks of disorder.

In 1768 John Wilkes, the famous pornographer, demagogue and champion of the free press and electoral rights, was arrested and held in the King's Bench Prison, which at this time was in the corner created by the meeting of Borough Road and Borough High Street (now the Scovell Street housing estate) on the eastern edge of St George's Fields. About 20,000 of Wilkes's supporters gathered outside the prison, and in dispersing them troops killed ten protesters. This was the famous St George's Fields Massacre of 10 May 1768. Twelve years later, on 2 June 1780, a demagogue of a different colour, Lord George Gordon, used the Fields to gather a vast crowd (60,000, it was said) in opposition to the government's 1778 Catholic Relief Act, which reduced the disadvantages experienced by the Catholic population. From Lambeth, the crowd marched across Westminster Bridge (opened in 1750) to chase and abuse MPs and ministers, then spread out to attack Catholic embassy chapels, Irish settlements and the London prisons, almost all of which were destroyed. On 7 June, when the Bank of England was attacked, the government called in troops, who stopped the disorder by killing nearly three hundred rioters.

The Fields were built over during the next half-century, and when the Chartists, still struggling for universal male suffrage, wanted a meeting place in south London in 1848, Europe's revolutionary year, they had to find somewhere further out. The great Chartist rally of 10 April 1848, which had all London in a panic, gathered on Kennington Common, which is now Kennington Park, at the junction of Kennington Park Road and Camberwell New Road, near the Oval. The famous photograph of the huge (perhaps 100,000) crowd, mostly in top hats or bowlers, listening to their leaders speaking, is one of the earliest of an important historical event.

In the west, as London spread, Hyde Park was the usual choice, within easy marching distance of Westminster and the West End. The eastern end of Hyde Park, near Park Lane, was a favourite place of assembly for discontented Londoners and the location of some of the most important Victorian riots and demonstrations. In August 1819 it was here, by Cumberland Gate, that the London mob stopped the funeral procession of Queen Caroline, George IV's wronged and popular wife (the Princess Diana of her day), and forced the government to reroute it through the City, where the crowds could see it.

On Sunday 1 July 1855 Hyde Park was the scene of a very large and effective protest against the proposed ban on Sunday trading. The police had banned demonstrations in the park, but the crowd defied the order and gathered to jeer and heckle the rich families parading in their carriages on the carriage drive near Park Lane. They defied a police order again in 1862, when great crowds met in Hyde Park in support of Garibaldi, and in July 1866, during the popular campaign for electoral reform. Finding Cumberland Gate locked against them, the huge crowd surged up to the railings along Park Lane and Bayswater Road and broke them down, effectively warning the government of what might happen if democratic hopes were disappointed. An Act of 1872 recognized the public's right of assembly in Hyde Park, so long as they obeyed the rules of the park.

Trafalgar Square was the other favourite West End meeting place, an even more strategic and contentious location. In February 1886 great crowds of socialists and the unemployed met in the square, and decided to go on a tour of West End gentlemen's clubs. They marched off down Pall Mall, turned right into St James's Street, left into Piccadilly, smashing windows along the way, and reassembled in the old radical meeting place, the north-east corner of Hyde Park. Despite occasional bans, Trafalgar Square has remained a focal point of marches and demonstrations ever since. There was a great battle between police and unemployed marchers in Hyde Park and Trafalgar Square in October and November 1932, and the square was the place where the annual Campaign for Nuclear Disarmament marches ended in huge rallies between 1958 and 1963.

*

Southwark is a good place to look for the remains of almost-vanished priories, playhouses and prisons. In the Middle Ages Southwark was outside the City's control, and those in authority there, including the Earls of Surrey and the Bishops of Winchester, allowed crime and prostitution to thrive. Even after the Reformation, when most of the Church estates along the southern bank of the Thames came under the City's jurisdiction, Southwark had a freer moral climate than the City proper. That, along with the accessibility of Bankside, explains the popularity of the area with Elizabethan and Jacobean theatrical entrepreneurs like Richard Burbage, Edward Alleyn and Philip Henslowe. Bankside had four playhouses, the Rose, the Globe, the Hope and the Swan, in James I's reign.

A walk along Bankside and through Southwark, starting at the southern end of the Millennium Bridge, takes you past the sites of three theatres, and of several Southwark jails and prisons. Take the steps from the bridge down to Bankside, and walk east. The site of the Swan, the only Elizabethan theatre whose interior we know from a contemporary picture, is to the west, in what was the Liberty (a personal or specific jurisdiction) of Paris Garden, beyond Hopton Street. Since there is nothing to see it is better to walk east along the river, with the Tate Modern a converted oil-fired power station originally built in the 1950s) on your right. You are in the Liberty of the Clink, a district of brothels, bear gardens and theatres, which was under the lax jurisdiction of the Bishop of Winchester. One of the first things you see after Tate Modern is a row of old houses, numbers 49–52, which date from about 1712. The blocked-off alley next to number 49 was Cardinal Cap Alley, which marked the beginning (going east) of the Bankside brothel district. A book by Gillian Tindall, *The House by the Thames*, tells the story of number 49, from its days as a brothel, the Cardinal's Cap, in the 1570s, and its rebuilding in brick in 1710, to its long history as a rich coal merchant's house, and its rescue from dereliction by the highly eccentric Guy Munthe in 1972. According to Ms Tindall, the vaulted cellars of the timber-framed Tudor house still exist under the present brick building.

Next, Sam Wanamaker's reconstruction of the Globe, a replica completed in 1996. The original Globe was constructed from the timbers of The Theatre, which were carried from Shoreditch by night by Richard and Cuthbert Burbage (James's sons) in 1599. It burned down in 1613, and the rebuilt theatre was closed for good in 1642.

The exhibition in the Globe brings the old theatre district to life, and makes understanding the rest of the walk easier. Continue east and take the second right into Bear Gardens, where a small square marks the site of the Southwark Bear Gardens, where muzzled bears were attacked by mastiffs. The Bear Gardens lasted from 1546 to 1656, but between 1613 and 1616 shared their building with Philip Henslowe's short-lived Hope Theatre. The bear pit reopened as Davies' Amphitheatre between 1662 and 1682, when the two great Restoration diarists Samuel Pepys and John Evelyn visited it.

Follow Bear Gardens round to the left into Park Street, where both the Rose and the Globe theatres were situated. The foundations of the Rose, which presented plays from 1587 to 1605, were discovered in 1989 on Park Street between Rose Alley and Southwark Bridge Road, where a plaque marks the site. The remains of the Rose, the first theatre on Bankside and the fifth in London, can be visited by pre-booked groups, and in the future perhaps by the general public. For information, go to rosetheatre.org.uk or www.shakespeares-globe.org. A short walk to the east, under the bridge, brings you to the true site of Shakespeare's Globe, partly under Southwark Bridge Road and Anchor Terrace, which was built in 1834. The exact location, established by excavation in 1989, is marked out in bricks and cobbles in Old Theatre Court, along with signs explaining the site.

A left turn down Bankend (previously Dead Man's Place) takes you back to Bankside, and to the Anchor, a fine late-eighteenth-century inn which stands on the site of a fifteenth-century inn, the Castle and the Hoop. Both the Anchor and its predecessor doubled as brothels. The Anchor brewery was owned by Henry and Hester Thrale ('Queeney'), who were very close friends of the great Dr Samuel Johnson. Johnson must have spent many hours here in the late 1770s, though he spent much more time at the Thrales' country house in Streatham, where he had his own apartment. Go under the railway bridge and you will see at least one sign marking the site of the Bishop of Winchester's prison, the Clink. Originally this would have been a cell inside the Bishop's Palace, which was built here in the early twelfth century and rebuilt in the fourteenth. In the sixteenth century, relocated again, the prison was used to hold those brave or foolish enough to resist the prevailing religion, and in the seventeenth century, when Winchester House was ruined by billeted Parliamentarian troops, the prison continued in use. It was unimportant by 1780, when the Gordon rioters burned it down. The Clink Prison Museum, which makes Southwark's penal history rather more gruesome and dramatic than it really was, probably stands on the site of the last Clink. The original was a little further east, through the canyon of Victorian warehouses, near the surviving fourteenth-century remains of Winchester House. The great early-fourteenth-century rose window, high on the west wall of the great hall, is one of the most striking sights in London. Now go past Southwark Cathedral and turn right on busy Borough High Street, one of London's most historic streets, once full of taverns and coaching inns.

As you walk south, as those leaving London for Canterbury, Dover and the south coast have done for a thousand years, you might notice the old inn yards on your left. King's Head Yard has an 1881 inn and a seventeenth-century head of Henry VIII, and White Hart Yard, whose old inn was demolished in 1889, was the scene of two famous fictional meetings, one between Mr Pickwick and Sam Weller, and the other (from Shakespeare's *2 Henry VI*) between Jack Cade and his rebellious followers in 1450, when Cade tried to persuade them not to desert his cause. Next comes the George Inn, the only seventeenth-century London coaching inn to survive, even in part. Only one wing of the inn exists now, to remind us of the courtyards in which plays were once acted, and of the sight which would have greeted a coach traveller when he arrived in London before the railways. The next alley is Talbot Yard, which was the home until 1873 of the Tabard Inn, in which Chaucer's fourteenth-century pilgrims gathered and agreed to entertain each other with stories on the road to Canterbury. Across the road there are a few more reminders of what Borough High Street must once have looked like: numbers 38–42 (in a branch of the High Street running up to Southwark Street) are early eighteenth century, and number 50 Calvert's Buildings has a courtyard with overhanging timber-framed buildings that survived the great Southwark fire of 1676.

Old Southwark had seven prisons, one run by the Church, others by the Surrey magistrates and others by the Crown. All of them are gone now, but it might interest you to see where they used to be. The Borough Compter, the ordinary local jail for debtors and petty offenders, had various locations, but in the seventeenth century it stood roughly where the war memorial now is, where the two branches of Borough High Street meet. Continuing to walk south on the east side of the High Street, you pass a late-seventeenth-century building that was once the Boot and Flogger inn at number 101, and St Christopher's Inn (once the Grapes Tavern) at number 123, with its handsome court. The Nag's Head, number 137, is gone, but its name is still carved in the kerbstone. The next turnings on the left, Newcomen Street, Mermaid Court, Chapel Court and Laytons Grove, between them held four prisons in the eighteenth and nineteenth centuries. Turn down Newcomen Street, where the King's Arms has an impressive royal arms (made in the 1730s) taken from the gatehouse of the old London Bridge when it was demolished in 1831.

If you walk down Newcomen Street, right into Tennis Street and right again into the still rather grim Mermaid Court, you have walked around the site of the first Marshalsea Prison, which was here between the 1370s and 1811. This was a royal prison, under the charge of the Earl Marshal, and once second only to the Tower of London in importance as a state prison. It held religious prisoners in the sixteenth century, and mostly debtors in the eighteenth. Queen Elizabeth's chief interrogator, Richard Topcliffe, tortured Catholic priests here in the 1580s and 1590s. When it closed in 1811 a new Marshalsea was opened a little to the south, nearer St George's church. This was the prison that held Charles Dickens's father as a debtor in 1824, and in which Dickens set the scene of Little Dorrit's birth and childhood. This is Dickens's description, from the opening of Chapter 6 of *Little Dorrit*: 'Thirty years ago there stood, a few doors short of the church of St George, in the borough of Southwark, on the left-hand side of the way going southward, the Marshalsea Prison ... an oblong pile of barrack building ... hemmed in by high walls duly spiked on top. Itself a close and confined prison for debtors, it contained within it a much closer and more confined jail for smugglers.' St George's, the 1730s church in which Little Dorrit was christened, is still in fine shape, 'massive and trustworthy' (Pevsner).

The block between Mermaid Court and the church of St George the Martyr on Long Lane held three prisons, the White Lion and the old King's Bench, as well as the new Marshalsea. The White Lion was a local lock-up in the sixteenth and seventeenth centuries, somewhere around Mermaid Alley, and the King's Bench was a state prison serving the royal court of that name. From the fourteenth century until the 1750s it stood a little south of Mermaid Court, where Layton's Grove has replaced King's Bench Alley. Right next to this, the new Marshalsea stood from about 1811 to 1842, when it was closed, and 1897, when it was demolished. But still, if you turn left from Borough High Street into Angel Place (just before Long Lane) you will see a long 5.5-metre-high brick wall, the southern wall of the final Marshalsea Prison and the last relic of the Borough High Street prisons. This must be one of the walls that Dickens found when he came to the Borough in 1856, while he was writing *Little Dorrit*, 'to see if I could find any ruins of the Marshalsea'.

Cross Borough High Street and walk down Marshalsea Road, next to Borough Underground station, and into Mint Street. Now you have entered the sanctuary of the Mint, a fearsome refuge of criminals, debtors and prostitutes in the sixteenth century, and a rookery in the early nineteenth. In 1832 London's first cholera cases appeared in the Mint, confirming the general low opinion of the area. As you walk along the streets now renamed Weller Street, Trundle Street and Pickwick Street you will not see much left of the old rookery, but plenty of evidence of how the Victorians got rid of it. There is a big Peabody estate on Mint Street and Marshalsea Road, and on Lant Street, a few metres to the south, there is an 1877 London School Board primary school, now named after Charles Dickens. Then go back up Weller Street and Mint Street to reach Ayres Street and Redcross Way, where the Victorian housing reformer and philanthropist Octavia Hill, who was employed by the Church Commissioners to manage their property in Southwark, built two rows of picturesque half-timbered terraces, Red and White Cross Cottages, in the late 1880s. The cottages were designed by Elijah Hoole, and the hall at the end of the terrace, also by Hoole, has interior decoration by Walter Crane. Octavia Hill Gardens, between Redcross Way and the cottages, has lost its original landscaping, but is still a pleasant haven in a very urban district. There are other examples of late-Victorian model dwellings in a similar style in the nearby streets. Gable Cottages, in Sudrey Street, off Lant Street, were built to Hoole's designs in 1889, and Whitehill Houses, on Sawyer Street (continuing Lant Street across Southwark Bridge Street), are working-class flats built by the Countess of Selborne in the same year. At the end of Sawyer Street, in Copperfield Street, are Winchester Cottages, built by the Church Commissioners in 1893, on Octavia Hill's advice.

All these replaced the notorious slums that filled these streets in the 1880s. This part of Southwark played an important part in the awakening of the late-Victorian conscience to the problem of poor housing and the desirability of council and charity housing to replace demolished slums. Two very important pieces of social reporting in 1883, George Sims's *Horrible London* and Andrew Mearns's *Bitter Cry of Outcast London*, were based on research done in this neighbourhood. Sims's account of 'darkest Southwark' was based on the Mint, and Mearns's influential little study was drawn from a visit to Colliers' Rents, a miserable alley off Long Lane between Tennis Street and Crosby Row, near the site of the second Marshalsea.

*

Westminster had its share of prisons, though only a few scraps of them now survive. Westminster Abbey had a jail in its fourteenth-century gatehouse, which straddled the road just before Broad Sanctuary divides into Tothill Street and Victoria Street, until 1776. This is where Walter Raleigh spent the night before his execution in 1618, and where the royalist poet Richard Lovelace wrote the famous prison poem, beginning 'Stone walls do not a prison make, Nor iron bars a cage', in 1642. In Little Sanctuary there is an old gateway, dated 1655, set into the side of the Middlesex Guildhall (facing the Queen Elizabeth II Conference Centre), all that remains of the Tothill Fields Bridewell, a prison for vagrants, prostitutes and petty offenders, offering (as the carved sign says) 'several sorts of work' for 'such as will beg and live idle in this city and liberty of Westminster'. This prison stood from 1618 to 1834 in Tothill Fields, the open space south-west of Horseferry Road, on a site next to the Greencoat School, roughly where Artillery Row (a turning off Victoria Street) becomes Greencoat Place. In 1834 this small, crowded and damp jail was replaced with a large cellular prison, reflecting in a half-understood way the latest theories of solitary confinement and the economical observation of radiating prison wings from a central point, the 'panopticon' principle. This large prison, called the Middlesex House of Correction or Tothill Fields Prison, was never a great success, and was demolished in 1884, making way for the new Westminster Cathedral on Victoria Street, which used some of the prison's foundations.

There was another huge prison built on the new panopticon principle in Westminster. This was Millbank Penitentiary, one of the biggest and most expensive buildings ever constructed in London and the first national prison in the country. Millbank was built on seven acres of marshy riverbank between 1816 and 1821, a hexagram with six huge projecting wings, like the petals of a flower, surrounded by a huge octagonal wall and a moat. Today the area it covered is marked roughly by Ponsonby Place, Regency Street, Vincent Street and Millbank. When it was finally demolished after an undistinguished career in 1892 enough land was freed to provide sites for the Tate Gallery, now Tate Britain, for a military hospital on one side and a barracks on the other, and for the LCC's large Millbank housing estate. The foundations upon which Millbank was built, both physical and criminological, were unsound, and it was never a success. It started sinking into the mud, and in 1842 lost its position as the national penitentiary to a new cellular prison, Pentonville, and was demoted to the status of a holding prison for those condemned to be transported to Australia. Its most visible physical remnant is a fat stone bollard or 'buttress' in the little riverside garden near Vauxhall Bridge, which stood at the head of the river steps from which prisoners embarked for exile in Australia or Tasmania until 1867.

The history of policing in London is connected with two famous places. In common speech, policing is (or was) as readily conveyed by the mention of Bow Street and Scotland Yard as medicine is by the name Harley Street, jewellery by Hatton Garden or journalism by Fleet Street. Bow Street is where the Middlesex magistrates, with responsibility for policing London north of the Thames and beyond the jurisdiction of the City, had their court and headquarters in the eighteenth century, supervising constables and nightwatchmen, hearing criminal cases and dispensing justice. The Bow Street Office, as it was called, was number 4 Bow Street, on the west side of the road, the fourth house (or 120 metres) north of the Russell Street corner. This is where Thomas de Veil lived and held his court in the 1740s, and Henry Fielding, lawyer, playwright, theatre manager and novelist, took up the position in January 1749. His blind half-brother John Fielding took over when Henry died in 1754, and continued in the post until 1780, when he died shortly after the Gordon rioters wrecked his court and destroyed his records.

In his short magistracy Henry Fielding created a small professional detective force, the Bow Street Runners, funded by rewards and secret government subsidies. The Runners, founded in 1749, consisted of six experienced constables or 'thief-takers' led by the redoubtable Saunders Welch, and had the job of investigating serious crimes, not patrolling the streets. The Bow Street Court remained the centre of an expanding system of patrols and police offices until 1829, when the new Metropolitan Police was established, under the control of two commissioners whose headquarters were in Whitehall. The old courthouse was demolished in 1887, and replaced by a new court on the other side of the road, which operated until 2006. Emmeline and Christabel Pankhurst, Roger Casement and Ivor Novello appeared there, and Oscar Wilde was held in a Bow Street cell after his arrest in April 1895, and endured three hearings in the court before his two trials at the Old Bailey. The court is now likely to become a hotel.

There were three connecting Scotland Yards off eighteenth-century Whitehall, one opposite the Admiralty, where the present Great Scotland Yard is today (but much wider), and two others, 'Middle' (now Whitehall Place) and 'Inner' or 'Little', between Whitehall Place and Horseguards Avenue, now under the Old War Office. Craig's Court, just to the north of Great Scotland Yard, gives an impression of what the three Scotland Yards might have looked like. It was laid out in the 1690s, and the house at the end, Harrington House, was built around that time. In 1829 the commissioners of the new Metropolitan Police were given an office in a house (number 4) on the north side of Middle Scotland Yard (Whitehall Place), which also had a police station and entrance on the south side of Great Scotland Yard. By the 1880s a bigger headquarters was necessary, and the force moved into a new Norman Shaw building on the riverfront north of Westminster Bridge, next to Portcullis House. New Scotland Yard is a big square building like a castle keep, around a central courtyard, in a mixture of domestic and institutional styles, including Shaw's favourite Queen Anne. Most of this much-imitated building is in orange brick with stripes of Portland stone, but the bottom two stories are of granite quarried by Dartmoor convicts, provided by the man in charge of English prisons, Sir Edmund du Cane. There is a relief portrait of Shaw under one of the balconies on the riverside frontage. The Metropolitan Police moved into their present Victoria Street headquarters, the tall modern building with a revolving sign so often seen on British news broadcasts, in the 1960s.

From 1839 the Metropolitan Police District covered a vast and mostly rural area of over 700 square miles, from Uxbridge to Dagenham, and from Chipstead to Cheshunt. There are Victorian police stations, some no longer in use, all over Greater London, and although they are not worth a special visit, you might notice them as you pass. The oldest seems to be the Hampstead Police Watch House at 4 Holly Place, off Holly Walk (west of Hampstead Underground station), a four-storey building dating from about 1830. Otherwise, the oldest police stations and police courts were designed by the first Metropolitan Police surveyor, Charles Reeves, between 1842 and 1866, and by his successor, Thomas Sorby, in 1867 and 1868. A few were built by Frederick Caiger in the 1870s, but far more surviving stations were the work of John Butler, surveyor from 1881 to 1895, and his son John Dixon Butler, whose unassuming and well-integrated stations still serve many London suburbs.

Charles Reeves's 1845 police station at 63–69 Rochester Row, Westminster, near Vauxhall Bridge Road, and his magistrates' offices round the corner at 66–67 Vincent Square are an interesting survival from the early years of professional policing, but the recent conversion and extension of the buildings for flats has obscured their original appearance and purpose. There is another police station from the Reeves era in London Road, Kingston, opposite the sculpture of leaning red phone boxes called *Out of Order*. The station was opened in 1864 and used until 1968. And on Holmes Road and Kentish Town Road (numbers 298–302) there is a police station built by Reeves and remodelled in 1894 by Norman Shaw, who thus established a style which influenced the Butlers in the many stations they built between 1881 and 1920.

Thomas Sorby's work also survives at 76 King's Cross Road in Clerkenwell, where he replaced Reeves's 1840 police court with a five-storey building in 1867–9 with a block of cells in the low building on its right. The station is now used as a traffic wardens' centre. Next door, on the corner of Great Percy Street, the newer Clerkenwell Magistrates' Court (now converted to other uses) is one of the finest buildings of John Dixon Butler, dating from 1906. There is a disused Sorby police station, built in 1869, in Vine Street (between Swallow Street and Regent Street), and a Sorby police court, dated 1869, in Renfrew Road, off Kennington Lane, near Elephant and Castle. In recent years this was used as a high-security court, dealing with IRA terrorists, the Kray twins and the gang that seized the Iranian embassy. It was closed in 1990, and five years later converted into a Buddhist centre, preserving the high court-room and the prison cells. There is now a nine-foot Buddha where the judge used to sit.

There are good examples of the late-Victorian and Edwardian police stations built by Butler and son all over London. Even in the middle of Hyde Park, which was often the scene of rowdy demon-strations in the late nineteenth century, there is a police station built by J.D. Butler in 1900. In Soho, 19–21 Great Marlborough Street (off Regent Street and opposite Liberty's) is a J.D. Butler magistrates' court and police station of 1913, now converted into the Courthouse Hotel (with its own prison cells), and a short walk down Carnaby Street and a left turn into lively Beak Street brings you to a J.D. Butler police Section house of 1909, at number 40. Other Butler police stations of interest include the 1904 station in Tooley Street (near its junction with Tower Bridge Road) and a fine 1908 baroque station and magistrates' court at the eastern end of Old Street, Shoreditch, opposite the town hall.

A building which represents the various forms of control to which the London working classes were subjected in the eighteenth and nineteenth centuries is the Vestry House in Vestry Road, Walthamstow (near Walthamstow Central station), in the interesting old village. This was built as a workhouse by the Walthamstow vestry (the local government of the parish) in 1730, on part of the village common. The message that paupers saw as they entered the workhouse is still there, on a stone plaque over the door: 'If any would not work neither should he eat.' The workhouse expanded in the eighteenth century, but in 1834, when the new Poor Law was introduced, paupers were moved to a larger building. From 1840 to 1871 part of the building was used as a police station, and one of their prison cells can still be seen, with authentic graffiti on its walls. In 1930, after various private uses, the Vestry House returned to the local authority, and is now a local history museum, open every day but Sunday, free of charge. Take a look through the door on the left of the Panelled Room, to see what was once the workhouse exercise yard. Walthamstow was an important centre for the early film, aviation and car industries, and the museum has on display the first motor car produced in London, made by Frederick Bremer between 1892 and 1894.

To see another side of Walthamstow's local government, walk up the Drive, which leads from the corner of Church Hill to Forest Road, to see the impressive town hall, which was built between 1937 and 1941. The architect, P.D. Hepworth, was influenced by a Swedish exhibition in London in 1931, but the building has a rather totalitarian look, a reminder of the years in which it was built.

*

Probably the most famous address in London law enforcement is a fictional one. In *A Study in Scarlet*, published in 1887, Sherlock

Holmes took an apartment at 221b Baker Street, 'a couple of comfortable bed-rooms and a single large airy sitting-room, cheerfully furnished, and illuminated by two broad windows'. When Arthur Conan Doyle invented this address the numbering of Baker Street stopped at 100, and the northern part of the street, where 221b might have been located, was called York Place and Upper Baker Street. When the whole street was renamed Baker Street and renumbered in the 1930s the Abbey Road (later Abbey National) Building Society got the number 221 (without the b), and took on the burden of answering letters written to the great detective. The building society moved out in 2002, and the task was picked up by the Sherlock Holmes Museum, which is at number 239 Baker Street but calls itself 221b. The display of Holmes exhibits that can be seen for a fee in the Sherlock Holmes Museum is rivalled by the one that can be seen for the price of a drink in the Sherlock Holmes public house in Northumberland Avenue, near Trafalgar Square. The publicans acquired the exhibition created for the 1951 Festival of Britain, and have used it to create a replica of Holmes's apartment in the upstairs restaurant. The pub has a Holmes connection because it was previously the Northumberland Hotel, which is where Sir Henry Baskerville stayed when he came to London to consult Holmes about the death of his uncle, apparently in the jaws of a gigantic hound.

*

Underneath the Arches

Questions 1 and 3 are not answerable at weekends and public holidays.

This little poem represents
A sort of rhyming questionnaire.
Excuse its simple rhythmic plan –
I got it straight from Rupert Bear.

On Holborn, west of Fetter Lane,
There's a fountainhead of knowledge.
Our walk starts there, at Barnard's Inn,
The present home of Gresham College.

Walking west towards High Holborn
You'll see some shops from Shakespeare's time.
Take the stone arch to the courtyard,
And date the thing you have to prime. [1]

Out again and cross the road
Where a dragon guards each light.
Briefly Brooke Street – who's the poet
Whose brothel home was on this site? [2]

Back on Holborn there's a Gothic
Temple to prudential trust.
Through the speckled marble gateway
Who lived here once, and now's a bust? [3]

East again, past Leather Lane
You turn left on the jewellers' route.
Who's that up there on the right,
Who made a nation of a boot? [4]

Forty paces on, a sign
Denotes the ruler of a see.
Take the passage, date the pub, [5]
And come out through the iron T.

Audrey points to Etheldreda,
Reversing old King Henry's script.
If it's open, count the columns
In the medieval crypt. [6]

Leave Ely Place and then follow
Charterhouse's meaty way.
Keep straight until you find Cold Storage
And the slogan of the PLA. [7]

Take West Poultry, then straight on,
A grimy ruin on your right.
Right on Smithfield, left on Snow Hill,
Justice looms up, golden bright.

Going east on Snow Hill, now,
Blue lamps denote the work within.
Before the station, whose head swung,
To signify a famous inn? [8]

Ahead towards St Sepulchre
Whose musicality's renowned.
But which of its parishioners
Said our blood goes round and round? [9]

To the left, just on this corner,
What's it here that needs replacing? [10]
And who's this most-loved essayist,
Tender, witty, self-effacing? [11]

Across the road, left of the tavern,
What's this place that villains hated? [12]
Then cross back, and north on Giltspur,
Find the fat boy who's gold-plated.

What caused the Fire of '66? [13]
And when this was Fortune of War,
Who sat lifeless round the walls,
And whose knives were they waiting for? [14]

Forward now to Haberdashers,
Then go right to see King Hal.
What's that sticking out at us,
Quite enough for any gal? [15]

Go through the arch to see the lovely
St Bartholomew the Less.
In this pretty church, uniquely,
What two functions coalesce? [16]

Back to Smithfield, then go right,
Along the wall, bomb-pocked, it's said.
Many folk were martyred here,
But what's the last day Wallace bled? [17]

Now go through the Tudor gatehouse
To see the City's oldest church.
Try the door, and if it's open,
Go inside and start your search.

By how much did Walter Mildmay
Outlive his wife, the fair Maria? [18]
And what day did the death occur of
The founder of the church, Rahere? [19]

Leave the church, go right and right,
To Cloth Fair's best house, forty-two.
A famous poet lived just near it,
Tell me where it was and who. [20]

Left before the Hand and Shears,
Where they knew fresh wool from shoddy,
To Back Passage and the Old Red Cow.
What's in Dick O'Shea's hot toddy? [21]

Cross Long Lane, and then take Hayne Street.
Halfway round the plague-pit square
You will find the ancient gatehouse,
Which guards the way to . . . tell me where. [22]

West now for the Fox and Anchor.
What's the date of this delight? [23]
And who rebuilt the Wicked Wolf? [24]
Now find St John Street on your right.

Then leftish for the same-named lane –
Horologists once ruled these acres.
Use your eyes as you walk north,
And find the names of three watchmakers. [25]

Date a Great War air raid here, [26]
Near the gateway of St John.
Once through it there's a cobbled square,
The priory precinct, now long gone.

North across a busy road,
Mix some guessing with research.
Looking at the ground below,
What shape was the vanished church? [27]

A passage called Jerusalem
Joined the homes of monk and nun.
We'll take it too, to reach our goal,
But not expecting so much fun.

The corner of this well-worn track's
The birthplace of the concert show.
Helped by one of London's plaques,
Name the impresario. [28]

Go left to find a greenless Green,
Where Twist learned how to spot a mark.
In which Georgian Marxist house
Did Lenin write for *Iskra* (*Spark*)? [29]

Pass the courthouse, then go right
To find a well that once ran clear.
Tell me who in Clerkenwell
Once 'esteemed the waters' here. [30]

The walking and the puzzling's done,
You've written all your answers down.
So go back to the Green again
And check them upstairs in the Crown.

*

CHAPTER NINE

Dickens's London

The gateway of St Olave Hart Street

ONE OF THE HOUSES occupied by the greatest Victorian Londoner, Charles Dickens, still exists, and is open to the public. Number 48 Doughty Street, near the junction of Gray's Inn Road and Guilford Street, is an ordinary middle-class house, built around 1808, with service rooms in the basement, living rooms on the ground and first floors and bedrooms on the second, but the fact that Dickens lived here from March 1837 to December 1839, and that it is his last surviving London home, the place where he finished *Pickwick Papers* and wrote *Oliver Twist* and *Nicholas Nickleby*, makes it special. This is the house in which Dickens's beloved sister-in-law, Mary Hogarth, died, causing him intense and lifelong grief. The house is now a museum, displaying many of Dickens's pictures, manuscripts and other possessions, and is open to visitors every day. Tickets cost about £5.

This house was saved by the Dickens Fellowship when it was threatened with demolition in the 1920s, but his other houses were not so lucky. Number 16 Bayham Street, Camden Town (parallel with Camden High Street), which Dickens's thriftless father moved into in 1822, and from which the young Dickens walked to Warren's blacking factory, near Charing Cross, was demolished in 1910. There is a plaque on the corner of Greenland Road to mark its site. It lives on as the Cratchits' house in *A Christmas Carol* and the Micawbers' house in *David Copperfield*, and other houses of the same type still exist in the street. Dickens drew on his knowledge of Camden Town in *Dombey and Son*, in which he described the devastating impact of the building of the Euston to Birmingham railway in 1836 on Staggs Gardens, where young Paul Dombey lived with his nurse. This was probably Park Street, now Parkway, which runs between Camden Town station and Regent's Park.

The Dickens family moved nine times between 1823 and 1834, pursued by creditors, and in 1834 Dickens took bachelor rooms in Cecil Street, off the Strand opposite Southampton Street, and in Furnival's Inn, Holborn, which was demolished to make way for the extension of the Prudential Building in 1897. There is a bust of Dickens at the far end of the Pru's magnificent pink Gothic courtyard. After Doughty Street, Dickens and his wife and children lived in two houses for substantial periods of time. The first, 1 Devonshire Terrace, was set back from the south side of the New Road (Marylebone Road), near the York Gate entrance to Regent's Park. Dickens lived here from 1839 to 1851, and wrote *The Old Curiosity Shop, David Copperfield* and *Dombey and Son* here. It was demolished in 1960 and replaced by Ferguson House, but a plaque with carved reliefs of Dickens and his characters marks the spot, near the corner of Marylebone High Street. Dickens set Mr Dombey's marriage and the christening and funeral of Paul Dombey in the parish church on this corner, St Mary, which is also the church in which Robert Browning and Elizabeth Barrett married in 1846. The second house was Tavistock House, on Tavistock Square in Bloomsbury, which Dickens leased from 1851 to 1860, when his marriage had broken up. The old house, in which Dickens wrote *Bleak House, Little Dorrit, Hard Times* and *A Tale of Two Cities,* and opened a little theatre with Wilkie Collins, was replaced by the grandiose red brick Tavistock House in 1938, now the home of the British Medical Association. From 1857 until his death in 1870 Dickens lived in Gad's Hill Place, Chatham, which is now a school, occasionally open to the public. He is buried in the south transept of Westminster Abbey ('Poets' Corner'), along with other great literary Londoners, including Chaucer, Dryden, Robert Browning and Samuel Johnson.

Although all but one of Dickens's many residences are gone,

London is so full of places he knew, described and made famous that he could share Wren's epitaph – *Si monumentum requiris, circum-spice,* 'If you seek his monument, look around you.' Almost any part of central London that has retained some of its old buildings evokes the spirit of Dickens and his novels, and is richer in our minds because of him: Clerkenwell, Covent Garden, Soho, Bloomsbury, Southwark, Bermondsey, Holborn, Fleet Street, Westminster, Lime-house and the City. When you are in Cavendish Square, remember Madame Mantalini's dress shop, where Kate Nickleby worked, and the wealthy Merdles (in *Little Dorrit*), who lived here. And in Golden Square think of the hanging body of Ralph Nickleby, or David Copperfield's discovery of Little Emily and Rosa Dartle in a squalid lodging house. Some of these Dickens associations are mentioned in other chapters (especially Chapters Four, Six and Eight), but there follows a suggested walk, beginning and ending in the Strand, which connects some of the more interesting locations, factual or fictional, in Dickens's life and work. All the Inns of Court locations will be closed at weekends and on public holidays.

*

Start on the Strand outside Charing Cross station, which occupies the site of the blacking factory in which Dickens worked as a boy, and which reappears as Murdstone and Grinby's wine warehouse, relocated to Blackfriars, in *David Copperfield.* At the Thames end of the station, where the new Hungerford (or Golden Jubilee) Bridge now crosses the river, were the Hungerford Steps, from which (in *David Copperfield*) Mr and Mrs Micawber embarked for a new life in Australia. Buckingham Street, two blocks to the east of the station, is where Mrs Trotwood found 'a singularly desirable and compact set of chambers' for David Copperfield, and where Dickens lived at number 15 in 1834, at the start of his writing career. His house is gone, but parts of the street are much as he knew it.

Then cross the Strand and go up the steps of St Martin-in-the-Fields, where David Copperfield, walking home one snowy night to

Buckingham Street from Doctor Strong's (where he worked in the evening), saw the prostitute Martha and met Mr Peggoty, who was looking for Little Emily. Copperfield took Peggoty to his inn, the Golden Cross, on the corner of the Strand and Whitehall, to hear about his search. Now take St Martin's Lane, turn right onto William IV Street and fork left onto Chandos Place and Maiden Lane, making for Covent Garden. The blacking warehouse moved to the far (eastern) end of Chandos Place (then Chandos Street), and Dickens used to work on the ground floor, at the second window from the corner of Bedford Street, where there is a plaque. With his friend Bob Fagin he bought his ale at the pub across the road. 'The stones in the street may be smoothed by my small feet going across to it at dinner-time, and back again.' All this has been rebuilt since Dickens's childhood, but if you walk ahead to Maiden Lane you can still find Rules, London's oldest restaurant, where Dickens, when prosperous, often ate. The restaurant, which was founded in 1798, now has a Charles Dickens private dining room, decorated with Dickens memorabilia. The stage door of the Adelphi Theatre, almost opposite Rules, was the scene of the sensational murder of the leading actor William Terriss by a jealous madman, Richard Prince, in 1897. Carry on into Tavistock Street, which brings you to Wellington Street, built to link Waterloo Bridge with Bow Street in 1833–5.

Dickens knew and loved Covent Garden, especially at sunrise 'when the fragrance of sweet flowers is in the air, over-powering even the unwholesome streams of last night's debauchery', and he was particularly fascinated by the jungle of streets around Seven Dials, to its north-west. One of the essays in *Sketches by Boz* evokes the exciting and lawless quality of the neighbourhood in the 1830s, and although the lamp-post leaners and fighting women are gone the streets and houses are not much changed: 'the streets and courts dart in all directions, until they are lost in the unwholesome vapour which hangs over the house-tops'. The grim slum called Tom-All-Alone's in *Bleak House*, where Jo the crossing-sweeper lived, 'a black, dilapidated street, avoided by all decent people', was a composite of the squalid housing in Covent Garden, Seven Dials and St Giles, all of which Dickens knew very well indeed.

In the 1850s Dickens wrote and published the magazine *Household Words* from an office (now gone) in 16 Wellington Street, and in the 1860s he produced *All the Year Round* from 11 Wellington Street, which is marked with a plaque. The Lyceum Theatre, rebuilt in 1834, staged a drama based on *A Tale of Two Cities* under Dickens's supervision. Leaving Seven Dials for another day, you could follow Tavistock Street past the most important theatre of Dickens's day, the Theatre Royal, and turn left onto Drury Lane, an ancient street that was mostly rebuilt in the 1880s and afterwards. Drury Lane Gardens, on your left, were once St Martin-in-the-Fields burial ground, and were probably the model for the 'pestiferous and obscene' churchyard in *Bleak House* in which Lady Dedlock's lover, Nemo (Captain Hawdon), was buried, and where she was later found dead. As the sign there tells you, this was one of the first London churchyards to be made into a public garden under the 1877 Open Spaces Act.

Go back (south) along Drury Lane to the Aldwych (which cut through the tangle of old streets Dickens knew so well), go left, cross Kingsway and go left on it, before turning right into Portugal Street. A left fork into Sheffield Street and a left turn into Portsmouth Street take you past the very old shop which claims to be (but is not) Dickens's Old Curiosity Shop, and along the western side of Lincoln's Inn Fields. This side of the Fields has some fine seventeenth- and eighteenth-century houses, including numbers 59–60, Lindsey House, the only survivor of the houses built around the square in 1640, and Newcastle House, in the far corner, partly Wren's work. Number 58, built in 1730, was once the home of John Forster, Dickens's close friend and biographer. Dickens knew the house very well, and gave a reading of *The Chimes* to a group of friends there in 1844. It was probably the model for Mr Tulkinghorn's house in *Bleak House*.

Go across to the east side of the Fields and enter Lincoln's Inn by the main gate. Straight ahead is the Old Hall, one of London's finest medieval buildings, which was built around 1490 and restored in the 1920s. The case of Jarndyce v. Jarndyce (in *Bleak House*) was held here, because this is where the Lord Chancellor's Court of Chancery sat until the Royal Courts of Justice opened in 1882. It is hard to gain entry to the Old Hall, but if you do you will see some beautiful linenfold panelling, a fine open roof, a 1624 gallery and Hogarth's huge painting of St Paul before Felix. Dickens had a job as a law clerk at number 8 New Square, south of the hall, in 1827. Walk down the east side of the square (by the pillar box), after a few metres turn left through the wrought-iron gates towards Hardwick Buildings, go right and out through the spiked gate, and right into Star Yard. This is where the *Bleak House* rag-and-bone dealer Krook had his shop, and died from spontaneous combustion. After another few metres go left through the busy unnamed shopping alley and left into Chancery Lane. Cross it and go right into Cursitor Street, and left into Took's Court, which Dickens calls Cook's Court, 'at most times a shady place', the workplace of the law stationer Snagsby in *Bleak House*. Most of the houses down here are nineteenth century, but numbers 14–15 were built in the 1720s.

Follow Furnival Street into Holborn and turn right to look into the courtyard of Barnard's Inn (on your right), which is where Pip (in *Great Expectations*) was taken by Wemmick, Mr Jaggers's clerk, to share the lodgings of Herbert Pocket, 'the pale young gentleman'. The discovery that this was not an inn in the usual sense of the word dashed the first of Pip's 'great expectations'. 'I now found Barnard to be a disembodied spirit, or a fiction, and his inn the dingiest collection of shabby buildings ever squeezed together in a rank corner as a club for Tom-cats.' The inn does not seem so bad today, and the memory that this is where Pip got his first foothold in London and heard from Herbert Pocket the story of the jilting of Miss Havisham might help you to enjoy it more. The hall on your right was built in the 1430s, and some of the buildings around the first courtyard were here, though not old, when Dickens arrived in London in 1822.

You could make a diversion here into the bloodstained world Pip found so repulsive when he first arrived in London. If you continue east past Holborn Circus and over Holborn Viaduct, turning left down Giltspur Street, you will come to West Smithfield where, in Dickens's day, animals were still sold and slaughtered for the London market. Dickens describes the scene in Chapter 21 of *Oliver Twist*, when Bill Sikes took Oliver on an expedition to Smithfield on a market morning. 'The crowding, pushing, driving, beating, whooping and yelling; the hideous and discordant din that resounded from every corner of the market; and the unwashed, unshaven, squalid, and dirty figures constantly running to and fro, and bursting in and out of the throng; rendered it a stunning and bewildering scene, which quite confounded the senses.' Continue with St Bartholomew's Hospital on your right, and turn right for a short distance into Little Britain, where Mr Jaggers, the powerful and sinister lawyer (a familiar Dickensian type), had his office. This struck Pip as a gloomy and threatening spot, placed as it was between two of London's most horrible places, Smithfield, where animals were slaughtered, and Newgate, where the victims were human. Smithfield, 'the shameful place, being all asmear with filth and fat and blood and foam, seemed to stick to me'. This is what it was like till 1855, when the animal market was moved.

Retrace your steps to Smithfield and into Giltspur Street, but quickly turn right into Cock Lane and left into Snow Hill. Here, on your left, is an elaborate 1920s police station. This occupies the site of the Saracen's Head, a famous coaching inn that was demolished in 1868. This was where Dickens met the illustrator Hablot K. Browne ('Phiz') on 30 January 1838 and planned a trip to York-shire to investigate the horrors of cheap boys' boarding schools. Like Dickens and Phiz, Nicholas Nickleby took the slow coach to Yorkshire from the Saracen's Head. This is also where the brutal schoolmaster Wackford Squeers stayed on his trips to London, and where Nicholas Nickleby rescued the recaptured Smike.

At the end of Snow Hill, turn right into Holborn Viaduct and cross Holborn Circus into Holborn. Go west along Holborn to look into the courtyard of Staple Inn, in the corner of which the lawyer Mr Grewgious had his chambers in *The Mystery of Edwin Drood*, with the inscription PJT 1747 over the door. Much has happened to Staple Inn since Dickens's days (including a V-bomb in 1944), but it is still, as he described it, 'one of those nooks, the turning into which out of the clashing street, imparts to the relieved pedestrian the sensation of having put cotton in his ears, and velvet soles on his boots'. The Prudential Building, which occupies the site of Furnivall's Inn, Dickens's home before and after his marriage, is across the road to your right, but cross Holborn and go left to find Gray's Inn Gateway, just before the Cittie of York pub. This takes you to the South Square (previously Holborn Court) of Gray's Inn, 'one of the most depressing institutions in brick and mortar known to the children of men', where Dickens worked as a solicitor's clerk for Ellis and Blackmore when he was 15.

Their office, 1 South Square, is still there, with TJW 1759 over the door, but number 2, where David Copperfield's friend Tommy Traddles began his married life, was rebuilt after bombing, like the rest of the square. Bombing also damaged the hall, which was built in the 1550s and restored after 1948. In December 1594 Shakespeare's *Comedy of Errors* had its first performance in this hall, by the Chamberlain's Men. It can only be visited by appointment, but the survival of its stained glass and fine Elizabethan screen makes the effort worthwhile. Go through the passage next to the hall to enter Gray's Inn Square. The archway on the left (built in the 1550s and restored after severe bomb damage) goes through to Field Court, with the Walks on the right. These were first laid out by Francis Bacon (whose statue you passed in South Square) in the 1590s, and improved by 'Capability' Brown in the 1750s, when they were a fashionable London promenade. You can walk in them too, but only between 12.00 and 2.30 on weekdays.

Return to Gray's Inn Square, leave it by the exit opposite (on the east side), cross Gray's Inn Road and go ahead into Baldwin's Gardens. Turn right into Leather Lane and left into Greville Street, crossing Hatton Garden, to find, on your right, Bleeding Heart Yard. This little yard, much changed but still there, was one of the main settings, along with the Marshalsea, of *Little Dorrit*. This is where the poor Plomish family lived, where Mr Pancks's agent struggled to collect his rents, where the injured Frenchman was looked after and hilariously patronized by the Bleeding Hearters (in Chapter 25), and where Little Dorrit's friend and admirer Arthur Clennam set up his engineering works with Daniel Doyle, helping to turn the yard into the industrial enclave which it is (architecturally speaking) today.

Carry on along Greville Street, turn right into Saffron Hill, and briefly follow Oliver Twist's walk towards his first meeting with Fagin, in Field Lane (*see* Chapter Eight). Cross Charterhouse Street, go a few metres right, turn left down Shoe Lane, sticking with it as it turns into a wider road and then an alley again. Just after Shoe Lane Library, turn right into Wine Office Court, and first left, when you see the sign of the Olde Cheshire Cheese, where Charles Darnay and Sydney Carton ate and drank together in *A Tale of Two Cities*. Enter Fleet Street, which is rich in Dickens associations. Cross over and go a few metres into Whitefriars Street, where Dickens founded and briefly edited the *Daily News*. Here, on the left, is Hanging Sword Alley, not as exciting as its name, where the bank messenger and grave robber Jeremiah Cruncher, in *A Tale of Two Cities*, lived.

Go no further, but return to Fleet Street, go west (left) and look at St Dunstan-in-the-West, preferably at a time when the clock (the oldest public clock in London with a minute hand) is chiming. Dickens used to watch the two fur-clad giants striking the bells when he was a boy, and he has David Copperfield and Betsey Trotwood do the same, catching them at midday, on their way to see Spenlow and Jorkins in Doctors' Commons. Another sight that mesmerized the boy here, the Temple Bar gateway, was taken away in 1878, but it has been recently re-erected between Paternoster Square and St Paul's Cathedral, and you can admire it again as Dickens did. Next to the church is the Gothic (1830) gatehouse of Clifford's Inn, all that is left of this old Inn of Chancery. This was where John Rokesmith drew Mr Boffin out of the noise of the 'roaring street' in *Our Mutual Friend* and asked for a job as his secretary.

Now take the gateway on the other side of Fleet Street into Middle Temple Lane, old even in Dickens's day, until you reach Middle Temple Hall. With luck this Elizabethan hall, one of the most magnificent places in London, will be open, but your Dickensian destination here is the fountain in Fountain Court. In *Martin Chuzzlewit* this is where Tom Pinch and his sister Ruth used to meet, as if by chance, and where John Westlock courted Ruth, making the fountain sparkle and laugh in a reflection of their joy. '"What a good old place it was!" John said. With quite an earnest affection for it. "A pleasant place indeed," said little Ruth. "So shady!"' Leave Fountain Court as Tom Pinch always did, by walking away from Middle Temple Gardens and taking the gate through to Devereux Court and back to Fleet Street. You could finish your walk with a drink in the charming Devereux pub (*see* Chapter Six), as Dickens or Tom Pinch might well have done, off the record. Your starting point, if you want to return to it, is at the other end of the Strand, ten minutes away.

*

Some London suburbs, including Teddington, Twickenham, Petersham, Richmond, Dulwich, Hampstead and Greenwich, have powerful Dickensian associations too. Mr Pickwick retired to Dulwich and spent his time in the picture gallery, and Mr Tupman took lodgings in Richmond, where he cut a dash on the Terrace, with its justly famous view of the Thames. The Meagles, in *Little Dorrit*, lived in Twickenham, and Dickens describes Arthur Clennam's walk from

London, through Fulham and across Putney Heath, to visit them there. Dickens knew this idyllic quarter of what is now (but was not then) suburban London very well. He regularly came to Petersham with his great friend John Forster to celebrate birthdays or a new publication, using the Star and Garter hotel which used to be at the top of the hill. In 1836 he stayed in Petersham, probably in the Dysart Arms, which is still on Petersham Road, and two years later he and his wife took a summer cottage in Twickenham, near St Margaret's station.

Dickens knew Hampstead well, and often took a walk on the Heath and a drink in Jack Straw's Castle or the Spaniard's Inn. Jack Straw's Castle was rebuilt in the 1960s, but the Spaniard's Inn is a very well preserved eighteenth-century Hampstead pub at the northern end of Spaniard's Road where it becomes Hampstead Lane, and the road is pinched into a bottleneck by the pub and an old toll house. Dickens used its garden in *Pickwick Papers* as the scene of Mrs Bardell's arrest for debt by Dodson and Fogg. Mr Pickwick, we know, was an expert on the source of Hampstead Ponds. A little south on Spaniard's Road turn right onto Sandy Road, which crosses the Heath towards the Bull and Bush pub. After a short walk the path meets North End Avenue, where you should turn right to find Old Wylde's Farm. This is the weatherboarded late-Tudor farmhouse where Dickens stayed for five weeks in 1837, trying to recover from the disaster of Mary Hogarth's death. In the 1880s the house was a meeting place for a Fabian socialist group called the Hampstead Historic Club, and in 1905 it was almost demolished for a car park. It was repaired after a fire in 1982 and is now a private house.

If you get lost (which is quite possible) you might remember that you are following in the footsteps of Bill Sikes, who fled here after murdering Nancy.

He went through Islington; strode up the hill at Highgate on which stands the stone in honour of Whittington; turned down

343

to Highgate Hill, unsteady of purpose, and uncertain where to go; struck off to the right again, almost as soon as he began to descend it; and taking the foot-path across the fields, skirted Caen Wood, and so came on Hampstead Heath. Traversing the hollow by the Vale of Health, he mounted the opposite bank, and crossing the road which joins the villages of Hampstead and Highgate, made along the remaining portion of the heath to the fields at North End, in one of which he laid himself down under a hedge, and slept.

Continuing your walk up to Hatfield, as Sikes did, is not recommended.

CHAPTER TEN

LONDON SCIENCE

A Greenwich Observatory telescope, 1883

THOSE WHO ENJOY the history of science and technology can easily pursue their interest in London, which has been the home of so many great scientists and scientific institutions. London has no ancient university, but it has medieval hospitals, which might, stretching a point, be called early scientific institutions. Medieval hospitals offered care and shelter – hospitality – rather than medical treatment, and even when medical treatment was offered it was based on principles and assumptions which had been inherited from the ancients rather than discovered or tested.

Three of London's present hospitals, St Bartholomew's, St Thomas' and the Bethlem, began as medieval monastic hospitals. The Bethlem hospital began as the Priory of Mary of Bethlehem in Bishopsgate in 1247, on a site now covered by Liverpool Street station, and began to specialize in sheltering the insane before 1400. Bethlem was the preferred official shortening of its title, and Bedlam the more popular and long-lasting. There is an old blue plaque in Liverpool Street, opposite White Hart Court. Bethlem survived Henry VIII's Dissolution of the Monasteries because it was too useful to abolish, and the Great Fire because it was in the north-east corner of the City, but it moved in 1676 to a palatial new hospital on Moorfields, built by the scientist Robert Hooke. This was abandoned as unfit for further use in 1812, and there is a plaque marking its site at Finsbury Circus near the corner of Circus Place. The third Bethlem building still exists, on St George's Fields (now the Geraldine Mary Harmsworth Park), on the Lambeth Road. It closed as a hospital in 1930 and reopened as the

Imperial War Museum six years later. Now Bethlem is in a country estate in Monks Orchard Road, Beckenham. There is a little museum (usually open Monday to Friday) which has some works by Richard Dadd, who was confined in the third Bethlem, and Caius Cibber's sculptures of *Raving Madness* and *Melancholy Madness*, which Hooke commissioned for the second Bethlem in 1680. The nearest station is Eden Park.

You are more likely to visit St Bartholomew's Hospital, which was founded on its present site as a monastery by the courtier Rahere in 1123 to thank God for his recovery from malaria while on a crusade. For over seven hundred years it shared its neighbourhood with the Smithfield animal market and annual August St Bartholomew Fair, and for the last 150 it has coexisted with the butchers of the wholesale meat market. Conveniently, butchers and surgeons share the same patron saint, and St Bartholomew stands, with his big knife at the ready, on the gatehouse of St Bartholomew-the-Great church. The hospital was refounded in 1546 by Henry VIII, whose 1702 statue stands above the main gateway of the hospital. The gateway, with its figures of *Lameness* and *Disease*, was designed by Edward Strong in 1702, and leads the way past the church of St Bartholomew-the-Less into a college-like courtyard which has buildings designed by James Gibbs between 1730 and 1768 on three sides. Having three separate blocks reduced the risk of fire or infection spreading through the hospital. The north block (the one you go through to reach the courtyard) has a fine staircase with two great canvases by William Hogarth (done without fee in 1735–7), *The Pool of Bethesda* and *The Good Samaritan*, and a Great Hall with a stained-glass window of Henry VIII, probably 1660s, and two wooden statues of a wounded soldier and sailor, maybe twenty years older. Bart's has a good little historical museum, which is open Tuesday to Friday, free of charge.

London's other medieval hospital, St Thomas', was founded in the twelfth century, a little later than Bart's. Its first home was next to the present Southwark Cathedral, but it moved to a site east of

Borough High Street, on the north side of St Thomas' Street, after 1300. It moved again in the 1860s, to make way for a railway line, to its present home between Lambeth Palace Road and the river. There are two statues of Edward VI, who refounded St Thomas' after the Reformation, one in stone dated 1682 outside the main entrance facing Westminster Bridge Road, and the other in brass, dated 1723, inside the entrance to the South Wing. The hospital also has a museum illustrating the work in England and the Crimea of Florence Nightingale, who founded the Nurses' Training School here in 1860 and guided its later development. The museum, which is on Lambeth Palace Road, costs about £6 to enter, and is open every day. The most interesting remnant of St Thomas' in Southwark is its Old Operating Theatre, which was rediscovered in 1956 in the attic of the 1702 church of St Thomas, a little way along St Thomas' Street from Borough High Street. The church was part of the courtyard of the hospital, and medicinal herbs were stored in its attic until 1815, when it was converted into an operating theatre. The horseshoe of seats gave plenty of room for medical students to watch the surgeons at work, and separation from the wards meant that other patients could not hear the screams of the star attraction. Such refinements as anaesthesia and antisepsis had not been introduced into English medicine by the time the operating theatre closed. The Old Operating Theatre is open every day from 10.30, and costs about £5 to visit.

Just across the road from the old St Thomas' is a much newer hospital, Guy's. Thomas Guy, a London bookseller who turned a small fortune into a huge one by selling his South Sea Company shares just before the Bubble burst in 1720, founded Guy's Hospital in 1721, initially intending it to be part of St Thomas'. Guy gave the hospital over £200,000, the last time a major hospital was founded in England on the strength of a single individual benefaction. Guy's, which you enter from St Thomas' Street, still has the two handsome courtyards built between 1721 and 1725, and east and west wings added in 1740 and 1775. In the first court there is a fine bronze statue of Guy in his guild livery made in 1734, ten years after his death, and a chapel with an impressive monument of 1779 by John Bacon of Guy holding the hand of one of the incurables for whom the hospital was originally intended. As the words on the monument say, 'Warm with philanthropy ... He established an Asylum for that stage of Languor and Disease to which the Charities of Others had not reached. He provided Retreat for hopeless Insanity, and rivalled the endowments of Kings.' The philosopher and mathematician Ludwig Wittgenstein worked here in 1939, the world's most intelligent hospital porter.

Guy's example might have inspired Thomas Coram, a wealthy merchant and promoter of American colonial settlement, to start raising money in the 1730s for a new hospital for London's many abandoned children. Coram attracted an enormous amount of fashionable support for his Foundling Hospital, enlisting 89 peers and 72 MPs onto its governing body. The hospital was demolished in 1926, and the children moved out of London. Now its grounds, Coram's Fields, are a children's park, enclosed by some of the original colonnades, and all that is left are the Coram's Foundation offices on Brunswick Square, a 1930s house which is now the Foundling Museum. Inside are some of the fittings rescued when the hospital was destroyed, and the paintings donated to Coram by Hogarth and other artists, including Hogarth's fine portrait of Coram. Roubiliac's 1739 bust of Handel is a reminder that he was a governor, and performed annual fundraising concerts here. Coram's art collection is regarded as England's first public art gallery, though the Dulwich Picture Gallery, founded in 1811 and still in its original John Soane building (repaired after war damage), also claims the title. The Coram Museum, which is a short walk from Russell Square Tube station, is open every day but Monday, and charges £5 to visitors over 16. Its website, www.foundlingmuseum.org.uk, gives details of special exhibitions.

The years between 1720 and 1750 were important ones in the history of London hospitals. The Westminster Hospital originated in a coffee house discussion in 1715 and opened in a house in Petty France in 1720; St George's (now in Tooting) was started by a group of discontented Westminster Hospital governors in 1733, on Hyde Park Corner; the London was founded in 1740; and the Middlesex was opened in Windmill Street, Soho, in 1745. The London Hospital (now the Royal London) on Whitechapel Road opposite Whitechapel Tube station still has some of its 1750s buildings and now has its own museum – entered from Newark Street – in the crypt of the former St Philip's church at the back of the hospital. This has an exhibition on East End health care, another on forensic medicine featuring famous London murderers (Jack the Ripper, Dr Crippen, John Christie), and material on Joseph Merrick (the 'Elephant Man'), who lived here, and on Edith Cavell, the nurse shot by the Germans in 1915. Her statue at the southern end of St Martin's Lane is inscribed with some of her final words, 'Patriotism is not enough.' The museum is open Monday to Friday, free of charge.

*

Many of the advances which started to turn medicine from a craft into a science and helped it break free of erroneous ancient assumptions took place in London. William Harvey discovered the circulation of the blood and the heart's role as a pump while he was a lecturer at the College of Physicians, and argued for his new doctrine in his lectures there. For its first century, from 1518 to 1614, the college met in Knightrider Street, which is between St Paul's and the Millennium Bridge, but in 1614, a year before Harvey's appointment, it moved to a building on Amen Corner, just off Warwick Lane, west of St Paul's. In the late 1670s the college moved into Robert Hooke's fine new building further up Warwick Lane, between Warwick Square and Newgate Street, and from 1825 to the 1960s it occupied the impressive building by Sir Robert Smirke on Trafalgar Square which is now, changed and enlarged, Canada House. In 1964 the college moved to a new building by

Sir Denys Lasdun in the south-east corner of Regent's Park, in St Andrew's Place. This much-admired building is worth a visit in its own right, and the college believes it might even represent the architect's interpretation of Harvey's work, 'with its two upper chambers, doors as valves and grill symbolising the pump action of the heart, [and] the Censor's Room is the heart of the College'. The Censor's Room contains panelling from Robert Hooke's building, and the college has an historical collection illustrating the work of its fellows since 1518, and especially the life and work of Harvey. Tours of the college are by appointment only, but sometimes there are open days or special visits. Go to www.rcplondon.ac.uk for details.

Harvey died in 1657, three years before the founding of London's greatest scientific institution, the Royal Society, now the oldest scientific society in the world. For its first fifty years, except for a few years after the Great Fire, the Society held its meetings in Gresham College, on Bishopsgate. The college, founded in 1579 by the merchant Sir Thomas Gresham, occupied his large mansion between Bishopsgate and Broad Street on the land that now supports Tower 42, previously the NatWest Tower. Its scientific professors included Christopher Wren (from 1657 to 1661) and Robert Hooke (from 1665 to 1703), who conducted most of his groundbreaking work on astronomy, microscopy, chemistry, engineering and physics in his rooms here.

Hooke and Wren worked in friendly cooperation as scientists and architects, and several of the City churches attributed to Wren are probably largely the work of Hooke. One of their joint architectural enterprises, the Monument to the Great Fire, on Fish Street Hill near London Bridge, was a sort of scientific instrument as well as a memorial. The Monument was designed as a giant telescope tube through which an astronomer (which both Hooke and Wren were) could view the heavens from an observatory dug out below ground level. It seems that the great stone telescope was not used because it vibrated, but Hooke certainly used the Monument for gravitational and barometric experiments, including dropping stones, swinging pendulums and measuring weight and pressure at different heights. At 62 metres, the Monument is the tallest pillar in London (12 metres higher than Nelson's Column) and the highest free-standing classical column in the world, and almost exactly the same height as the tower of old St Paul's, which Hooke and his friends had used for height experiments before the Great Fire destroyed it. You can climb the Hooke/Wren Monument, the product of the engineering and building skills of two of our greatest scientists, for £2, any day of the week, and enjoy a great view.

There is an even better view from the top of Wren's masterpiece, St Paul's Cathedral. The entrance fee of about £10 allows you to climb the 530 steps to the Golden Gallery, which is at the top of the dome and 85 metres above the ground. As you climb from the stone gallery, over 30 metres below, you can see at close quarters what Wren did to make his vast dome, one of the biggest in the world, so graceful and strong. The staircase takes you between the timber and lead outer dome, the one you can see from all over London, and the brick cone which supports the lantern (the cathedral's highest point) and the outer dome. The best way to see all the wonders of Wren's work is to pay a little extra for a guided tour of the cathedral. A Triforium tour, which costs about £4.50 on top of the usual admission price, takes you into the Library, with its 1709 panelling, and the Trophy Room, which houses Wren's Great Model (the cathedral as he wanted to build it), and gives you a glimpse of the famous geometrical staircase, a stone spiral round an open well, and a wonderful view of the nave from the west end. This tour is available Monday and Tuesday at 11.30 or 2.00, and Friday at 2.00. See the website, www.stpauls.co.uk, or phone 020 7246 8357 for details.

Gresham's mansion was demolished in 1768, and the Royal Society moved its meetings to a Wren house (now gone) in Crane Court, off Fleet Street (near Fetter Lane), in 1710. After long spells in Somerset House (1780–1845) and Burlington House, which still houses several learned societies, in 1967 the Royal Society moved into its present home, four Nash houses (numbers 6–9) on Carlton House Terrace. The Royal Society does not have a museum, but group tours of the society buildings, booked in advance, cost about £7 per person.

Another important scientific group in seventeenth-century London was the Guild of Apothecaries, those who prepared and sold medicinal drugs. The guild, or Worshipful Company, got a royal charter, enabling it to control entry to the profession, in 1617. The Apothecaries' Hall, rebuilt a year or two after the Great Fire, survives in Blackfriars Lane, near New Bridge Street and Carter Lane, a beautiful surprise in a dingy street. This is the oldest livery hall in the City of London, and it is possible to visit it by arranging a tour in advance, or by going to one of the Society's public lectures, which are listed on the company website, www.apothecaries.org. The apothecaries' greatest gift to London was the medicinal herb garden they founded, mainly for educational purposes, in 1673. Chelsea Physic Garden, four acres on the Chelsea riverfront just east of the Albert Bridge, is one of London's most magical places. The apothecaries ran the garden until 1899, paying £5 a year in ground rent to Sir Hans Sloane and his successors, but now it is administered by a charity, which maintains its medicinal and educational purpose. It is open to the public on Wednesday, Thursday, Friday and Sunday afternoons, from April to October, for a fee of £7, which is not much for a trip back to the London of Charles II and Samuel Pepys. Friends of the Garden have much fuller access all year round for a modest annual fee. There is an historical walk in the western part of the garden which is described on the website, www.chelseaphysicgarden.co.uk.

As a scientific institution Chelsea predates London's more famous botanical garden, in Kew, by a century or more. Kew began as a royal park, and its accumulation of palaces, temples and follies dating from the eighteenth century is almost as interesting as its wonderful collection of botanical greenhouses, added in the nineteenth and twentieth. Sir William Chambers' 1761 Chinese Pagoda, which I am looking at as I type these words, is one of London's most spectacular buildings, even without the eighty enamelled dragons that it once had.

Kew's life as a botanical garden began in the 1740s, through the interest of Augusta, the wife (and widow) of Frederick, Prince of Wales, and mother of George III. Under the influence of the botanist and politician Lord Bute, Augusta extended the gardens and employed Chambers to beautify them. In 1773 George II put the gifted amateur botanist Joseph Banks, who had been around the world with Captain Cook, in charge of the gardens, and their history as a scientific institution began. Banks initiated the role of the gardens as the hub of a system of botanical transmission and exchange between one suitable territory and another, and as a centre for the storage and study of unfamiliar species. But the gardens as we know them today were the product of a later and more intensive period of expansion and scientific development, when Kew passed from royal to government control in the 1840s and Sir William Hooker, an academic botanist, was director from 1841 to 1865. In the 1840s the gardens grew from 11 to 280 acres, the entrance gates on Kew Green were erected, an arboretum planted, and Decimus Burton's magnificent Palm House was built by Richard Turner. The Temperate House followed in the 1860s, a great lake fed with Thames water was dug in 1861, and Kew was opened to the public every afternoon. Hooker's son Joseph collected plants for the Kew Herbarium all round the world, and was Kew's director from 1865 to 1885. One of his main achievements was to defend Kew's role as a scientific institution against those, especially Richard Owen, who wanted to transfer Kew's work and collections to the Natural History Museum, which opened in South Kensington in 1881.

So now the Royal Botanic Gardens in Kew are a most beautiful and absorbing place to visit, but also contain the largest collection of living plants in the world and a research centre of the greatest international importance. Kew's entry price is now nearly three thousand times what it was in the early 1970s (when it was a pre-decimal penny), but it is one of the wonders of London, nonetheless. The gardens open at 9.30 every day, and close at 4.15 in winter, 5.30 in February and March, 6.30 from April to early September (7.30 at weekends), and 6.00 in September and October. But those long summer evenings we used to enjoy are just a memory now, unless we pay through the nose for entry to a special event.

In the middle of Chelsea Physic Garden there is a replica statue of Sir Hans Sloane (1660–1753), the physician and collector who owned the garden and leased it to the apothecaries, and the only person to have been Secretary of the Royal College of Physicians and President of the Royal Society. Sloane's vast collection of botanical and geological objects, books and antiquities was bequeathed to the nation on his death in 1753, and led directly to the foundation of the British Museum that same year. The original of Sloane's statue, and his collection of books and documents, are in the British Museum, but when the Natural History Museum became a separate institution his plant collection was moved to South Kensington, where it is still carefully preserved for specialist study. You can look at the collection online, by going to www.nhm.ac.uk and putting Sloane Herbarium into the search box. If you would like a more tangible reminder of Sloane's work, eat a bar of milk chocolate, which Cadbury's started making to Sloane's recipe in the nineteenth century. The many streets around Sloane Square that bear Sloane's name reflect the fact that his daughter married into the Cadogan family, which owned and developed this area.

Another great eighteenth-century scientific collection is still on public display in London. John Hunter, a Scottish military surgeon and anatomist, became one of London's most respected and innovative surgeons in the 1770s and 1780s, and taught his craft to some of the greatest surgeons, including Edward Jenner. He also accumulated a vast and varied collection of anatomical and natural history specimens in his large house on the east side of Leicester Square. On his death in 1793 the collection was left to the (Royal) College of Surgeons, which eventually built a museum for it in its head-quarters on the south side of Lincoln's Inn Fields. Two thirds of the collection was destroyed in an air raid on 10 May 1941 (the last and heaviest raid of the Blitz), but what is left is now well displayed in the college's Hunterian Museum, which is open Tuesday to Saturday, free of charge. There is a free guided tour on Wednesdays at 1.00, for which it is best to book. The college's website is www.rcseng.ac.uk/museums. There is a plaque marking the site of John Hunter's house on 31 Soho Square, and a bust of the surgeon in Leicester Square. His equally famous surgeon brother Sir William had a house and anatomical museum on the east side of Great Windmill Street, and the building is still there, marked with a plaque and altered to serve as changing rooms for the Lyric Theatre on Shaftesbury Avenue.

There is a much greater, though less idiosyncratic, historical medical collection on display in two London museums. The Well-come Trust lent its famous history of science collection to the Science Museum in South Kensington in 1976, and a small propor-tion of it is on show there. The collection was assembled by the American pharmacist and businessman Sir Henry Wellcome (1853–1936), who created in 1913 a museum of the history of medicine at 183 Euston Road, where the Wellcome Institute, with its magnificent new library, still stands. The refurbished building, near Gordon Street and opposite Euston station, has an important display based on Sir Henry Wellcome's unrivalled collection, with exhibits including (according to its advance publicity) Darwin's walking stick, Napoleon's toothbrush, a French Revolution guillo-tine blade and a giant jelly baby. Both collections are open without charge, every day.

The surgery pioneered by the Hunters needed two further advances to make it really useful to living patients. One of these, anaesthesia, was introduced into Britain by Dr John Snow, who first used ether in operations in St George's Hospital (now the Lanesborough Hotel) on Hyde Park Corner in 1847. Snow's equally famous work on the transmission of cholera through the water supply is commemorated in Broadwick Street in Soho, where there is a replica of the Broad Street pump which carried the cholera bacillus in 1854 until Snow removed its handle. Incidentally, anyone reading the blue plaque on 52 Gower Street would see that the first use of ether as an anaesthetic in Britain was here, by the dentist James Robinson in December 1846. The other important advance, antisepsis through carbolic acid, was pioneered in Britain (at Glasgow University) by Joseph Lister, who lived at 12 Park Crescent, at the top of Portland Place, in the last decades of his life, 1877–1912, when he was a professor at King's College. A bronze plaque marks the house of the man who at last persuaded doctors to wash their hands.

A medical pioneer of a later age, Alexander Fleming, is remembered in St Mary's Hospital, Praed Street, Paddington, where he spent most of his career. The hospital has restored the laboratory in which he made his revolutionary observation of the antibacterial effects of an accidentally grown mould, *Penicillium notatum*, in September 1928. The recognition and development of penicillin as an antibiotic were the work of others, but Fleming's range of achievements was impressive, and his dingy little laboratory, restored to its original condition, is an historic and moving place. It is open for about £2 from Monday to Thursday, between 10.00 and 1.00.

A giant in another field, Sigmund Freud, spent his last years in London, having fled Austria in 1938, when the Germans invaded. Freud only lived for another fifteen months, but his Hampstead house, 15 Maresfield Gardens, has become a museum of his life and work. His library and study have been kept as he left them, and his analyst's couch, along with the chair he used to sit on, taking notes, is there. The museum is near Finchley Road Underground station and it is open Wednesday to Sunday, from 12.00, at a cost of around £5.

*

London is especially strong in scientists who advanced the theoretical and practical understanding of electricity. There is a museum devoted to the life of the American Benjamin Franklin, who worked on the electricity of lightning in his house in Craven Street, west of Charing Cross station (*see* Chapter Three). As a young man Franklin worked as a printer in the Lady Chapel of the church of St Bartholomew-the-Great, before it was reclaimed for the church. The rich and reclusive Sir Henry Cavendish (1731–1810) worked on electricity as well as the chemical composition of air and water and the density of the earth in his home and laboratory at 11 Bedford Square, on the corner of Montague Place.

The life of one of the greatest British scientists, Michael Faraday, can be followed in several London locations. He was born in 1791 at the Elephant and Castle, where Faraday Square and Faraday School commemorate the district's second most famous son, after Charlie Chaplin. The new Cuming Museum, at 151 Walworth Road (in Newington Library, about a quarter of a mile from the Elephant), has a small Faraday exhibition as part of its much larger collection on the history of Southwark. It is open Tuesday to Saturday, free of charge. Faraday's family moved to Marylebone when he was five, and lived in various houses near Manchester Square. Faraday was apprenticed to a bookbinder at 48 Blandford Street, north of Manchester Square, and lived there from 1805 to 1812. There is a plaque on the house. In 1812 a customer gave Faraday tickets to Humphry Davy's lectures at the Royal Institution, changing his life and the history of English science.

In 1813 Faraday got a job with Humphry Davy as a laboratory assistant, and by 1821 his great gifts had secured him the position of acting superintendent of the house of the Royal Institution. Faraday lived in the Royal Institution in Albemarle Street until 1858, when the Queen gave him a house on Hampton Court Green, which is now called Faraday House. To discover the full range of his work on electricity, chemistry and physics you should visit the Royal Institution, which has a Faraday Museum, with a large collection of his apparatus and a reconstruction of his laboratory. The Royal Institution, where many of the most important advances in nineteenth-century science were achieved or announced, was founded in 1799 in two early-eighteenth-century houses, 20 and 21 Albemarle Street. The houses were given their impressive classical front by Lewis Vulliamy in 1838, and were renovated in 2006–7. For details of Christmas lectures (begun by Faraday in 1825), events and museum opening times and prices, go to www.rigb.org.

London scientists were at the forefront of the development of the theory and practical applications of electricity. As well as Benjamin Franklin, Henry Cavendish and Michael Faraday, there were William Thomson, Lord Kelvin (1824–1907), mathematician, physicist and inventor of the electric telegraph, who lived at 15 Eaton Place, Belgravia, and James Clerk Maxwell (1831–1879), who developed the theory of electromagnetism, and lived at 16 Palace Gardens Terrace, Kensington, in the 1860s. Nearby, in Kensington Court, a cobbled alley off the eastern end of Kensington High Street, there is an interesting reminder of the early days of commercial electrical generation. In 1886 an electrical pioneer, Colonel R.E.B. Crompton, started producing electric power for his neighbourhood from a generating station at 46 Kensington Court. It became a substation in 1900 and the interior was stripped out in 1985, but the building still bears the words Electric Lighting Station on its front. Round the corner, Crompton's house and laboratory, Thriplands (number 48), is one of the earliest houses in London to be built (in 1888) on a framework of steel girders. And to confirm that important technical advances can take place in unlikely places, number 35 Kensington Court Place, at the far end of Kensington Court (next door to T.S. Eliot's house), was built in 1884 as a hydraulic power station, providing water power for the lifts in the nearby apartment blocks of Kensington Court. In these early years London was something of a pioneer in electricity. The greatest practical exponent of electricity, Thomas Edison, opened the world's first steam-powered public electricity-generating station on Holborn Viaduct in January 1882, and the Savoy Theatre was the first in the world to be lit entirely by electricity.

London also has its share of great engineers. Number 8 Adam Street (off the Strand) is the fine house owned between 1789 and 1792 by the inventor of the water frame and pioneer of factory cotton spinning Sir Richard Arkwright, one of the creators of industrial Britain. Other great engineers and industrial pioneers who lived in London include Robert Stephenson, who died at 35 Gloucester Square, near Paddington Station, in 1859, and the two Brunels, Marc and his son Isambard Kingdom (builder of Paddington station), who lived at 98 Cheyne Walk, Chelsea.

You can see an interesting example of the Brunels' work by going to Railway Avenue, Rotherhithe, the southern entrance to their Wapping to Rotherhithe tunnel. This was dug as a pedestrian tunnel, was the world's first tunnel under a navigable river, and the first dug with a tunnelling shield, Marc Brunel's own invention. Work was begun by Robert Vazie in 1805, continued by Richard Trevithick in 1808, abandoned, taken up from 1825 to 1828 by Marc Brunel (a pioneer in both senses of the word), and completed, with great difficulty, between 1835 and 1843. His son Isambard helped him, and learned his craft on this, their only joint enterprise. The huge bore hole was divided into two 4- by 5-metre tunnels, 365 metres long, and these were converted for the East London Railway, the first true 'tube' train, in 1865. The horseshoe-shaped tunnels are still more or less as Brunel made them, and they can be glimpsed from Wapping station. Once these tunnels were regarded as a miracle, but now they are almost forgotten, though they are still in daily use. There is a small museum now in Brunel's engine room, which once pumped out any water that leaked into the tunnels. Next to it is the circular tunnel access shaft (covered over) through which the tunnels were dug. The museum is open every day, for a fee of £2, and also offers special trips along the tunnels. See the website, www.brunelenginehouse.org.uk/index.asp, for details.

Rotherhithe Street, right next to the engine house, gives a good impression of what the old industrial riverside looked like before river trade collapsed, with high brick warehouses now surviving as flats, workshops or offices. The Mayflower pub is the descendant of the Shippe Inn, which was here when the *Mayflower* set off on the first stage of its voyage to America in 1620, and though it has been twice renamed and rebuilt it manages to evoke the atmosphere of the seventeenth-century riverfront, and still has tremendous views over this historic riverscape. Captain Christopher Jones of the *Mayflower* is buried over the road in St Mary's church, which has some fine nautical monuments.

The next foot tunnel under the Thames was not constructed until 1870, when James Greathead, using his own much more efficient shield, tunnelled under the river near the Tower of London. The tunnel was abandoned when Tower Bridge was built in 1894, and now carries cables and water mains. You can see its northern exit, a short circular brick tower, in the open area west of the Tower of London. There is a fine statue of Greathead, whose shield was used for digging the deep-level tube in the 1890s and 1900s, in Cornhill next to the Royal Exchange. There are still two foot tunnels under the Thames, both built by the London County Council before the Great War. The Greenwich Tunnel (1902) runs from the Isle of Dogs, near the Island Gardens terminus of the Docklands Light Railway, to Greenwich Pier, and the Woolwich Tunnel (1912) connects Pier Road, North Woolwich, with Ferry Approach, Woolwich. The entrances to both tunnels are marked by glass domes or pagodas, and both are free.

I.K. Brunel's masterpiece in London is Paddington station, built as the London terminus of his magnificent Great Western Railway between 1850 and 1854, when the influence of Paxton's glass and iron Crystal Palace was at its strongest. The three great iron-roofed sheds (a fourth was added in 1913) are not quite as Brunel made them, and Brunel's cast-iron columns have been replaced with steel, but this is still one of the most important buildings of the early railway age. The Great Western Hotel on the front, built in the early 1850s, was the first of the big London railway hotels. Robert Stephenson's Euston station was much earlier (1833–7), but it had no hotel and was demolished in 1961, and Sir William Cubitt's King's Cross station, built by the Great Northern Railway in 1851–2, has a fine functional front rather than a fancy hotel. To see the railway hotel at its most fantastic, go to St Pancras, where Sir George Gilbert Scott's Midland Grand Hotel (1868–74) has been restored as the Renaissance St Pancras Hotel. When it reopens in 2009 it should be possible to visit the magnificent public rooms, with their vaulted ceilings, marble columns and wall paintings. The hotel hides William Barlow's huge railway shed, whose 73-metre-wide and 210-metre-long roof, without supporting columns, was the largest in the world when it was built in 1866–8. When you are waiting for a train to the East Midlands or the Continent, look up and admire this wonder of Victorian engineering.

You can find other examples of Isambard Kingdom Brunel's work in east and west London. Between Ealing Broadway and Southall stations the Great Western Line crosses the Brent Valley on the eight brick arches of the beautiful Wharncliffe Viaduct (1835–8), Brunel's first large structure and a model for his later viaducts. About half a mile away, where Windmill Lane crosses the Grand Union Canal and the Great Western Railway at the northern corner of Osterley Park, you can see Brunel's last bridge design, which was completed just after his death in 1859. This is Three Bridges, where the canal is carried over the railway in an iron trough, and the road crosses both on an iron bridge.

One of the most famous events in Brunel's life, the construction and launching of the vast iron steamship the *Great Eastern*, took place on the other side of London, at the Millwall Ironworks on the Isle of Dogs. On Burrell's Wharf, on the riverside path near the southern tip of the Isle of Dogs, some old shipyard buildings have been incorporated into a modern apartment and leisure development. One of these, the Plate House, seems to have been built in 1853–4 to assemble and accommodate the gigantic paddle engines for the *Great Eastern*, the largest ever made. Nearby, between Burrell's Wharf and Napier Avenue, there is a section of the slipway that was built to allow the giant ship to be launched sideways in January 1858, after thirteen earlier attempts at a conventional launch had failed. The vast chain lying next to the slipway looks exactly like the one in the most famous photograph of Brunel, top-hatted in front of the *Great Eastern*. All around here there are reminders that east London once had an important shipbuilding industry, and that this was a centre of industrial production of all sorts. Taffrail and Slipway Houses were built in 1906 as plywood workshops, numbers 264–266 Westferry Road were the 1854 Counting House of the shipbuilder Scott Russell and Co., which was bankrupted by the building of the *Great Eastern*, and across the road the single-storey building dated 1860 was the forge and girder workshop of C.J. Mare and Co., the only one of its kind left in London. This area is easy to reach, by taking the Docklands Light Railway from Bank or Tower Hill to Mudchute, or taking a river boat from Savoy Pier to Masthouse Terrace Pier, which takes about 30 minutes. It is also only a short walk west from the northern exit of the Greenwich Foot Tunnel.

A few stations north on the Docklands Light Railway, near West India Quay station, the Museum in Docklands is a large and impressive collection of material on London's river trade and industry, mostly collected when the docks were closing down in the 1970s and 1980s. The museum has trading, passenger and pleasure vessels, implements for cargo handling and riverside industries, and artefacts illustrating every aspect of river life. Its entrance fee, which gives unlimited visits for a year, is modest (£5, and free for students), and it is open every day. There can be no better way to understand the trade and industry of east London, which sustained much of London's economy for two hundred years, but which is now almost vanished. It is in a warehouse on the West India Docks, which were built in 1802, the first of London's new wet docks and at that time the largest such structure in the world.

The western terminus of the Docklands Light Railway is near one of London's most famous engineering masterpieces, Tower Bridge. Although the steel skeleton was encased in Gothic stone-work to harmonize with the Tower of London, the bridge used the latest technology when it was built in the 1890s by the architect Sir Horace Jones and the engineers Sir John Barry and George D. Stephenson. It is a 287-metre suspension bridge with two opening leaves, or bascules, to give ships entering or leaving the Pool of London (between London and Tower bridges) an opening 61 metres wide and 47 metres high. The two mighty towers, under their Gothic disguise, used to house steam engines that could raise the leaves of the roadway in 90 seconds. Electric engines replaced the steam ones in 1976, but some of the old machinery can still be seen if you pay about £6 to go into the Tower Bridge Exhibition, which also gives you a history of the bridge and the right to walk along the high-level walkway.

London has been a huge city, too big for most people to walk across, since the nineteenth century, and its growth and prosperity were more dependent on the development of new forms of transport than any other city of its time. London has some of the earliest canals (on the River Lea) and great railway termini, the oldest underground railway system (over thirty years ahead of the next), the first underground stations, the first and oldest underwater tunnels, and the first electric deep-level tube lines. Some of the stations, lines and tunnels are still in use today, but thankfully the vehicles have all been changed, and you can only see the originals in museums. The Science Museum has a good transport collection, including the world's first commercially successful steam train,

Puffing Billy (1813), Stephenson's *Rocket*, a brougham carriage, one of the original 1890 electric underground locomotives and a Rover safety bicycle, while London's specialist London Transport Museum, which has an excellent collection of horse and motor buses, horse and electric trams, underground trains and cabs, is in the old Covent Garden Flower Market.

✳

London has two suburbs with a notable scientific history. Greenwich has one of Britain's oldest surviving purpose-built scientific buildings, the Royal Observatory, and a naval museum which has important exhibitions on astronomy, navigation, cartography, geographical exploration and the measurement of time and space. The Royal Observatory, on a hill in the middle of Greenwich Park, consists of Flamsteed's House, built by Hooke and Wren in 1675, and the buildings added in the eighteenth and nineteenth centuries as Greenwich's activities grew. The exhibition inside the observatory includes many of the instruments used by the early Astronomers Royal, including Thomas Tompion's 1676 year-going clock and Edmond Halley's 8-foot (2.4-metre) iron quadrant, and Sir George Airy's 1850 telescope with an 8-inch (20-centimetre) object lens, right on the meridian line. The museum of navigation and marine timekeeping has clocks by the greatest English clockmakers, including several illustrating John Harrison's path towards an accurate maritime longitude clock.

One of the most interesting scientific instruments here is London's only public camera obscura, in which light comes through a lens in a turret into a darkened room, projecting a faint but clear image of the outside world onto a white screen. The lens revolves, enabling the observer to see the view to the north over Greenwich, the river and the great city beyond. From the terraces outside, of course, the view is even better. Painters once used this device for capturing accurate images, but astronomers used it for looking at the sun. The National Maritime Museum administers the observatory, the Queen's House (*see* Chapter Three) and the main museum, which is in the old Royal Hospital School, which moved out to Suffolk in 1933. Greenwich was only accepted as the world's prime meridian, latitude 0 degrees, in a world conference in 1884, when Britain was the world's leading maritime nation.

The grand set of buildings between the Queen's House and the river were built as the Royal Naval Hospital, the maritime equivalent of the Chelsea Royal Hospital, and conceived, like Chelsea, in imitation of the Hôtel des Invalides in Paris. The imitation was very successful, and there is not a more impressive architectural sight in London. It is marvellous to stand in the space between the main hospital blocks, with views across the Thames to Canary Wharf, east London, the City and the distant Hampstead and Highgate hills in one direction and the Queen's House and the hilltop observatory behind it in the other. The work was commissioned by William and Mary, carried out between 1693 and 1708 by Christopher Wren and Nicholas Hawksmoor, and completed over the next few decades. The hospital became the Royal Naval College in 1873, and was entrusted to the Greenwich Foundation in 1998, when the college moved out. Now it is occupied by the University of Greenwich and Trinity College of Music, but the finest parts, especially the Painted Hall, Sir James Thornhill's baroque masterpiece, and the chapel, beautifully rebuilt by James 'Athenian' Stuart and William Newton after a fire in 1779, are open free of charge every day. The chapel's curved ceiling gives it excellent acoustics, and this is appropriate because it has a 1787 Samuel Green organ, one of the biggest and best baroque organs in the country in its original site and condition. The paintings in the hall, which were done between 1708 and 1712, show William and Mary bringing peace and liberty to Europe, and Louis XIV crouching under their feet. The later paintings in the upper hall, done between 1718 and 1725, attempt the difficult task of making George I and his family look charismatic.

When you have seen all this you could reward yourself by walking east down to the river where, next to a terrace and a statue of Nelson, you will find the grand Trafalgar Tavern, which was built with iron balconies overlooking the river in 1837. Walk a little further east to see Trinity Hospital, founded in 1613 but given a Gothic makeover two hundred years later.

London's other scientific suburb, South Kensington, was transformed in the 1850s, when Prince Albert, Henry Cole and the 1851 Exhibition Committee decided to spend the exhibition's profits on an 87-acre estate in Brompton between Cromwell Road and Kensington Road, and to turn it into a great centre of scientific and artistic learning. Most of what is there now was built after Albert's death in 1861: the Albert Memorial and the Albert Hall in the 1860s, the Natural History Museum in the 1870s, the Royal College of Music and the Royal College of Organists in the 1880s, the Imperial Institute (of which only the tower remains) around 1890, the Victoria and Albert Museum in the 1900s, the Royal School of Mines (next to the Royal College of Music on Prince Consort Road) between 1909 and 1913, and the Geological and Science Museums in the 1920s and 1930s. In the 1950s most of the Imperial Institute was demolished to make room for the growth of the Imperial College of Science and Technology.

There can hardly be another place in the world where such rich and interesting collections on the history and practice of science can be studied or enjoyed in such detail and with such convenience. The Science Museum covers almost every area of science, from the history of medicine to space exploration. It has one of the oldest Boulton and Watt rotary steam engines, Crick and Watson's 1953 DNA model, the Apollo 10 Command Module, a German V2 rocket, the first genetically engineered mice (freeze-dried) and many other treasures. See www.sciencemuseum.org.uk/collections/treasures for more details. Like most of London's major museums, it is free and open every day.

The Science Museum is linked to the Geological Museum, also on Exhibition Road, and the Natural History Museum, on Cromwell Road, which specializes in botany, biology, zoology and palaeontol-

ogy. Alfred Waterhouse's vast 1870s Romanesque building, terracotta slabs on an iron frame, is one of the most impressive in
London. Inside and out, the building reflects the beliefs of its creator
and first superintendent, Richard Owen. Outside, there are carvings
of extinct animals on the east wing and living creatures on the west.
Inside, decorations and carvings indicate the original layout of the
museum, though inevitably advances in scientific understanding and
in museum design have changed the appearance of the museum and
the arrangement of the collections.

London's other great scientific collection is in the Zoological
Gardens in Regent's Park, the successor to the various menageries
that had entertained Londoners of earlier generations. London Zoo
was initiated by the newly founded London Zoological Society in
1828, when the architect Decimus Burton started laying out the
site. The last remaining animals in the Tower of London menagerie
(founded in the early thirteenth century) were transferred to Regent's
Park in 1832, but this was from the start a scientific enterprise, and
the paying public was not admitted until 1847. The opening of
Whipsnade in 1928 allowed the society to keep larger mammals in
more open conditions, and London Zoo has increasingly concentrated on smaller creatures and educational work.

Several of the original Decimus Burton structures remain, including the clock tower, the raven's cage (on the Fellows' Lawn), the
East Tunnel (linking the Zoo's two halves), the giraffe house and
Three Island Pond, which now has flamingos and pelicans. Notable
twentieth-century additions include the Mappin terraces, artificial
mountains of hollow reinforced concrete to make bears feel at home,
which were built in 1914. They are now used for sloth bears. The
zoo has two of London's most famous 1930s modernist buildings,
both by Berthold Lubetkin's Tecton group, the Round House and
the Penguin Pool, which now houses porcupines. The early 1960s
contributed Lord Snowdon's aviary, a great tent in which a netting
skin is held over a frame of poles by cables, and the Casson Pavilion,

whose concrete exterior was meant to suggest the appearance of the elephants that used to live in it. It costs about £12 to go into the zoo, and last entry is at 3.00 in winter, 4.30 in summer.

The man whose work did most to change our understanding of the development of species, Charles Darwin (a fellow of the Zoological Society), had a house in the Kent countryside which is now in London, if we take the Metropolitan Police District as its outer limit. Downe House, in Luxted Road, Downe (near Biggin Hill), Darwin's home from 1842 to 1882, is now a Darwin museum, preserving the study where he did the work that changed our intellectual world, and the garden walks he took to collect his thoughts.

*

London is especially well supplied with museums that examine and sometimes celebrate the military uses of science and technology. As well as the Imperial War Museum, there is the National Army Museum in Royal Hospital Road, Chelsea, and the Royal Air Force Museum in Grahame Park Way, which is quite near Colindale Underground station, but is easier to drive to. These fascinating collections are free and open every day. Less well-known is the Royal Artillery Museum, now called Firepower. This used to be in the Rotunda, an extraordinary John Nash building which was erected in St James's Park as a mock tent for victory celebrations in 1814 and moved to its present site on Woolwich Common (near Green Hill) five years later. Now the collection is in the Paper Cartridge Factory of the Woolwich Royal Arsenal, off Beresford Street, near the ferry terminal. It is open Friday to Sunday in the winter (November–March) and Wednesday to Sunday in summer, 10.30 to 5.00, and costs about £5 to go in. The Woolwich Arsenal was one of the greatest concentrations of industrial and military power in Britain, and London's biggest industrial employer. During the Great War 80,000 munitions workers were employed there. But it declined after 1945, and in 1967 over four hundred years of arms production at Woolwich came to an end. The area is now being redeveloped as housing, but some of the old buildings have survived, either converted into housing or used for museum storage. The 1717 Royal Brass Foundry, probably by Vanbrugh, is now utilized by the National Maritime Museum, and several of the older buildings are used by Firepower. The best way to understand this large and changing site is to visit the Royal Arsenal exhibition in the Greenwich Heritage Centre in Artillery Square (on Warren Lane Gate, next to Firepower), which is open from Tuesday to Saturday, 9.00 to 5.00, free of charge.

CHAPTER ELEVEN

*

LONDON'S WATERWAYS

Old Holborn Bridge and the River Fleet, 1844

LONDON HAS ONE great waterway whose contribution to its history and prosperity has been enormous. The fact that the Thames could be bridged between Cornhill and Southwark, and nowhere further downstream, led the Romans to establish a permanent settlement there, and for nearly two thousand years the Thames has been London's chief trade and supply route and the main source of its prosperity. For most of that time the Thames was also London's main highway, and for a long time its chief sewer and water supply.

The efforts of two men turned a filthy and dangerous river into a relatively clean waterway in the middle of the nineteenth century. Dr John Snow's research on the relationship between different drinking water sources and cholera deaths in the epidemic year of 1854 proved that cholera was waterborne. The area whose deaths he mapped was in Soho, especially between Great Marlborough Street, Regent Street, Wardour Street and Brewer Street, and his main focus was on Broad Street (now Broadwick Street), where the public pump at the end of Lexington Street was proved to be the main source of infection. There is a memorial to Snow and the famous pump there now, and a pub named after him. So when you are looking round Soho or shopping in Regent Street, take a drink there to one of the greatest and most beneficent of all British doctors, whose other achievements include the introduction of anaesthetics into English surgery. Snow's house in Frith Street, nearby, is marked with a blue plaque.

Snow's work helped to shape the climate of opinion in which the other creator of the modern, cleaner Thames could do his work.

The sewer system designed and built by Joseph Bazalgette between 1858 and 1865 is the network Londoners still rely on, and his work is visible all over London. Bazalgette's six main intercepting sewers, which pick up (or intercept) the contents of thousands of miles of main and local sewers, often follow London's main streets. His Northern High Level Sewer runs from Kentish Town, through Stoke Newington, Hackney and Stratford. The Middle Level Sewer runs under Bayswater Road, Oxford Street, Clerkenwell Road and Old Street, joining the High Level Sewer at the south-east corner of Victoria Park, and the Low Level Sewer follows the Embankment and Upper Thames Street most of the way from Chelsea to the City, before swinging north through Bow to meet the other two at Stratford. After this, the combined tunnel known as the Northern Outfall Sewer runs through Plaistow and East Ham to Beckton, near Barking Creek. The Albert, Chelsea and Victoria Embankments were all built by Bazalgette (as chief engineer of the Metropolitan Board of Works) to contain the sewers, and to narrow and tame the river. So he is the creator of the modern Thames in more ways than one. South of the river, Bazalgette's intercepting sewers start in Putney, Balham and Herne Hill, meet at Greenwich, cross Woolwich and the Erith Marshes and enter the Thames a little further downstream than the Northern Outfall.

The most impressive visible features of Bazalgette's work are the pumping stations which raise the level of the sewage at various points on its route, to enable gravity to keep it flowing. The best of these, the Abbey Mills Pumping Station, Stratford, which lifts the sewage in the lower level to meet the outfall sewer near West Ham station and Three Mills Island, is a fabulous mixture of Gothic, Byzantine and Russian styles, 'exciting architecture applied to the most foul purposes' (according to Pevsner). The architect was not Bazalgette but Charles Driver (1832–1900), who later designed engineering-related buildings all over the world. You can see his 'Cathedral of Sewage' from the Greenway, a well-marked public path that follows the outfall sewer for 4.4 miles from Wick Lane,

Hackney Wick, to Royal Docks Road, Beckton. Its partner across the Thames, also built by Driver in the 1860s, is the Crossness Pumping Station, on the Erith Marshes north of Thamesmead, at the end of the Southern Outfall Sewer. There are other pumping stations in London, but none is as impressive as Abbey Mills.

In west London the best place to visit is the Pumping Station at Kew Bridge (near Kew Bridge station), which was built in the 1830s to draw relatively clean water from the Thames for the Grand Junction Waterworks Company. The building is impressive, especially the very tall standpipe tower (1867), and the pumping engines inside the building, which is now a steam museum, are unequalled in London as a record of Britain's industrial history. There is an 1820 Boulton and Watt beam engine, an 1837 Maudslay engine, a rare 1855 Bull engine, and two Grand Junction Cornish-type beam engines, one with a 90-inch (229-centimetre) cylinder diameter, the other with a 100-inch (254-centimetre), which are respectively the largest working beam engine and the largest beam engine in existence. Some of the engines are in operation every weekend, and you can usually enjoy the unique sight of the vast 90-inch engine in motion. Check the museum website, www.kbsm.org, for details. Bazalgette's house is 17 Hamilton Terrace, a fine early-nineteenth-century street in St John's Wood, running parallel to Maida Vale, and there is an impressive monument to him on Victoria Embankment, near Embankment Underground station. The inscription, *Flumini Vincula Posuit*, means 'He put chains on the river.'

The Thames has (or had) many tributaries, and these, though some are now lost or forgotten, played an important part in London's history. There are dozens of little rivers in the Greater London area, on or beneath the surface, some flowing into sewers, some running directly into the Thames, others feeding its bigger tributaries, the Lea, Brent and Wandle.

When London was small, during the first half of its history, only two tributaries, the Walbrook and the Fleet, mattered. The

Walbrook, now completely lost, ran through the middle of the Roman city, between Ludgate Hill and Cornhill. For London's first hundred years the Walbrook was used by Roman manufacturers for water and power, but then it seems to have silted up, although the pattern of ninth- and tenth-century Saxon roads suggests that the stream was still a barrier, and Walbrook is a Saxon name. In the Middle Ages the river was covered and built over, so that the historian John Stow, in the 1590s, did not know exactly where it was. Maps and modern excavations make it possible to follow its course, beginning near Shoreditch High Street, where a well or spring known as Holywell might have been its source. The river ran along Curtain Road, through the swampy area called Moorfields (now occupied by the Broadgate Centre), down Blomfield Street, under the Bank of England, a little to the west of the City street called Walbrook and Dowgate Hill, reaching the Thames between Cannon Street station and Southwark Bridge. Though you cannot see the river, you can visit the church that bears its name. St Stephen Walbrook, in Walbrook (near Bank, next to the Mansion House), is one of Wren's largest and finest City churches, with a beautiful dome on which Wren practised the techniques he later used in St Paul's. It is open every weekday, 10.00 till 4.00.

The Fleet was important for much longer and could be seen (and smelt) until it was covered over in the eighteenth century. In Roman and medieval times the Fleet was the natural western boundary of the City, just outside the walls, and had important and often conflicting uses as an industrial resource, a harbour, a water source and a drain. Its value as a drain eventually overwhelmed its other uses, and the foul and polluted lower reaches of the Fleet ditch were covered over and turned into a sewer. The section from Ludgate Circus to Holborn was covered by the Fleet Market (later Farringdon Street) in 1733, and the lower stretch by New Bridge Street in 1764, when Blackfriars Bridge was built. What is left of the lower Fleet flows into the London sewers, and thus into the Thames. The Fleet may be lost but its valley is not, and anyone walking down Ludgate Hill from St Paul's or down Snow Hill to Farringdon Street is walking into it. Holborn Viaduct was built in the 1860s to bridge the valley, and is about 9 metres above Farringdon Street, which follows the Fleet. In its upper reaches, north of Holborn, the Fleet was called Hole Bourne or Turnmill Brook, and it has therefore given its name to at least seven London streets: Fleet Street, Fleet Lane, Holborn, High Holborn, Holborn Viaduct, Turnmill Street and Fleet Road, Hampstead. In its cleaner northern reaches it was an important provider of power for mills and the source of the 'restorative' waters dispensed by several north London spas in the eighteenth century. It also marks the boundary between the boroughs of Islington and Camden (previously St Pancras) from King's Cross to the City.

We can still swim in the waters of the Fleet, at its source on Hampstead Heath. Its eastern branch flows from Highgate Ponds (one for women swimmers, another for men), which are themselves fed by springs in the grounds of Kenwood House, and its western branch comes from Hampstead Ponds, which are fed by a stream flowing from the Vale of Health. One of the Hampstead Ponds, near South Hill Park, has mixed bathing. The two branches run underground, the Hampstead branch following Fleet Road, skirting Lismore Circus and Malden Road, and the Highgate branch running east of Highgate Road and west of Kentish Town Road. They meet, still underground, near the junction of Camden Road and Camden Street (deep underneath the Grand Union – or Regent's – Canal), and follow the meandering course of St Pancras Way and Pancras Road down to King's Cross. Battle Bridge Road, off Pancras Road, refers to a bridge that once crossed the Fleet here. The river goes round the western side of the high ground of Mount Pleasant Sorting Office, and swings east to meet Farringdon Road at its junction with Clerkenwell Road, and then follows Farringdon Street and New Bridge Street down to the Thames.

The Hampstead heights are the source of two more London rivers, the Tyburn and the Westbourne, both of which still play a

part in London life. The Tyburn flows in two branches from a
source near Haverstock Hill, crosses the Regent's Canal in an
aqueduct built into John Nash's bridge (near Charlbert Street), and
feeds the boating lake in Regent's Park. From the south-western
side of the park the Tyburn flows underground down Gloucester
Place, then swings east to meet the northern end of Marylebone
Lane. This old and winding lane followed the stream almost down
to Oxford Street, the Tyburn Road. The Tyburn crossed Oxford
Street near South Molton Street, flowed under Berkeley Square,
Green Park and Buckingham Palace, and then divided into several
branches, which reached the Thames either side of the Houses of
Parliament and probably near Vauxhall Bridge. The two Westminster branches created Thorney Island, the dry ground in the Westminster marshes on which Edward the Confessor built his abbey
and palace in the 1050s, using a site previously used by Offa in the
eighth century. The lake in St James's Park, which was created as a
canal for Charles II in the 1660s and formed into its present shape
by John Nash in 1827–8, is artificial, although the Tyburn used to
flood into the marshy deer park that was here in the sixteenth
century.

The Westbourne has several sources, one on Hampstead West
Heath, near West Heath Road and Whitestone Pond, others on
Frognal, near Finchley Road. The branches unite near Kilburn High
Road station, and run together under Kilburn Park Road before
turning south past Paddington station and flowing into the Serpentine, which was formed in 1730 for George II's queen, Caroline, by
damming the Westbourne. So we can swim in the Westbourne too.
Leaving the Serpentine through the Dell at its south-eastern end,
the Westbourne passes under Knightsbridge (which was built to
cross it in the eleventh century) and runs near Sloane Square and
under the grounds of Chelsea Hospital. The large pipe that you can
see at the western end of the platform of Sloane Square Underground station is the conduit carrying the lost Westbourne. Once
it flowed prettily through Ranelagh Gardens and tastily into the

Chelsea Waterworks' reservoir, but now it passes quietly and unseen into the Thames.

Away from the city centre, north London's rivers have retained more of their natural quality, though they have been polluted by urban drainwater. The main river of north-west London, Dollis Brook/the Brent, rises in Arkley, between Chipping Barnet and Elstree, and flows east through Barnet and south through Whetstone, and along the western edge of Finchley, picking up the Mutton Brook on the way. After this confluence the river, now called the Brent, runs close to the North Circular from the Great North Way (the A1) to the Edgware Road (the A5), where it flows into the Brent reservoir, the Welsh Harp. This reservoir was created in the 1830s by damming Dollis Brook and the Silk Stream (flowing south from Edgware and Colindale), which met here, to supply water to the Paddington Canal. When the Brent emerges from the western end of the reservoir, it flows between Neasden and Wembley Park, alongside the North Circular to Hanger Lane, and through parkland north and west of Ealing until it merges with the Grand Union Canal at Hanwell. From there it continues south to join the Thames at Brentford Marina, which was once Brentford Dock.

For much of its route the river can be followed on a series of well-marked long-distance paths, the Dollis Valley Greenwalk, the Brent River Park Walk and the Capital Ring. You could join the Dollis Valley Greenwalk from High Barnet Underground station (half a mile to the north) or Totteridge and Whetstone station, which is a few metres east of the path. The riverside walk ends at the junction of the North Circular and Golders Green Road, a mile away from the reservoir, unless you choose to turn east just after the A1 (at Bridge Lane) to follow Mutton Brook to Hampstead Garden Suburb. The walk along the Brent is mostly through very pleasant parkland and golf courses, beginning in Pitshanger Park, not far west of Hanger Lane Tube station. Just before the walk reaches the Uxbridge Road it goes under I.K. Brunel's Wharncliffe Viaduct, which is described in Chapter Ten, and shortly afterwards the walk joins the Grand Union Canal towpath on its way into industrial Brentford.

*

From the south, the Thames is fed by seven rivers or streams, some flowing openly, others hidden or lost. Beverley Brook rises in Nonsuch Park and flows through Stoneleigh and Worcester Park before meeting the Pyl Brook (rising in Sutton) in New Malden. These two brooks used to be heavily polluted by sewage works at Worcester Park and Sutton, but they have become much cleaner since water treatment changes in 1998, and there is a seven-mile waymarked walk all along the Beverley, from New Malden station to the Thames. The brook roughly follows the Kingston Bypass, runs along the western boundary of Wimbledon Common and the eastern side of Richmond Park, leaves the park near Roehampton Gate, and crosses Palewell Common and some sports grounds. The path does not follow the brook through Barnes, but joins it briefly where it passes between Barnes Green and Barnes Common, and then finds it again when it flows east across Barn Elms sports fields to join the Thames at the western end of Putney Embankment.

The Hogsmill begins in a pond in Bourne Hall Park, next to the High Street in Ewell Village, which is fed by a chalk spring. Then it flows through open land in Ewell, Tolworth and Malden, and joins the Thames at Kingston, where it is crossed by the twelfth-century Clattern Bridge, one of the oldest in Britain, on the High Street. Nearby, in the riverside window of John Lewis, are the remains of the medieval bridge over the Thames. An easily followed footpath, part of the London Loop, follows the Hogsmill's course from Ewell to Kingston, with some deviations along residential streets. Like other small London rivers, the Hogsmill had the power to turn apparently rustic backwaters into small manufacturing cen- tres. The river powered two watermills in Ewell, one for grinding corn, the other making paper, as well as providing water for a brewery and power for a gunpowder mill in West Ewell.

The Wandle, which begins in chalk springs and ponds in Carshalton, Croydon, Waddon and Purley, is a much bigger and more important river, over sixteen miles long. The course of the Wandle can easily be followed on roads, footpaths and cycleways from Waddon Park (north of Waddon station) through Beddington Park to Hackbridge, where it meets a second branch flowing from ponds by Carshalton High Street. From Carshalton there is a ten-mile waymarked foot and cycle trail that runs all the way to the Thames. You can find details of this trail at www.wandletrail.org. The river flows roughly north through Mitcham, Morden Hall Park, Merton and South Wimbledon and Earlsfield. Just after Wimbledon greyhound track the Wandle joins its longest tributary, the Graveney, which has made its way from Thornton Heath, about six miles to the south-east. Flowing through Garratt Park and King George's Park into Wandsworth, the Wandle, now in two channels, goes under the High Street (where there has been a bridge since 1602) and finally reaches the Thames in an inaccessible industrial stretch of the river a little to the west of Wandsworth Bridge.

Wandsworth gave its name to the river, rather than the other way round, but the Wandle made Wandsworth prosperous. The river was once famous for its trout, and it has provided power and water for Wandsworth's industries for over six hundred years. As you walk the pleasant banks of the Wandle you might notice remnants of the very large number of industrial enterprises it used to sustain. In 1805 it powered forty industrial works, and maps of the 1960s, before London's industries declined, show a succession of corn mills, dyeworks, paperworks, leatherworks, printworks, calico works, breweries and watercress beds. The Wandle helped make Victorian Wandsworth an important industrial suburb, famous in the 1870s (according to James Thorne) for 'corn mills, distilleries (Messrs Watney's), maltings, dye works, chemical works, colour factories, cloth printing and bolting mills, match factories, artificial manure works, and so forth'. Upstream, the Wandle made late-Victorian Merton, Morden and Mitcham into manufacturing centres, specializing in varnish, floor coverings, felt, leather, flour-milling, bleaching and calico-printing. In Morden Hall Park, a short walk from Morden Tube station, there are the remains of a water-powered snuff mill that was in operation from the eighteenth century until 1922 and is now an education centre. One of the two great iron waterwheels is still there, along with the tobacco-drying kilns and two old mill cottages. The eighteenth-century Hall, rather spoiled by Victorian stucco, is now used for council offices, but the National Trust park is a lovely mixture of marsh, meadow, woodland and gardens, and the Wandle meanders beautifully through it.

There is another impressive industrial site a few hundred metres downstream. Calico-bleaching and printing works were established inside the grounds and ruins of Merton Priory, on the east side of the Wandle, in 1724 and 1752. A large new mill, Bennett's Mill, was built nearby in 1802, and in 1875 the Littler family, which had owned the print works since 1833, started printing fine fabrics for Liberty's, the newly opened West End department store. Within 15 years Merton was printing all Liberty's fabrics, and in 1904 the store took the works over. Liberty's sold the factory in 1972 and it closed in 1982. The surviving buildings, which include the 1740s Colour House, as well as many of the buildings erected by Liberty's, are now used for a lively market known as Merton Abbey Mills. The other Merton Priory works, those established in 1752, eventually became a tablecloth-printing works, which in 1881 was sold to the socialist designer, writer and businessman William Morris. This is where William Morris's beautiful tapestries, fabrics and stained glass were produced until 1940, when the factory was closed. A little further north, before the river passes Wimbledon greyhound track, Coppermill Lane, a left turn off Plough Lane on the east bank, has an early-nineteenth-century mill cottage and mill buildings, the remains of a leather works. And the Wandle has another interesting literary connection. In 1859–60, when George Eliot was writing *The Mill on the Floss*, she was living in Holly Lodge, Wimbledon Park Road, Southfields, and her local river was the mill-rich Wandle.

Going east, the next open river in south London is the Ravensbourne, about eight miles away. Between these two there are four hidden rivers, the Falcon, the Effra, the Neckinger and the Peck. The Falcon brook flowed from Tooting Bec Common and Streatham Hill, through Balham and under Clapham Junction, then divided into two branches, making Battersea an island, which is what the 'ea' or 'eie' on the end of its name means in Old English. One branch turns north-west across York Gardens and enters the Thames at Battersea Creek, near the Heliport, and another swung east, the other side of Battersea Park and Power Station, to flow into the Thames in a ditch at Nine Elms.

The Effra was a longer and more important river, which flowed openly until the nineteenth century and still has one open stretch. It rises from springs in Upper Norwood (or Crystal Palace), runs steeply downhill to Norwood Cemetery and cuts across West Dulwich to find Croxted Road. In Dulwich, on the corner of Thurlow Park Road and Gallery Road, its waters feed the long ornamental lake in Belair Park, before resuming their progress down Croxted Road to Herne Hill. The Effra skirts the east and north sides of Brockwell Park and crosses Brixton Water Lane and Effra Parade to reach Brixton Road, where its valley is visible on the east side of the road. Before Kennington Park it swings west around the Oval, to reach the Thames in a creek just south of Vauxhall Bridge. The Effra was once a charming and fast-flowing river, but its lower reaches were a sewer by 1700, which did not stop the Vauxhall Water Company from selling its untreated waters to customers in the early nineteenth century. Its waters were unpredictable and liable to flood, to the great inconvenience of the growing suburb of Brixton. Therefore it was filled in and enclosed in the later nineteenth century, leaving only Belair as a reminder of its ancient charm.

The River Peck, which gave its name to Peckham, rose south of Peckham Rye Park, and flowed through the park along a visible (but now dry) watercourse near its western edge. The lake and water features in the park are still fed by the Peck. The name Rye is derived from the Old English *ripe*, a brook. The underground stream flows north towards Bermondsey, and at Rotherhithe New Road joins another underground stream, known as the Earl's Sluice, which begins on Denmark Hill, near Ruskin Park, and flows under Albany Road and Rolls Road. In Rotherhithe the river finds its way into the ditches, streams, canals and docks that still criss-cross the area, and makes its way to the Thames, either near the Rotherhithe Tunnel or further downstream near South Dock and Greenland Pier.

It is possible that some of the Peck's waters flow into the Neckinger, a little river which begins on St George's Fields, in front of the Imperial War Museum, or perhaps in Lambeth Marsh, near Waterloo station. Flowing under Brook Drive, past the Elephant and Castle, and near the New Kent Road, the Neckinger briefly follows Tower Bridge Road up to the site of Bermondsey Abbey (Bermondsey Square) before turning north-east under Abbey Road and meandering around Jacob's Island (*see* Chapter Eight) before reaching the Thames at St Saviour's Dock. It is said that the wharf on the Thames here, Neckinger Wharf, drew its name (and thus the river's) from the Devil's Neckinger, neck-cloth, or noose, a reference to the old practice of hanging Thames pirates at the gallows here. The Neckinger was once important to the leather industry that dominated Bermondsey until the Second World War, providing the water that the tanneries needed. It was also a source of power for mills grinding corn, peas and spices. The river was diverted in the early Middle Ages to serve the corn mills of Bermondsey Abbey, and little Millstream Road, between Druid Street and Maltby Street, marks its course. Later, the mill on Millstream Road became a pioneering water-powered gunpowder factory. The circuitous course of the river to the east of St Saviour's Dock, which formed Jacob's Island, was created in the seventeenth century to serve the needs of millers and tanners, and recent excavations have discovered a network of man-made watercourses.

The last southern tributary, the Ravensbourne, flows through London's south-eastern suburbs, forming a network, with its tributaries, the Quaggy (Kyd Brook), the Pool and the Beck, of over forty miles of rivers. The sources of all the rivers are on the North Downs: the Ravensbourne starts at Caesar's Well, Keston Common, the Pool near West Wickham, the Quaggy at Locksbottom, south of Bromley Common. The Pool and Ravensbourne meet just south of Catford station, and the Quaggy joins them at Lewisham station, about two miles south of Deptford Creek, where the river enters the Thames. In the twentieth century large sections of the Quaggy and Ravensbourne were diverted into concrete channels to reduce flooding, but in recent years there has been progress in returning them to their natural state. There are foot and cycle paths along the Pool from Penge to Catford, and along the Ravensbourne from Keston Common to Bromley, and from Catford to Deptford. The Sustrans national cycle network (www.sustrans.org.uk) includes the Pool and Ravensbourne path in its well-marked route 21.

*

No Thames tributary has played such an important part in London's recent history as the Lea, or Lee. The Lea rises in springs north of Luton, and flows about fifty miles through Hertfordshire and Greater London, meandering and dividing in a broad flat valley through Waltham Abbey, Enfield, Edmonton, Walthamstow, Leyton, Hackney and Bow, before joining the Thames at Canning Town. For the Romans, the Lea was a wide and useful waterway, as well as an obstacle which land transport had to negotiate. The lowest point at which the Lea could easily be crossed was Old Ford, where the Roman road to Colchester crossed the river. Plentiful evidence of a Roman settlement here has been found, including herringbone brickwork on the bed of the river. After Alfred the Great defeated the Danes in 886, the Lea formed part of the boundary between the

Anglo-Saxon kingdom and the Danelaw, and later it was the border between Middlesex (and Hertfordshire) and Essex, and, from 1888 to 1965, the eastern limit of the London County Council.

Most settlements along the Lea, which are now densely populated East End suburbs, began as river crossings. Stratford-le-Bow, like all England's Stratfords, was on a Roman road as it crossed a river (Street-ford), and the Bow here, like that of Bow and Bromley-by-Bow, refers to the arched bridge that was built across the Lea in the reign of Henry I (1100–35). The Lea's riverside settlements became manufacturing and market towns for London, handling or processing the grain, malt, wool, dyestuffs and garden produce that came down the river from rural Hertfordshire. Milling, baking, brewing, fulling and dyeing remained the main industries of the Lea settlements into the eighteenth century, but they did not prevent the area from attracting wealthy Londoners who needed a peaceful rural retreat.

The Lea's importance as a trade route meant that it long ago lost its natural shape. It was managed and improved even in the fifteenth century, and in 1577 a pioneering pound lock, probably the first in England with two sets of mitred gates, was constructed at Waltham Abbey. In the 1760s, near the start of the Canal Age, a survey conducted by the great engineer John Smeaton proposed a series of new channels to speed the passage of vessels from Waltham Abbey to the Thames. After the River Lea Act in 1766 eleven miles of new channels were built under the supervision of Smeaton and his assistant Thomas Yeoman. One of the new canals, the Limehouse Cut, connects the Lea at Bromley (near Three Mills Island) with the Thames at Limehouse, allowing ships to avoid the very sinuous lower reaches of the Lea, and another, the Hackney Cut, joins Lea Bridge and Old Ford, bypassing the Lea's meandering course across the Hackney Marshes. The Lea Navigation was improved during and after the Great War to allow 130-ton ships to reach Enfield (an important centre of the armaments industry), and for the next fifty years the canals were an important route for the London timber trade. Now their value is mostly recreational, and walkers and cyclists can now follow the Lea, along the canals and most of its natural course, from the Thames to its source at Leagrave.

Most of the visible evidence for the earlier history of the Lea valley settlements was destroyed by very rapid urban and industrial growth in the late nineteenth century. Only a few pre-Victorian buildings survived the Victorian and twentieth-century destruction of Bow. The late-medieval church of St Mary, on a traffic island in Bow Road, near the bridge over the Lea, survived because the Victorians never managed to find the money to rebuild it. Number 43 Gillender Street, between the Lea and the Northern Approach to the Blackwall Tunnel, just south of Bromley-by-Bow Tube station, is Bromley Hall, a Queen Anne house which recent rescue work has revealed as a remodelled remnant of an early-Tudor brick manor house which was built by Holy Trinity Priory in the 1490s and seized and refurbished by Henry VIII in the 1530s. It has been converted into offices for local businesses. Stratford, on the other side of the Lea, was a little luckier. The Broadway, Stratford's old market street, still has a few Victorian pubs, and its continuation, Romford Road, has some older houses, especially number 2 and number 30, the Old Dispensary, a timber house built around 1700.

The best remnant of the lost world of the pre-Victorian Lea is Three Mills Island, a short walk north-east from Bromley-by-Bow Tube station, by Hancock Road and Three Mill Lane. If you are walking the Lea Valley Walk, Three Mills Island is a little to the north of Bow Locks, where the Limehouse Cut joins the River Lea. The mills were built on this man-made island to take advantage of the tidal flow of the Lea. In the 1720s they were bought by Huguenots, who used them for grinding grain and distilling it into gin. The House Mill, the largest tide mill in Britain, which now contains the museum, was built in 1776 and rebuilt after a fire in 1804, and the Clock Mill was rebuilt in 1817. They remained in use for much longer than most tide mills, prospering because they performed milling and distilling on one unified and very conveniently located site. Milling and distilling ended in the 1940s, but the mills were saved from demolition and converted into a museum and film studios. The House Mill Museum opens on Saturday and Sunday afternoons (2.00 to 4.00), from June to October.

In the later nineteenth century the Lea became the centre of London's dirtier industries – chemicals, gas, soap, paint, glue, fertilizers, solvents, dyes and explosives. Its riverside settlements grew into industrial giants, Walthamstow, West Ham and Canning Town, where London's industrial development would be carried forward when its old crafts declined. So since the late nineteenth century the Lea has been a highly urbanized, industrialized and polluted river, and even today, despite efforts to improve the condition of the river and its environs, the walker here is as likely to smell sewage as new-mown hay. Much will change, no doubt, when the Lea Valley is cleaned up before the 2012 Olympic Games.

The smell of the Lea matters, because for nearly four hundred years Londoners have been drinking its waters. Between 1609 and 1613 the New River Company, led by Hugh Myddleton, dug a channel from some springs in Hertfordshire, at Amwell and Chadwell, to Clerkenwell, to give Londoners a fresh and clean water supply. This first channel was 38 miles long, and ran over several wooden aqueducts, dropping only six metres over its whole length. Half the capital for this vast project was supplied by King James I, who took half the profits and helped Myddleton overcome the opposition of local landowners. In 1618 the New River was connected to the Lea, which has been supplying London with water ever since. Today about 48 million gallons of water a day come from the Lea and the Hertfordshire springs via the New River, making up about 8 per cent of London's daily supply. Since Londoners used the New River (as they used all their rivers) for bathing and waste disposal, its waters did not stay clean for long, and Tobias Smollett described it in 1771 as 'an open aqueduct, exposed to all manner of defilement'.

To discover whether the New River has improved since 1771,

you can now walk a 28-mile path along its banks. The path follows
the New River for much of its length, using nearby roads and lanes
when there is no access to the river. The Hertfordshire section is
about 14 miles long, and the London section, not all along the
riverbank, is another 14 miles. Details of this walk are available
from Thames Water, whose online guide can most easily be found
by putting New River Path into a search engine.

The New River walk begins near Hertford East station, where
the A10 meets the Hertford Road, crosses the M25 by an aqueduct
near its junction with the A10, runs south through Enfield, Bush
Hill and Palmers Green, and goes into a tunnel (built in 1859)
between Myddleton Road, Wood Green and the reservoirs on the
eastern edge of Alexandra Park, which were part of the old Hornsey
waterworks. Then, in a section followed by the New River Path, it
crosses the northern corner of Finsbury Park and loops east to run
alongside the two Stoke Newington reservoirs which are now the
finishing point of the New River as far as London's water supply is
concerned. But it flows on, mostly unseen and underground, through
Clissold Park (where ornamental waters indicate the river's old
route) and Canonbury, and there is a good walk along the river
through a little park between St Paul's Road and Canonbury Road,
starting near Canonbury station in the north. The housing to its east
is the Marquess Estate, the first big estate built by Islington council
after the new borough was created in 1965.

The New River is piped through Islington, crossing Regent's
Canal and the City Road, finally reaching the New River Head in
Hardwick Street (near Rosebery Avenue), where Hugh Myddleton
built his Round Pond and the Metropolitan Water Board had its
offices. The Metropolitan Water Board buildings are still on Rosebery Avenue, now converted into flats, preserving a richly plastered
1690s boardroom, the Oak Room, in their centre. You can see the
buildings that once housed the New River Company's pumping
machinery by going down Myddleton Passage (off Myddleton
Square) to the visitor information point in the Nautilus House

Garden, which is open from 8.00 to 4.00, or till 7.00 in the summer. There is a little single-storey circular brick building, the base of a windmill, built around 1708, which was meant to pump water to the Upper Pond in Claremont Square, 300 metres to the north. The wind pump was not a success, and the engineer John Smeaton designed a steam engine to do the job. His tall brick engine house of 1768 is still standing here, along with the larger engine house built between 1784 and 1796 for more powerful Boulton and Watt steam engines. And there is the Inner Pond, the last remnant of the Round Pond, which gave Londoners water for nearly four hundred years, and Water Board offices of 1919 and 1938. If the passage is shut, you can see most of this from Amwell Street, near the primary school.

There is another link between central London and the Lea. Between 1812 and 1820 the Regent's Canal was built by John Nash's assistant James Morgan, linking the Paddington arm of the Grand Union Canal with the Thames at Limehouse in an arc around what were then the northern and eastern edges of London. The Regent's Canal turns south at the southern corner of Victoria Park, through Globe Town and Mile End, but in 1830 the 1.5-mile Hertford Union Canal (or Duckett's Cut) was dug along what is now the southern edge of Victoria Park to link the Lea at Hackney Wick with the Regent's Canal, and thus with the Grand Union Canal and the national canal network. The walk from Hackney Wick to Paddington along Duckett's Cut and the Regent's Canal is a very pleasant and interesting day out, and takes you through a variety of London districts, from South Hackney, Haggerston, Hoxton and Islington to Pentonville, King's Cross, Camden Town, Regent's Park, Little Venice and Paddington. Hackney Wick (which is also on the Lea Valley and Greenway walks) is a station on the Silverlink Line, and it is easy to find the start of the walk where the Hackney Cut of the Lea Navigation goes under White Post Lane (Carpenter's Road), a few metres east of the station.

The route along the canal is marked and explained by dozens

of useful signs along the way, and there are several opportunities to explore the surrounding neighbourhoods as you pass them. You could get some refreshment in the cafe by the lake in Victoria Park, or try your luck in F. Cooke's Pie and Mash shop on Broadway Market in Shoreditch, where you might find that the 'liquor', despite its lurid green colour, adds very little flavour to a bland minced beef pie. After going under Kingsland Road the canal runs between Hoxton (to the south), a Victorian industrial and residential district which retains some vestiges of the original seventeenth- and eighteenth-century hamlet, and de Beauvoir Town, which was developed as a well-planned estate of modest villas in the 1830s and 1840s by its landlord, Benyon de Beauvoir. After passing the City Road Basin, once an important freight handling centre, the canal enters a long tunnel under Islington. The quickest way to find the canal as it reappears near the Caledonian Road is to go ahead on Duncan Street, turn left into Upper Street, go right opposite the Angel station into White Lion Street, and right again into Rodney Street.

At King's Cross, soon after rejoining the canal, you will pass the London Canal Museum, which is on the Battlebridge Basin and New Wharf Road. You can find it by going left (south) on York Way, left into Wharfedale Road and left again into New Wharf Road. It is open every day except Monday, and costs about £3. Details are on its website, www.canalmuseum.org.uk. The museum is in a warehouse built in the 1860s by Carlo Gatti for storing the ice he imported from Norway to sell to London restaurants. The ice arrived at the Limehouse Basin and was taken by horse-drawn barge along the canal to King's Cross, to be stored in ice wells, one of which is still visible. The Gattis were the most successful Italian family in Victorian London, with major interests in the ice-cream, restaurant, music hall and theatre businesses, and a house on Bedford Square.

The canal then takes you through the acres of railway land behind King's Cross and Euston stations, up to the lively markets of Camden Town, through London Zoo, with Lord Snowdon's aviary on the right and some mammal enclosures on the left. The bridge you go under just after the zoo (going west) is the handsome Macclesfield Bridge (with iron Doric columns), which was built in 1816 and rebuilt after a gunpowder boat exploded under it in 1874. The millionaire's mansions you can see from the canal, just before you catch sight of the London Central Mosque, were built around 1990 by Quinlan Terry, who specializes in recreating the classical styles used by John Nash when the park was first developed. The canal runs south of Lord's cricket ground and St John's Wood, and reaches the busy stretch known as Little Venice (a comparison first suggested by Robert Browning), where the Regent's Canal meets the Paddington Basin and joins the Grand Union Canal. If you leave the canal here it is a short walk to Warwick Avenue or Royal Oak Tube stations. For those with the time and energy, the Grand Union Canal Walk continues through west London into the Midlands, arriving in Birmingham 145 miles later. Or you could turn off past Greenford station, at Greenford Road (the A4127), and follow the Capital Ring walking route for nearly two miles to reach the Brent River Walk, which joins another branch of the Grand Union Canal and eventually reaches the Thames at Brentford.

Despite its age, the New River is not London's oldest man-made waterway. The Duke of Northumberland's River, which connects the River Crane in Twickenham with the Thames at Isleworth, dates back to the late fifteenth century, probably the reign of Henry VII. The river was cut to provide water and water power to Syon Abbey, on the Thames at Isleworth, which became part of the Duke of Northumberland's estate after the Dissolution of the Monasteries. You can follow the Duke's river from Church Road, Isleworth, along Mill Plat, where the river-powered mills used to be, passing some early-seventeenth-century almshouses, then down Riverside Walk, through the Mogden Sewage Works (not as bad as they sound), past Twickenham rugby ground and Kneller Hall, to join the River Crane alongside Kneller Gardens. The River Crane walk continues as part of the well-marked London Loop,

going through some parkland, until it joins up with the Grand
Union Canal walk at Bull's Bridge, a little north of exit 3 on the
M4. In Crane Park, just west of the Great Chertsey Road, there is a
24-metre shot tower, dated 1828, part of Hounslow Powder Mill,
which produced gunpowder here from the sixteenth century, or
perhaps earlier, until 1927. Around the tower there are a few other
remnants of this industry, which needed water power and an open
site away from dwellings. An explosion in 1772 blew out some of
the windows of Walpole's Strawberry Hill, over a mile away. From
here, you could turn back and follow the river east to the Thames
at Brentford, about a mile north of your starting point. There may
not be any nightingales in Berkeley Square, but thanks to the work
begun by Dr John Snow and Joseph Bazalgette there are still
kingfishers on the banks of the Crane.

Answers to the Walking Quizzes

1 Hubert Le Sueur
2 Royal Marines
3 The goddess Athena
4 Robert Falcon Scott
5 John Nash, 1821
6 Sir John Vanbrugh
7 Sir Herbert Tree
8 Ho Chi Minh
9 Plaque on the back of the Theatre Royal, Haymarket, which staged two Wilde plays, in 1893 and 1895
10 Richard Dadd
11 Sir Mortimer Wheeler
12 Tommy Cooper, in the Hand and Racquet
13 Tom Cribb, world bare-knuckle champion
14 Piccadilly Number 7 Piano Bar, the Comedy Upstairs Downstairs
15 On the corner of Lisle Street and Wardour Street
16 Number 9 Oxenden Street, the Exchange and Bullion Office, 1798
17 Samuel Johnson, Joshua Reynolds and the Club
18 Number 40 Gerrard Street, King's silversmith Paul de Lamerie
19 John Dryden
20 Willy Clarkson, perruquier (Sarah Bernhardt and Henry Irving)
21 King Theodore of Corsica
22 William Hazlitt
23 Dorothy L. Sayers (Lord Peter Wimsey)

24 Thomas Hearne, watercolourist
25 Number 69 (actually on Dean Street)
26 1732
27 Karl Marx, above Quo Vadis
28 Dog and Duck, Bateman Street
29 Mozart (20 Frith Street) and Ronnie Scott
30 John Logie Baird (22 Frith Street)
31 The snail rider at L'Escargot
32 St James and Soho Club, 1864, Greek Street
33 Josiah Wedgwood
34 The House of St Barnabas
35 Charles II
36 Edward VI, in his 1550 charter, on the French Protestant church
37 Regent Sounds Studio
38 Elms Lesters Painting Rooms
39 The Odeon's history of entertainment
40 Queen Beatrix of the Netherlands
41 B. Flegg, saddler
42 Thomas Chippendale

PINOLI is written on the top of numbers 17 and 21 Wardour Street, near the Exchange and Bullion Office. The walk finishes in the Salisbury on St Martin's Lane and St Martin's Court, one of the finest of the West End public houses built in the gin palace style in the 1890s.

LAWYERS, PRINTERS AND MONKS

1 1902
2 King's College
3 William Lilly, 1602–81
4 Strand station
5 Roman baths
6 Cabmen

7   International Institute of Strategic Studies

8   She represents the Loyal Temperance League

9   *Qualitas et Servitium*

10 Cherubs

11 Grecian Coffee House

12 Robert Devereux, Earl of Essex

13 Nicholas Barbon

14 Nine

15 Yellow

16 Mrs Thrall (or Thrale)

17 A golden lion

18 1717

19 Lloyds Bank

20 The Great Fire

21 Child's Bank, now RBS, at number 1 Fleet Street

22 Lawyers of the Middle Temple are symbolized by the Lamb and Flag

23 Samuel Pepys (though his exhibition is in Prince Henry's Room)

24 The Automobile Association

25 Hoare's Bank

26 Alfred Harmsworth, Lord Northcliffe

27 Izaak Walton

28 Elizabeth I

29 *Alere Flammam* (feed the flame [of truth])

30 Dr Johnson's cat, whose statue is in the square. Boswell records in his *Life*: 'I recollect him one day scrambling up Dr Johnson's breast, apparently with much satisfaction, while my friend smiling and half-whistling, rubbed down his back, and pulled him by the tail; and when I observed he was a fine cat, saying, "Why yes, Sir, but I have had cats whom I liked better than this;" and then as if perceiving Hodge to be out of countenance, adding, "but he is a very fine cat, a very fine cat indeed."'

31 The Olde Cheshire Cheese

32 London's first Irish pub

33 Thomas Tompion and George Graham, clockmakers

34 Samuel Pepys
35 *Sunday Times*
36 Bridewell Palace, now St Bride's Institute
37 The Punch Tavern, where *Punch* magazine began
38 The Old Bell Tavern, built to feed and lodge St Bride's builders
39 The Blackfriars or Dominicans, 1278–1539
40 The King's Wardrobe in Wardrobe Place
41 St Anne's Blackfriars and the Provincial's Hall of Blackfriars Priory
42 The Worshipful Company of Spectaclemakers, who share the Apothecaries' Hall

The walk finishes at the Black Friar public house (1873), which owes its fame to a complete makeover by members of the Arts and Crafts movement in 1905. The Grotto behind the main bar, which is even wittier and more unrestrained than the work of 1905, was done in 1917–21.

UNDERNEATH THE ARCHES

1   1937
2   Thomas Chatterton
3   Charles Dickens
4   Giuseppe Mazzini
5   1546
6   Six
7   *Floreat Imperii Portus*
8   Saracen's
9   William Harvey
10 Cup in drinking fountain on churchyard wall, Giltspur Street
11 Charles Lamb
12 Giltspur Street Compter
13 Gluttony
14 'Resurrected' corpses and St Bart's surgeons

15 Henry VIII's codpiece
16 Hospital church and parish church
17 23 August 1305
18 13 years, 2 months and 24 days
19 20 September 1143
20 Sir John Betjeman. Number 43 Cloth Court (Betjeman's)
21 Ginger wine base plus secret ingredient
22 Charterhouse, or Thomas Sutton's charity
23 1898
24 J.H. Schrader
25 Thomas Tompion, Joseph Simms, Christopher Pinchbeck, James
    Upjohn, John Cranfield, Edward Massey, John Moor and Dan
    Parkes
26 18 December 1917
27 Round
28 Thomas Britton, the musical coalman
29 37a Clerkenwell Green, Marx Memorial Library
30 Benedictine nuns and prior and brethren of the Order of St John

Bibliography

Adcock, A.S. – *Famous Houses and Literary Shrines in London.* 1929.

Ashley, P. – *London Peculiars: Curiosities in a Capital City.* 2004.

Barker, F., Jackson, P. – *The History of London in Maps.* 1990.

Barker, F., Silvester-Carr, D. – *The Black Plaque Guide to London.* 1987.

Barkshire, P.D. – *Unexplored London.* 1988.
 – *Other London.* 1989.

Barton, N. – *The Lost Rivers of London.* 1962.

Bell, W.G. – *Unknown London.* 1919.
 – *More About Unknown London.* 1921.

Camden History Society – *Streets of Bloomsbury and Fitzrovia.* 1995.
 – *East of Bloomsbury.* 1998.
 – *Streets of Old Holborn.* 1999.
 – *Streets of St Giles.* 2000.

Clunn, H.P. – *The Face of London* (n.d.).

Culbertson, J., Randall, T. – *Permanent Londoners. An Illustrated Guide to the Cemeteries of London.* 1991.

Dark, S. – *London.* 1924.

Draper-Stumm, T., Kendall, D. – *London's Shops.* 2002.

Duncan, A. – *Secret London.* 1998.
 – *Walking Village London.* 2003.
 – *Walking Notorious London.* 2004.
 – *Walking London.* 2006.

Fairfield, S. – *The Streets of London.* 1983.

Fletcher, G. – *The London Nobody Knows.* 1962.
 – *Offbeat in London.* 1966.
 – *Pocket Guide to Dickens' London.* 1969.

Forshaw, A., Bergstrom, T. – *The Open Spaces of London*. 1986.

Gibson, P. – *The Capital Companion*. 1985.

Girouard, M. – *Victorian Pubs*. 1975.

Glinert, E. – *The London Compendium*. 2003.

Guillery, P. – *The Small House in Eighteenth-century London*. 2004.

Hare, A. – *Walks in London* (2 vols, 1884).

Harwood, E., Saint, A. – *London* (*Exploring England's Heritage* series; 1991.

Horwood, R. – *The A to Z of Regency London*. 1985.

Inwood, S. – *A History of London*. 1998.
— *City of Cities*. 2004.

Jackson, P. – *Walks in Old London*. 1993.

Jones, E., Woodward, C. – *A Guide to the Architecture of London*. 2002.

Kent, W. – *An Encyclopaedia of London*. 1951.
— *Walks in London*. 1951.

Lambert, S. – *New Architecture of London*. 1963.

Lee, E. – *Musical London*. 1995.

Lillywhite, B. – *London Coffee Houses*. 1963.

Nairn, I. – *Nairn's London*. 1966.

Panton, K. – *London. An Historical Companion*. 2003.

Pearce, D. – *The Great Houses of London*. 1986.

Pevsner, N., Bradley, S. – *London 6: Westminster*. 2003.

Pevsner, N., Bradley, S., Rowan, A. – *London 2: South*. 1983.
— *London 1: City of London*. 1997.

Pevsner, N., Cherry, B. – *London 3: North-West*. 1991.
— *London 4: North*. 1999.

Pevsner, N., Cherry, B., O'Brien, C. – *London 5: East*. 2005.

Phillips, H. – *The Thames About 1750*. 1951.
— *Mid-Georgian London*. 1964.

Rennison, N. – *The London Blue Plaque Guide*. 2003.

Rocque, J. – *The A to Z of Georgian London*. 1982.

Rosen, D., Rosen, S. – *London Science*. 1994.

Saunders, A. – *The Art and Architecture of London*. 1984.

Schofield, J. – *The Building of London, from the Conquest to the Great Fire*. 1984.

Scimone, G.M.S., Levey, M.F. – *London Museums and Collections*. 1989.

Shuckburgh, J. – *London Revealed: Uncovering London's Hidden History*. 2003.

Smith, S. – *Underground London*. 2004.

Stapleton, A. – *London Lanes*. 1930.

Sumeray, D. – *Track the Plaque*. 2003.

Summerson, Sir J. – *Georgian London*. 1962.

Tagholm, R. – *Walking Literary London*. 2001.

Thornbury, W., Walford, E. – *London Old and New* (6 vols, 1883–5.

Timbs, J. – *Curiosities of London* (1885.

Trench, R., Hillman, E. – *London Under London*. 1993.

Turner, C. – *London Churches Step by Step*. 1987.

Venables, S., Williams, S. – *Still Open: The Guide to Traditional London Shops*. 2006.

Weinreb, B., Hibbert, C. – *The London Encyclopaedia*. 1993.

Williams, G. – *Guide to Literary London*. 1973.

Young, G. – *Walking London's Parks and Gardens*. 1998.

Those whose appetite for information is greater than these books can satisfy should turn to the *Survey of London*, a series of architectural, topographical and historical studies started in 1894 and now into its 45th volume, but still unfinished. It is in most public reference libraries, but its practical value has been increased enormously by the fact that about 20 volumes are now digitized and freely available and searchable, at www.british-history.ac.uk. The rest should be online by the time this book is published. The same site, a joint enterprise of the Institute of Historical Research, the History of Parliament Trust, the Centre for Metropolitan History and the Victoria County History, has a large and valuable collection of sources on the history and topography of London which is growing bigger by the month. At present they include the *Victoria County Histories* of Middlesex, Essex and Surrey, Thornbury and Walford's *Old and New London*, H.A. Harben's *Dictionary of London*, and the most important printed records of the medieval City.

Index

100 Club 201
2i's coffee bar 55
A Tale of Two Cities 334, 337, 341
Abbey Mills Pumping Station 376
Abbey Road studios 199
Academy of Ancient Music 180, 218
Acton 116
Adam, Robert 71, 72, 95, 97, 99, 102, 108, 115, 128, 132, 143, 145, 149, 267
Adelphi Terrace 143–4
Adelphi Theatre 336
Albany 100
Aldgate 5, 80, 211, 218, 285, 299, 301
Aldwych 72, 153–5, 253, 260, 337
Alfred the Great 123
All Hallows Barking 22
All Hallows on the Wall 5
All Hallows Staining 21
All Saints, Carshalton 36
All Saints, Edmonton 30
All Saints, Kingston 36
All Saints, West Ham 29
Almack's Assembly Rooms 185
Amwell Street 153
anaesthesia 357
Anchor inn 312
Apothecaries' Hall 17, 354, 407
Apsley House 95
Archer House 126

Argyll Arms 213, 228, 270
Argyll Rooms 187
Arkwright, Sir Richard 361
Arne, Thomas 184
Athenaeum 148
Aubrey, John 51, 216
Austin Friars 9, 19

Bach, JC 175, 184, 185, 204
Bagnigge Wells 42
Baker Street, 221b 323
Banister (or Banester), John 177–9
Bank of England 52, 116, 309, 378
banks 217, 219, 233, 253, 303
Banks, Joseph 355
Bankside 193, 241, 279, 305–6, 310–3
Banqueting House 67, 87, 288
Barbon, Nicholas 53, 72, 79, 80, 82, 135, 136, 180, 223
Barking 22, 28, 75, 233
Barking Abbey 22, 28
Barnard's Inn 78, 338
Barnes 36, 199, 382
Barnet 30, 381
Barnett, Henrietta 157–9
Barnett, Samuel 157–9, 299
Battersea 163, 385
Battersea council housing 163
Battersea Park 46–8
Bazalgette, Joseph 376, 377, 395

Beatles 199–200, 269–70
Beddington 74
Bedford Park 155–7
Bedford Square 1, 137, 359, 393
Bedford Square residents 137–8
Beecham, Sir Thomas 190–1
Beggar's Opera 181, 183, 204
Belair Park lake 385
Belgrave Square 140, 259
Belgravia 139, 259, 360
Berkeley Square 97, 131–3, 230, 380
Bermondsey 18, 248, 284, 386
Bermondsey Abbey 386
Bermondsey Priory 8, 18
Bermondsey Square 18, 248, 386
Bethlem hospital 347–8
Bethnal Green 55, 116
Bexley 37, 74–5
Black Friar pub 213, 225
Blackfriars 9, 17, 225, 294, 354
Blake, William 97, 269
Bleak House 334, 336, 337–8
Bleeding Heart Yard 341
Bloomsbury Group 139, 145
Bloomsbury Square 136, 204, 260
Blow, John 176, 177, 178
Bond Street 200, 238, 272–3
Booth, Charles 281
Boston Manor House 84

Boswell, James 2, 53, 54, 59, 217, 306, 407
Bow 29, 388–9
Bow Street 181, 242, 318–9
Bow Street Court 319
Bramah Tea and Coffee Museum 56
Brent 32, 381
Brent River Walk 381, 394
Brent Valley 363
Brentford 35, 84, 203, 381–2, 394
breweries and brewing 92, 109–10, 210–11, 227, 312, 383
Britannia Saloon 193
British Museum 3, 356
Britton, Thomas 179, 296
Brixton 249, 260, 263, 385
Broadcasting House 149
Bromley 241, 387
Bromley-by-Bow 80, 388, 389
brothels 283, 286, 303, 305, 306, 311, 312
Brunel, Isambard Kingdom 48–9, 106, 361–4, 381
Brunel, Marc 106, 361–2
Bruton Street 132, 230
Bryanston Square 141
Buckingham, George Villiers Duke of 76
Buckingham Palace 42, 119, 147
Buckingham Street 76, 82, 336
Bunhill Fields 97–8
Bunyan, John 97
Burgh House, Hampstead 89
Burlington House 99–100
Burlington, Earl of 12, 99–100, 108–9, 183
Bush House 154
Byrd, William 176

Café de Paris 198
Café Royal 149, 304
Camden Town 333, 378, 393–4
Canal Museum 393

canals 389–94
Duckett's Cut 392
Duke of Northumberland's river 394
Grand Union 363, 381, 392–4
Lea 389
Limehouse Cut 215
Regent's 215, 392–4
Canonbury 391
Canons 182
Carew Manor 74
Carlile House 185
Carlyle, Thomas 107, 128
Carlyle's house 107
Carshalton 36, 383
Cartwright, John 139
Cato Street Conspiracy 292, 308
Cavell, Edith 351
Cavendish Square 130, 267, 335
Cavendish, Sir Henry 359
Chandos House 99
Chandos, Duke of 99, 131–2, 182
Change Alley 51–2
Chapel Royal 75, 176, 177
Chaplin, Charlie 248, 251
Charing Cross Road 82, 184, 194, 198, 306
charitable housing 159–60
Charles I 66, 67, 85, 146, 231, 288
Charles II 83, 110, 126, 127, 147, 176, 255, 287, 305, 380
Charlton Manor House 85
Charterhouse 9, 15
Cheam 36, 73
Cheapside 25, 81, 123–4, 216–7, 237–8, 288
Chelsea 70, 105–7, 185, 354
Chelsea Physic Garden 354
Chelsea Royal Hospital 45, 88
Cheyne Walk 105–7
Chiswell Street 92
Chiswick 35, 108–11

Chiswick House 108–9
Christ Church, Spitalfields 93
Christchurch, Newgate Street 19
Church Row, Hampstead 104
Churchill, Sir Winston 190, 301
City of London churches 24–7
Clapham 160, 163, 304, 385
Clattern Bridge 382
Clerkenwell 8–9, 15–6, 42–3, 54–5, 152, 179, 282, 289, 292
Clerkenwell Green 297
Clifford's Inn 342
Clink, Liberty of 279, 311
Clink Prison 23, 312–3
Clink Street 23
Clissold Park 391
Cloth Fair, Smithfield 14, 79, 221, 239
coffee bars 54–6, 201
coffee houses 15, 50–4, 56, 106, 111, 130, 223, 227, 257
Cold Bath Fields 297, 307–8
Coliseum 194
College of Physicians 146, 351
Collins music hall 192
concert halls 178–80, 184–90
concerts 178–80
Constable, John 44, 104
Cooper's Row 4
Coram museum 350
Coram, Thomas 350
Cornhill alleys 50–2, 219
courtesans 305
Covent Garden 124–5, 178–9, 180, 181, 183, 190, 225, 241–2, 258, 306, 336–7, 366
Covent Garden Opera House 181
Coward, Noel 204–5
Craven Street 91, 359
Crayford 38

Index

Cremorne Gardens 42
Crewe House 97
criminal sanctuaries 278–80
Crippen, Dr 257, 302
Crompton, REB 360
Cromwell, Oliver 66, 210
Cromwell, Thomas 287
Crosby Hall 70, 106
Crosby, Sir John 20
Crouch End 232
Crown and Anchor 180, 217
Croydon 37, 69, 383
Cruikshank, George 153
crypts 25
Crystal Palace grounds 48–50
Cubitt, Thomas 139–40, 241
Cuper's Gardens 42
Curtain Street 193
Curtain theatre 193

Dagenham 29, 75
Dance, George (younger and elder) 5, 7, 95, 116, 293–4
Dartmouth House 119
Darwin, Charles 370
David Copperfield 333–6, 340–2
Dean St 55, 101, 130, 199, 201, 255–6
de Beauvoir Town 393
Defoe, Daniel 85, 97, 285
Denmark Street 198–9
Dennis Severs House 93
department stores 261–71
Deptford 387
Devereux Court 81
Devereux pub 53
Devonshire Square 92
Dickens, Charles 129–30, 314–5, 333–44
Dickens' houses 333–4
Diorama 150
Disraeli, Benjamin 118, 134
docks 23, 46, 214, 281, 284, 298–9, 364–5, 381, 386
Dollis Valley Greenwalk 381

Don Saltero's coffee house 106
Dorset Square 142
Doughty Street 333
Dove Coffee House 111
Downe House 370
Droop Street School 160
Drury Lane 337
Duckett's Cut 392
Dufferin Court 98
Duke of Northumberland's River 394
Duke's Place 5, 17
Dulwich 342, 350, 385

Ealing 32–3, 116, 202, 363, 381
Ealing churches 32–3
East End Farm Cottage, Pinner 32
East Street 247–8
Eastbury Manor House 75
Eaton Square 140
Edgware Road 142, 192, 290, 381
Edison, Thomas 361
Eel Pie Island 202
Elder Street 93
Eleanor Crosses 31
electricity 359–61
Elephant and Castle 321, 359, 386
Elephant Man 351
Eliot, George 106, 385
Elizabeth I 10, 113, 287, 289–90, 292, 293, 314
Elsing Spital 16
Eltham Palace 69–70
Ely Place 24, 221, 326
Embankments 376
Enfield 30, 87, 388, 391
engineering 361–6, 377
Epping Forest museum 31
Essex Street 81
executions
  at Newgate 292
  at Tyburn 290, 291
  in Kennington 288
  in Smithfield 289
  in the Tower 287

in Whitehall 288
on Tower Hill 287
Exeter Hall 187

Faraday, Michael 359–60
Farringdon Street 379
Fenton House, Hampstead 88
Festival of Britain 47, 54, 323
Field Lane 284
Fielding, Henry and John 318–9
Finchley 158–9, 358, 380–1
Finsbury 92, 97, 151–3, 164–5, 347
Firepower 371
Fisher's Folly 79
Fitzrovia 228–9
Fitzroy Square 145
Fitzroy Tavern 228
Flamsteed's House, Greenwich 86, 366
Fleet Street 18, 25, 79–82, 179, 217, 223–4, 238, 253, 285, 293, 303, 341–2
Fleming, Alexander 358
Fleming's laboratory 358
Fornum and Mason 261
Forty Hall 30, 87
Foundling Hospital 350
Franklin, Benjamin 92, 359
freemasons 220, 296
Freud's house 358
Fulham Palace 68

Gamages 263
garden suburbs 155–9
Garraway's coffee house 52
Garrick, David 53, 109
Gatti family 138, 254, 393
Gay, John 181, 183
Geffrye Museum 94
Gentleman's Row, Enfield 87
George and Vulture 51
George inn 56, 212
George III 50, 136, 185, 186
George IV, Prince Regent 119, 146–7, 305, 309

Gerrard Street 53, 54, 101, 202
Gibbons, Grinling 26, 129, 178, 182
Gibbons, Orlando 176
Gilbert, WS 117
gin palaces 213
Golden Square 129, 335
Golders Green 158, 381
Goldfinger, Erno 89
Gordon Riots 293, 309, 313, 319
Gordon Square 139
Gordon's Wine Bar 232
Gower, John 22
Grand Union Canal 392–4
Granville Square 42, 152
Gray's Inn 340–1
Great Eastern steamship 363–4
Great Expectations 215, 338–9
Great Fire, rebuilding after 80–1
Great Ormond Street 82–3, 136
Great Russell Street 137, 280
Grecian coffee house 52
Greenway, the 376
Greenwich 56, 84–6, 102–3, 249, 362, 364, 366–8, 371
Greenwich Observatory 86, 366–7
Grims Dyke, Harrow 116
Grosvenor Square 133, 308
Guildhall 7
Guildhall Art Gallery 67
Gunnersbury House 116
Guy's Hospital 349–50
Guy, Thomas 349
Gwynn, Nell 43, 305

Hackney 72–3, 195–6, 376–8, 392
Hackney Empire 195–6
Hackney Wick 376–7, 392
Hall Place, Bexley 74–5
Ham House 83
Hammersmith 54, 111, 197, 303

Hammersmith Palais 197
Hampstead 44, 88–90, 105, 343–4, 358
Hampstead Garden Suburb 157–9
Hampstead Heath 344, 379
Hampstead Wells 44
Hampton Court 70, 360
Handel, George Frideric 177, 179–82, 189, 203–4, 218, 350
Handel's house 182
Hanover Square 131
Hanover Square Rooms 185
Harmondsworth 34–5
Harris, Renatus 129, 178, 189
Harrods 262–3
Harvey, William 351–2
Haydn, Joseph 186, 203
Haymarket 127, 180–2, 184, 186, 250, 259, 304, 306
Haymarket Theatre 259
Headstone Manor 69
Hendon 370
Hendrix, Jimi 182, 199
Henrietta Maria 85, 127
Henry VIII 67, 69, 70, 75, 105, 176, 286, 289, 294, 313, 348, 389
Her Majesty's Theatre, Haymarket 181, 182, 304
Hertford House 99
Hickford's Room 184
high-rise housing 163–5
Highgate 72, 165, 343, 379
Highgate Ponds 379
Hillingdon churches 34
Hippodrome 194, 197
Hogarth, William 15, 35, 98, 109, 280, 338, 348, 350
Hogarth's house 109
Holborn 77–8, 341, 379
Holborn Empire 192
Holborn Viaduct 361, 379
Holland House 83–4
Holland Park 84

Hollar, Wenceslaus 23
Holy Trinity Priory 5, 8, 9, 17, 389
Home House 97
Hooke, Robert 51, 86, 124, 347–8, 351–3
Hoop and Grapes 80, 218
Horniman Museum 203
Hornchurch 28–9
Hornsey 43, 391
hospitals 347–51
Hounslow churches 35
Hounslow Powder Mill 395
houses
  eighteenth-century 89–116
  medieval 65–70
  nineteenth-century 116–9
  seventeenth-century 79–89
  sixteenth-century 70–79
Hoxton 192–3, 393
Hoxton music hall 192
Hoxton Street 193
Huguenots 93, 389
Hungerford Steps 335
Hunter, John and William 356–7
Hunterian Museum 357
Hyde Park 305, 309–10, 321
Hyde Park Gate 190
Hyde Park Square 142

Inner Temple 18, 19, 79
Inns of Chancery 78
Irish in London 223, 224, 247, 292, 309
Isle of Dogs 364
Isleworth 72
Islington 43, 245, 393

Jack Straw's Castle 343
Jack the Ripper 93, 299–301, 351
Jacob's Island 284, 386
Jamaica Wine House 51
jazz 197–8, 201–2
Jermyn, Henry 127, 129
Jerusalem coffee house 52

Jews 243, 301
John Croxton 7
John Lewis store 264, 267, 382
Johnson, Dr Samuel 2, 82, 102
Jones, Inigo 1, 67, 83, 85, 87, 105, 113, 124, 177, 217, 241
Jordan de Bricett 8, 15, 16

Keats, John 89
Keats House, Hampstead 89
Kelvin, Lord 360
Kensington 88, 117, 189–90, 203, 246–7, 260, 264, 356–7, 360–1, 368
Kensington Court 360
Kensington Gardens 88
Kensington High Street 264
Kensington Palace 88
Kentish Town 232, 321, 379
Kenwood House 102, 379
Kettner's restaurant 304
Kew 35–6, 71, 84, 203, 354–6, 377
Kew Bridge Steam Museum 377
Kew Gardens 84, 354–6
Kew Palace 84
King Street, Covent Garden 126
King's Bench prison 308, 315
King's Cross 42, 151–2, 321, 363, 379, 393
Kingsland Road 94–5
Kingston 36, 241, 320, 382
Kingsway 153–5
Knights Hospitaller 8, 15
Knights Templar 8, 15, 18, 19, 34
Kray twins 302

Lamb's Conduit Street 136
Lambeth 44–5, 248, 309, 347–9, 386
Lambeth Palace 23–4
Lambeth Wells 44

Lane, Allen 101
Lansdowne House 132
Latchmere Road estate 163
Latin America 145
Lauderdale House 72
LCC estates 160–4
leasehold system 137
Leicester Square 126–7, 194, 306, 357
Leighton House 117–8
Lenin 152, 296
Lewisham 387
Liberty's 149, 272
libraries 14, 24, 128, 296, 353, 357–9
Limehouse 215, 216, 388–9, 392
Lincoln's Inn 134–5, 338
Lincoln's Inn Fields 98, 116, 124, 135, 181, 287, 337, 357
Lincoln's Inn Fields theatre 181
Lindsey House 106
Linley Sambourne House 117
Little Dorrit 315, 334–5, 341, 342
Little Venice 394
Littlewood, Joan 196
Livery Company halls 8
Lloyd Baker estate 152
Lloyd's Coffee house 51
London Hospital 351
London Loop 382
London Palladium 194
London Pavilion 194
London Philharmonic Orchestra 191
London Pride 205
London Symphony Orchestra 188
London Transport Museum 366
London Zoo 369–70, 394
Long Lane 80
Lord Mayor *see mayors of London*
Lord's cricket ground 44, 142
Lower Robert Street 144

Lyceum theatre 195
Lyric theatre 197

Mall, the 147
Manchester Square 99, 141, 359
Manor Farm Barn, Harmondsworth 34–5
Mansion House 95
maps 2
Marble Hill House 114
markets 236–49
    Berwick St 245
    Billingsgate 240
    Borough 241
    Brick Lane 243
    Brixton 249
    Camden Lock 246
    Camden Passage 245
    Covent Garden 242
    East Lane 248
    Greenwich 249
    Leadenhall 239
    Leather Lane 244
    New Caledonian 248
    New Covent Garden 240
    Petticoat Lane 243
    Portobello Road 247
    Ridley Road 244
    Smithfield 240
    Spitalfields 242
    Strutton Ground 245
    Walthamstow 244
    Whitechapel 243
Marlborough House 95–6
Marquee club 201
Marshalsea Prison 279, 314–5, 317
Martin Chuzzlewit 342
Marx, Karl 255, 296
Marx Memorial Library 296
Marylebone 42–4, 130–1, 141–2, 150, 213, 228–9, 334, 359, 380
Marylebone Gardens 42
Marylebone Road 151, 334
Mayfair 130–4, 230, 272–3, 305
Mayflower pub 362
Mayors of London 7, 21, 28,

Mayors of London (*cont.*)
30, 74, 81, 95, 113,
221, 239, 289, 290
medieval churches 19–25,
27–38
Merchant Taylors Hall 8
Mermaid Tavern 215–6
Merton 36, 383–4
Merton Abbey Mills 384
Merton Priory 384
Metropolitan music hall 192
Metropolitan Police 319–22
Metropolitan Water Board
391
Middle Temple 19, 53, 80,
233, 253, 342
Middle Temple Hall 19, 342
Middle Temple Lane 80
military museums 370–1
Millbank Penitentiary 317–8
Ministry of Defence 67
Mint, the 316
Mitcham 383–4
Mitre Square 17, 301
Mitre Taverns 217
modernist architecture 369
monasteries and religious
communities 8–20
Montagu Square 142
Monument, the 286, 352–3
Morden Hall Park 384
Morris, William 111–2, 135,
384
Mount Street, Mayfair 134
Mozart, Wolfgang Amadeus
184–5, 256
Mrs Salmon's Waxworks 79
Mulberry Gardens 42
murders 297–303
Museum in Docklands 364
music halls 191–6, 204
musical instruments 203
Musical Museum, Kew 203
Myddleton Square 153, 391
Myddleton, Hugh 390

Nash, John 119, 145–51,
370
National Maritime Museum
86, 366

Natural History Museum
368–9
Nelson, Admiral 12, 200,
250–1, 272, 367
New Oxford St 251–2, 280
New River 87, 152, 390–2
New River Company 152
New River Head 391
New Square 135, 338
Newman Arms 229
Newport Court 82
Nicholas Nickleby 129–30,
253, 335, 339–40
Northfields 84

Old Bell Tavern 224
Old Dr Butler's Head pub
218
Old Ford 387
Old Mitre Tavern 25, 221
Old Nichol 161–2
Old Operating Theatre 349
Old Palace School 69
Old Vic 195
Olde Cheshire Cheese
223–4, 341
Oliver Twist 282–3, 296,
341
opera 176, 181–3
orchestras 187–91
organs 178, 367
Orleans House 114
Orpington 37
Osterley House 72
Outer Circle, Regent's Park
150–1
Owen, Sir Richard 49–50,
369
Oxford Circus 149, 200,
228, 230, 271
Oxford Street 130, 185, 201,
238, 265–71, 291, 380

Paddington 233, 358, 361,
362–3, 380, 392, 394
Palace Theatre 194
Palewell Common 382
Pall Mall 75, 127, 146, 231,
251, 305, 310
Pantheon 185, 270

Park Crescent 146, 149, 358
Park Lane 118, 134, 309,
310
Park Village 151
Pasqua Rosee's Head 51
Peasants' Revolt 289
Pellicci's 55
Pentonville Road 43, 152,
165
Pepusch, Johann-Christoph
179, 180, 181
Pepys, Samuel 21–2, 45, 79,
82, 217, 312
Percy Circus 152
Peter Jones 264
Petersham 343
Pevsner, Nikolaus 15, 23, 26,
53, 79, 85, 88, 165,
219, 222, 228, 266,
315, 376
Piccadilly 55, 99–100, 129,
148–9, 153, 187–8,
194, 211, 259–60, 310
Pickwick Papers 211, 220,
313, 333, 342–3
Piers the Ploughman 210
pillories 283, 285–6
Pinner 32, 68–9
Pitshanger Manor, Ealing
116
Pitshanger Park 381
Playhouse Yard, Blackfriars
17
pleasure gardens 41–50
police stations 104, 295,
318–22
policing 318–22
Pope, Alexander 115
Poplar 240
popular music clubs 200–3
Portland Place 146
Portman estate 142
Prince Henry's Room 19, 79,
218
prisons 292–7, 310–8
Bridewell 295
Clink 23, 312–3
Fleet 295
Ludgate 293
Millbank 317–8

Newgate 294
  Southwark 310–8
  Wellclose Square 294
  Westminster 318
Promenade concerts 188–9
Prospect of Whitby pub 215
prostitution 305–07
Prudential Building 334, 340
public houses 209–233
  16th-century 210
  18th-century 210–11
  Art Nouveau 213, 265
  Borough High St 314
  boxing 226
  City 216–20
  coaching inns 212
  Covent Garden 225–6
  East End 214–6
  Fitzrovia 228–10
  Holborn and Fleet St
    221–5
  Marylebone 228–30
  Mayfair 230
  Medieval 209–10
  Smithfield 221
  Soho 225–8
  St James 230–1
  suburban 232–3
  Victorian 212–3
  Westminster 231–2
Purcell, Henry 175–7
Putney 36, 268, 288, 343,
    382

Queen Anne's Gate 90
Queen Square 136
Queen's Hall 188
Queen's House, Greenwich
    85–6
Queen's Park estate 160
quiz walks 2, 57–61,
    167–171, 325–29

railway stations 362–3
Rainham Hall 29, 103
Ranelagh Gardens 44–5
Rangers House 102
Ratcliffe Highway murders
    297–8
rebuilding after 1666 81

recording studios 199
Red Lion pub 231
Red Lion Square 135
Reeves, Charles 321
Regent Street 148–9, 271–2
Regent's Canal 215, 246,
    392–4
Regent's Park 46, 150–1,
    352, 394
Rich, John 181
Richmond 112–3, 202, 303,
    342
Richmond Green 113
Richmond Palace 113
Richmond Park 382
riots 307–10
rivers 375–95
  Beverley Brook 382
  Crane 395
  Dollis Brook or Brent
    381–2
  Effra 385
  Falcon Brook 385
  Fleet 378–9
  Hogsmill 382
  Lea, or Lee 387–90
  Neckinger 284, 387
  New 390–2
  Peck 386
  Quaggy 387
  Ravensbourne 387
  Thames 180, 298, 306,
    361–2, 375–6, 377
  Tyburn 380
  Walbrook 378
  Wandle 382–5
  Westbourne 380–1
rock music 198–200
Roehampton estate (Alton
    East and West) 163
Rolling Stones 198, 202
Roman amphitheatre 6
'Roman Baths' in Strand Lane
    76
Roman fort 6
Roman wall 3–6
Ronnie Scott's club 202
rookeries 279–84, 299–301,
    315–6
Rose Theatre 312

Rotherhithe 361–2
Rotherhithe foot tunnel 361
Rothschilds 96, 97, 116, 159
Roubiliac, Louis-François
    177, 182, 350
Royal Albert Hall 186, 189,
    197
Royal Artillery Museum 370
Royal College of Music 190,
    203
Royal College of Surgeons
    357
Royal Exchange 237
Royal Institution 360
Royal Naval Hospital 367
Royal Observatory,
    Greenwich 86, 366–7
Royal Philharmonic Society
    187
Royal Society 352, 354
Rules restaurant 336
Russell Estate 136–9
Russell Square 138

Sadler's Wells 186
Saffron Hill 282–3, 341
St Alphage London Wall 16
St Andrew Undershaft 21,
    178
St Andrew, Enfield 30
St Andrew, Hornchurch
    28–9
St Andrew, Kingsbury 32
St Barnabas House 101
St Bartholomew the Great 14
St Bartholomew's Hospital
    348
St Botolph 13
St Bride 25
St Dunstan and All Saints,
    Stepney 29
St Dunstan-in-the-West 341
St Dunstan, Cranford 34
St Ethelburga 21
St Etheldreda 24
St George Hanover Square
    132, 182
St George-in-the-East 298
St George's Fields 308–9,
    347

St George's Hospital 358
St George the Martyr,
    Southwark 308, 314,
    315
St Giles Cripplegate 5
St Giles rookery 280–1
St Giles, Ickenham 33
St Helen and St Giles,
    Rainham 29
St Helen Bishopsgate 20, 21
St James Clerkenwell 179
St James, Friern Barnet 30
St James Garlickhythe 26
St James' Church 129
St James' Hall 187
St James' Palace 75, 118,
    176–7
St James' Park 147, 380
St James' Place 96
St James' Square 127–9
St James' Street 250–1
St John of Jerusalem priory
    15
St John the Baptist,
    Hillingdon 33
St John the Baptist, Pinner
    32
St John, Smith Square 91
St John's Church, Hampstead
    104
St John's Gate 53
St Katherine Cree 178
St Lawrence, Cowley 34
St Magnus the Martyr 178
St Margaret, Barking 28
St Martin-le-Grand 8
St Martin, Ruislip 33
St Mary Abchurch 26
St Mary Aldermary 26
St Mary Clerkenwell 16
St Mary Magdalene, East Ham
    28
St Mary the Virgin, Bexley
    37
St Mary Walthamstow 27
St Mary-at-Hill 26
St Mary-le-Bow 25
St Mary, Barnes 36
St Mary, Beddington 37
St Mary, Bow 29

St Mary, East Barnet 30
St Mary, East Bedfont 35
St Mary, Harefield 33
St Mary, Harmondsworth 34
St Mary, Harrow 32
St Mary, Hayes 34
St Mary, Ilford 27
St Mary, Merton 36
St Mary, Neasden 32
St Mary, Putney 36
St Nicholas, Chislehurst 37
St Nicholas, Chiswick 35,
    110
St Olave, Hart St 21
St Pancras 30, 229, 363, 379
St Pancras church 30
St Paul's Cathedral8, 10, 12,
    178, 353
St Paul's Deanery 80
St Paulinus, Crayford 37
St Peter and St Paul,
    Dagenham 29
St Peter and St Paul,
    Harlington 34
St Peter Vere St 131
St Sepulchre 178, 189,
    290–1
St Stephen Walbrook 378
St Thomas's Hospital 348–9
Salisbury pub 226
Salomon, Johann 177
Sambourne, Linley 117
Saracen's Head 339
Sargent, Sir Malcolm 190
Savoy Chapel 76
Savoy Palace 76
Savoy Theatre 197, 361
science 91–2, 347–71
Science Museum 357, 365,
    368
Scotland Yard 318–20
Seckforde estate 16
Selfridge, Gordon 133
Selfridge's 269
Senate House 1, 138, 154
Serpentine, the 380
Seven Dials 142–3
Seven Stars pub 222
sewers 375–7
sex scandals 303–6

Shaftesbury Park Estate 160
Shaftesbury Avenue 148,
    197, 280
Shakespeare 19, 193, 216–7,
    312–3, 340
Shaw, Norman 117, 149,
    156, 320
Shepherd Market 133
Shepherd, Edward 133
Shepherd's Bush Empire 195
Sherlock Holmes 322–3
shopping arcades 258–61
shops 139, 236–7, 249–73
    18th-century 238, 250–3
    Bond St 272–3
    City 252–3
    Covent Garden 254
    department stores 261–72
    Fleet Street 253
    Jermyn St 260–1
    Kensington High St 265
    medieval 237–9
    Regent St 271–2
    Soho 255–7
    Strand 253–4
    umbrella 252
    Whitechapel 252
Shoreditch 94, 161–2, 378,
    393
Siege of Sidney Street 302
Sloane Square 356
Sloane, Sir Hans 356
Smeaton, John 392
Smith Square 91
Smithfield 13–14, 78–80,
    221, 239, 283, 287–9,
    339, 348
Snow, Sir John 358
Soane, Sir John 5, 30, 35,
    98, 116, 117, 128, 350
Soane's House 98
Soho 53–55, 101–2,
    129–30, 148–9, 162,
    184–5, 200–202,
    227–8, 245, 255–7,
    287–9, 295, 321, 358,
    375
Soho coffee houses 53–5
Soho Square 130, 185, 255
Somerset House 98

songs about London 203–5
Sorby, Thomas 321
South Kensington museums 368–9
South Molton St 269
Southside House, Wimbledon 90
Southwark 56, 211–2, 241, 279–80, 288, 310–16, 349, 359
Southwark Cathedral 22–23
Spa Fields 16, 307
Spa Green estate 164
Spaniard's Inn 343
Spencer House 96
Speyer, Sir Edgar 188
Spitalfields 93, 252
Spohr, Ludwig 187
Spring Gardens 42
Staple Inn 77, 340
Stephenson, Robert 361
Stepney 28–30, 216, 301–2
Stoke Newington 391
Strand 76, 79, 82, 98, 153–5, 179, 180, 187, 195, 197, 213, 217, 237–8, 250, 253–4, 258–60, 263, 286, 304, 335
Strand palaces 76
Stratford-le-Bow 388, 389
Streatham 198, 312, 385
Streatham Locarno 198
Stuart, James 'Athenian' 96, 128, 367
suburban churches 27–38
Sutton House 72
Sweeney Todd 303
swimming 379–80
Sydenham Wells Park 50
Syon House 72

Tabard Inn, Bedford Park 156
Tabard Inn, Southwark 313
Tallis, Thomas 176
Tavistock Square 139, 334
Templars 8, 15, 18, 169, 178
Temple Bar 285

Temple Church 19, 178
Temple Fortune Lane 159
Thames Valley University 202
Theatre Royal Drury Lane 176, 181, 184, 190, 254, 259
Theatre Royal Haymarket 181–2, 304
Theatre Royal, Stratford East 196
Theatre, the 193
theatres 180–2, 191–6, 259, 311–2
Three Bridges (Brunel) 363
Three Mills Island 389
timber-framed houses 77–80
Tooting 233, 303, 385
Tothill Fields Bridewell 317
Tottenham 196, 232
Tottenham Court Road 229, 263, 265, 291
Tottenham Palace Theatre 196
Totteridge and Whetstone 381
Tower Bridge 365
Tower Hill 3, 4, 287
Tower of London 4, 78, 278, 287, 292
Town Of Ramsgate pub 214
Toynbee Hall 299
Trafalgar Square 146–7, 310
Trafalgar Tavern, Greenwich 368
transport 2, 365–6
tunnels under the thames 361–2
Turk's Head 53
Twickenham 113–6, 202–3

underground stations 271, 380
University of Greenwich 367
Upper Brook Street 134
Upper Norwood 48–50, 385

Valence House, Becontree 88
Vanbrugh, Sir John 103, 181, 259, 371

Vanbrugh Castle, Maze Hill 103
variety theatres 193–6
Vauxhall Gardens 41, 45–6
Vendu (concert room) 180
Vestry House, Walthamstow 322
Victoria and Albert Museum 31, 79–82, 128, 182, 203, 368
Victoria Embankment Gardens 77
Victoria Palace Theatre 194
Victoria Park 376, 392, 393

Waddon Park 383
Walker, Emery 111
walks
Aldwych and Kingsway 153–5
Battersea Park 47–8
Beatles sites 199–200
Bedford Park 156–7
Beverley Brook 382
Boundary Street 161–2
Camden markets 246
Chelsea houses 105–7
Chiswick houses 108–11
City houses 92–3
City pubs 219–20
City, Strand and Covent Garden shops 252–4
Clerkenwell squares 151–2
Crane river walk 394–5
Crystal Palace 48–50
Dickens' City and Covent Garden walk 335–42
Dickens' Hampstead 343
East End pubs 214–6
Fleet valley prisons 294–7
Greenway sewer walk 376
Greenwich houses 85–7
Greenwich science 366–8
Hampstead Garden Suburb 158–9
Hampstead houses 88–90, 103–5

Index

walks (cont.)
  Holborn and Fleet St pubs 220–1
  Holborn shops 134–139
  Jack the Ripper 299–301
  Jacob's Island 284
  Kingsland Road 94
  Marylebone and Bayswater 141–2
  Mayfair and St James' pubs 230–1
  medieval City churches 21–22
  monasteries near Fleet St 18–19
  Nash's Regency London 145–51
  Newgate to Tyburn 290–1
  New River walk 391–2
  Oliver Twist's Saffron Hill 282
  Oxford St and Bond St shops 265–73
  Piccadilly houses 99–100
  Ratcliffe Highway and Wapping 298–299
  Ravensbourne river walk 387
  Regent's Canal 392–4
  Richmond and Twickenham houses 112–115
  Roman wall 3–6
  St James' houses 95–7
  St James' shops 250–1
  Shoreditch theatres 192–3
  Smithfield and Clerkenwell monasteries 12–15

Soho pubs 225–8
Soho shops 255–7
Southwark criminal sites 310–16
Wandle walk 383–5
West End squares 125–34
Westminster Abbey 10–11
Wren churches 25–7
Wallace Collection 99
Walpole, Horace 45, 98, 108, 115–6
Waltham Abbey 31, 388
Waltham Cross 31
Walthamstow 27–8, 56, 111–2, 322
Walworth Road 247–8, 359
Wandsworth 383–4
Wapping 298–9, 361
Wapping High Street 214–5
Water Rats pub 43
Waterloo Place 148
Waterlow Park 72
Well Walk, Hampstead 44
Wellcome Trust 357
Wellington, Duke of 95, 250, 251, 305
Wellington St 337
Wembley 381
Wesley's House 97–8
West Ham 29, 233, 376, 390
West India Docks 365
West Kilburn 160
Westminster 82, 90–1, 245, 317–20
Westminster Abbey 10–12, 176–7, 279, 285, 287, 380
Westminster Hall 65–7

Westminster Palace 65–7
Wharncliffe Viaduct (Brunel) 363, 381
Whistler, James McNeill 107
White Conduit Gardens 43
White Swan Inn 114
Whitechapel 93, 243, 252, 281, 299–302, 351
Whitefriars 18
Whitehall Palace 67–8
Whiteley's 262
Wig and Pen Club 79
Wigmore Hall 189
Wilde, Oscar 107, 149, 251, 304, 319
Wilkes, John 308–9
Willesden 32
William III 70–1, 88, 128, 176, 367
Wilton Crescent 140
Wiltons music hall 192
Wimbledon 90
Winchester Palace 23, 313
Woburn Square 139
Wood, Henry 188–9
Woolf, Virginia 139, 145
Woolwich 241, 362, 370–1
Woolwich Arsenal 370–1
working-class housing 159–65
Wren, Sir Christopher 25–6, 95–6, 70, 86, 88, 129, 224, 352–3, 366–7, 378

Yeats, WB 157, 223–4
York House, Twickenham 114
York Watergate 76